STRAVINSKY

Other books by this author include the following
collections of essays:

Prejudices in Disguise (1974)

Present Perspectives (1984)

Current Convictions (1972)

Small Craft Advisories (1989)

ROBERT CRAFT

Stravinsky:
Glimpses of a Life

St. Martin's Press
New York

Library of Congress Cataloging-in-Publication Data

Craft, Robert.
    Stravinsky : glimpses of a life / Robert Craft.
      p.   cm.
    Includes index.
    ISBN 0-312-08896-5
    1. Stravinsky, Igor, 1882–1971. 2. Composers—Biography
3. Craft, Robert. I. Title.
ML410.S932C85   1993
780'.92—dc20
    [B]   92-34388
                                               CIP
                                               MN

First published in Great Britain by Lime Tree.

First U.S. Edition: February 1993

10 9 8 7 6 5 4 3 2 1

CONTENTS

CONTENTS

ACKNOWLEDGMENTS

I am indebted above all to Alva Minoff ('thou hast put off my sackcloth and girdled me with gladness'), and, for editorial suggestions, to Elsbeth Lindner, Robert Gottlieb, Robert Silvers, Barbara Epstein, Eva Resnikova, and my sister, Phyllis Crawford. Special credit is due to my niece, Kristin Crawford, for her help in translating documents and letters from the French, particularly in connection with the various drafts of the *Histoire du soldat* libretto. I am grateful to Mme Lucia Davidova for her translations from the Russian correspondence of Vera and Igor Stravinsky, and to my editor, Robert Weil, and my representatives Fifi Oscard and Kevin McShane, for having brought about the publication of the book in America.

PREFACE

A book that is half biography and half musical commentary might seem to have been directed toward two different kinds of reader. But in this instance the essays on Stravinsky's music were chosen for their glimpses of the creative-genius side of his personality. The penultimate one, on the *Symphonies of Wind Instruments,* was included because my association with Stravinsky began with this work.

Of the purely biographical essays, the most important, and most painful, are the two that conclude the second part of the book. I wrote the longer of them, '*Cher père, Chère Véra*', because I was the only witness to most of the events it records. Another observer, even one with the same documentation, or even more of it, and with other sources of testimony, would not be able to reconstruct more than a very fragmented history of Stravinsky's life *vis-à-vis* his two families during the years 1950–71.

The Catherine Stravinsky story, on the other hand, might well be re-examined now from a different hypothesis: that the primary motive of her letters, conscious or otherwise, may have been to punish her husband with feelings of guilt. When I wrote that Catherine was apparently not jealous of his love for Vera Sudeikina, I had not yet seen Vera's diaries, and the entry of 22 October 1923: 'Igor writes constantly about Ekaterina Gavrilovna's jealousy.'

But apart from the sad revelations in Catherine's 1930s letters, I know little about her. Nor, let me emphasize, did I know the Stravinsky to whom it would be possible for her to complain that 'I've been without money the last few days; 3

francs remain in my purse'; that their elder son should meet her 'Wagon-Lit 3rd Class', because she does not have enough money to tip the porter; and that she gave short answers during a long-distance telephone conversation because 'you did not want to go beyond three minutes.' The Stravinsky I knew was parsimonious but also capable of great generosity, and he was never self-indulgent.

But I should have balanced the Catherine story with a Vera story, one that would show the tormented as well as the passionate side of Stravinsky's love for her and hers for him, and describe the early stages of their romance until, with Catherine's knowledge and consent (under duress), they lived together. I shall attempt to do that here in very abbreviated form.

When Serge Diaghilev introduced Stravinsky to Vera Sudeikina, in an Italian restaurant in Montmartre, 21 February 1921, Stravinsky, married and the father of four children aged seven to fourteen, fell head over heels in love. With the recurrence of his wife's tuberculosis in 1914, his conjugal sex life had apparently come to an end. After that date, in any case, he engaged in affairs with, among others, Coco Chanel, Lydia Lopokova (later the wife of John Maynard Keynes), and a cabaret dancer whose theme song he added to the trombone part in the orchestration of his four-hand Polka. Vera was also, and in a homologous sense, unsatisfactorily married, to the painter Serge Sudeikin (1882–1946). (John Bowlt's forthcoming *The Salon Album of Vera Stravinsky*, Princeton, 1993, documents some of the Sudeikins' amatory inconstancies.) But whereas the Sudeikins lived together underfoot in a hotel, Stravinsky, for at least part of the time, was enviably footloose in his Paris atelier, joining his family for the other part in a home at first in Biarritz, and later in Nice and Grenoble. In the first fourteen years after meeting Vera, he shuttled between two addresses and two existencies.

Less than a week after the Montmartre dinner, Boris Kochno, a Russian-refugee poet all of seventeen years old, told the Sudeikins, whom he had known in the Caucasus in

1917 and 1918, of his consuming desire to meet Diaghilev. Kochno's memoir of how this came about differs obliquely from Vera's. He claims that Sudeikin 'asked me to see Diaghilev on his behalf concerning. . .a revival of [*The Tragedy of*] *Salomé* [with Sudeikin's decors].' Sudeikin's entrée was that he had been Diaghilev's lover in Paris in 1906.

Vera's version is that one day she had asked Diaghilev to come to tea and invited Kochno as well. The young man arrived before the hour complaining that the barber shops were closed because it was Sunday and asking to borrow a razor. Thinking that he had not made a very strong impression, she was surprised when Diaghilev invited him to lunch, and when, a few weeks later, in early April, he was in Seville with Diaghilev and Stravinsky.

Meanwhile, not long after the evening in Montmartre, Stravinsky and Vera seem to have rendezvoused; at any rate, the formal 'to Madame Sudeikina' on a calling card saying that he is waiting for her in his car in the street, and dated by her '1921', was probably written before he inscribed the initial theme of *Firebird* in her album and the dedication: 'To the lady, this one, charming one, this one, beautiful one . . .Vera Sudeikina, Paris, March 1921.' (Sudeikin painted a raptorial and mean-looking 'firebird' over the music.) In a later 1921 album Stravinsky penned some lines of Dada-like verse and filled the rest of the page with a passage from *Les Noces*, the text of which reads: 'This one is fantastically good. If you don't touch her she costs one ruble, but if you fuck her she costs two rubles.' One doubts that this was written in Sudeikin's presence, or, to judge by the mistakes in notation, in an entirely sober state, no matter where.

Diaghilev, back from Spain, confided in Vera that he had found Kochno distastefully, ferally furry, but would retain him as a secretary. In London, at the beginning of June, Stravinsky invited Kochno to write a libretto for a one-act chamber opera based on Pushkin's *The Little House at Kolomna*. Obviously the favour to Kochno, Vera Sudeikin's 'friend from childhood', as he calls her, was not coincidental, and neither, perhaps, was the subject, in which a man in woman's clothes is discovered shaving.

As already indicated, Sudeikin was bi-sexual. During most of his first marriage, to Olga Glebova, 1907–1916, the homosexual poet Mikhail Kuzmin shared the Sudeikin apartment and, with Glebova, though for a long time unbeknownst to her, Sudeikin himself.

Vera's letters to Stravinsky from July to September 1921 – in later years they celebrated their 'marriage' on Bastille Day, 14 July – pretend to convey Sudeikin's affectionate regards along with her own, but are ill-disguised *billets-doux*. They mention Kochno repeatedly and in a way to indicate that he had become her confidant. On her nameday, 30 September, Kochno and Stravinsky inscribed one of her albums on the same page, Stravinsky with a short and less audacious quotation from *Les Noces*.

At the beginning of October, Diaghilev invited Vera to play the mimed role of the Queen in his revival of *The Sleeping Beauty*, which was to begin a long engagement in London on 2 November. She was there for rehearsals on 27 October when Kochno, failing to perceive the depth of Stravinsky's feelings, warned her that the composer could be fickle (Kochno knew about Stravinsky's and Robert Delaunay's visit to a Madrid bordello in April):

V.S.

Dear friends of my childhood
What is new in [the Ballets Russes]?
What about Lydia Lopokova
And Igor – the old friends?
I find things out by chance
I was blessed with a gift of omniscience.
And for you, what could be nicer than a family of
Friends, like Vera, from childhood.

Five days later, Stravinsky, in London for the premiere of the ballet – he had orchestrated two numbers that Diaghilev had been able to obtain only in piano score – arranged with Kochno to act as go-between with Vera. Stravinsky would send letters to him containing letters to Vera, some of them to be handed to her and some mailed: 'Give the enclosed yellow letter to Vera, post the other one with an English stamp and write the address so that the handwriting will not be recognized.' Her communications would be sent to Stravinsky poste restante, Biarritz.

The absurdity of the subterfuge is not so much in the unlikelihood of Sudeikin appearing in London and intercepting Stravinsky's letters as in the evident fact that the cuckold had long since guessed or been told the truth. Soon after Stravinsky's return, Sudeikin confronted him in his studio, but parted from it 'in harmony and peace, and seemingly reconciled,' as Stravinsky wrote to Vera on 17 November. Uxoricide had been threatened, it is true, and Stravinsky repeats this to her as a real possibility. (One wonders what Stravinsky said to mollify him.) In the same letter, Stravinsky expresses 'uneasiness' at not having heard from Sudeikin since their meeting, and two days later asks if she has had any details of it from him. On this same day (19 November), Sudeikin telegraphed Diaghilev asking him to 'send my wife back.' She returned in December.

The irony of the story is that while processing Stravinsky's love letters to Sudeikin's wife, Kochno was sending love letters of his own to Sudeikin. The precocious poet-lover piningly addresses Sudeikin as 'my darling', and vows, in verse, never to 'betray the memory / Of those last / Hours. . . / But my darling! / There is no / End, my dear, to these felicities!' The reference is to the sessions in which Kochno posed for Sudeikin's heavily lipsticked profile portrait of him. Kochno signs himself ' "Mavra" ', the name of the in-drag shaver in the opera.

Vera's Paris diary for the first months of 1922 records only a few token social engagements with Stravinsky, but surely others are hidden behind such entries as 'Visit with Koussevitzky', whom she would hardly have seen without Stravinsky. Kochno and Diaghilev appear frequently, the latter in a depressed state over the financial fiasco of *The*

Sleeping Beauty. Stravinsky wrote to him on 23 February: 'If I cannot help you with my music, what can I help you with? Despite my admiration for my male member I am not willing to offer you consolation with it.'

The spectacle of Stravinsky, in his fortieth year and the most reticent of men, confiding in a seventeen-year-old is astonishing: 'I am in a very anxious state of mind . . . Vera writes to say she can no longer bear the separation.' He thanks the teenager for his 'thoughtful phrase, "You have to believe in a profound and disturbing love at the present time",' and is uncharacteristically gentle in criticizing his young collaborator: the duet for *Mavra* is 'not a duet (and what you brought me is not a quartet), it is dialogue.' Incredibly, he had sent more than forty such letters.

Stravinsky's letters to Vera are those of a man tortured by love: 'I have a colossal lump in my soul . . . my love for you tied to this agonizing and unbearable separation . . . We love each other too much and I want it to be like this, and like this it will be' (30 November). He writes twice on the same day (19 November), telling her, first, that they cannot live together, not yet, and that she must return to her husband: 'I agree with you that one cannot build one's happiness on the grief of another.' The second letter says that one of her questions, '"Will I love you whatever happens?",' was 'so dear to me . . . that for twenty-four hours I have had it with me and repeated it and carried the letter in my pocket'. But his most remarkable declaration is that 'my words are less than what is going on inside me and what I feel—music is . . . instinctive . . . for which reason to express oneself in it is less embarrassing.' Richard Wagner might have written the first part of this, but the 'embarrassment' part is uniquely Stravinskyan. A note in Stravinsky's hand, probably from the 1950s, reads: 'Musical Art must be as indifferent to the element of motive as the church is to love or to any other reason for which people wed. After all, you do not tell a priest that you are in love. He does not need to know that, and if you did tell him you would embarrass yourself before God.'

Stravinsky had to face a more terrible encounter than Vera could have experienced with Sudeikin even at his most murderous. Sometime in the spring or summer of 1922, Stravinsky told his wife about his love for Vera, and that he could not live without her. He described the anguished scene that followed in a letter to Vera that she destroyed at his wish.

Vera left Sudeikin shortly after 4 June 1922. In the summer she moved to Deauville where, on 12 August, Alfonso XIII, King of Spain and Stravinsky's fervent admirer, called on her. She seems to have been in Deauville on 19 August when Sudeikin most conveniently left for America, and, as it happened, for good.

The love affair did not inspire a *Tristan und Isolde;* music further from *Mavra* is inconceivable. But Stravinsky's next creation, the Octet, written with the throes behind him, is one of his happiest. The lineaments of gratified desire are audible in every phrase.

PART ONE

Life in America

I

A CENTENARY VIEW, PLUS TEN

The following remarks are more personal than they might have been had I not made so many stand-in conducting appearances for Stravinsky in the year of his centenary, and not also begun to sort out my mementos, most of which had been stored away in the decade since his death. Looking through these again, I was engulfed by a wave of affection, surprising in view of the estrangement I had felt of late as a result of annotating his 1930s correspondence, in which he sometimes scarcely resembles the man I knew. Seeing the memorabilia, however, I was transported back to the events and emotions of our first years together.

Of course I did not save everything. No one could have been thinking constantly of Stravinsky's immortality while living with him – sharing three meals a day, spending most evenings together, and travelling all over the planet in automobiles, trains, ships and aeroplanes. But in perusing the contents of these old packing cases, I was more poignantly touched by his mortality than at any time since his death on 6 April 1971. Here were those neatly typed letters – some with drawings: a heart in red ink, a California desertscape in spring – and the calligraphically addressed postcards sent during later separations. (He kept *my* cards, too, even pasting some of them in a music sketchbook – not for their contents, but as exhibits of my engineering skill in cramming two hundred words into a three-by-four-inch space!) Here, too, were those sheets of my questions with his answers, later destined for books; on one page that I had asked him to return urgently, he wrote: 'You cannot complain.'

I was particularly moved to find again the manuscript copies that he made for me of a canon by Mozart, three pieces by Lasso, and Gesualdo's *Io pur respiro*, all given to me on special occasions, as well as scores of his own music, always with original dedications: on the first page of the *Monumentum*, for instance, he wrote: 'To Bob, who forced me to do it and I did it, with love, I.Str' – a statement that might have been inscribed on *The Flood* and the *Requiem Canticles* as well, and that could serve as an *apologia pro vita mea*. The boxes also contained lists of passages in scores to be rehearsed; scraps of paper with messages, passed across the aisles of aeroplanes or from adjoining seats in concert halls; and menus, paper napkins, backs of envelopes on which he had jotted down bits of music. What disturbed me enough to make me stop this nostalgic rummaging was the sight of my baggage tags filled out by him in July 1951 before we left California for Venice and the premiere of *The Rake's Progress*, these and packets of pills that he had given me for pre-concert nerves. To reiterate, my deepest feelings for Stravinsky have returned and have inevitably influenced these observations about him.

Our present view of Stravinsky is almost exactly the opposite of what it was when I met him in 1948. In the 1940s, it often seemed that rather than pursuing an inner-directed course, he was allowing himself to be led by circumstances, composing music that diverged widely in subject and form from what was thought to be his proper genus. The man who during the late 1920s and early 1930s had been inspired by the Psalmists, Homer (*Perséphone*), Sophocles (*Oedipus Rex*), Virgil (*Duo concertant*) and Petrarch (*Dialogue between Joy and Reason*) was now writing a vocalise (the 1940 Tango),[1] reharmonizing our sprawling national anthem, fulfilling commissions for the 'big bands' of Paul Whiteman and Woody Herman, providing a polka for pachyderms, and composing music for the cinema (none of it used for that purpose, but converted into concert pieces in the *Ode*, *Norwegian Moods*, *Scherzo à la russe*, the 1945 *Symphony*). Stravinsky was also writing for the symphony orchestras of Chicago, Boston and

New York; for Balanchine's ballet; and for the church. The extravagant variety of these other works bewildered even his most faithful followers. The first composition of his American period was the song, inspired by a sign posted at Harvard, 'DO NOT THROW PAPER TOWELS IN TOILET', but most of the pieces from his first dozen years in America, including settings of the Elizabethan poems 'Dancing Day' and 'Westron Wind', are based on Russian folk songs.

Only now do we see how these diverse creations both fit together and integrate with Stravinsky's earlier and later music. Thus a figure in the 1965 Variations (bar 103) is borrowed from the 1957 *Agon* (bars 498–500); the two-note dirge-rhythm in the *Requiem Canticles*'s Interlude had already appeared in the *Symphonies* of 1920; and the 'Te Deum' in *The Flood* (1962) recalls *Les Noces*. *The Flood*, moreover, is best described by the subtitle of *Histoire du soldat*: 'to be read, played and danced'. These random examples show that new departures in Stravinsky's art are often tied to older ones.

A change came about in the 1950s; Stravinsky was finally conceded to have found a path, or vehicle, when he jumped on the twelve-tone bandwagon. Few people liked this new music, but by 1956, with the *Canticum Sacrum*, his use of series was clearly no mere experiment but had come to stay. At this point I must emphasize that Stravinsky's *modus vivendi* in the first half of the 1950s differed in almost every respect from that of the monumentalized master of the late 1960s. In the early 1950s not much of his music was performed, and the popular audience was aware of him only as the composer, probably dead, of *Firebird, Petrushka,* and *The Rite of Spring*. Having been with him during this period of trial, watching him struggle to support his family—which he did by conducting, not composing—yet steadily advancing from the Septet (1952–3) to *In Memorium, Dylan Thomas* (1945), the *Canticum* (1955–66), and *Agon* (1957), I believe that this last was the turning point in Stravinsky's later life and art.

Ironically, *Agon*'s success came about through Balanchine's smash-hit ballet, and not through concert performances of the score. Today, according to publishers' royalty
statements, the piece in either form is one of Stravinsky's
most popular. And today no one seems to notice a Webern
influence, though this was a principal objection at the first
audition; we now recognize Stravinsky's characteristic gestures, temperament and energy on every page of the score.
Most of it was written during a period of recovery from a
near-fatal stroke, and though the first performance took place
on the composer's seventy-fifth birthday, the music from
beginning to end, especially in its fleetness, is that of a young
man. The rhythms, sonorities, harmonic structure, canonic
games, contrasts, and the shapes of individual dances as well
as of the work as a whole link *Agon* to *Histoire du soldat*—
to name only one predecessor: I am thinking of the parallel
function of the castanet part in 'Bransle gay' and the string-
bass part in the '*Marche du soldat*'.

Agon is now regarded as a comfortable classic, but, as
could be expected, the audience at the concert premiere
grasped none of this. And with *Agon*, other composers began
to fellow-travel with Stravinsky in his idiosyncratic use of
tone-rows, for it is true that he did not keep abreast of
developments in academic serial theory but simply borrowed
what he required in order to write masterpieces.

Stravinsky's eightieth-birthday year was marked by another
turning point, the return of the native to Russia for the first
time since 1914. That deep-freeze in which his music had
been stored since the early days of Stalin began to thaw. It
did not matter that while Stravinsky was being welcomed by
Khrushchev in the Kremlin, the fifty-one-volume Soviet Encyclopedia (1958 edition) did not even contain the composer's name; or make any difference that he was not permitted
to play his post-*Agon* music—which by then included Movements and *The Flood*—for the reason that audiences were not
prepared for it anyway. But now, belatedly recognizing their
greatest son in the arts of this century, the Russians are

performing not only *The Rake's Progress* (in their own language) but also the *Requiem Canticles*, and are publishing more studies of his music than any other country in the world.

What did Stravinsky believe to be his place in music history, in the sense that Schoenberg viewed himself as the bridge into atonality and saw his twelve-tone row as ensuring the supremacy of German music for another hundred years? In relation to Stravinsky the question is more complex, first because his notion of what constituted music history was so much larger than Schoenberg's, extending not only backward to Machaut and earlier (music that Schoenberg regarded as of no more than antiquarian interest), but also outward to Oriental and other ethnic art. Stravinsky maintained that the motets of Josquin should be heard at least as frequently as Brahms *Lieder*, Monteverdi madrigals rather more often than anything by Dvorak. But Stravinsky's affinities, technical and aesthetic, are closer to the composers of the Renaissance than to those of the late nineteenth century, although in old age his catholicity expanded to include that period as well: finally, he gave up referring to himself as Wagner's Antichrist and even learned to appreciate Mahler's Ninth Symphony.

Whatever Stravinsky thought of Schoenberg before 1950, after that date the Russian-American regarded the Austro-American not as the embodiment of an antithesis but as a great colleague from whom he could and did learn. (It is important to remember that Stravinsky was always a student, never a teacher; he had a perpetually acquisitive mind equipped with the keenest antennae.) If Stravinsky is the centre of excitement in twentieth-century music—try to imagine it without him!—that is not only by virtue of his innovations and power of personality, but also because he captured more of the whole contemporary world, American as well as European, than did his counterpart. When I speak of synthesis, therefore, I am referring not to any merger with the school of Schoenberg but rather to the assimilation of a vast range of elements filling the sound waves of the last seventy-five years, from Ukrainian folk music to Broadway variety shows, ragtime to Kabuki. I realize that I have not answered the question, but I cannot, and when I once asked it of Stravinsky himself, he replied, 'That is for history to decide.'

That Stravinsky saw his place in his *own* time is clear. In Munich, 1 February 1933, he told an interviewer:

> Audiences want the familiar, that to which they are accustomed. . . People feel confident in putting the great masters of the past against a musician of today, against a 'cultural Bolshevik', as I am called. Perhaps in twenty-five years, my works, which will then have become familiar, will be held up as examples of *real* music to younger composers.

A week later, when a reporter in Milan addressed him, as 'the recognized leader of modern music,' he responded, 'Perhaps, but there are *good* and *bad* modern musicians. I am Stravinsky and that is enough.' Although some would attribute this remark to egotism, I believe it to be the honest statement of a man with rare self-knowledge. Stravinsky knew the value of what he was doing and was simply asserting that his music would endure. The retort was also a way of refusing the crown and sceptre of a school or movement. To these characteristic rejoinders, one should be added from the rehearsal record in CBS's thirty-one-disc Stravinsky album, where he can be heard correcting a musician, then saying, 'Excuse me, please, but I *like* my music.'

Looking backward from the 1980s, we can also see that Stravinsky's music interacts more organically with architecture, choreography, painting and poetry (in three languages) than that of any other composer. This is a subject for another occasion; all that can be said here is that he was at the hub of the arts, both bestowing and receiving inspiration thereby. It is well known that the five domes of St Mark's suggested the five-movement form of the *Canticum Sacrum*. But Palladian principles, such as surrounding a central axis with rooms of sequentially different sizes, also influenced Stravinsky, who was familiar with many of the great architect's villas, as well as with his Venetian churches. (The *Canticum* even has a portico.) Besides the *Canticum*, with its 'Trinity of Virtues' as the centerpiece, the Cantata (the tenor ricercar), *Agon* (the *pas de deux*), *Threni* (the middle section of the second part), and *Requiem Canticles* (Interlude) have axial movements. Fewer listener-viewers are aware that the orthogonal style of *The Rite of Spring* and the falcate one of *Apollo*, determined the choreographic postures that Nijinsky and Balanchine created for these works.

Poetry and its relation to Stravinsky's music is a still larger subject, and, because both are formed with sounds, more closely connected. Some musicians have even detected in parts of *The Rake's Progress* an intuited comprehension of Chomsky's deep-language structures in Stravinsky's use of words; but however that may be, Stravinsky did borrow technical concepts from verse patterns and poetic forms, Pushkin and Boileau in *Apollo*, Gide's Alexandrines that the music of *Perséphone* sometimes duplicates, and Auden's haiku. Moreover, the changing metres, unequal time-intervals, and shifting accents in Stravinsky's music are devices comparable to the rhythmic innovations of the poets of the time, Americans as well as Russians, though no modern writer, including Pound, understood Stravinsky's techniques to the degree that he had understood theirs. Still another parallel could be mentioned between Stravinsky's pilferings from the past and Eliot's chrestomathy (*The Waste Land*).

What are some of the principal reasons for Stravinsky's preeminence? First, he continued to grow, as minor artists do not. *Abraham and Isaac* (1963), the masterpiece of his final years, is more concentrated music than he had ever written before, as 'passionate' as *Oedipus Rex* and utterly new in sonority, rhythm and the reduction of the harmony to largely two and three parts. The *Requiem Canticles* (1966), composed at the end of a sixty-five-year evolution, is a no less astonishing epiphany from a man of eighty-four than that of *Firebird* from a man of twenty-seven. The *Requiem* combines a new Stravinsky—in, for one example, the melodic intensity of the music for four solo flutes—with such of his older, though mutated, devices as the verse and response in the Lacrymosa, the ostinato with concertante upper parts in the Prelude, and the apotheosis of bells in the Postlude. When the *Requiem* was first given by the Los Angeles Philharmonic, Harris Goldsmith remarked that Stravinsky chose the minatory rather than the consolatory portions of the text.[2] In fact, *I* chose them, not Stravinsky, as the libretto, excerpted from Verdi's *Requiem* and containing Stravinsky's markings, drawn over but not fully deleting mine, reveals; but this does not change the truth of the observation, since I was guided by the conviction that he was becoming more defiant and less mellow with age—as well as by the realization that the octogenarian was naturally somewhat short-winded.

Another reason why Stravinsky is one of the dominating artists of his century is that he introduced a new musical medium, as did Wagner in his century. True, Stravinsky composed, in Mozartian variety, operas, oratorios, cantatas, melodramas, symphonies, concertos, overtures, sonatas, incidental music, divertimentos, songs, string quartet pieces. Yet his epochal creations were ballets, or 'choreodramas', as he called them. It cannot be coincidental that he is also music's greatest revolutionary in rhythm, in which dimension, but not only, he irrevocably altered our lives.

Finally, Stravinsky was a great artist because he knew that depth of allusion can be attained only by using the past, and that creation depends as much on the old as the new.

To turn to the forward view, what should be placed on the Stravinsky agenda for future generations of music lovers? First, his published music is an unspeakable condition. The example that comes to mind is the 1919 *Firebird*, with its more than three hundred errors;[3] but this is not atypical, since every Stravinsky score has quantities of them. To some extent the Russian Revolution is to be blamed, having deprived the composer of copyright protection in much of the world and exposed his music to legalized piracy. Despite his

American citizenship and the new US–USSR copyright agreement, the abuse continues; in their original versions, all of his pre-1931 compositions are permanently in the public domain in the United States. Even so, a 'complete works' must be begun, the variorum edition that his publishers promised him in November 1968. Some of Stravinsky's arrangements of his own and other people's music (Chopin, Grieg, Sinding) have never been published at all, while some pieces that were in print have long been unavailable, which explains the absence of an accurate catalogue, let alone a corrigenda.

The first step in correcting this situation would be a search for markings, traceable to him, in the scores of vocalists, instrumentalists, and conductors—Monteux, Ansermet, Malko, Rosbaud, Desormière, Dorati, Goossens, Collaer, Molinari—whose libraries should be examined for information. For one example, Stravinsky rewrote some of *The Rake's Progress* harpsichord part for piano, in Sante Fe in July 1957; the pianist kept the manuscript, which surely still exists and can be found.

Stravinsky's recordings are both a help and a hindrance to the improvement of performances of his music. Norman del Mar's book *Orchestral Variations* (London, 1981) demonstrates how the composer's recordings of *Apollo,* the *Etudes* for Orchestra, and *Danses concertantes* not only correct but also supplement the published scores. What Mr del Mar overlooks are the obstacles that arise when Stravinsky's recordings of the same work contradict each other. At first, Stravinsky believed that he could establish performance traditions through his recordings. But he did not tell us which tempo we are to follow for the final section of the *Symphony of Psalms,* whether that of the recording he made closest to the time of composition, the twice-as-fast version released in March 1949, the still-different tempo of the suppressed recording, made in Los Angeles in June 1961, or that of the one taped in Toronto in the spring of 1963, after he had had the most experience conducting the piece (*mutatis mutandis* concerning the advancement of technological influence and the dangerously enlarged co-conductor role of the recording supervisor).

The aforementioned CBS album credits me as the conductor of several pieces under the composer's 'supervision', though in some cases the supervising was remote indeed.[4] Naturally I tried to carry out what I believed Stravinsky wanted, but who knows how different his performances might have been if he had broken ground with them and done all of the conducting himself (i.e., if I had not rehearsed them and inevitably suggested tempos and other questions of interpretation)? The facts are that when Stravinsky *wanted* to record, in the early 1950s, Columbia would not support his projects, and that in the 1960s when the money was offered him, he no longer believed in the recording process.[5]

The next item on the Stravinsky agenda should be the completion of the oral history. When London Weekend Television began its 1982 Stravinsky documentary, only three survivors with pre-World War I connections could be located, and, since then, two, Dame Marie Rambert and Michel Pavloff, the Diaghilev dancers, have died. Some seventy interviews were taped with people who had known the composer in various degrees of intimacy; but seventy is far below the actual number of those who might have contributed, and this quotient excludes some valuable witnesses, a Dominican Sister living in Wisconsin, for instance, and a violist living in California, both in their nineties, both *compos mentis*, and both directly involved with Stravinsky premieres.

To judge from the London Weekend videotapes, this now-popular method of manufacturing history should be classified in this instance as a branch of autobiography, since the participants only recount incidents in their own lives, with little bearing on Stravinsky's. What struck me is that certain apocryphal stories revealed more significant truths about his character than some of the readily verifiable material. Thus Kyra Nijinsky, daughter of the dancer and an incontinent reminiscer, first saw Stravinsky when she was two, and only once or twice in later life. This does not prevent her from describing an encounter with him in Venice in September 1937, walking between his actual wife, Catherine, and his common-law wife, Vera, both of whom he introduced as if such public threesomes were the foundation of respectability. But in truth Catherine was in a tuberculosis sanatorium at the time, and though she and Vera were friends and did take walks together, Stravinsky never promenaded with both women at once.

The anecdote is not without value, since it describes behaviour that anyone who knew Stravinsky would agree is characteristic of him and of his logical, as opposed to psychological, mind. The concocted story was based on well-known true ones. In 1920, at the beginning of his affair with Chanel[6], he immediately told his wife, because, as he said, she was the person most concerned. A few months later, he again fell in love, this time with Vera Sudeikina. He again told his wife, and for the same indisputably logical reason. Soon after, he brought the two women together, insisting that since they were the people he most cared for, they really had to know each other. The logic is still consistent, yet something seems to be wrong!

The last item on my Stravinsky agenda concerns publications, musicological, analytical, and—most difficult for all biographical. Such technical works as Allen Forte's of the harmonic structure of *The Rite*, set new and high standards. But a comprehensive biography is still far from being a possibility, for the reason that the crucial information about Stravinsky's formative years through the period of *Firebird* is lacking. We need a book similar to that of Bronislava Nijinska about her brother.[7] The diary of Stravinsky's father, which covers Igor's life until age twenty in great detail, especially its financial aspects, provides some but not all of the essential clues, and the few Russian musicologists who have had access to the volume do not employ an even remotely psychoanalytical approach to the biographical material about the infant and the young child.

This, I submit, is central for a man who was extremely

anal, exhibitionistic, narcissistic, hypochondriacal, compulsive and deeply superstitious. He was also quarrelsome and vindictive, which is stated not as moral judgment but merely as description of behaviour. The probable cause of all this goes back to the cradle, and the deprivation of the mother. Indeed, the patterns of Stravinsky's Oedipal conflict can be seen both in family relations and in choices of subjects (Orpheus, the punishment of Jocasta, the sacrifice of the virgin in *The Rite* and *Noces*). But we do not have the evidence; no observation of the infant Igor has so far surfaced, or, at least, been made available to the West. The combative relationship existing between the young boy and his parents extended, throughout his life, to others in authority, most prominently music teachers and orchestra conductors. He repeatedly said that he wrote *The Rite of Spring* in order 'to send everyone' in his Russian past, Tsar, family, instructors, 'to hell', in other words, all who failed to recognize his genius. *The Rite is* music's masterpiece of iconoclasm.

Finally, who is qualified to write Stravinsky's biography, in the sense of Boswell's claim to have written 'not only a history of Johnson's visible progress through the world . . . but a view of his *mind*'? To any suggestion that I might be, let me answer with an analogy to the obstacles encountered by Flaubert's niece in describing the initial inaptitude of the future author of *Madame Bovary* in his attempt to master the alphabet, and consequent backwardness in learning to read. First, her main source was Flaubert himself, and, second, she had to find an objective and unobtrusive way of presenting herself. My difficulty is of the same order, since I play a very large part in the narrative from which, to achieve perspective, I would have to detach myself. I was too close to Stravinsky to do this, and I do not yet understand the real relationship between us, personal, professional, psychological, cultural, not to mention the irrational, such as 'karma' and Hamlet's 'there's a divinity that shapes our ends'.

Why Stravinsky in my life, and why me in his? The question

paralyzes me now more than it did while he was alive. After all, we came from opposite ends of the earth, had entirely different backgrounds, and were forty-two years apart in age—though this last was a factor only very near the end, for generation gaps did not exist with Stravinsky. (The poet Eugenio Montale, describing the dress rehearsal for *Threni* in Venice, 24 September 1958, wrote: 'The frequent interruptions showed that the good preparatory work done by the young Craft in pulling it all together was thrown to the winds by the still younger Stravinsky . . .') But in many ways we were also alike. A biochemist at the Massachusetts Institute of Technology, the late Max Reinkel, one-time physician to us both and a man of uncommon insight, noted that our nervous systems and temperaments were virtually the same. We were similarly ironic, hypercritical, perfectionist (in our unequal ways), intransigent, and our eupeptic-dyspeptic cycles usually coincided. Moreover, our taste in people as well as in music, art, literature, and cuisine, was amazingly compatible.

Stravinsky's personality was overwhelming and dominating, of course, and I had to seek refuge from it in order to preserve my identity. Yet my personality—whose features, as I see them, where my certainty about musical values and my crippling Libran indecisiveness and procrastination in most other things—must actively have contributed to the relationship. It goes without saying that Stravinsky shared the first of these qualities but not the second (did anyone ever act so positively and immediately?), which probably promoted our friendship. As it flourished, Stravinsky discovered that I was more independent than he had first supposed, and markedly unlike his children and numerous acolytes schooled by Nadia Boulanger. Yet I think that, after an initial shock, he welcomed this difference in me. No one before ever seems to have contradicted him, or questioned a patently foolish statement (of which he was as capable as anyone else). No doubt my bad manners were to blame when I talked back, as much as the feeling that disagreement should not always be swalᴗu. But we did adjust to each other.

What was the magnet that brought us together? Our letters immediately before and after we met reveal conscious and unconscious motives on both sides that helped to establish the basis of the twenty-three-year symbiosis. But Stravinsky's correspondence also exposes a prescience concerning me, at least to my hindsight, that goes far deeper. Was I looking for vicarious or reflected glory? I don't think so, and certainly I succeeded in avoiding it in the formative period to which I am referring, that of the private, even hermetic three years during which Stravinsky composed the *Rake* and began the Cantata, years interrupted only by rare forays for conducting engagements. The sole observer present then, when we stayed home together, and crossed the continent five times by auto-mobile, and took innumerable other trips exploring the West-ern states, was Mrs Stravinsky, and she alone understood our relationship. From the first, she believed that I, or someone like me, was essential to her husband if he were to remain in the midstream of new music. She sensed—as she had done in the early 1920s, when she introduced Arthur Lourié to Stra-vinsky—that he needed a musical confidant and sounding board, which is not to say that my role was comparable to that of Lourié, who had a family life of his own and was near to Stravinsky in age and cultural background. In any case, and as their correspondence shows, Lourié was never as close to Stravinsky as I was from the beginning.

When I met Stravinsky, in the spring of 1948, his fortunes were at a low ebb. Most of his music was not in print, he was not recording, and concert organizations wanted him to conduct only *Firebird* and *Petrushka*. More important, he was becoming increasingly isolated from the developments that extended from Arnold Schoenberg and had attracted the young generation. Stravinsky was aware of this despite the acclaim for *Orpheus*, his latest composition, and if he wanted to understand the other music, he did not know how to go about it. I say in all candour that I provided the path and that I do not believe Stravinsky would ever have taken the direction that he did without me. The music that he would otherwise have written is impossible to imagine.

The 1948 meeting occurred at a propitious time and place—a crossroads—in other ways as well. Until then, the Stravinskys had lived largely in a world of non-English-speaking refugees, most of whom were returning to Europe. On the very day we met, Stravinsky received the English libretto of his next work, which automatically made me useful to him. Interactions began to take place, and, inevitably, he was Americanized through the exposure—to the extent that this transmogrification can be said to have taken place. Finally, though scarcely believable today, Stravinsky in 1948 lacked performing champions of his music, and was himself its only specialist conductor. He saw me, at first and increasingly in later years, as an interpreter of his works.

Music historians are aware that understanding my role is their greatest obstacle, and I dread to contemplate their prurient hypotheses and tendentious projections concerning the nature of the glue that held us together. What I can say with certainty is that my friendship with Igor Stravinsky endured because of continuing exchange; because of an ever-increasing mutual dependency; and, above all, because of an affection that, though not always visible to others, was abiding and profound.

Notes

1 'The music of my little Tango was composed in 1940 with a view to cabaret performaces. The publisher was supposed to have commissioned the words from a "song writer" with whom he never reached an agreement. For this reason my Tango remained in a provisional form (a kind of piano reduction) until last year, when I decided to make a special instrumentation.' (Letter to Hans Rosbaud, 13 July 1954.)

2 *Performing Arts Magazine*, March 1970.

3 On 8 March 1952, Stravinsky wrote to Willy Strecker of B. Schotts Söhne: 'Last year in the Augusteo in Rome, the parts of the 1919 version were in such poor condition and so full of mistakes that [Paul] Kletzki, who happened to be there before

my arrival, had the kindness to devote an entire rehearsal to correcting the parts.'

4 The notion that I might conduct recordings under Stravinsky's supervision was inadvertently suggested to him by David Oppenheim of Columbia Records, in a letter of 25 August 1954: 'I am wondering whether you are planning to conduct at the recording sessions or whether Bob will do that. I have not the slightest reservation about the kind of job Bob would do. It occurs to me that in this series we are making absolutely authentic performances under the supervision of yourself.' I had already conducted *Three Songs from Shakespeare* in a Los Angeles concert and was about to conduct *In Memoriam Dylan Thomas* in another one. Stravinsky, who had not had any performing experience with either piece, wanted me to record them but finally did it himself. In a letter to Columbia, 27 October 1966, Stravinsky protested against the pretence 'that I conducted the Capriccio [recording].'

5 By contrast, in the 1940s Stravinsky's records were remarkably popular and accounted for a major part of his income. Between 1940 and 1944, more than 28,000 sets of *The Rite* and 11,148 sets of *Petrushka* Suite were sold, and, within six months of release (January 1947), 25,000 albums of *Firebird*. But the most surprising figure is the 7,237 copies of Symphony in Three Movements sold within one month of its appearance (May 1947). In later years Stravinsky became convinced that the danger of misrepresentation through bad performances was not offset by 'documentary' value, and he wrote to Columbia, 27 February 1967, asking the company not to release the *Requiem Canticles* recording: 'The contralto and bass solos are faulty in intonation, and there are a number of wrong notes and other errors . . . an immature performance: you are quite right in opposing any recording of any new piece on its trial run . . .''

6 Misia Sert has introduced Stravinsky to Gabrielle Chanel in May 1920. In September Chanel invited the composer to live in her *art nouveau* villa in the Paris suburb of Garches. She became his mistress soon after, and in December sponsored Diaghilev's revival of *The Rite of Spring*. The furtive affair lasted only to February 1921, but the two were lifelong, if distant, friends, and Chanel helped Stravinsky and his family until the mid-1930s.

7 *Early Memoirs*, translated and edited by Irina Nijinska and Jean Rawlinson. New York, 1981.

2

ENCOUNTER AND METAMORPHOSIS

In the following pages I attempt to describe the reverse side of my relationship with Stravinsky, the effect that he had on me, from the moment that I first heard his music to the impact of the first face-to-face meetings. My biography is of general interest, of course, only where it intertwines with his, yet to clarify that connection, more of it must be told than can be found in parentheses and footnotes in writings about him. Though my upbringing in provincial pre-electronic America must resemble that of countless others, my peculiarly American artistic and intellectual rags-to-riches story-that-could-not-happen-but-did provides a study in culture shock that may have an interest of its own.

Stravinsky's origins and mine could hardly be more disparate. Kingston, New York, at the time of my birth there, had been a prosperous Hudson River port since the seventeenth century. The pace of life that I knew was slow, the economy being based on farming, river trade, and small manufacturing. New York City, ninety miles away, was another world, to be visited only on special occasions for viewing such wonders as skyscrapers, Chinatown, elevated trains, double-decker buses, and the Bronx Zoo. In contrast, Kingston retained its colonial Dutch flavour in the many old stone houses surrounding the beautiful Reformed Church, whose spire is still the city's chief landmark, and one of whose congregation, in 1942, earned the admiration of Wallace Stevens for having a pamphlet with the phrase, 'When Spinoza's logic went searching for God'. The society in which I was reared, however, was pure Babbittville.

My paternal great-grandfather Craft, in appearance a Biblical patriarch, was a prodigious reader and a failed writer. My grandfather Craft established stores in the Far West for the Great Atlantic and Pacific Tea Company and barely escaped with his life during the San Francisco earthquake. My grandmother Craft's great-grandfather played in the Royal Philharmonic in Haydn's time. His son emigrated to the United States, fought in the Civil War, and survived imprisonment at Andersonville. The paternal ancestors of my mother's father came to America with a grant from Queen Anne for what is now Coney Island, and on the maternal side he was descended from Huguenots turned Quaker. His mother had met General Lafayette. Among my maternal grandmother's ancestors were three Huguenots who emigrated from the area near Lille in the seventeenth century and with nine other families founded the village of New Paltz: Hugo Frère (the progenitor also of Charles Lang Freer of Freer Gallery–Smithsonian fame) and Chrétien and Pierre Deyo, lesser noblemen from the eleventh-century Château Donjon at St Pol, near Lille. My other maternal ancestors were early Dutch and English settlers who owned small farms, based their lives on the ethics of Protestantism, and fought in the Revolutionary and Civil Wars. Though my mother, a chip off Plymouth rock, was a Daughter of the American Revolution, she was a woman totally without prejudice who took very seriously the virtue of loving one's neighbour.

For their time and class, my parents were somewhat better educated than most of their peers in the small city of Kingston, my father having attended Syracuse University and my mother a teachers' college. As a stock investor, my father was sufficiently prosperous to afford private schooling for his three children, a Cadillac and chauffeur, a live-in maid, a tennis court, family photographs by Bachrach – in other words, the trappings of the bourgeois *nouveau riche*. (I did not realize my true social status until I went to boarding school, where my classmates included James Farley, Jr – son of the Postmaster General – the Shattucks of Schrafft's, the

Philadelphia Annenbergs, and the scions of South American dictators: therein was born a lifelong sense of social aggrandizement that turned me inward.) In the Great Depression my father lost everything except our home, though his son and two daughters were hardly aware of the straitened circumstances and remained sheltered from life's realities. As a businessman he had imagination and vision, quickly seeing, after a visit to one of the new 'supermarkets' in Philadelphia, that this way of merchandising was the wave of the future. In the Hudson Valley (Albany to Poughkeepsie) and Western Massachusetts (Great Barrington, North Adams), he opened the first supermarkets in the North-east and worked prodigiously to pay his creditors. Though the stores flourished, his generous heart and lack of ruthlessness militated against a return to our former affluence.

Both of my parents had musical talent and could play the piano, my mother with sufficient promise to win acceptance at the New England Conservatory of Music. As children we were taken to the Metropolitan Opera, the New York Philharmonic, and chamber-music concerts, as well as to local musical events. The most important factor in our early education, however, was my mother's dedication to her profession of schoolteaching. She read to us and made us study, taught us to speak grammatically, to attend church, and, above all, to be punctual – the root, no doubt, of my 'deadline' neurosis. My father, too, always stressed the importance of knowledge and education, taking us to every historic and culturally interesting location within a five-day drive of our home.

Our childhood home was a handsome fourteen-room Victorian residence whose secret passageways, dumbwaiter, tiled fireplaces, bay-window seats, and hideout attic-above-the-attic still haunt my dreams. By good fortune, most of the furnishings had been purchased along with the house from the estate of a widely travelled collector of Oriental art. As I became conscious of the mysterious treasures surrounding us – a carved Chinese dragon chair, Indian incense burners and cobra-shaped candelabra, Siamese teakwood objects, samurai swords, tooled brass and copper wares from Egypt, Persian rugs – I began to fantasize about them. Our most conspicuous European antiques were some faded seventeenth-century French tapestries – distinctly not the fashion in a 1920s provincial American town. None of this exotica reflected the tastes of my parents, but it stimulated my imagination, desire to travel, passion for the visual arts, and future hobby of collecting Indian miniatures.

The most consequential part of the previous owner's legacy was a large library containing Shakespeare, Dickens, Scott, Byron, the Brontës, George Eliot, Ruskin, Hawthorne, the 1893 edition of Emily Dickinson's *Letters*, Cooper, Stevenson, Mark Twain, and Thackeray; I still remember *Vanity Fair* more vividly than any other novel. The history books and those about African explorers were particularly engrossing, as was the four-volume *World of Today* illustrated with colour photographs. To these my parents added dictionaries, Compton's *Picture Encyclopedia*, and *My Book House*, an anthology of fairy tales, myths, and fables. No music corner existed until I began to read biographies of composers and to collect Eulenburg pocket scores. In the enjoyment of all of this, I had the guidance and companionship of a sister two years older whose dominant interests were also literature and music. Together, over the years, we added Everyman and the Modern Library to the Victorians.

Of inspiring teachers I remember only one, the organist and director of the choir at St John's Episcopal Church, in which, at age six, I became boy soprano soloist. Here I learned Bach's Mass and Passions, and sacred classics by Mendelssohn, Gounod, and César Franck. This choirmaster convinced my parents that my musical gifts were worthy of training. Luckily they were able to follow his advice because of the proximity of Woodstock, where a colony of musicians from New York had summer homes. I not only attended concerts there, but also, between the ages of ten and thirteen, was enrolled in a nearby music school whose faculty included Percy Grainger, Henry Cowell, the cellist Horace Britt, the concertmaster of the

Metropolitan Opera Pierre Henrotte, and the flautist Georges Barrère. Not until years later did I learn that Barrère had been coached by Prokofiev in a performance of Stravinsky's *Pribaoutki* in New York in 1919. Had anyone told me this, I would have questioned Barrère about it, for by age twelve I already knew that my goal in life was to study with Stravinsky. As the first step in this direction, I approached the head of the school, a former member of the Philadelphia Orchestra when Stokowski was introducing Stravinsky's music in America. My aspiration was ridiculous, I was told, and not for the expected reason – lack of preparation – but because Stravinsky's music was horrible noise!

Meanwhile, I had written songs and an elementary, over-orchestrated tone poem. Eric Leidzen, composition teacher at the camp, sensibly informed my disappointed parents that these efforts showed no evidence of unusual talent. Nor did they betray any influence of the Cowell experiments, which fascinated me, let alone of the music I loved most, *Firebird*. At this stage and from then on I was spending all of my time studying scores and applying myself to exercises in harmony and counterpoint. My academic grades suffered accordingly, and in order to qualify for the Juilliard School, which I entered in 1941, I had to enlist the help of another Woodstock resident, a friend of my father, the historian and Columbia professor James T. Shotwell.

I should also mention the yeast that was entering upstate cultural life in the persons of refugees from Germany, whose cosmopolitanism contrasted sharply with the narrowly circumscribed world of the natives. One elderly ex-Berliner's reminiscences about Salzburg and Bayreuth made me especially aware of my limitations as a small-town American. (Coincidentally, Woodstock was also the home of the painter Serge Sudeikin, ex-husband of Vera Stravinsky, but this I learned years later.)

Like other young musicians, I suffered one infatuation after another among the great composers: the Tchaikovsky mumps, then the Brahms measles, and the Wagner scarlet fever. (An exception: I discovered Beethoven's quartets at an early age, and my love for them has never diminished.) When I heard recordings of *Les Noces* and *Histoire du soldat*, I was more thrilled by this music than by even the greatest classics, and I realized that the moderns, Stravinsky above all, exerted the strongest appeal for me. The two decisive listening experiences in my adolescence occurred within the same year, the Sunday-afternoon New York Philharmonic broadcast (7 April 1940) of Stravinsky conducting *The Rite of Spring* which I followed in a Kalmus miniature score, and the recording of *Pierrot Lunaire*, made after Schoenberg's Town Hall performance (7 November 1940). No score of *Pierrot* being available, I stole the one from the 58th Street Music Library.

I first glimpsed Stravinsky in the flesh in January 1946, when he led the New York Philharmonic in the premiere of his Symphony in Three Movements. He seemed very tall, and his sandy hair surprised me, since photographs showed it to be dark. He walked faster between the wings and podium than any conductor I had ever seen. (Until he underwent a prostate operation shortly after his seventy-first birthday, his movements were remarkably rapid, which contradicts the impression conveyed by his late-in-life television documentaries.) After the performance of the Symphony, I waited outside Carnegie Hall's stage door in the bitter January cold, but when Stravinsky finally emerged, I did not immediately recognize him beneath his high fur collar and with his head swathed in scarves and towels. His height, which seemed hardly more than half that of his closely protecting wife, misled me. I followed them at a respectful distance as they walked to the corner to a waiting car, which, as I learned years later, took them to their hotel, the Sherry Netherlands.

When I next saw Stravinsky, again in Carnegie Hall, on 8 February 1946, he was playing the piano, and Joseph Szigeti the violin, in *Duo concertant*. The composer's brisk, detached stage presence and businesslike reading of the music were utterly different from the emoting of most soloists. Unsmiling and aloof, he acknowledged the applause, right hand above his heart, with a single deep bow—which I assumed to be the Russian style, Rachmaninov having done the same when I had seen him in a concert with Ormandy and the Philadelphia Orchestra in October 1941.

Juilliard had been a terrible disappointment to me, partly for the reason that Stravinsky's music was almost totally ignored there. The discussion that followed a classroom reading of *The Rite*, played four-hands by pupils of Frederick Jacobi, was jejune, and the analysis of the Capriccio in one of Bernard Wagenaar's composition classes was confined to a superficial examination of the orchestration. Compositions by William Bergsma, Robert Ward, and William Schuman were played by the student orchestra, but why, I wondered, did it never attempt the *Symphonies of Wind Instruments* and *Pulcinella*? I tried to remedy this by organizing a chamber ensemble, which presented Stravinsky's Octet and, later, *Histoire du soldat* and the Concerto in E flat. I cut classes to give time to this, as well as to explore New York's art museums and galleries, and to earn money by playing trumpet in the Radio City Music Hall touring orchestra. Here I lost all contact with Stravinsky's music except for a Philharmonic broadcast heard while our orchestra was on a three-week tour. I must also mention my lost year as a draftee in the US Army, a period during which I heard no music above the level of 'You Are My Sunshine', and managed to survive only by reading Stendhal and Proust.

I spent the summer of 1946 at Tanglewood, already familiar because I had hitch-hiked to Boston Symphony concerts there since its inaugural years. I soon met a young musician, Claudio Spies, who was as fanatically devoted to Stravinsky as I was, who knew as much about his music, and who was my undisputed cultural superior. A refugee from Germany by way of Chile, Spies's multilinguality intimidated me, as this accomplishment has always done. Moreover, he knew the Stravinskys and had actually had lunch with them and Alexis Haieff a few months before. Another Stravinskyite at Tanglewood, Harold Shapero, was enough older to attract his own generation of followers, but all of us were insufferable prigs, snobbish in our tastes for Stravinsky as well as the music, such as Monteverdi, that he was known to admire. (After giving a concert in Madison, Wisconsin, in February 1982, I was told by the director of the orchestra that he recalled Spies and me, in that summer of 1946, pronouncing all non-Stravinsky-lovers 'dunces'.)

In January 1947 I was able to observe Stravinsky at close hand during rehearsals for Ballet Society's *Renard*, performed on the 13th at Hunter College Playhouse, and during rehearsals and a studio broadcast performance of *Perséphone* two days later. As Leon Barzin conducted *Renard*, Stravinsky, towel around neck, rushed down the aisle complaining in French about the tempo and shouting in Russian to George Balanchine, who staged the work. The voice was a deep basso whose timbre and volume seemed incongruous issuing from such a small man. The composer spoke to the orchestra players and the singers in heavily accented English, and, going on stage, mimed movements for the dancers. The focus of attention at every instant, he interrupted frequently with a loud '*Non, Non*,' less often with '*Da, Da*'. A music stand with a light had been installed for him a few rows from the orchestra pit, and I found a place directly behind him. He licked his thumb before turning the pages of his score and, each time he looked up, exchanged his reading glasses for the spectacles on his forehead. He beat time and counted metres aloud. But it was his speed and energy as he bobbed up and down from his seat that distinguished him from everybody else.

Two years later I learned from him that he had not noticed me at either the *Renard* or the *Perséphone* rehearsal. During the latter I managed to squeeze myself into a group photograph with him and to watch him change his shirt and undershirt, at which time I caught a glimpse of his naked torso, and of the gold cross and cluster of religious medals suspended around his neck. After he had dried his back with a towel, like a shoe-shine boy's polishing, and had doused himself with '4711', his wife handed him dry clothes, a flask, and a cigarette and holder. The *Perséphone* performance made me determine to see the as-yet-unpublished score, and the next day I went to Juilliard's dean, Mark Schubart, to ask him if he could arrange to borrow a manuscript copy for me to study. He very kindly did this, procuring the one that Stravinsky himself had used. (Is it ungrateful to repeat Stravinsky's remark at a later date when someone mentioned Juilliard: 'Oh, that's the place with the wrong Schubert, the wrong Schumann, and the wrong Wagner!'?)

The year 1947 is the crucial one in my story. That summer I had gone to Maine to study conducting with Pierre Monteux but dropped out when I realized that, whatever my aptitudes, I wanted to concentrate on certain music only, and not on the pop masterpieces. Returning home, I was amazed to find a letter from Stravinsky. Having written to him previously without a reply, I was so nervous that I waited hours before opening it. Although this letter has long since been published, the one from me that provoked it has not, and this makes clear that Stravinsky was responding primarily to my request to borrow the parts for the *Symphonies of Wind Instruments*. Strange as it seems now, apparently nobody else took any interest in the piece, and, as he told me later, on the very day that he received my letter he was going over a proof score of the unpublished original version. The possibility of a performance by my Chamber Arts Society evidently motivated him to rewrite the work.

Between that day in August 1947 and our meeting in Washington, DC, 31 March 1948, our letters became increasingly friendly, and to a degree unparalleled in any of Stravinsky's other relationships. Why did he offer to conduct the new *Symphonies* for me, gratis, when he had been known to spend as long as six years in litigation to collect a fee, and had given only one charity concert (for war relief) in all of his years in America? Why did he share a programme with me conducting the second half? My letters to him contain no clue to this, and they are certainly not impressive. I know that he received favourable reports about my performances of his music in a New York concert in the autumn of 1947, but this hardly explains his generosity. He never told me why he did it, and it remains a mystery.

Although my book *Chronicle of a Friendship* describes our first meeting, from today's perspective I would see it very differently. Now I ask myself how I found the courage to go at all, and managed to brazen my way through it. One explanation is that the presence of W. H. Auden helped to shield me, since he was speaking English and was almost as awkward and shy as I. Stravinsky must have noticed that although I was tongue-tied with him, I could talk freely with Auden, at least about literary matters. Undoubtedly this made me look better than I would have otherwise, given Stravinsky's enormous regard for the poet's intelligence.

The *Chronicle* does not show any awareness of *my* effect on Stravinsky, but at the time I could not tell. Furthermore, only after living with him did I learn that he could wear many masks, for initially I would not have guessed that he could be anything but straightforward and ingenuous; certainly on that day he was without equivocations. He was the most gracious man I had ever met, and I was reminded of Saint-Simon on the Roi Soleil: '*Jamais homme si naturellement poli.*' I was immediately conscious of being an entirely new breed to him, quite unlike his Harvard pupils (in 1939–40) and the privileged young people that he had known while being entertained in wealthy American homes. From today's distance, the most striking thing about him was the intensity of his concentration. Unlike others, he did not switch from subject to subject but pursued each one to the end, demanding definite, not provisional answers. 'Do you know the best way to render "*se rendre compte*" in English?' he asked, and of course I did not, in spite of five years of school French. (Auden was equally nonplussed.) When our forthcoming Town Hall concert came under discussion, Stravinsky asked how many strings I would have and how much rehearsal time. Knowing that both were insufficient, I feared that he would cancel. His animal energy seemed to be on the verge of exploding, and he expressed his impatience with grunts, headshaking, and knee slapping. (I am not sure that I ever adjusted to this quality in Stravinsky the man, but I never ceased to admire the supreme patience of the artist, who could wait calmly for days until he had found the right note in a chord.)

After lunch I walked along the Potomac, elated but also apprehensive about the fate of my concert. When I returned to the Stravinskys' hotel suite, I could see that whatever they had concluded about me, their curiosity had been aroused, and so, I felt, had their affection.

Of the culture shocks that took place during the next four and a half weeks in New York, the most painful was the luncheon to which I invited the Stravinskys and their friend Lisa Sokolov. I chose the wrong restaurant, the now-defunct Town and Country on Park Avenue, my mother having mistakenly believed that they might enjoy American cooking, and paying no heed to Saint Paul's advice to Timothy: 'Drink no longer water, but use a little wine for thy stomach's sake.' There was no wine list, but plenty of popovers, and the stiff and prim waiters disapproved of these loud, Russian-speaking autocrats. Although Mrs Stravinsky tried to subdue her husband, he did not conceal his desire to leave and go to an Italian or French café, no matter how poor. My blunder embarrassed me, the more so because we had become the cynosure of the room. The Stravinskys forgot the incident an hour after it had happened, but it has stayed with me until now. I was soon converted to their kind of cuisine but never became accustomed to their dining-out etiquette – hitting a glass with a fork to get a waiter's attention, complaining audibly about anything that did not please them – all so very unlike my own family's meek and easily intimidated restaurant manners.

Some of the events of the next three and a half months are related in published correspondence, but not our next two encounters, in Denver on 20 July, and in the Stravinsky

Hollywood home ten days later. Despite the warmth of the interim correspondence, and the reiterated invitations to make these trips, I felt upon arrival that I was not quite so important to them as I had seemed at their leave-taking in New York after our wonderful weeks together in the spring. They had left a message at their Denver hotel for me to meet them at the home of the conductor Saul Caston, where Soulima Stravinsky had been practising the Capriccio on the piano with his father conducting him, in preparation for their concert at Red Rocks. For lunch we went to a country club as guests of a wealthy, well-bred American who had just returned from travels in Africa. Being politically and socially left-wing, I considered our host to be the kind of effete dilettante who should be overthrown, and Stravinsky dismayed me by referring to him as the paragon of American gentility. (*My* idea of a true American aristocrat was Stravinsky's good friend Stark Young, an articulate and learned Southern gentleman who was even permitted to call him 'Mr Igor'; it seems ironic that I should have met this fellow-countryman through Stravinsky.)

Another culture shock occurred in the evening as the Stravinskys and I were window-shopping. Seeing some modern American paintings, I voiced my preferences, unasked, and was gently rebuked and told that I knew nothing about art. This was true, not in the sense of book knowledge or even in the amount of time spent looking at masterpieces, but in my lack of expertise and discrimination. Stravinsky saw with his eyes as he heard with his ears, and viewed any painting, or scene in nature, as a composition. Sitting at a table he would habitually rearrange the objects on it, placing them in relationships that enhanced their individual forms and resulted in new designs. His own drawings of people, of Diaghilev, Picasso, and Ramuz, for example, reveal his perception and gift for capturing essential features. He could have been a brilliant cartoonist.

The young Igor Stravinsky *had* been a painter and had wanted to study the art. As a guide, his criticisms cut directly to the bone and were always illuminating – which I say because visits to exhibitions were to become an important part of our life together. His tastes, from textiles to Piero della Francesca, were catholic (with the exception that, when I first met him, his admiration for Picasso and the School of Paris left no room for Klee, Kandinsky, Mondrian). Visiting the temples of Kyoto, the Cairo Museum, the Villa Giulia, and the Scythian collection in the Hermitage with Stravinsky was one of the great privileges of my life.

In Denver, Stravinsky had talked about Mexico, not the pre-Columbian, but the Baroque, encouraging me to take a side-trip there *en route* to Hollywood. He urged me to go by train from Juarez to Mexico City in order to see the villages. I followed his advice, and experienced a new culture shock, less that of the usual tourist's reaction to the country than bewilderment at what Stravinsky had found most interesting. What had fascinated him, and no doubt reminded him of tsarist Russia, was the picturesque, the old people begging from the train passengers and the crippled children pointing to maimed limbs to indicate that they could not earn money. I was appalled, and even more so at Guadalupe, which he had placed at the top of my itinerary as an awesome holy site. I could hardly wait to leave Mexico, which I did on 30 July. (Twelve years later, when I returned to Guadalupe with Stravinsky and saw him kneel next to praying peons, I realized that I had changed, at least to the extent of believing in his belief.)

My plane put down in Nogales and then in Los Angeles, and I arrived in time for dinner at the Stravinsky home, where I was overwhelmed with their Russian hospitality, unlike any I had ever known in America – another kind of cultural difference. Stravinsky showed me through his studio, familiar from photos, but still the *sanctum sanctorum* for me. I slept on the couch in his den, after my height had been recorded on its closet door, several inches below the tallest marks, for Charles Olson and Aldous Huxley. The next morning Stravinsky took me to the studio and played his recently completed Mass, as well as what he had composed of *The Rake's Progress*. He sang various parts, groaned while searching for notes, and looked very pleased afterwards when I showed how deeply I was moved by the beauty of both works. This view of creation from the inside was the peak experience of my early musical life.

When I finally returned to New York, I had indeed undergone a metamorphosis. From being with Stravinsky at his rehearsals in Washington, New York, and Denver, I had learned more about music than in my entire life until then, and I knew that I had sat at the feet of a man whose horizons were broader and further away than those of other men.

As for my own horizons, they had expanded far beyond my means, or so my friends and family quickly noticed and I myself realized. But my uprooting was forever.

3

INFLUENCE OR ASSISTANCE?

Mikhail Druskin's *Igor Stravinsky: His life, Works, and Views*, first published in the USSR in 1974 and now in the United Kingdom and United States in a translation by Martin Cooper (Cambridge University Press), has provoked me to give a long-overdue account of the part I played in the composer's life during the early 1950s' crisis in his development. After this and until the mid-1960s my main function was to rehearse and co-conduct his concerts and recording sessions.

Druskin's survey allots considerable space to the music of Stravinsky's final years, unexpectedly giving it a higher value than such accepted masterpieces of the 1930s as *Perséphone* and the *Concerto per due pianoforti soli*. The book's emphasis on aesthetics rather than biographical detail is also surprising, in view of the crippling limitations imposed in the Soviet Union on serial and all other 'socially reactionary' music. Not surprisingly, the bibliography is small; the principal studies on the composer (especially the Boretz and Cone *Perspectives on Schoenberg and Stravinsky*) are still unavailable, or untranslated, there. Druskin met Stravinsky briefly – in Berlin, in 1931[1] – but no subsequent contact occurred between them, and even the film documentaries, which present Stravinsky best, seem not to have been shown in Russia.

Druskin's greatest handicap is his inability to transcend his Marxist orientation, surely a necessity in attempting to understand a composer for whom religious beliefs are at the core of both life and work. Forced to skirt the issue, albeit forgiving Stravinsky on the grounds of his being a victim of his capitalist environment, Druskin develops the notion that the composer was perpetually homesick for Russia, could not adjust to the United States, and compromised his art when he tried to do so. But despite these misleading interpretations (and not to mention numerous factual mistakes), Druskin impresses the reader as a fair-minded critic who has thought deeply about Stravinsky.

This said, some of the book's premises are based on erroneous assumptions that must be corrected and that compel me to cite certain historical facts that Druskin strives conscientiously, but perforce blindly, to understand and explain. He writes:

> In the composer's own hallowed phrase, quoted by Craft, '[The] Rake's Progress was an end.' After this there was an abrupt change in Stravinsky's [style]. He wrote first the Cantata . . . and then the Septet, in which he experimented for the first time with the use of a series. From now onwards his whole attitude to the New Viennese School was different . . .
>
> What had in fact happened? Had Schoenberg's death had such a deep effect on him? Had he in fact wished to study dodecaphonic methods earlier and been embarrassed by the existence of a rival whose death alone could liberate him from this inhibition? There is no answer to a psychological question of this kind . . .

The questions that Druskin raises *do* have answers, some of them matters of record, to which he simply had no access. It is true that Schoenberg's death affected Stravinsky, but hardly to the degree suggested here. The composer of *Sacre* had such a powerful ego that he could soon put any death behind him, even that of his beloved daughter, after whose passing he almost immediately resumed work on his Symphony in C.

It is true that Stravinsky and Schoenberg had been cast in opposition for four decades, their so-called feud being most publicized during the eleven years when they were neighbours in California. But they had not met in all this time, and had glimpsed each other infrequently. Although Stravinsky had always held his counterpart in the highest esteem, he could not have felt a deep personal loss when there had not been a personal association. Druskin's description of the reaction as 'mourning' is inappropriate.

When I first entered Stravinsky's household, in 1948, Schoenberg was never mentioned. Sol Babitz and Ingolf Dahl, who were Stravinsky's closest musical associates at the time, did not tell him of their connection with the father of twelve-tone music. Babitz had played Schoenberg's Violin Concerto in Hollywood (25 May 1941, Evenings on the Roof, later the Monday Evening Concerts) and managed to conceal this from Stravinsky, and Dahl was no less secretive about conducting *Pierrot Lunaire*. Why, I wondered, did these two friends of Stravinsky, the first to whom he introduced me in California, whisper and tiptoe when I raised the subject of Schoenberg? It was not long before I discovered what everyone else knew: that the name had been *verboten* for years. This explained Samuel Dushkin's flustered and embarrassed manner when I ran into him in April 1950 at a New York performance of *A Survivor from Warsaw*: he realized that I would mention the meeting to Stravinsky. What still seems incredible is that Stravinsky never knew that Erich Itor Kahn, Dushkin's accompanist, who had worked with the composer on the piano reduction of his *Jeu de cartes*, belonged to the Schoenberg school.

Visitors to the Stravinsky home, including Darius Milhaud, also refrained from mentioning Schoenberg to Stravinsky, though I knew from Mrs Schoenberg that Milhaud regularly called at their house when he was in Los Angeles. Even the far-from-surreptitious Otto Klemperer never pronounced the name Schoenberg to Stravinsky. One day when the eminent conductor came to lunch, I greeted him with, underarm, a score I was to conduct in an 'Evenings on the Roof' concert. He grabbed the music, glanced at it, pointed to the first notes, counted aloud from one to twelve, and said to me in his stentorian voice: 'Nowadays no one is doing anything else.' Stravinsky overheard this but made no reference to the twelve-tone vogue. During the meal, he did not inquire about Schoenberg, probably assuming that Klemperer would be going to his house as well. When Klemperer had left, Stravinsky and I examined the score together, but its serial aspect did not interest him at all.

An incident told to me by Dahl indicates that Schoenberg's followers were as cautious as Stravinsky's in mentioning the 'enemy' name. One day in June 1949 when David Diamond knocked at the Schoenberg door, Richard Hoffman, a pupil and distant Viennese relative of Schoenberg, opened it and exclaimed: 'Zomeone from ze ozzer camp.' I did not find the story unusual, having heard many like it. But I did wonder if the cold war were being fuelled by disciples, especially when I learned that Schoenberg defended Stravinsky against René Leibowitz's abuse and also received me so cordially, despite knowing which 'camp' I was in. But then, Schoenberg realized that the motive for my visit was pure admiration, and some member of his family must have told him that Mrs Stravinsky had driven me there and waited in the car.

Nonetheless, subordinates usually echo their masters, and in this case must have known that no love was lost between them. It is reasonable to assume that the rivals themselves were jealous of each other: Schoenberg of Stravinsky's popularity, Stravinsky of Schoenberg's mystique with certain musical élitists. I think that I alone was aware that neither composer knew anything about the other's music, having recognized that each of them had been unwilling to examine his own prejudice – Schoenberg's being that Stravinsky depended on formulas and a bag of tricks, Stravinsky's that Schoenberg was a slave to an abstract system.

When did Stravinsky begin to explore Schoenberg's music and methods? The question is important, since Mikhail Druskin hypothesizes that Schoenberg's death was the crucial factor in 'freeing' Stravinsky to do so. To me, Druskin's Freudian interpretation of Stravinsky's *volte-face* as a case of 'creative mourning. . .the ego's identification with the lost object' is wholly mistaken. Another of Freud's theories is the one that really applies: relief at the death of someone perceived as a threat.

Let me recall the events of the morning of 14 July 1951. After the secretary of the 'Evenings on the Roof' concerts telephoned me with the news of Schoenberg's death during the night, Mrs Stravinsky went to her husband's studio to inform him and came back saying that he was deeply shocked. Within a few minutes, he had sent a telegram of condolence to the widow. During lunch he hardly spoke, but he resumed his work in the afternoon. Later in the day, I heard indirectly that his message had been the first to be received, and that it was greatly appreciated. Later still, a member of the Schoenberg household told me about the memorial service, hinting that Stravinsky's attendance would be a welcome gesture. Though I think Stravinsky wanted to go, he did not, his sense of irony probably intervening. The two men having avoided each other for so long, the survivor's attendance might seem insensitive.

On 19 July, when the Stravinskys and I were dining at the house of Alma Mahler-Werfel, her sculptress daughter, Anna, unexpectedly stopped by on an errand. She had Schoenberg's death mask with her and offered to show it to Stravinsky. He expressed interest, but upon seeing the image was visibly upset. Here, a foot away, was the face of the man who had haunted his thoughts since 1912, but whom he had scarcely seen, and never, since that date, at close range. Schoenberg was the one composer who challenged Stravinsky's supremacy in twentieth-century music. Furthermore, the sculptress, who had taken the impression, told Stravinsky he was the first to see it. As a superstitious man and a believer in patterns of coincidence, he must have been struck with thoughts of his own mortality.

I have already said that Stravinsky could quickly turn his energies to new projects; he had done so a few weeks before, after the death of Koussevitzky, a friend since pre-World War I days – though it must be admitted that in this instance what most unsettled Stravinsky was the harassment of reporters requesting statements. He was not asked for any tribute to Schoenberg, however, for which reason *I* wrote one (for the *Saturday Review*). Schoenberg's death receded rapidly in Stravinsky's mind as he prepared to leave for Europe two weeks later.

In September, in Venice, *The Rake's Progress* was received by most critics as the work of a master but also a throwback, the last flowering of a genre. After the premiere, conducting concerts in Italy and Germany, Stravinsky found that he and Schoenberg were everywhere categorized as the reactionary and the progressive. What was worse, Stravinsky was acutely aware that the new generation was not interested in the *Rake*. While in Cologne, he heard tapes of Schoenberg's Violin Concerto (played by Tibor Varga) and of Hermann Scherchen's Darmstadt performance of 'The Golden Calf' (from *Moses und Aron*); he listened attentively to both, but without any visible reaction. (In an interview in Seattle not long after, Stravinsky said that 'the endless quality of atonality' was 'repulsive' to him.) In contrast, a few days later, in Baden-Baden, when a recording of Webern's orchestra Variations was played for him, he asked to hear it three times in succession and showed more enthusiasm than I had ever seen from him about any contemporary music. In Rome, Stravinsky learned that even his future biographer Roman Vlad wrote twelve-tone music, and that Luigi Dallapiccola, a Schoenberg follower, had become Italy's most esteemed composer.

Back in the United States, Stravinsky was preoccupied with the Metropolitan Opera's plans to produce *The Rake's Progress* and with conducting for the New York City Ballet. Schoenberg and Webern were momentarily set aside. Then, on 24 February 1952 at the University of Southern California, I conducted a performance of Schoenberg's Septet-Suite (in a programme with Webern's Quartet, Opus 22), with Stravinsky present at all the rehearsals as well as the concert. This event was the turning point in his later musical evolution.

On 8 March,[2] he asked to go for a drive to Palmdale, at that time a small Mojave Desert town, where the Stravinskys liked to eat spareribs and drink Bordeaux from thermos bottles in a cowboy-style restaurant. On the way home he startled us, saying that he was afraid he could no longer compose and did not know what to do. For a moment he broke down and actually wept, whereupon Mrs Stravinsky convinced him that these feelings and the musical problems, whatever they were, would pass. He referred obliquely to the powerful impression that the Schoenberg piece had made on him, and when he said that he wanted to learn more, I knew that the crisis was over; so far from being defeated, Stravinsky would emerge a new composer.

To divert him, I suggested that he undertake an orchestration of one of his pieces, advice he would have given someone else in the same situation. I said that the Concertino for String Quartet was a work that the younger generation admired, and perhaps he could reinstrumentate it, employing winds from the Octet and Cantata, works that he had agreed to conduct in a Los Angeles Chamber Orchestra concert in November. The next day, he started work on the Concertino. He gave me a manuscript page of the first ricercar of the Cantata, with the setting of the words 'and through the glass window shines the sun,' inscribing it – I believe in reference to the crisis – 'To Bob whom I love'.

In Paris, in May 1952, Stravinsky watched the same audience that had cheered Berg's *Wozzeck* hiss and boo Cocteau narrating *Oedipus Rex* – though the target was not only Cocteau but the piece itself and its aesthetics, as I think the composer understood. In the same month, in Brussels, Stravinsky heard dinner-table discussions about Webern between me and Paul Collaer, as well as a tape of Webern's *Das Augenlicht*, which he borrowed. Collaer's comparisons of this music to that of the Flemish masters of the Renaissance held Stravinsky's attention – as did Ernst Krenek's talk on the same subject later.[3] Back in Hollywood, Stravinsky completed his Cantata and began the Septet, in which, for the first time, he used a series, and, in the last movement, suspended most references to the tonal system.

In the autumn of 1952, I conducted four Schoenberg memorial concerts at 'Evenings on the Roof'. Stravinsky attended these, as well as the rehearsals and the subsequent recording sessions of the Septet-Suite. All of the music was new to him, and he was so taken with the Serenade, which he had already heard at a rehearsal of mine on 12 April, that he used a mandolin in *Agon* and a guitar in his instrumentation of his Four Russian Songs. Yet the Septet-Suite, with its serial language, had the more profound influence on him, its Gigue movement directly inspiring the one in his own Septet. Writing to me on 24 August 1982, one of the players in those concerts of thirty years ago, Don Christlieb, remembers 'the musicians' awareness of the miraculous transformation in Stravinsky. We noticed that he could not resist looking at the scores you would lay on the table. We knew how involved he was becoming when we were rehearsing the Schoenberg Quintet. He sat on the couch with the score and after the second day said, "It is the finest work ever written for this combination."'[4]

In April 1953, while Stravinsky was in Caracas for concerts, I arranged a meeting between Mrs Stravinsky and Mrs Schoenberg. This was made possible because of my acquaintance with Nuria, Schoenberg's attractive daughter, whom I had occasionally escorted to concerts, restaurants, and movies, and through whom I became a regular visitor to the Schoenberg house. While there, I learned a great deal from her mother, who knew her husband's music so well that in a matter of moments she could locate any passage in his sketchbooks; for example, when I showed her a sheet of manuscript for *Moses und Aron* that I had acquired, she immediately found its place in the score. On one of my first visits, she gave me a paper on which Schoenberg had written: 'Do not discourage people, friends. They will "break" the Schbrg clique. Encourage Craft.' (Schoenberg realized that the possessiveness of his 'old guard' was against his best interests; the note was in response to a criticism of me from Erika-Wagner Stiedry.)

Influence or Assistance?

I asked Mrs Stravinsky to invite Nuria and her mother to dinner. On 12 April, when we greeted them at the door, Mrs Schoenberg said, very movingly, 'This should have happened years ago.' She asked to see Stravinsky's studio, and looked at everything very carefully. During dinner, at the Knicker-bocker Hotel, the talk centred on the personal and character similarities – which proved to be more important than the differences – of their husbands. Mrs Schoenberg had brought a gift for Stravinsky, a bottle of Schoenberg's favourite Knize toilet water, and was delighted to hear that it was also Stravinsky's brand. (On 13 April, Mrs Schoenberg wrote to Mrs Stravinsky: 'Thank you for taking the initiative and for the wonderful evening I and Nuria enjoyed in your company. Hope to see you again in my house. With *herzlichsten Grüssen*.')

In spite of the existence of some common ground between the two men, Mikhail Druskin is mistaken in his conclusion that Stravinsky was 'attracted to Schoenberg's personality, his rock-like conviction, his inflexible will.' To Stravinsky, the personality, as expressed in the music and in what he had read about Schoenberg, was not sympathetic. The real reason for Stravinsky's avowals of admiration later on was his indignation at the neglect and ill-treatment Schoenberg had suffered. Stravinsky was pleased to hear about the evening, and soon the three of us went to the Schoenbergs' for dinner.

When George Balanchine came to Los Angeles in the summer of 1953 for a season at the Greek Theater, he got in touch with Mrs Schoenberg because he wanted to choreograph one of her husband's pieces. She invited Balanchine to dinner (which the guest himself barbecued) on 29 July. She also invited me, as a friend of his and because I could act as a bridge between the Russian and Austrian cultures and between the two arts – she being ignorant of ballet, he of Schoenberg's music. Stravinsky, in hospital after a prostate operation, was of course not asked to come, but his presence would have inhibited Balanchine. During the evening, I convinced both Balanchine and Mrs Schoenberg that the best choice would be the *Begleitmusik*, Op. 34. Balanchine avoided telling Stravinsky about the episode, and when I did it was evident that Stravinsky was upset. Yet this latest proof of the increasing general interest in Schoenberg's music motivated Stravinsky to study such books as Jelinek's analyses of chordal construction in the Septet-Suite.

In the autumn of 1954 Stravinsky declined Mrs Schoenberg's invitation to hear a tape of *Moses und Aron* in company with other people, and relations cooled. He sent her a courteous note, but a little later she refused his request for a copy of an early letter from him to her husband. Several years passed before they met again, this time at a dinner in the Stravinsky home, for which occasion she gave him a facsimile of the *Jakobsleiter* score and a tape of the BBC performance. Perhaps Schoenberg's death did 'liberate' Stravinsky, but not in Druskin's 'psychological' sense. What really happened is that Schoenberg's music began to be performed only after his death – in those first few years, more of it by me, I am proud to say, than by anyone else. After that, the story switches from private to public annals. Upon hearing the *Canticum Sacrum* and *Threni*, the poet Eugenio Montale wrote: 'By adopting the twelve-tone system, Stravinsky took the most perilous step in his career.'

Now to the remainder of Mikhail Druskin's thesis:

People sometimes talk as though Craft were a kind of 'tempter' in Stravinsky's life, the man who 'converted' him to the serialist faith. This is manifest nonsense. When Craft first met Stravinsky, who was already a world famous composer, he was twenty-four years old. He was gradually to become the composer's indispensable assistant, his travelling-companion, a not unbiased witness and correspondent of Stravinsky's last years, a kind of Eckermann to his Goethe, though a much more enterprising and masterful personality than Eckermann. . . But can anyone seriously suppose that a composer who all his conscious life had composed in accordance with an inner artistic law which he had deliberately imposed on himself, who was spontaneous and impulsive in his aesthetic tastes – that such a man would be untrue to his own character and allow himself to be persuaded by a young man who had not as yet in any way proved himself as an artist? Assistance must not be confused with influence. Craft could help Stravinsky to become better acquainted with the works and the methods of the New Viennese School. . .but he could not, of course, direct or control the spiritual interests of a composer of genius.

Whether or not I was an artist at age twenty-four – or ever – is inconsequential. What matters is that Stravinsky valued my musicianship enough to write to Toscanini asking him to give me an opportunity to guest-conduct the Symphony in C with the NBC orchestra; that Schoenberg not only expressed his confidence in me in letters but encouraged me to direct his *Pierrot Lunaire* and Septet-Suite; that Schoenberg's pupil Eduard Steuermann, who had played the piano parts in the premieres of both works, would not have agreed to perform them under me if, during rehearsals, he had not found me capable of conducting them; and that Edgard Varèse chose me to record *Arcana* in preference to Leonard Bernstein and the New York Philharmonic, who had already performed the piece several times (whereas my recording had to be made in three hours with a sight-reading orchestra). But how would Druskin know anything about all of this?

Surely it is a quality of youth to be strong in convictions, partly because of limited knowledge and experience. Another quality of twenty-four-year-olds, at least one of them, is outspokenness; I always revealed openly to Stravinsky my preferences in any music we discussed, including his. Having tried to compose before I met him, I regarded music with a composer's rather than a conductor's eye. He understood that I had nothing to say *in* music, but he must also have sensed that I had something useful to say to him *about* it. During our first sessions together at the piano, I began to realize that he trusted my judgement when he asked my opinion about doubling a note in a chord, choosing between alternative courses in a modulation, or the advisability of repeating a figure. I was dumbfounded. Here was the man I had worshipped since my twelfth year, the man who *had* to know more about every aspect of music than I could ever learn. Was it possible that in the very crucible of his creation he was really seeking *my* confirmation?

In fact, Stravinsky was seeking my opinion precisely because of my age, my lack of position, and my nonalignment with any academic or other organization. I was slow to understand this, and that my elders had axes of their own to grind: careers as composers, conductors, and performers. If I had been his near contemporary, as was Arthur Lourié, his amanuensis in the 1920s, Stravinsky would probably not have exposed himself in this way. Moreover, since his coevals knew less than he did, had less imagination, and came from the same European culture, they had no new perspective to offer. He quickly saw that a member of a much younger generation, and a native American at that, could react in fresh and possibly stimulating ways. What must be admitted is that Stravinsky *wanted* to be influenced.

As I grew older, I suffered from, to borrow Harold Bloom's phrase, 'the anxiety of influence', because I *had* 'directed' Stravinsky – and who could want the responsibility of advising a great composer in any way related to his art? In the years immediately following his death, I was torn with doubts, wondering whether I had been right, not about repeating a phrase of music but in urging him to compose one piece rather than another; for, in truth, every Stravinsky opus, after and including *Three Songs from William Shakespeare* (1953), was undertaken as a result of discussions between us. The texts of *A Sermon, a Narrative and a Prayer* were partly my choice. Stravinsky's publisher was alarmed by an article submitted for its house review, entitled '*In Memoriam Dylan Thomas*: Stravinsky's Schoenbergian Technique', but by this date Stravinsky was pleased to be described as a Schoenbergian and annoyed with his publisher.[5]

Apart from the subject matter, I sometimes went so far as to suggest forms that new pieces might take. A year or two after Stravinsky died, I looked through his manuscript sketchbook for *The Flood* and saw that in the centre of it he had pasted several pages of my notes to him concerning the work, whereupon I impulsively tore them out. A few minutes later, I was distraught at what I had done, recognizing that he had wanted to give me credit for my contribution. My notes dealt with technical questions as well as musical symbolisms, mentioning, for one example, the music in the film sequence in *Lulu* as a model retrograde for the Biblical storm scene in *The Flood*. I did not want my part in this to be known, but *he* did – and it *will* be, since the manuscript had already been preserved on microfilm, a fact I had forgotten.

A full account of what most readers would call my 'influence' on Stravinsky is too extensive for this article. I can only repeat to Druskin that without me Stravinsky would not have taken the path he did after *The Rake's Progress*. Those music lovers preferring another opera, more *pas de deux*, and some additional concertos, will feel that they have been cheated; others, admirers of *Abraham and Isaac*, of *The Flood* and *Requiem Canticles*, will thank me.

I understand the wishes of a Druskin to believe that their hero always discovered, cogitated, and acted completely independently. But Druskin's assertion that Stravinsky was already 'acquainted' in 1948 with 'the works and the methods of the New Viennese School' is breathtaking in its ignorance not only of Stravinsky but of American musical life from 1948 to 1953. When I met Stravinsky, he did not know a single measure of music by Schoenberg, Berg, or Webern, had no copy in his library of any of their pieces, and did not understand the meaning of the word 'tone-row'. Shortly before my arrival in June 1949, Benjamin Bok, brother of Harvard's President Derek Bok, and an aspiring young musician, son of a close friend (Peggy Kiskadden) of both the Stravinskys and the Aldous Huxleys, had come for lessons in composition. As it happened, the young man was uniquely interested in twelve-tone technique, and after a single session did not return, telling his mother, who told me, that Stravinsky did not know the first thing about this music.

Not only Druskin but most people do not realize how little the 'New Viennese School' was known before the past decade, and how infrequent were the opportunities to become acquainted with it. In Stravinsky's entire career of concert touring in Europe and the United States before 1951, he had heard performances of only *Pierrot Lunaire*[6] and the Chamber Symphony of Schoenberg, possibly of the early string quartet and violin pieces by Webern (at any rate, these were on programmes with his own works), and of nothing at all by Berg; *Der Wein* shared a programme with Stravinsky's Capriccio in Venice in 1934, but Stravinsky was present only when conducting his own work. In Venice three years later, he happened to hear a rehearsal of Schoenberg's Septet-Suite and told interviewers afterward that this was an experiment, not music.

In the survey 'Stravinsky in Los Angeles',[7] Lawrence Morton, a musicologist who from 1956 to the late 1960s knew Stravinsky better than anyone else outside the household, devotes several paragraphs to my position, calling me the last of a breed of associates cultivated by the composer since the early 1920s. I differed from the others, Morton says, in remaining very much longer than my predecessors, in being younger, and in having the status of an adopted child. But the Stravinskys and I were more like companions than parents and son. This was particularly evident in our almost constant travels. Although it was *his* as much as *my* avidity for new experience, without me Stravinsky probably would not have gone to African game parks, Inca ruins, or on one of the first flights across the North Pole. Morton also notes that one of the advantages of belonging to the Stravinsky ménage was the opportunity it gave me to mingle with the artistic and intellectual élite.

Stravinsky never shed his Russian culture, of course, and in his exclusively refugee circle in Hollywood, 1940 to 1947, he was more French than American.[8] It was my ignorance of his other languages that forced on Stravinsky the Anglo-American dimension, which eventually became more important to him than any except the Russian. When I entered the home, the library contained only a handful of books in English, whereas in a few years there were thousands, on every subject. In fact, the Stravinskys soon sold their eighteenth-century Voltaire *Oeuvres complètes* to make room for Henry James, Thoreau and Melville, as well as many British authors. Stravinsky was a rapid learner, and English soon became the language of his professional and literary life, though he continued to count money and baggage, and to converse with his wife, in Russian. Was his English sufficiently fluent to write books of 'conversations' without me? The answer is 'no', for which reason I helped him, as must always have been obvious to those familiar with the idiosyncratic wording in his correspondence ('I would like to be through with the recording work that same day at lunch time, because I do not want to kill entirely myself').[9] Druskin quotes from these books as if my part in them were exclusively that of the interrogator, but, though I no longer remember my exact contributions, certainly there were *some*, and without both of us the books would not exist.

Did I influence Stravinsky's politics? Yes, but I am not certain that I succeeded in converting him to democracy. The Russian Revolution, depriving him of his property, had turned him into an admirer of strong conservative governments, and therefore of Mussolini. Only a few weeks before coming to the United States in September 1939, he planned and agreed to conduct a concert in Venice and asked his Paris publisher to procure an Italian visa. The answer was that a new rule had gone into effect that anyone seeking a visa would 'have to come for it personally. . . I told [the official] that this was impossible since the person involved was in the Haute-Savoie in a sanatorium, and could not come to Paris. . . I took on the official again [and] to his question as to why an exception should be made, I explained that Il Duce knew you personally and has often given you an audience. That made an immediate impression and, instead of replying, the official gave me a form to fill out and said that the visa would be granted the next day. I have just returned from the consulate, where they delivered your passport to me with a kind smile.' By the end of 1935, Stravinsky was defending Italy against the 'misunderstanding democracies'. In a letter to Yakov Lovovich Lvov, in Trieste, 5 December 1935, Stravinsky says: 'It is a great pity that I cannot accept the kind invitation of the Ministry of Propaganda for the performance of *Oedipus* set for 15 March,' and he goes on to express sympathy for 'the difficult position that Italy, glorious and unique, now rejuvenated and thirsting for life, has been put in by worldwide obscurantism. . .'

I do not think that Stravinsky would have returned to his native land in 1962, particularly when his White Russian friends were opposing the trip, without encouragement from me. And, finally, is it plausible that without some very strong influence he would have outgrown his inherited Russian religious prejudices and composed a cantata in Hebrew, travelling to Israel for its performance?

I am indebted to Mikhail Druskin for inspiring me to 'pull back the curtain' in my relationship with Stravinsky. Some readers will think I have pulled it back too far, and that I should not be my own advocate ('*Le moi est haïssable*'). But no one else knows the facts. I am aware of the opinion that my life has been spent basking in his fame. In truth, it has been spent, since his death, receiving brickbats, most of them vicariously aimed at him. But if this is the price of twenty-three years with Igor Stravinsky, I am willing to pay it. Not a day has passed since his death in which I have not sorely missed the exciting originality of his mind, the weight and concentration of his intelligence, the infectiousness of his buoyant spirit, and the guidance and the joy of making and listening to music with him.

Notes

1 F. V. Weber of the Russischer Musik Verlag wrote to
   Stravinsky from Berlin, 8 April 1931: 'On Saturday, 11 April,
   the pianist Druskin (remember, he was in your hotel in Berlin)
   is playing your Concerto in Königsberg on the radio.' (Weber
   added: 'Today I am sending you the pocket score of Schubert's
   Octet.') On 1 February 1932, Weber wrote again: 'In January
   Druskin played your Concerto, and it was very successful, with
   both the public and the press. He played truly well and
   accurately, but the conductor was awful.'

2 On 25 February, Stravinsky had played me his setting of
   'Tomorrow shall be my dancing day'. By 4 March, after having
   spent four days in bed with influenza (26–9 February), he had
   added two oboes to the ensemble of flutes and cello. On his
   return from concerts in Mexico (22–30 March), he
   reorchestrated 'The Maidens Came' for the same ensemble. He
   played 'Westron Wind' for me on 5 April and on the 8th told
   me that he intended to complete the Cantata with instrumental
   chorales as prelude, interludes, and postlude. Other entries
   from my diary during this period remind me that I was reading
   Heinrich Zimmer's *Philosophies of India* to Stravinsky, and
   that this provoked him to state many of his own beliefs, for
   example, in 'the physical Devil . . . The Devil wants us to
   believe he is only an idea, since this would make it easier for
   him.' On 6 April, Stravinsky came to the conclusion that
   'angels do not have to breathe'. On the 9th, the manuscript of
   Auden's *Delia, A Masque of Night* arrived.

3 In an article on the best-selling song-writer Warren Zevon
   (*New York Times*, 18 July 1982), Robert Palmer wrote: 'Mr
   Zevon has been a composition student of Robert Craft and a
   frequent visitor at Igor Stravinsky's house. . . Mr Zevon has
   been writing classical music since his teenage years, when his
   composition class with Mr Craft included poring over the latest
   Stockhausen and Berio scores *with the perpetually curious
   Stravinsky* [looking on].' (Italics added.) I quote this because
   the adverb and adjective describe a characteristic of Stravinsky
   as a listener in conversations and because Zevon, who was
   thirteen at the time, has observed Stravinsky exactly as he was,
   and, unlike many other interviewees, has not falsely claimed a
   relationship with him. I remember receiving a remarkably
   intelligent, informed and discriminating letter from the young

Warren Zevon. He seemed to have been familiar with my
recordings of contemporary music, and he wanted to consult
me for advice about his musical future. Could I recommend
teachers? Should he go abroad and perhaps study with
Stockhausen? In any case, he would like to discuss the present
state of music with me. I answered, fixing an appointment. He
arrived late one afternoon at the Stravinsky Hollywood home,
1260 North Wetherly Drive. Though much younger than I had
expected, he was self-possessed and articulate beyond his years.
After some conversation, I played recordings of contemporary
pieces, not available commercially and unknown to him. He
was keenly attentive and his responses were unambiguous; very
young people tend to be judgemental, but his judgements were
supported with acute arguments. We followed scores of
Stockhausen's *Gruppen* and *Carree* as we listened to air-checks
of German radio performances. After an hour or so, Stravinsky
came into the room – *his* living room – and I made
introductions. As always, Stravinsky was warm and hospitable,
and Mr Zevon, whatever he felt and thought, was in perfect
control. Part of Stravinsky's late-afternoon post-work ritual
was to drink Scotch and eat a piece of Gruyère, or some
smoked salmon on small squares of black bread. I might be
conflating this first of Mr Zevon's visits with a later one, but I
think that Stravinsky invited his young guest to join him in the
nourishment. Mr Zevon betrayed no effects from the liquid. We
chose a time to meet again the following week. Our 'lessons',
repeated several times, were confined to analyzing scores; I
think that at that time Mr Zevon was not interested in much
music before, or of a lesser quality than, Webern. I suggested
that he study with Nadia Boulanger to acquire a foundation in
traditional harmony and counterpoint, and, at the same time,
with Luciano Berio, but whether or not he followed my advice I
do not know since I soon departed on a concert tour.
Stravinsky was always interested in the opinions and reactions
of the young, and I believe that that was his interest in me
when I first met him. Mr Zevon on that first visit reminded me
of my own first meeting with Stravinsky, though I had been ten
years older and much less intelligent.

4 Mr Christlieb's memories of the two great Los Angeles
composers should be preserved by oral historians. He wrote to
me, 25 November 1982: 'When Schoenberg was invited to

conduct his *Pelleas*, we combined three Works Progress Administration orchestras, which included twelve horns, and gave a performance. You can imagine the instrumentalists of that time. Nevertheless, Schoenberg's face was love-in-communication such as I have only experienced once again – with Stravinsky. We broke for lunch, and Schoenberg sat with us at a great table in the Trinity Auditorium (near Ninth and Figueroa). During one of these lunches, Schoenberg asked me if it would be possible to perform the Beethoven Septet for his composition class. We did it, and I asked him if he would be interested in hearing a rehearsal of his Quintet, which we were preparing for a performance. This rehearsal took place in his home, where his daughter was asleep in a crib next to us. On a card table nearby was a manuscript. Schoenberg explained that he was preparing a string quintet version of the piece simply in the hope that he would be able to hear the music once again. . . At that time Julius Toldi (you remember him, the violist in the Bing Crosby radio orchestra) was delivering weekly 'CARE' packages to Schoenberg because his yearly salary was $2600.'

5 *Tempo*, Spring 1955. Stravinsky even sent the author of the article the negative Boston reviews of the piece with a note: 'Excellent idea to (ab)use* them in your book.
[*Better without the parentheses.]'

6 In 1924 the German critic Walter Tschuppik questioned Stravinsky closely as to which Schoenberg pieces he had heard, and the answer was 'Only *Pierrot Lunaire*.'

7 Los Angeles Philharmonic Association, 1982.

8 In indexing Stravinsky's books in 1948, I was amazed at the preponderance of titles concerned with Dominicans: *La Retraite aux hommes chez les dominicains*, for example, with a dedication by the author, André David (1944). Stravinsky's funeral took place in the Dominican church of Saints John and Paul. There was also an eighteenth-century volume of the *Sermons* of Massillon, and René Bazin's life of the hermit Charles de Foucauld.

9 Letter to Columbia Records, 1 December 1953.

4

STRAVINSKY AND DYLAN THOMAS

Andy Cartwright   Whose idea was it to bring Stravinsky and Dylan Thomas together to collaborate on an opera?

Robert Craft   Michael Powell, the film director, proposed the collaboration, but for a film, not an opera. Late in 1951, Powell wrote to Stravinsky asking him to look at a scenario by Simon Harcourt-Smith based on the *Odyssey*. When this arrived in Hollywood, 10 January 1952, I read it and told Stravinsky that the storms, gods, combats and spectacular landscapes were more in Wagner's line. Two months later, Powell wrote requesting a meeting. The Stravinskys had seen his *Red Shoes* and were filled with nostalgia by the views of Monte Carlo and its theatre, with Leonid Massine bringing the Diaghilev years back to life; Stravinsky was delighted to receive the director. I was present 19 March 1952 when the meeting took place. By this time, after four years with Stravinsky, his ear was so attuned to my upstate New York accent that he found British visitors difficult to understand and wanted me to assist in his interviews with them. Powell offered him a commission to compose a film score for an episode from the *Odyssey*, but the narration was now to be written by Dylan Thomas. Stravinsky answered that he would be interested in composing an incidental song to Thomas's words. But Powell did not write for more than a month, and when he did, Harcourt-Smith was back in; I remember a lunch with him at the Plaza Athénée, Paris, in early May.

Script prepared for a BBC interview (Savoy Hotel, London, 11 October, 1989), but not used. Mr Cartwright's questions were taken from a letter.

AC   When and how was Stravinsky introduced to Thomas's work?

RC   I had read some of it to the Stravinskys in the summer of 1949. They were in transition from Russo-French to Anglo-American culture at the time, and were trying to enlarge their English vocabularies by speaking, reading and writing English only. During January 1950 both of them memorized 'In My Craft or Sullen Art'. Their recitations of the poem would seem strange to you, particularly Stravinsky's; his Russian accent was thicker than hers and his 'Ws' (pronounced as 'Vs') were more guttural, an inheritance from his Prussian nurse. In March 1950 the Stravinskys went to Urbana for a concert and discovered that Thomas was there to read his poetry. Stravinsky could not attend because his rehearsals were in the evening, but Mrs Stravinsky went and gave him an enthusiastic account. On their return to New York, they described Thomas's performance to me as the highlight of the trip. I should add that Auden had talked to Stravinsky about Thomas either shortly before or after Urbana. I remember Auden coming to the Lombardy Hotel one afternoon to work with Stravinsky on the *Rake* and saying that 'Dylan, the poor dear, is in bad shape.'

AC   How did the meeting between Stravinsky and Thomas in Boston a year later come about?

RC   In January 1953 Boston University invited Stravinsky to conduct *The Rake's Progress* in Sarah Caldwell's opera workshop. The fee was substantial, but his primary reasons for accepting were his dissatisfaction with the Metropolitan Opera production and his desire to show how good the opera can be even in a student performance. Another factor in his decision is that, at the time, Boston was Stravinsky's city in America. He had conducted the Boston Symphony numerous times between 1935 and 1949, and lectured and taught composition at Harvard in 1939–40. And, during the war, Nadia Boulanger, at the Longy School, helped to cultivate a Stravinsky audience.

At the end of April 1953, Stravinsky was in New York recuperating from a concert tour in Havana and Caracas. I went to Boston ahead of him to prepare the orchestra, chorus and principals. A few days before the performance (17 May), Caldwell asked if I thought Stravinsky would accept a commission for another opera. Knowing that he would not undertake a work of any length, I said only that he might consider a theatre piece of some kind. I was thinking of *Delia*, the Auden–Kallman masque that Stravinsky did not compose, partly because the libretto had arrived in the mail, a *fait accompli*, whereas he always chose his own subjects and collaborated in the scenarios. A different librettist would have to be found, therefore, and I suggested Thomas. Caldwell tracked him down – to New York – through the Boston University English department and John Malcolm Brinnen.

AC   Stravinsky was ill when Thomas came. Was this a consequence of the *Rake* performance that he conducted?

RC   Of the second one. When the first quickly sold out, the university decided on a repeat, but with an entirely different cast. Stravinsky should not have agreed to this without rest and rehearsals with the new singers. The first performance, a Sunday matinee, went smoothly and he was delighted with it. Friends came up from New York to see it, Lincoln Kirstein and Kallman among them – Auden was away teaching – and everyone was enthusiastic. But the performance on the following night was a disaster. The singers, understudies, were inexperienced college students, excited to be working with Stravinsky, but also jittery, and they had not been adequately prepared. Cues were missed and more than once the performance ground to a halt. Stravinsky was tired and very tense. He was not a regular conductor and not at his best in an opera pit. When he foundered in his changing metres, as he often did, professional orchestras could carry the music, but not students.

Back in the hotel, Mrs Stravinsky called Dr Max Reinkel, Stravinsky's physician in Boston since February 1949, well known a few years later for his experiments with LSD at the Massachusetts Institute of Technology. He sentenced the composer to a teetotal regime and to bed, which is where he was four days later when Thomas arrived.

AC Can you add any details to the description of the meeting in your diary?

RC Anything I say will sound like hindsight, but I am certain that from the moment Thomas entered the room I realized that the collaboration would not take place. This was not because of a premonition that Thomas would not live long, though he was frail and shaky, his left arm was in a sling, and his skin was red, pimply and badly blotched from his too evident bibulousness. My thought was simply that Stravinsky was so punctilious in his habits that he would not have been able to work with anyone who might turn up late and hungover. A 'lost weekend' would have exasperated this compulsive worker, who strictly apportioned all of his time, and an explosion would not have been long in coming.

Thomas arrived perfectly sober, but in a bad state of nerves. Stravinsky, in bed with a thermometer in his mouth and a beret on his head – he always wore a beret in bed when afraid that a cold might be coming on – poured a tumbler of whisky and handed it to Thomas, expressing genuinely painful regrets at not being allowed to join him. Thomas had inspired a fatherly, protective feeling in him. Mrs Stravinsky, trying to put the guest at ease, talked about life in Los Angeles. Thomas had been there once for a reading when we were abroad.

Thomas said that he had heard the *Rake* broadcast from Venice and had thought the libretto 'wordy'. 'Auden is the most skilful of us all,' he went on, but 'he should have knocked some of those speeches on the head.' Knowing that Stravinsky did not accept any criticism of the libretto, I broke in here and asked Thomas if he had any ideas for a musico-theatrical work. Two, he said, but the one that interested him more was about the rediscovery of love and language in what might be left of the world after the bomb. Stravinsky replied that he would be interested to see what could be developed from this theme, adding that he and Thomas should explore it together in California in the autumn.

Smoothed out by the whiskey, the jumpiness and edginess gone, Thomas began to unbutton about personal problems: his wife was going mad, he had no money to support his children, his gout required daily injections from doctors' 'bayonets'. He would have to return to England, but another American trip was planned for October. At this, Stravinsky invited him to stay in his Hollywood home and offered to pay his travel expenses – though at that time the Stravinskys were hard put to meet their own financial obligations.

Mrs Stravinsky began to describe their Los Angeles circle of English friends, not seeming to realize that the prospect of spending an evening with a deadly sober polymath (Aldous Huxley) could only appal Thomas. When she mentioned that Christopher Isherwood was a regular, twice-a-week dinner companion, Thomas's response, 'You know, I am not at all like Auden and Isherwood,' made clear what he meant. When he said that he did not know much about opera but was fond of Puccini, Stravinsky interjected that he liked Puccini, too, but 'we must first be fond and more of Mozart.' Thomas then switched to Yeats, claiming that he was 'the greatest lyric poet in English since Shakespeare,' and giving a spontaneous and very moving recitation of 'The Wild Old Wicked Man'. The voice, unlike the voice of the recordings, was without the boom but a little tremulous. When he had finished, Mrs Stravinsky said that the doctor was expected, and she repeated the invitation to stay with them in Hollywood. Thomas promised to come. He said that he intended to stay in New York a little longer 'to escape the Coronation' – which we watched on television in a hotel in Amarillo, Texas, wondering whether he had gone back.

AC Thomas's two letters reveal nothing about the development of his idea. Did you ever learn about it?

RC Two months after Boston he was in Ireland with the American poet Theodore Roethke, to whom he talked quite freely. Roethke then talked no less freely to Auden and Kallman, and in September or October I received a card from Kallman containing the slightly sour words, 'What's this we hear from Ted Roethke about space cadets?' When I saw Kallman next, Thomas was dead and neither of us ever mentioned the matter.

AC What were Stravinsky's impressions of the poet?

RC He cherished the memory of the meeting, and obviously did not think Thomas incapable of creative work.

A week after the visit, Dr Reinkel advised Stravinsky to cancel some upcoming concerts in Chicago and return home and rest; the doctor told me that a prostate operation would soon be necessary. Back in Hollywood – we crossed the country by car, which explains the night in Amarillo – the Stravinskys, using money from an Italian prize, engaged an architect and contractor to build an extension to the back of their house. The new room, completed in the autumn and ever thereafter called the Dylan Thomas Room, expanded the dining-room area, which was directly inside the front door. By mid-October the new room had dark green walls, a sofa, a table and several paintings.

AC How did Stravinsky react to the news of Thomas's death?

RC I received the cable at nine o'clock in the morning. It was from London, the BBC or a newspaper, asking for a comment about the death, which Stravinsky did not know had occurred. We called New York for confirmation, and, when it came, Stravinsky wept, went to his studio and closed the door. That night we tried to listen to one of Thomas's recordings but could not. A little later Aldous Huxley gave us details by way of Edith Sitwell, who had been in New York at the time and was in California for readings.

AC   When did Stravinsky start to compose *In Memoriam Dylan Thomas*?

RC   At the end of December he went to New York to conduct concerts there and in Washington – the premiere of his Septet at Dumbarton Oaks. I wrote to him suggesting that he compose a piece in Thomas's memory and asking him to look at 'Do not go gentle into that good night'; I still have this letter – he gave it to me years later – in which he had underlined the title of the poem in red pencil. I had considered, of course, that the form of the poem, the repetition of the 'Rage, rage' refrain, would appeal to him as well as the subject. He composed the song at the beginning of March, after his return to California, and the Prelude toward the end of the month, after the other music on the programme had been chosen. From the first he had wanted the premiere to take place in the Hollywood chamber-music series called Monday Evening Concerts. When I told him that we would also perform Heinrich Schütz's *Fili mi Absalom* – the father mourning his son – for bass voice and four trombones, Stravinsky added the canons for string quartet and trombones. The Postlude was written in June, after a concert tour that ended in Lisbon. I have a postcard from him in Lisbon saying that he had just read *Under Milk Wood*.

AC   Can you describe the atmosphere at the first performance, which you conducted in September 1954?

RC   The concert drew an overflow audience, the largest in the history of MEC. Stravinsky was, as he used to say, very 'emotioned' by the occasion, as I could tell from the warm telegram he sent me. Aldous Huxley gave a brief, moving talk, emphasizing how rare a phenomenon was a lyric poet, and referring to Keats. As I recall, he spoke without a text; he could do that. The programme was made up of favourite pieces, including a group of Gesualdo madrigals in which the mezzo-soprano part was sung by a twenty-year-old who was to become one of the great vocal artists of the second half of the century, Marilyn Horne.

I should have mentioned that the *In Memoriam* rehearsals took place in the Stravinsky home and that Stravinsky himself coached the players and the tenor, Richard Robinson, in every detail. From the first tryout, all of us felt the emotional power of the music. The audience did, too, and the piece had to be repeated in the concert. Not coincidentally, I think, this intensity of feeling emerges again in Stravinsky's next father-and-son piece, *Abraham and Isaac*, at least at the end, when the angel comforts the would-have-been filicidal Abraham.

AC In Memoriam uses serial technique. How do you explain this change in direction and style in a composer seventy-two years old?

RC In the sense of technique, the turning point in Stravinsky's musical evolution would have occurred in whatever he might otherwise have composed after the *Shakespeare Songs* – which, by the way, were written between the Boston meeting and Thomas's death, partly as an exercise in setting English. The evolutionary line goes from the tenor ricercar in the 1952 Cantata through the Septet and *Shakespeare Songs*, but, unlike those pieces, *In Memoriam* is entirely serial and its procedures are more sophisticated. For one thing, the four-part counterpoint in the dirge-canons employs all four forms of the five-note series simultaneously – though Stravinsky used the term 'theme' instead of 'basic set'. The pitch-derivation of this theme is from the music for the words 'meteors and be gay'; I do not know if any significance is attached to this, but only that the first notation for the song was for these words. A small point: the last four bars of the Postlude are divided into three units of, respectively, three minims, two minims, and three minims, so that the number '5' is obtained by '3' plus '2' from both the 'theme' and its retrograde direction. The manuscript reveals this calculation; but again, I do not know whether this has any symbolic meaning.

What remains to be said is that *In Memoriam*, with its treatment of strings and trombones as equal antiphonal choirs, points ahead to the *Canticum Sacrum*, Stravinsky's next completed composition, and the musical style of the Basilica of St Mark's in Venice. Perhaps *The Flood*, with its Garden of Eden scene and the idea of a new world after a catastrophe, owes something to Thomas's vision of the rediscovery of love and language after the bomb, but this is speculation.

5

CONVERSATIONS WITH STRAVINSKY

If God wills me to live a very long time, I will write many more things, because I still have many more things to say.[1]

Apart from programme notes and 'open' letters, the 'conversations' books are the only published writings attributed to Stravinsky that are very largely by him. Unlike the entirely ghosted *Poétique musicale* and *Chroniques de ma vie*, the pamphlet on Pushkin and the essay on Diaghilev, most of the 'conversations' – for which many of the manuscript and typescript drafts survive – were in fact written or dictated by the composer.

Although six 'conversations' books were published in America (1958–69) and only five in the UK (1958–72), the British edition is more complete.[2] The titles and most of the contents of the first four are the same in both the Faber & Faber and Doubleday editions. Stravinsky signed the contracts for *Conversations with Igor Stravinsky* with Doubleday on 31 March 1958, and with Faber on 29 April 1958. Dr Donald Mitchell edited all of the Faber books, the late Herbert Weinstock the third and fourth Doubleday volumes and the Alfred A. Knopf *Themes and Episodes* and *Retrospectives and Conclusions* – books five and six – published in 1966 and 1969, respectively.[3]

Only a fraction of the contents of books four, five and six (in the American series) was devoted to my questions and Stravinsky's answers, the larger part consisting of excerpts from my diary. Faber consolidated books five and six into one volume entitled *Themes and Conclusions*. In order to include the interviews, reviews, letters, and programme notes of the last years, the publication was delayed, for which reason this posthumous edition (1972) is the most thorough. By my own request, my diaries were excluded from *Themes and Conclusions*; as early as 1961, I had wanted to effect this separation, as my correspondence with Virginia Rice, Stravinsky's literary agent, reveals.[4] On 17 May of that year, answering her inquiry 'When will I receive the chapter from Volume 4 about *Oedipus Rex*?', I wrote:

> The *Oedipus* section has grown so large that we will need two more weeks. . . It is obvious that my 'questions' are *ex post facto*, and, followed by such long answers, they look idiotic; yet they must be retained, if only as a device to switch subjects. . . I do not want this business in dialogues to drag on, and I do not want it to conflict with my own book [on modern music]. [3 June 1961]

Shortly after Stravinsky's death, when Knopf was preparing a selection of my diaries for publication,[5] I wrote to Weinstock (who had left Doubleday for Knopf) proposing that Knopf follow Faber's example, even though

> this might damage my own book and would raise the cry that Stravinsky had written my stuff or that I had written his, though surely the separation would draw a line between his mind, packed with absolutes, and my bagful of doubts. [9 September 1971]

But *Retrospectives and Conclusions* was selling too well – 'Herbert says that if this keeps up, they will go into a second printing,' Miss Rice wrote to me on 11 May 1970 – and my suggestion was rejected. Nevertheless, when the books began to be padded with my diaries, many readers assumed that Stravinsky was actually the author of my contributions, as I first realized at a dinner in New York in November 1963, when Luigi Barzini complimented Stravinsky on *his* description of his return to Russia the year before.

The subject matter of Faber's *Themes and Conclusions* stems in large part from three centres of interest: Stravinsky's medical experiences (he was engrossed in the treatment of his polycythemia); from his reading (which was his chief diversion after 1966, when he stopped composing); and from the music he listened to and played: not many days, including those spent in hospitals, were without concerts listened to on record, nor did he neglect his daily diet of Bach on the small muted piano that was installed in his bedroom in each residence. Many of Stravinsky's comments about scientific developments, people, television, and New York City in the vicinity of the Essex House can be traced to entries in the logbooks of his nurses. But since much of the language of the books is mine, Stravinsky's spontaneity may not be discovered. Compensation may be found, however, in the acute irony that emerged as the composer lost tolerance both for the musical scene and for his tribulations at the hands of doctors.

The *Themes and Conclusions* interviews tend to follow a formula, the one noted in my reply to a letter from Miss Rice:

> I just had a phone call from Murray Fisher . . . about the delivery of the interview. . . Murray implores you to mention all of his questions, and if Mr Stravinsky does not want to answer some of them – as, for example, the question on rock'n'roll – will he please say why. He can be as brusque as he wants to be, but it seems that the readers, and many of them are very young, will be eager to hear Mr Stravinsky's reaction to popular music. . .

I answered:

> I can do nothing about Fisher's questions . . . since they arouse no interest in Mr Stravinsky. Moreover, they do not fit in with the mood of the piece. Perhaps this has become stereotyped: a 'sardonic' first part, a 'serious' middle, a 'personal' ending. But the ending, Stravinsky's old-age view of his childhood, is the justification of the whole, and I do not want to destroy its effectiveness.

And, of course, these reminiscences will provide whatever lasting interest the books may have, regardless of the slips of memory and other inaccuracies exposed by subsequent studies (such as the annotated omnibus of the conversations published in the USSR in 1973). The 'conversations' capture some of Stravinsky's feelings about his past and the people in it, something far beyond the power of biography.

In April 1956, Deborah Ishlon of Columbia Records in New York wrote to Stravinsky asking him to read passages from his books for a record of his voice. He answered, from Hollywood, on 18 April:

> A few days ago. . .I read through the possible material, a lecture I delivered at various American universities and the *Poetics of Music*. My feeling is very strong that this material is inappropriate for recording. More than that, I no longer would say the same things in the same way. . . A further problem is that when I wrote these lectures over a generation ago I was entirely at the mercy of translators for my English style. I do not like reading myself in another person's style. And now for me to compose in English, which would be the only suitable thing to do, is too great a labour to undertake just at this time. . .
>
> . . . I do not consider the project as definitely closed. I am indeed very interested in it and would like to do it at a later date when there is more time. It would certainly be of more interest to you to have a statement from me in my own style and from my present point of view. I will try to write this during the free time on our travels, and I can work on it with Bob Craft during our concert tours. . .

In New York, in late June, at the start of a six-month tour, Stravinsky consented to talk to Miss Ishlon. The tape-recorded results had been destined for *Newsweek*, whose music and dance editor, Emily Coleman, was a friend of Miss Ishlon. Stravinsky spoke at length, but only a fraction of his comments were transcribed, and he did not allow these to be published:

> To be a good listener you must acquire a musical culture. . .you must be familiar with the history and

development of music, you must listen. The person with the subscription ticket for concerts is not necessarily a musically cultured person. He is musical only because the music is performed in front of him. To receive music you have to open the ears and wait, not for Godot, but for the music; you must feel that it is something you *need*. . .To listen is an effort, and just to hear is no merit. A duck hears also.

The larger the audience, the worse. I have never attached much importance to the collective mind and collective opinion. . . Music never was for the masses. I am not against masses, but please do not confuse the value of music addressed from one ear to a million ears. . .Do not make the mistake of merely multiplying.

No audiences are good anywhere, but. . .the best musical level is that of the Germans. They have a higher level of listeners because of their musical history and musical culture. . . In the seventeenth and eighteenth centuries, the people who listened to music were much more learned; music was for them a language which they knew well. They knew not only by passive listening but by active playing. Everybody played – harpsichords, organs, flutes, violins. They had the habit of music played with their own hands.

. . . Now we hear music by the gramophone. This gives maybe more people a connection with music, but the result is not the same because the passive is not the active. . .

We think that very difficult works, like all the last works of Beethoven, are better understood now. No, people are simply more accustomed to them. It isn't that they understand better. . . A composer thinks about the audience, but not primarily. If you think about audiences, you do not think about your work, but about a reaction. . .If the audience is yourself that is quite different, but to be the audience yourself is difficult [for] it is difficult to multiply yourself.

Clearly, Stravinsky's conversational partner would have to be someone who was almost constantly in his company.

The next development occurred on 3 December 1956, in the Ritz Hotel, Paris, where I met with Pierre Suvchinsky, Pierre Boulez, and Gerard Worms of the Editions du Rocher (Monaco). Worms commissioned me to write a book, *Avec Stravinsky*, and tried to persuade me to obtain a preface to it by its subject. When I mentioned the matter to Stravinsky, who had been visiting Pavel Tchelitchev in another part of the hotel, he suggested instead that he contribute a dialogue touching on a variety of subjects. Much of the result, 'Answers to Thirty-Six Questions', was written during Boulez's visit to Los Angeles three months later, and under his influence.[6] He promised to translate the text into French and to check the French version of the remainder of the book (which was published in German as well). 'Answers to Thirty-Six Questions' appeared in several languages at the time of Stravinsky's seventy-fifth birthday (June 1957) and became the cornerstone of the 'conversations'. A televised 'conversation' between Stravinsky and myself in NBC's 'Wisdom' series, filmed at the same time, provided impetus to continue. The questions for the NBC chat came from Robert Graff, the director of the film. Here are some of them with Stravinsky's written but unused and heretofore unpublished answers:

Q. Where do musical ideas occur to you?
A. Well, sometimes in the bathroom.
Q. Do you write them down?
A. Sometimes.
Q. Does chance or accident play a role in musical ideas?
A. Of course.
Q. How do you know when a work is finished?
A. Because I finished it.
Q. Of all of your music. . .which [piece] do you like best?
A. All of them, when composing them.
Q. Do music critics perform a useful function?
A. They could if they were competent.
Q. How does a composer of serious music survive economically in our time?
A. The same as in any time, very badly.
Q. How would you define music?
A. An organization of tones.

Stravinsky, soon besieged with requests for more 'interviews', realized that he had found a way of controlling their contents, and a gainful enterprise. His acumen in discerning what should be published is evident from the deletions, rephrasings, underlinings, marginal comments (*'ridicule'*, *'non'*) in his hand on the contract with Editions du Rocher for the 'Thirty-Six Questions' (superseding the agreement signed by myself).

By December, Stravinsky had completed additional sets of answers. On the second of that month, Miss Ishlon wrote to him:

> I find each set even more interesting than the previous one and I especially admired your answer about the false 'limitations' on music and the stagnation of one-time explorers. I have, in fact, placed this answer at the end of the manuscript. . .

A 'book of dialogues of mine', as Stravinsky described the 'conversations' in a letter to T. S. Eliot, was offered to Faber & Faber in January 1958. Two months later, after Doubleday had purchased the American rights, the question of the title and accreditation of authorship arose. On 25 March, Stravinsky wrote to Doubleday's Ken McCormick: 'Columbia wants to record me reading excerpts from the book [and] we can't have "Conversations with Igor Stravinsky by Igor Stravinsky" but really should call the book "Conversations with Igor Stravinsky by Robert Craft".'

McCormick counterposed 'Afternoons with Igor Stravinsky', or 'almost anything but "Conversations"', since we already have another title with this word on our fall list'. On 18 April, he suggested 'Dialogues with Igor Stravinsky, edited by Robert Craft', which 'does away with the cumbersome repetition of your name and gives Mr Craft proper credit.' Stravinsky objected, giving his reason that 'a dialogue must involve two people'. But the word 'edited' had been anathema to him ever since the Russian Revolution had rendered him a stateless person, and his music publishers customarily appended 'edited by . . .' to his works in an attempt to copyright them under a different name.

On 6 June, Richard de la Mare of Faber & Faber wrote to

me: 'Our suggestion is that the main title should be given as: "Conversations with Igor Stravinsky", and that we should then put as a sort of sub-title "Igor Stravinsky and Robert Craft", with a short rule, perhaps, between the two, but not, we think, "by".'

Mr de la Mare wrote in the same letter: 'I spoke to Mr Eliot, who is now home again from America, about those queries you raise in the Satie letters, and his opinion was that the original words could be quoted without undue offence. His opinion was that to omit them and to insert dots should be a mistake, but he suggested that the words immediately preceding the offending words in those letters in the French originals should be substituted for the English translation.'

Stravinsky wrote to McCormick that the book should appear at the time of 'the first performance of a new work of mine, *Threni*' (on 23 September 1958); but since a letter dated 10 June directs the publisher to send the proofs to Venice, the impossibility of this conjunction must already have been recognized. On 27 August, Stravinsky wrote to Miss Ishlon from Venice: 'As Bob has already gone to Hamburg and instructed me to open his mail, I answer you in his place about the photos. It seems to me ridiculous not to use photographs of the people discussed in the text. . .and silly to use photographs of Prokofiev, Gide, Cocteau, who do not figure in this book but only in the one we are now preparing.'

As was the case with the 1935 *Chroniques*, the first instalment of the 'conversations' was too slender and failed to embrace any subject in sufficient depth, despite which the book received wide attention and favourable, if puzzled, notices. One source of controversy was Stravinsky's endorsement of the Schoenberg school and certain of its younger progeny. The response of William Schuman, for instance, betrayed his irritation with the apparent turnaround. When McCormick was soliciting favourable pre-publication reviews for the second book, Stravinsky asked Doubleday to try to place it in the hands of general reviewers rather than music critics. 'The second volume is even less specifically musical than the first,' he wrote, and, 'the reactions of the New York music critics to my works are as automatic as the Russian veto at the UN.'

Stravinsky's outspokenness about his contemporaries and collaborators, particularly in the orginal text of *Memories and Commentaries*, led to some unfortunate bowdlerizing of the autobiographical portions of this and later books. McCormick sent a copy of the composer's remarks about Nijinsky to the dancer's widow, provoking a letter from her San Francisco attorneys, Erskine, Erskine and Tulley (28 July 1959) with-holding permission for the publication of any of her husband's correspondence with Stravinsky unless he deleted the comment 'although it is true that Nijinsky's brother became insane. . .' and certain allusions to stories of intimacies with Diaghilev. Stravinsky complied, and his excisions, now irreparable, included valuable information about such matters as Nijinsky's hereditary syphilis, something about which few others would have known.[7] The composer wrote to McCormick, on 2 August:

> I regret Mrs Nijinsky did not see the entire chapter of my book. . .for she would there see that the Nijinsky portion of it is, or so I think, very fair and very friendly. In fact, I had expected her to regard my discussion of Nijinsky here as something of a retribution for my remarks about him in my Autobiography – which she did not like. . . I even hesitated to include Nijinsky's letter because of the damage it might do to Diaghilev. But it seemed to me such an extraordinary document, and so entirely favourable to Nijinsky's reputation, that I decided to publish it.

In retrospect, I regard the 'conversations' as a monument to a million missed opportunities. But at the time that the books were written, Stravinsky resisted efforts to explore his past. Furthermore, he refused to open his archives even to verify matters of fact. *His* interest in the 'conversations', unlike mine, was not to continue his autobiography, but to air his critical views, and the books provided an ideal rostrum from which he could express his musical opinions. It must also be said that he

was not indifferent to the pecuniary potential: his correspondence concerning this aspect of the publications is nearly as
long as the dialogues themselves.

Notes

1 Stravinsky in *La Liberté*, Paris, 27 April 1935, apropos the
   publication of *Chroniques de ma vie*.
2 One chapter, 'Some Observations on V.D.', in the Knopf *Themes
   and Episodes*, was omitted from the British edition of the book
   as too specifically American in interest.
3 Knopf had wanted to publish the first book but did not meet
   Stravinsky's financial terms.
4 In February 1979, shortly after Miss Rice's death, her executor,
   Judge Morris Lasker, released to me the files of her thirteen years
   of work for Stravinsky and myself.
5 *Stravinsky: Chronicle of a Friendship, 1948–1971*. New York,
   1972.
6 Stravinsky wrote to Deborah Ishlon, 14 March 1957: 'May I ask
   you to note a change in the last frase [*sic*] of the questionnaire?
   Here is the new text: "Webern is for me just before Music (as
   man can be 'just before God') and I do not hesitate. . ." etc. till
   the end. I made this change because the French [*juste*] was not
   clear enough for the reader and the sentence is so important to
   understand. . .' A letter to Boulez from Miss Ishlon, 8 April
   1957, establishes that Stravinsky had entrusted her with the
   preliminary editing of his manuscript. On 21 March, she
   telegraphed to Stravinsky: 'Weinstock interested republishing
   Chroniques with questions [and] new updating chapter. . .'
   Stravinsky answered the same day that no more 'answers' would
   be forthcoming until he had finished *Agon*.
7 On 4 May 1934, Stravinsky had received a letter from Romola
   Nijinsky asking him to conduct *Petrushka* as part of a charity
   gala at Covent Garden on 3 July to raise money for her husband.
   In the same letter, Mme Nijinsky says that she is requesting the
   composer's support because she knows he was 'a friend and
   comrade of my poor husband'. Evidently Stravinsky did not
   reply, which may in part explain the widow's reluctance to
   condone his statements about Nijinsky.

PART TWO

Life in France

6

STRAVINSKY, STOKOWSKI
AND MADAME INCOGNITO

In July 1923, Leopold Stokowski became the intermediary – or so he said – for a woman who wished to make a twice-yearly gift of money to Stravinsky for a period of three years. The events that followed form one of the stranger chapters in Stravinsky's biography, partly for the reasons that his benefactress insisted on remaining anonymous, did not commission any music with the money, and never met the composer or answered his letters. The six thousand dollars that Stravinsky eventually received is a larger sum than he would have earned from concerts with the Philadelphia Orchestra that Stokowski had already invited him to conduct.

The story of 'Madame', as Stokowski referred to her, and as Stravinsky addressed her in letters of thanks, must be told against the background of the composer's negotiations for an American tour. These had begun in August 1921, when Walter Damrosch asked Stravinsky to conduct programmes of his works with the New York Symphony Orchestra. Whatever the reasons, for this correspondence Stravinsky used the address of Mme Sudeikina, Hôtel Elysée, 100 rue La Boëtie, Paris. Stravinsky refused Damrosch's proposal, but another one soon came from Stokowski, who, in May 1923, discussed with Stravinsky, in Paris, the possibility of conducting a series of concerts in Philadelphia. The terms are found in a letter of 29 September 1923, from Arthur Judson, manager of the Philadelphia Orchestra, and in another letter of the same date from Stokowski, who mentions that he will conduct *The Song of the Nightingale* in October.

On 3 June 1923, Stravinsky and Stokowski concluded an

agreement that gave Stokowski the rights to the American premiere of the *Symphonies of Wind Instruments* for one hundred dollars. Stravinsky invited Stokowski to attend the first performance of *Les Noces* (13 June), but the conductor telegraphed from Bordeaux saying that he was ill and would come later, and telegraphed again, on 25 June from Quimper, saying that he would arrive in five or six days. On 5 July he deposited the one hundred dollars in the Bankers Trust Company, Place Vendôme. Then, on 14 July, he sent a cheque for one thousand dollars, claiming that it was the gift of a woman who was an admirer of Stravinsky's music and who promised to send, anonymously, through Stokowski, a total of six thousand dollars in six-month instalments. Stravinsky could express his gratitude, Stokowski added, by writing to 'Madame' at the Philadelphia address of Stokowski, who signed his letter, 'With the profoundest admiration for your music'. (The correspondence is in French.)

Stravinsky wrote to Stokowski from Biarritz on 21 July:

How to express my appreciation to you and to your so generous friend, who has made this rare gesture of coming to the aid of another person and yet remaining unknown! Thanks to your so friendly and so effective intervention, you have given me three years of relief, which I greatly need.

A letter was enclosed for 'Madame':

Monsieur Stokovsky [*sic*] has forwarded $1,000 to me, saying that you wish to give a sort of pension to me of $2,000 a year for three years ($1,000 every six months, of which I have had the first instalment) and that you are doing this to procure for me the tranquillity indispensable for my work and for the realization of my artistic ideas.

I cannot convey to you, Madame, all the gratitude that I owe you, and my appreciation, not only of your so generous gesture, but also of the way in which it was made, which is to say, without self-interest. . . For my part, I will not conceal from you the very strong desire that I have to know you and to thank you in my own voice, if I ever have the opportunity of meeting you. . .

On 13 September, Stravinsky sent the orchestra parts of his *Symphonies* to Stokowski, with a letter asking for news of the American audience's reaction to the piece.

Stravinsky soon began to suspect that the mysterious donor was actually Stokowski, who was subsidizing him to secure American premieres of his new works, as well as his approval. A letter from Carlos Salzedo in Maine to Stokowski in Paris, 26 June 1923, may be interpreted as supporting this theory. Salzedo explains that the International Composers' Guild in New York, of which Edgard Varèse was the founder and chairman, intends to perform Stravinsky's *Renard* but lacks the money to meet his conditions:

> . . .As our principal offering last year was *Pierrot Lunaire*, so this year we would like to give *Renard*. Would you intercede with Stravinsky and find out his terms for [exclusive rights] for the American premiere? . . . We could organize a tour for him, but, as you know, we are beholden to two parvenues, Mrs Reis and Mrs Wertheim, whose only interest is in social climbing, who understand absolutely nothing in contemporary music, and who support only what that boring Louis Gruenberg writes. . . I thank you in advance for your ambassadorship.

In view of Stokowski's meeting with Stravinsky at this time, and of the circumstance that Salzedo's letter could not have been received much more than a day or two before 14 July, the sudden appearance of a wealthy enthusiast for a composer still scarcely known in America, and certainly not popular in Philadelphia, is suspect. Stokowski *does* seem the most probable source for the stipend.

On 8 September, Salzedo wrote directly to Stravinsky, saying that the scores and parts for *Renard* had come from London, and that the important question of the conductor must now be decided – either Stokowski or Monteux, since Ansermet (who had led the premiere) was unavailable. Whether or not Stravinsky realized that Stokowski had been the foregone choice, the composer learned that Stokowski would conduct the piece when Salzedo sent the programme (9 November), and learned, too, that the concert would take place in the Vanderbilt Theater, New York, on 2 December, and that in addition to *Renard*, music by Schoenberg, Bartók, Hindemith, Lourié, and Delage would be heard.

'Stokowski gave a marvellous performance of *The Song of the Nightingale* and he will give a perfect one of *Renard*,' Salzedo added. But Stravinsky had already received the first part of this news from Stokowski himself, in a letter dated 27 October. The conductor, however, attributed the 'decided success of the piece with the public – far more than the newspaper clippings that I am sending would indicate' – to the many extra rehearsals. 'The performance of *The Nightingale* was a good one.'

Stravinsky was more interested in 'Madame'. He wrote from Paris on 4 November, mentioning the 'very lively success' of his Octet, and the composition of the Piano Concerto, the first performance of which, in Paris in the spring of 1924, he invited Stokowski to attend; but the purpose of the letter was to ask Stokowski to arrange for the second instalment to be sent in dollars to Lloyds' Banque [*sic*], Biarritz. Writing again on 15 November, Stravinsky expressed his 'great pleasure in the success' of *The Song of the Nightingale*, and announced that, since his prior obligations to his American manager, A. F. Adams, no longer obtained, the Philadelphia engagements in January and February 1925 could now take place. He waited four days before writing to Stokowski asking him to arrange an earlier payment of the January instalment from Madame.

This 19 November letter crossed with one from Stokowski which was dated 24 November and which revealed that at the premiere of the *Symphonies* the day before, the audience had been very antagonistic, even though

I conducted a great many rehearsals. . .and I feel that it was a good performance. The public was simply unable to understand the music at a first hearing . . . I am conducting [the piece] again tonight . . . Your letter to Madame was placed faithfully in her hands, and she was happy to hear from you. . . She is most enthusiastic about *The Nightingale* and the *Symphonies*.

This report also describes rehearsals for *Renard*, and the difficulties with the cimbalomist – 'I am searching all over America to find a better man in time for the concert' – concluding with the statement, 'I have had the most profound musical pleasure in studying your work this season, and although the public is hostile, I shall continue to perform it.' Stravinsky's next letter, on 30 November, reveals that he had asked his ex-manager, A. F. Adams, to guarantee twenty-five American engagements, at a thousand dollars each, as soloist in the Piano Concerto, and ten conducting engagements, at five hundred dollars each. That Stravinsky's fee for conducting an entire concert was half of that for a quarter of an hour of piano-playing is less surprising than his in-principle acceptance of a new proposal from Judson (1 December) offering a mere five thousand dollars for six concerts with the Philadelphia Orchestra. But on 22 December, Stravinsky sent a counter-offer – repeated in a letter directly to Stokowski on 1 January 1924 – demanding that his travel expenses be paid, not only from Europe and back, but also within the United States. Judson did not respond until 12 March, and whatever the new proposition, Stravinsky refused it in a one-word cable, writing later to Stokowski: 'I prefer to talk about the matter with you in Paris, where I hope to see you in May or June.' Stokowski had sent the January 1924 instalment on 14 December, which again suggests that the money was at his immediate disposal, since Stravinsky's request could hardly have reached Philadelphia more than a day or so before. Stokowski's accompanying letter characterizes the *Renard* performance as a sensational success, even though the cimbalom part had to be played on the piano by Salzedo, whose own account of the event, on 17 December, confirms the conductor's and informs Stravinsky that *Renard* and Schoenberg's *Herzgewächse* had had to be repeated, that Stokowski took seven curtains calls after *Renard*, that friends who heard the Paris performance had attested to the superiority of the one in New York, and that 'the occasion was a triumph for contemporary music.'

The failure of the audience to understand the *Symphonies* did not dampen Stravinsky's enthusiasm for his new champion:

> Your letter referring to my *Symphonies* has given me very great pleasure. It is of no importance that a symphony-concert audience has received this work badly. With a man such as yourself, I have nothing to fear. You will finish by convincing these good people. Nevertheless, I wait impatiently for news of the second performance. Thank you for having given my letter to Madame. Tell her how happy I was to know that she likes not only my *Nightingale* but also my *Symphonies*. . .

No doubt because of this encouragement, Stokowski decided to play the *Symphonies* again in Philadelphia on 1 and 2 February 1924, and in New York on 5 February (letter of 11 January). But the Orchestra Committee unanimously vetoed his plan to repeat the piece locally, and, according to a letter from Stokowski on 26 February, after the New York performance

> there was a great deal of hissing and a great deal of applause. But although the reception was only half good, I feel that your music is gaining in understanding in America. In a few weeks I am going to play your *Renard* twice in Philadelphia and once again in New York.

Writing on 14 April, Stokowski expressed his desire to conduct the *Scherzo fantastique*, and on 20 April, his hopes of giving *Les Noces*. Stravinsky replied on 3 May, asking the conductor to bring the parts of the *Symphonies* with him to Europe, for the reason that 'the work has not yet been published and there are many difficulties with it.' Stravinsky also explained that his publisher, J. & W. Chester, had neglected to ask for his author's rights for the New York performance of *Renard*, and, since he had received nothing from this 'sensational premiere', he asked for Stokowski's help. Whatever the outcome of this request, when the conductor arrived in France, Stravinsky taught him *The Rite of Spring*.

On 2 September Stravinsky wrote that he had signed a contract for an American tour, in the period January–March 1925, and was therefore free to appear with the Philadelphia Orchestra during that time as guest conductor and pianist. In the same letter, Stravinsky also asked Stokowski to try to procure the January 1925 instalment from Madame on 1 October, 'my expenses having been augmented because of my forthcoming move to Nice.' Neither in this nor in any subsequent letter does he refer to 'Madame'. The money, sent on 16 September, was tied to a request by Stokowski to conduct *The Rite* in Philadelphia, unless Stravinsky intended to do so himself. The composer answered on 8 October:

> . . .As for *Le Sacre*, knowing the great desire that you have always had to conduct it, and also knowing the zeal with which you studied the score with me, I really do not have the courage to take the lead from you and to conduct the work myself. Therefore I will not conduct it this year with your orchestra, but instead, as they say, pass the baton to you . . . I hope that my guest tour with your orchestra has been well arranged for me. Waiting for your good news, I send you, dear Mr Stokowski, *amitiés*.

In his next letter, 20 July 1925, four months after the American tour, Stravinsky asked Stokowski to pay the January 1926 instalment together with the current one, so that I can draw on the sum of $2,000 by the first of September, on which date I have very large financial obligations to meet. These two payments will be the last from the generous unknown person for whom I will always feel the greatest gratitude. Permit me to tell you, with the frankness that has always existed between us, that despite my profitable tour in America, I must again, this last time, ask for the help that has been so generously given me these three years. It is because I must liquidate, as quickly as possible, the numerous debts that I have accumulated during the last years, and because I must give the money that I earned in America to my numerous family . . . Hoping you will understand the reasons that have forced me to write this letter, and that you will not condemn me, I send you, dear friend, my most devoted regards.

Stravinsky understood that he was in a position to request the remainder of his 'pension' half a year in advance as the result of a letter from Louis Bailly of the Flonzaley Quartet, sent from Corsica on 20 June. Bailly wrote that Stokowski 'would be infinitely pleased to have the red ribbon of the Legion of Honour.' But a campaign to gain support for this, launched in November, had come to nothing, Alfred Cortot having complained that 'too many Americans have received the ribbon recently.' According to Bailly, Stokowski believed that a few words from Stravinsky would accomplish the desired result. Stravinsky wrote to Stokowski on 6 July 1925:

Recently I saw M. Bailly, who told me that there was a question of the Legion of Honour being awarded to you, but that the matter has been dragging since November. Since you are an American citizen, the question is in the hands of the Minister of Foreign Affairs. Knowing many people in this ministry, and knowing that to receive this award would please you, I spoke to one of the most important functionaries and asked him to speed the process. I am happy to tell you that he received my request very favourably and promised to see to it immediately. . . Hoping to have good news from you, I send you, dear Mr Stokowski, my best *amitiés*.

Stravinsky, Stokowski, and Madame Incognito

Stokowski acknowledged this letter on 16 July, and on 8 September wrote to say that he was hoping for a reply from Madame 'in about two days'. Stravinsky did not write again until Christmas day, at which time he excused his long silence because of a concert tour:

> Returning from this trip, I push myself to reply to your nice letter with the cheque and to send great thanks to you and to the person who has so generously supported me through these three years. . .

Surely this person was Leopold Stokowski.

7

LA POÉTIQUE MUSICALE

At the end of March 1939, Stravinsky was invited to give Harvard's Charles Eliot Norton Lectures for the academic year 1939–40. His in-principle acceptance had been conveyed to the university by Nadia Boulanger months earlier, however, and Stravinsky had undoubtedly turned his mind to the subject matter in the autumn of 1938.

Stravinsky actually wrote only some fifteen hundred words for *La Poétique musicale* (as the published lectures were called), and in verbal note form: not a single sentence by him actually appears in the book of which he is the nominal author.[1] The thirty-thousand-word text was written by Roland-Manuel,[2] with assistance, in the lecture on Russian music, from Pierre Suvchinsky. But to distinguish Stravinsky from his ghostwriter is possible only by examining Roland-Manuel's transcriptions of his discussions with Stravinsky, which may or may not have been preserved.

The aim of this essay is simply to translate and publish Stravinsky's own words, leaving the discovery of the ideological differences between his annotations and Roland-Manuel's book to the reader. At the time when both were written (April–August 1939), Roland-Manuel seems to have been preoccupied with Freud, Suvchinsky with Sartre, Stravinsky with Nicholas of Cusa (particularly with the idea of the *coincidentia oppositorum*) and with Nesmielov's *The Science of Man*,[3] a book in line with, and making as little sense as, Bossuet's *Politics Drawn from Holy Scripture*, which Stravinsky might also have read.

Why did Stravinsky not write the lectures himself? Chiefly because he had begun to compose the second movement of the Symphony in C and had no time for any other work. Why, then, did he accept the lectureship? The answer is that he needed the money ($10,000), or at any rate believed that he did. In countless letters to concert agents of the period,[4] he states his minimum terms for a transatlantic tour at $15,000 after expenses. The money from Harvard, together with fees for conducting the Boston Symphony Orchestra while in residence at the university, would match this figure.

The point of departure for the lectures was a polemic by Roland-Manuel[5] challenging Boris de Schloezer's classification of Stravinsky as a Pelagian,[6] 'who relies only on himself and on his prodigious technique.' The truth, of course, is that Stravinsky's profoundest belief was in the divine nature of artistic inspiration, and in St Paul's 'I know that in me dwelleth no good thing: for to will is present with me! . . .' Stravinsky's struggle to castigate his will was lifelong.

Maurice Ravel introduced Roland-Manuel to Stravinsky in 1911. On 26 May 1913, this future biographer of Ravel sent a postcard to Stravinsky: 'From Liège, whither the magical sonorities of the *Firebird* have pursued me, I cannot resist the temptation to remind you of the admiration of Roland-Manuel.' A decade later, Roland-Manuel wrote to the composer of *Mavra*, before it was publicly performed, bravely dissenting from his views about the merits of Tchaikovsky. After *Le Baiser de la fée*, a second letter came on the subject:

Mon cher maître,
On 6 January 1922, you wrote to me about *Mavra*. . . What goodness and generosity in that letter. . .which I now see as clearly prophetic. *Le Baiser de la fée* is a success that surpasses success, as do all works marked with perfection. The powerful emotion that it inspires in me results from the unity of substance in the diversity of the objects. Everything that one loves in you is here retained, linked up, synthesized. And how could I deny that the 'catalyzing' element in this splendid composition is the very Tchaikovsky that I did not

like? In my eyes, *Le Baiser de la fée* justifies all of the [developmental] steps in your art that I was somehow unable to appreciate. This work explains everything to me. I demanded this revelation from your art because of my unshakeable confidence in your artistry. . . Two days ago this marvellous work provided this vision, and so forcefully that I cannot restrain myself from thanking you from the bottom of my heart and with all of my affection. [30 November 1928]

Then, in 1936, Roland-Manuel's intelligent review of *Chroniques de ma vie* caught the composer's attention, no doubt the following lines in particular:

The more the master of the *Symphony of Psalms* composes, and the more he expatiates on his art, always concerned to purge it of all that is not purely musical, the more his aesthetic resembles an ascesis . . .

Durus hic sermo. We must continue to point out to our Aristotelian, however, that a piece of music is inevitably expressive. Whether or not its author wishes it to be, it expresses him.[7] [*Courrier Royal*, 4 January 1936]

Stravinsky chose Roland-Manuel rather than Suvchinsky to write the lectures because the former was a professional musician (composer) and author-critic as well as a native speaker of French, the language in which, by stipulation, the *Poétique* had to be written. Suvchinsky's roles were those of adviser on the state of music in the USSR[8] and translator of the Russian words and phrases in Stravinsky's notes. A substantial passage near the end of 'The Avatars of Russian Music' was also Suvchinsky's work, and he wrote a seventeen-page draft in Russian for this lecture.

I should also mention that in December 1938, Stravinsky read an essay by Suvchinsky, 'Reflections on the Typology of Musical Creation: The Notion of Time and Music', and recommended it to Charles-Albert Cingria with a view to publication in *La Nouvelle Revue Française*. Though a regular contributor to the *NRF*, Cingria wrote to Suvchinsky on 15 January 1939, disclaiming any influence with Jean Paulhan, the editor, and revealing that a similar article by himself, likewise based on the Stravinsky–Scriabin polarity, was already due to appear in the periodical. Cingria explained that Gide and Schloezer, Stravinsky's nemesis among the music critics of the moment, were certain to oppose the essay, whereupon, at Stravinsky's request, Cingria met with Victoria Ocampo in an effort to promote the publication through her. In a letter of 25 January to Madame Ocampo, The French poet Jules Supervielle quotes Paulhan: 'Suvchinsky is too quick to apply what he thinks he has discovered, and in any event, his piece is too abstract.' From Suvchinsky's essay, nonetheless, Stravinsky borrowed the word 'typology' for the title of his fourth lecture, and the composer's study of Nicholas of Cusa must be attributed to the influence of his compatriot.

In September 1938, Stravinsky visited Roland-Manuel at his home in La Roche Saint-Pierre (Fontainebleau), after which their friendship became more intimate. On 3 November, Stravinsky dined with Roland-Manuel at the Restaurant Weber in Paris, and the younger man kept notes on the composer's conversation. A card from Roland-Manuel, 20 February 1939, informing Stravinsky that 'I will come to see you on Thursday', helps to date the next batch of notes to have survived.[9] Stravinsky's written notes must date from late February, for the reason that he was unable to work for several weeks after his wife's death on 2 March. Seriously ill himself, Stravinsky left Paris for Sancellemoz on 15 March. A letter from his daughter-in-law to Nadia Boulanger, in Boston, of 23 March, reveals that he had suffered 'a pulmonary incident [lesion] like the one he had in America two years ago. The doctors have warned him that he must take his condition seriously. At first, they foresaw the possibility of having to perform a pneumothorax.'

Roland-Manuel wrote to Stravinsky on 24 March, and the composer jotted a *pensée* for the lectures on the back of the envelope:

The musician can approach the words that he puts to music in two ways. First, the word can be treated as sonorous material of expression itself. . . Second, the word can determine the meaning of the music, [in which case] it is left meaningless without the word. The second approach is the passive one. The active approach is that of the musician who employs the word as sonorous material *only*, taking no account of its literal significance.

Stravinsky's characteristic presentation of his arguments is through such dialectical distinctions. Though the use of this form is more manifest in his notes than in their elaboration in the lectures, Roland-Manuel followed the composer's subject outline almost without deviation.

The following chronology of the composition of the lectures has been excerpted from correspondence, including two letters from the composer's mother, of which the one dated 15 May reveals something of the character and critical propensities of this eighty-five-year-old woman.

23 March 1939 Boston. Edward Forbes sends Stravinsky an official invitation to give the Charles Eliot Norton Lectures and describes the terms.

24 March Paris. Roland-Manuel to Stravinsky: 'I have assembled my notes and begun to organize them. This gives me the feeling of being near you and makes me very happy. I have not forgotten that I must send certain books to you, above all Dalbiez on Freud and Chesterton's *Chaucer*.'

4 April Paris. Suvchinsky to Stravinsky: 'I stopped by at [Henri] Sauguet's today to ask for the piano score of the *Chartreuse [de Parme]* for you. Recently I had dinner with Cingria. He claims not to have enough money to buy a stamp.'

11 April Sancellemoz. Stravinsky cables his in-principle acceptance to Forbes.

25 April Paris. Anna Stravinsky, the composer's mother, living at 7, rue Antoine-Chantin since the death of her daughter-in-law, writes to her son: 'Today is Radonitsa,[10] but I was unable to go to church, much less to the cemetery. . . Father Vassily went, and I was sad not to be able to visit our graves to put Easter flowers on them. . . We have had no news from you for almost a week, my Gimurochka. All that has arrived is a letter from Fedya in which he asked about your shirts, but he does not write about any of you. . . I seem to remember that you will be X-rayed on Wednesday. No later than Thursday, then, we hope to have a letter from you, which, God willing, will cheer us up.'

26 April   Paris. Suvchinsky writes:

> Roland-Manuel leaves on Saturday morning and will be there
> by evening. You should be able to accomplish a lot in six
> days together – enough, in any case, so that you will not
> have to trouble yourself any further in this matter. The
> second (and probably the last) trip that Roland-Manuel
> makes will depend entirely on you. He is free at the
> beginning of June. He should turn out to be more useful than
> I because of his French and for a variety of other reasons. I
> unfolded the plan and character of the lectures to him in
> general terms. I am happy for you, and for Roland-Manuel,
> though disappointed that circumstances have made it
> impossible for me to go in his place.

27 April   Sancellemoz. Stravinsky cables his acceptance to Forbes.

29 April   Paris. Suvchinsky writes:

> I have explained everything to Roland-Manuel – that you
> will take on the cost of the trip, the stay in Sancellemoz, the
> purchase of books, up to 10,000 francs. Within a few days
> you will see whether you can work with him satisfactorily.
> Whether or not I continue to participate in this affair will
> depend on your determination.

5 May   Paris. Suvchinsky writes: 'Sauguet is thrilled that you like his opera. How is your work with Roland-Manuel going?'

7–17 May   Stravinsky is in Italy, conducting in Milan on the 12th, in Florence (*Perséphone*) on the 16th.

13 May   Paris. Roland-Manuel writes to thank Stravinsky for his hospitality during the sojourn. 'I will work with Suvchinsky tomorrow or the next day and explain your point of view precisely. . . The first movement of the Symphony in C is so masterful that it discourages the rest of us from writing our music.'

15 May   Paris. Roland-Manuel writes: 'I saw Suvchinsky, and we sorted out the difficulties in the lecture on typology. I gave him a copy of the first lecture and of the first part of the second.'

15 May   Paris. Anna Stravinsky writes to her son in Florence:

> Gimurochka . . . thank you for your letter-postcard, which I received this morning . . . I was happy to hear that your health is good, and of the great triumph of your concert. Let us hope that the one in Florence enjoys equal success. The Florence orchestra must be good, too; in fact, you are probably already familiar with the orchestra, so working with it will not be too difficult . . . I hope, my Gimurochka, that you will write in greater detail about the Milan concert. . . According to this morning's *Le Matin*. . .'*L'Université de Harvard annonce aujourd'hui que le fameux compositeur Igor Stravinsky a été nommé professeur à l'Université. . .*' Why '*professeur*'? Is there no more appropriate title? It also seems odd to me that they should say *fameux* – which sounds strange, somehow – ironic – instead of *célèbre*; evidently the translator took the word straight from the dictionary.

18 May   Florence. Stravinsky sends a postcard to Roland-Manuel (a photograph of Pope Pius XII).

23 May   Paris. Suvchinsky writes:

> I was about to send the material for the last part of the fifth lecture, but, instead, I decided to work on it myself first, to

facilitate things for you. If you find the result suitable, I will show it to Roland-Manuel, and we will endeavour to translate it into French before he leaves to visit you. He has shown the first lecture to me. I think it is good, but too much material is presented all at once; some should be transferred to the second lecture.

25 May   Paris. Suvchinsky writes:

How happy I am that you liked my text. . . I am glad that certain things which no one has wanted to state openly will finally be said. How wonderful that you are the person to say them. . . While preparing for the fifth lecture, I read almost the whole of Soviet musical/critical literature. . . I will meet with Roland-Manuel today to discuss the translation. . . Perhaps in the first lecture, where you talk about 'artistic appetite', something should also be mentioned about the *presentiment of discovery*. Roland-Manuel will paraphrase my thoughts on this subject to you.

25 May Sancellemoz. Stravinsky telephones Dagmar Godowsky,[11] in New York, asking her to fix the dates of the lectures with Edward Forbes. (Stravinsky wrote out his four-page telephone message in advance, in German.)
30 May   Roland-Manuel returns to Sancellemoz.
3 June Sancellemoz. Stravinsky writes to Forbes: 'The titles of the lectures have not yet been established, and for me to deliver more than six is impossible.'
7 June Paris. Anna Stravinsky dies of pneumonia at 3 p.m.[12]
10 June Paris. Stravinsky attends his mother's funeral service, in the Russian church, 32, rue Boileau. (Catherine Stravinsky's funeral had taken place in the same church on 4 March.)
17 June Sancellemoz. Stravinsky sends the titles of the six lectures to Forbes.
18 June Paris. Roland-Manuel writes to Stravinsky: 'I continue to work on the sixth lecture and to see to the typing of all

the texts. I have a typist who knows literary English perfectly and who could translate the summaries.'

21 *June* Suvchinsky writes: 'Do not even dream that you have reached a "dead end". In the first place, what is happening to you is a transition from one cycle to another.[13] I have found out from Roland-Manuel that the lectures are finished, and I eagerly await an opportunity to read them as a whole.'

22 *June* Paris. Roland-Manuel writes: 'I met with Suvchinsky this morning, and we have adjusted the last details of the fifth lecture, to which he has added an appendix.[14] The sixth lecture is almost ready.' Roland-Manuel acknowledges Stravinsky's payment of five thousand francs.

23 *June* Paris. Suvchinsky writes:

It occurred to me that the fifth lecture has no ending, and that perhaps a return to the general questions is desirable. I wrote a conclusion and am sending it to you. . . Roland-Manuel has made a few revisions in the sixth lecture, some of which, in my opinion, are not quite correct. When I mentioned them to him, he agreed. Thus he wrote '*seminaristes exaltés*' where I think it should be '*paradoxalement athées*'; concerning Tolstoy, he wrote '*de la genèse de la création artistique*' where I think he ought to have said '*de la genèse de toute création*'; and on *Eugene Onegin* he has: '*réaliste et ethnique*' where I would have said '*de mœurs réalistes*'. Further on, he writes '*ce fût le contraire*', but it would be more precise to say '*c'était aussi*, etc.'; finally, he wrote '*les différentes cultures régionales se transforment et s'amplifient en s'agglomerant*', where I would have said '. . .*et s'amplifient pour s'intégrer*'.

24 *June* Sancellemoz. Stravinsky writes to Roland-Manuel: 'I impatiently await the sixth lecture. When will I have it? Agreed for the English translation of the summaries – a sum of about 500 francs.'

28 *June* Paris. Suvchinsky writes:

This very day I composed the addition [to the fifth lecture] and sent it to Roland-Manuel. He and I have read all of the lectures together, one after the other. I think that this book came out very well. Do you agree that it would be more correct to describe the 'Piatyorka' as 'musical populists' instead of 'musical slavophiles'? Almost all of them were 'nevyis', weren't they? And in Pskovityanka, the 'Gosudari-Pskovichi' was sung by the students as a revolutionary song.

29 June Paris. Roland-Manuel writes to Stravinsky: 'I read the sixth lecture to Suvchinsky before having it typed, and I showed him the third lecture, which he had never seen. We made a final appendix together for "The Avatars of Russian Music". . . I put the summary of the sixth lecture in the margin, and I am finishing the other summaries.'

29 June Paris. Suvchinsky writes to Stravinsky: 'Yesterday Roland-Manuel gave me 1,000 francs, according to the terms of our agreement, thus settling the matter satisfactorily.'

3 July Paris. Roland-Manuel writes to Stravinsky: 'The work on the summaries is progressing.'

5 July Paris. Suvchinsky writes to Stravinsky: 'I suggested to Roland-Manuel that he put in a comment about "artistic effort" and "chance in the artistic process", since chance is inherent in it and differs from "invention". I will discuss this with him when we meet.'

17 July Paris. Roland-Manuel writes to Stravinsky: 'I believe that you have received the sixth lecture. . . Here is the fifth. I have kept copies in which to insert your corrections. The typist has the manuscript of the fifth, so I cannot rectify what I suppose to be an error on page 22, line 5.' The manuscript is a fifty-six-page draft in the hand of Soulima Stravinsky, on which Roland-Manuel has made one hundred and sixty changes (stylistic improvements). On pages 50 and 52 (pages 148 and 150 of the 1969 bilingual edition), Stravinsky has marked the places for inserting the titles of contemporary Russian operas, from a list in Suvchinsky's hand. Beneath this list, the composer has reminded himself, in Russian, to 'verify the transliterations'.

2 *August*   Sancellemoz. Stravinsky writes to Compagnie Transatlantique, Paris: 'I need a round-trip ticket, since I will be returning from America in May 1940.'

9 *August*   Paris. Roland-Manuel writes to Stravinsky: 'I have the copies of the three lectures that you still lack. The translations of the summaries are under way . . . I hope that the weather permits you to take walks with Madame Sudeikina. . .and that your daughter's health permits her to leave her bed.' (Milene Stravinsky was still in Sancellemoz when Stravinsky and Madame Sudeikina returned to Paris at the beginning of the war.)

20 *August*   Paris. Roland-Manuel writes to Stravinsky: 'I am sending the second and third lectures by the same post. Now you have the complete course. . . An American painter here tells me that the word "*pompiers*" is understood [in his country] by everyone at all conversant with the arts. . . I am impatient to hear the Symphony in C.'

24 *August*   Stravinsky acknowledges Roland-Manuel's letter of the 20th and the typescripts of the second and third lectures, encloses a 490-franc cheque for the copyist, and suggests a new beginning for the fifth lecture: '*Aujourd'hui donc, tout comme autrefois, du temps de Stassoff et de Moussorgsky (musicien de génie, certes, mais toujours confus dans ses idées), l'intelligence [rationalisante] prétende assigner à la musique un rôle et lui attribuer un sens totalement étrangers, à sa vrai mission et dont elle est en vérité fort éloignée.*'

29 *August*   Paris. Roland-Manuel writes to Stravinsky: 'I thank you for your letter and for the unexpectedly large cheque.'

7 *September*   Paris. From Paul Valéry's notebook for this date: 'At Nadia Boulanger's [Gargenville], Stravinsky. Conversation in the twilight about rhythm. He goes to fetch the texts of the lectures that he has just written and will give at Harvard. He calls them *Poétique*, and his first ideas are more than analogous to those of my courses at the college.'

End of September   Paris. Valéry writes to Gide: 'Stravinsky read us his future *Cours de Poétique* (he too!) *musicale*, which has analogies with mine – something very curious.'[15]

No doubt scholars and cryptographers will some day be able to fill in the blank spaces in the following transcription of Stravinsky's notes, but Roland-Manuel himself encountered difficulty in deciphering many words, to judge by his more legible versions in the margins. Stravinsky's quotation marks and italics have been preserved throughout.

Stravinsky's notes for *La Poétique musicale*

Second part of the first lecture
I am obliged to speak polemically, first to cover the inversion and transferral into music, and second because the lectures have a first-person perspective. [Illegible] Since the beginning of my career, my musical biography, my work (which is not a passing whim, and I am not about to consider it simply a fortunate coincidence), has, for this reason [polemics], been termed 'reactive'. This 'reactive' [element] is in contact with the musical reality surrounding me, and with the milieu of ideas and people, whose reactions [to me] have been as violent as they have been misdirected. Perhaps one should say that they were misaddressed. Such erroneous reactions are serious, for they demonstrate the vice that resides in the whole musical conscience, and thanks to which all ideas, themes, judgements, opinions about music and art, one of the principal faculties of the human spirit, are falsified. It must be remembered that at the time when *Petrushka, The Rite of Spring*, and *The Nightingale* appeared, many things changed, not on the aesthetic level but in the mode of expression. The changes to which I refer took place together with a general revision of the basis of the art of music and its primary elements.

The question of the phenomenon of music has begun to interest me personally insofar as it emanates from an integral man, i.e., a man armed with all the resources of our senses, our psychic faculties, and intellectual means.

Above all, I declare that the phenomenon of music is one of speculation (see my interview with [Serge] Moreux), a speculation consisting of sound and time.

The *Chronos*. [In the typescript, Stravinsky has elaborated in Russian: 'an analysis of the elements of time and movement, indicating either Lento or Presto in music.']

(1) The dialectic of the creative process in music. The principle of contrast and similitude in music and creation: my attitude toward 'variety' and 'similitude' (polychromy, monochromy).

(2) Meditation in active and passive music (author–listener).

(3) Musical emotion (see interview).

(4) The limits of the art of music: pure music and descriptive music. (I discuss realizations and give examples in Lecture 4.)

I contend that the general change, begun in the period of [*Sacre*], continues its development endlessly, and the conjunction of certain concrete facts and events in the musical life that we have all witnessed testifies to this continuum.

I know that a popular interpretation of my development is: Revolution at the time of *Sacre*, and assimilation of the revolutionary conquests now. This interpretation is wrong.

I admit that my course will be extensive, not in order to defend myself, but rather to defend music and its principles verbally as strongly as I do through my musical compositions.

Now allow me to outline my course. It will be divided into eight[16] lectures, and each one should have a title. (I will then name them.) The first, which has just been given, is nothing more than 'Getting acquainted'. The second [illegible]. The third [illegible].

As you will see, this '*Explanation*' of music that I undertake before you and with you will, I hope, be a systematic synthesis of views, beginning with an analysis of the phenomenon of music and ending with the problem of performance. I warn you that in this instance I have not chosen the standard method, which consists in developing a thesis using the general as a departure point and finishing with the particular [detail]. On the contrary, I plan to follow the method of 'sychronization', meaning that I will discuss the general and particular at the same time, supporting the one with the other, because it is only by virtue of practical necessity [i.e., the particular] that we are challenged to distinguish, discern things, arranging them in purely conventional categories, such as primary, secondary, principal, subordinate, etc.

[Illegible] The real hierarchy of phenomena and things and also the relationship of things takes form, incarnates, on a completely different level. I nurture the hope that this theme will be elucidated, for that is what I desire most from the course.

Second Lecture: The Musical Work (Elements and Morphology)
(a) the sonorous scale
(b) interval, chord
(c) mode, tonality
(d) melody, theme, motif; phrasing, period, development, *reprise*. Cite examples: sonatas, cantatas, etc. Do not forget *Variations*.
(e) harmony
(f) modulation
(g) movement in time, metre, rhythm
(h) sonority: pitch, register, timbre of the sound
(i) the instrument producing the sound and the human voice. The human voice: the word and the syllable. Intonation (keeping in mind the accent, which is to say, sometimes strong, sometimes weak, but not a dynamic element).
(j) scheme, form, system (coexistence in a mechanical or organic unit of different forms)

The Phenomenon of Music
(a) That which does not constitute music: noises, even the songs of birds. What music *is*: sounds organized by the conscious action of man. I admit that I have no taste for the problem of 'origins' and 'prehistory'. Alas, such an excursion into the depths and shadows of the past, which claims to possess the qualities of an exact science, too often is nothing but an *interpretation* of little-known facts. The interpretation has *its* origin in ideas and points that were clearly preconceived. Example: I am a materialist. Long live Darwinism, therefore, and I search, consequently, for the monkey in question rather than the man.

(b) To formulate the origins of music in magic, incantations, etc.

Third Lecture: the Métier *of Music, or, rather, 'On Musical Composition'*
(a) The composition of a work: the implication is that the work is a *piece* that is composed.
(b) [Taken literally and from this departure point], the term *composer* has a pejorative sense, as a reproach: see my interview with Moreux (artist, artisan, etc.).
(c) The invention, the imagination (self-expression), intellectual imagination.
(d) The will and the accidental in the creative process.
(e) The writing – musical invention (tightened [illegible]: easy or expanding sequences, Wagner, etc.).
(f) Inspiration.
(g) Culture and taste. The culture *of* taste. One searches for good taste, imposes it upon oneself and upon others. That is cultural and traditional. [In Russian:] I am in the process of creating, and at a certain moment it begins to happen automatically. Rarely can one invent a law about creative processes.
(h) Order. As rule and as law; external and internal orders. Order and disorder. The realm of necessity and the realm of liberty. [In Russian:] Dialectics supposes that art is synonymous with free creation, but this is not so. Art is more free when it is more limited, more finished, canonical, dogmatic.

Fourth Lecture: Musical Typology (that which is established by tracing history) [original subtitle]
Making synoptic, synchronic, and parallel analyses, in order to arrive directly at the problem of *style*, which is very difficult, if not impossible, to define. The question of musical history, the problems of continuity and discontinuity;[17] evolutions [versus] evolution in history; the determinate and the indeterminate; chance (miracle; the accidental) and genesis (origin; *rapport causal*). Haydn–Mozart are of common origin, but each has his own miracle: the phenomenon is determinate and indeterminate at the same time.

Before discussing such arbitrary classifications as, for example, Classicism and Romanticism, I would like to expound on the law to which any art must subject itself, the phenomenon of submission and ascendancy, the yielding and the unyielding. [In Russian:] The subordinate and the independent. Cite Sophocles (from the interview).

Distance [of the classical rules] demands of music things that are beyond its jurisdiction – the principle of illustration imitation (leitmotif). Example of the *negative*: Wagner–Strauss (epigone), *Symphonia Domestica*; and the *positive*: Beethoven *Pastoral* Symphony; Verdi, the storm in *Rigoletto*; *gesetzmässig*. With this in mind, return to the discussion of Classicism and Romanticism. Examples, a slow movement by Haydn and one by Chopin. Then compare two Romantics, Chopin and Weber. Also mention Schumann and Brahms. The commonplace and the platitudinous [illegible].

'*Courant*': This is the contrary of duration – without limit and without end.

Two words on the subject of 'modernism' and academicism. What an ineffectual word, 'modernism'.

The two academicisms. I have nothing against the good one, which can do no harm and always renders a certain service. Pedagogy. I am not a modernist. *I have always been taken for what I am not.* I am not revolutionary, nor am I conservative.[18]

Fifth lecture: Russian Music
Why do I suddenly launch into a discussion of Russian Music? Not because I am Russian or because I value it more than other music. Also, do not think that I oppose that manifestation of nationalism, since such a thing is of course subconscious. I do not pretend to be a citizen of the world, as the Russian revolutionaries of the nineteenth century fancied themselves.

Folklore and musical culture. Plainchant, sacred and profane music. The Italianisms, the Germanisms, and the Orientalisms of nineteenth-century Russian music. The continuity of Russian culture. The two Russias, the Russian revolutionary and the Russian conservative – the two disorders, which collided tragically before World War I: *Glinka, Tchaikovsky* = order; Scriabin = disorder (religious, political, ideological, psychological, and musical).[19]

Mussorgsky [is] between the two. [Present-day] Russia as the third Rome, [including] Rozanov's very just description: 'Russia lost its colours in three days, if not two.'

The new Soviet Folklorism: Ukrainian, Georgian, Armenian, Azerbaijanian, etc., and the degradation of values.

Sixth Lecture: On Performance

Being, nothingness, and reality [are] simultaneous in a musical work. Music exists while it is played and exists when it is played again. Between these two moments, music does not exist, whereas a painting or a sculpture does exist.

Interpretation and execution.

The performers, the listeners, and the public. Presence and absence in respect to the music.

Passiveness and activeness of the public toward the music. The problem of musical criticism, its aberrations, the classical bewilderment. ['*Klassische Kritiken*': ask Strecker.[20]) And now the Epilogue.

The true meaning of music. Like all the creative faculties of man, music is a quest for unity, communion, union with fellow beings and with Being [illegible word], Monism, the Creator.

Postscript: The Janin Edition of *La Poétique musicale*

On 12 February 1945, Roland Bourdariat, of the Radiodiffusion Française and the publishing firm of Janin, cabled Stravinsky from Paris requesting permission to publish a special edition of the *Poétique musicale*. Stravinsky, at the Hotel Drake, New York, cabled his authorization to Bourdariat after confirming that no copies remained of the 1942 Harvard University Press edition. On 28 February, a representative of HUP wrote to Stravinsky and asked for permission to publish an English-language edition. Bourdariat wrote to Stravinsky on 25 April saying that Louis Jouvet,[21] returning from America, had brought a copy of the book,

which I have just read with great joy and emotion. When I wrote to you about making a French edition, I was not aware that the book consisted of texts by Roland-Manuel and Suvchinsky. . . Musicians here are divided into partisans for

or against Messiaen and the chapel of ridiculous disciples
that surrounds him, hypnotized by him, and in which, like
Father Divine, he preaches a pseudo-mystical jargon. The
religiosity of his sermons cannot hide an unbelievably vulgar
sensuality, as well as false and absurd doctrines. These pupils
hail *The Rite* and *Noces* . . . but create scandals at
performances of every other work of yours. Western music
does not interest them, but only so-called Hindu rhythms and
pseudo-Oriental melodies. . . For these Messiaenists, the
greatest modern composer is Schoenberg. . .[22] but then, apart
from Poulenc and Françaix, we have no musician of value to
oppose and resist this current. . . Turning to the subject of *La
Poétique musicale*, the text will be sent to the printer in a few
days, and I hope that the work will appear in June.

Bourdariat wrote again on 16 May to ask Stravinsky if he
would allow the publisher to omit the chapter on Russian
music, since, apart from the 'violent polemics that it would
certainly provoke, the censor might ban the book; Roland-
Manuel and Suvchinsky are of the same opinion.' This letter
was delivered to Stravinsky in person by Nadia Boulanger,
who must have been in accord with the suggestion; she helped
to persuade Stravinsky to suppress the 'Russian chapter', a
decision that he cabled to Bourdariat on 18 June. On 16
August, Stravinsky wrote to his younger son:

> I never received the contract that Bourdariat promised me in
> his letter of 25 April. . . A month ago, I entrusted the
> producer John Houseman (who was leaving for Europe) with
> a gift for Bourdariat, the recording of my *Scènes de ballet*
> that I made with the New York Philharmonic last February.
> Was this gift received?

Whatever Stravinsky thought of Bourdariat's report on the
musical situation in Paris and of other accounts of the protests
– hissing, booing – that greeted *Danses concertantes* at its
Paris premiere on 23 February, the composer responded with
denigrations of Messiaen. Regarding Messiaen's *Petites Litur-
gies*, Stravinsky wrote to Suvchinsky on 18 November 1946:

'Why compose such rubbish, anyway? Who needs it?' But Stravinsky did not comment on Suvchinsky's observation (in a letter of 11 November) that 'the *Poétique* was not properly published in France. It needed one or two more chapters, and a new preface' – or on Suvchinsky's remark, 'After much agonizing thought I have decided not to return to Russia.' (Could Suvchinsky seriously have considered living in Stalin's Russia?) On 20 September, Bourdariat wrote to Stravinsky thanking him for the recording, praising the score, promising that it would be performed at the end of November at the Théâtre des Champs-Elysées, and inviting him to conduct his new symphony in Paris. The letter also said that the proofs of the *Poétique* were due any day, and that the book would be published on or about 15 October.

Stravinsky received the contract on 5 October and immediately cabled that it was unacceptable since it failed to specify that Janin's rights applied only to France. Janin settled the matter directly with Harvard University Press, and a new contract was sent by mid-November. On 8 November, the critic Claude Rostand wrote to Stravinsky requesting permission to publish two excerpts in a new review—and also reminding the composer that they had been introduced by Poulenc and Sauguet at the Princesse de Polignac's ('I will never forget the day when I had the joy and honour to approach so great a master'). The book was printed by 7 December, and a copy was sent to Stravinsky. On the 11th, the widow of Ricciotto Canudo[23] sent a letter to Stravinsky saying that she had worked on the book for Janin, though in fact she appears to have headed the company.

According to a letter from Bourdariat, 9 September 1946, the edition of five thousand copies, which was released at the beginning of March, was sold out in three weeks. This letter also refers to the critical acclaim that the book received, though most of the reviews would be more accurately described as mixed. Meanwhile, the English translation had been entrusted to the Gide expert Marie D. Molles Stein, wife of Schoenberg's assistant, Leonard Stein. When Mrs Stein wrote to Stravinsky on 26 December expressing regret that she was too busy to complete the task, Stravinsky asked Ingolf Dahl to undertake it. Dahl agreed on condition that he could collaborate with Arthur Knodel, the authority on Saint-John Perse. By the summer of 1947, Janin had defaulted on the payment of royalties. Stravinsky sued the publisher, who then declared bankruptcy. Stravinsky tried to attach the company's assets, and the litigation lasted until December 1951. In 1952, free to issue the book in French through another publisher, Editions le Bon Plaisir, Stravinsky restored the chapter on Russian music. By this date, of course, the Cold War had intensified.

Notes

1 Nevertheless, Stravinsky was to write to the Czechoslovakian publisher of the book: 'The translation ought to be entrusted to a person thoroughly versed in French. . .because of the highly subtle, idiomatic language I used.' (10 February 1947).

2 Pseudonym of Alexis Manuel Lévy (1891–1966).

3 Stravinsky used the third edition (2 vols; Moscow, 1905) and wrote extensive marginal commentaries.

4 N. Zborovsky and Severin Kavenoki, among others. It was Kavenoki who, in 1937, introduced the composer to Max Manischewitz, the wine manufacturer, who became a good friend and who sent a moving letter to Stravinsky after the death of his wife.

5 Roland-Manuel's article and one by Suvchinsky – the latter with an epigraph from Sartre – were published in the special Stravinsky number of *La Revue Musicale*, May–June 1939.

6 After conducting the 'Dumbarton Oaks' Concerto at the Salle Gaveau in June 1938, Stravinsky wrote to Vittorio Rieti: 'I was very surprised by the success of my new Concerto and not at all surprised by the press: with a few exceptions. . .an attack (Schloezer, *bien entendu*). . .' When Boris de Schloezer sent his monograph on Stravinsky to the composer (25 May 1929), Stravinsky seems not to have acknowledged the book and, instead, filled his copy with marginalia: '*Quelle sottise!*' '*Complètement faux*', '*Quel bavardage!*', '*Pas si simple que ça*', etc. Schloezer had inscribed the book: 'For Igor

Stravinsky, this work of admiration and of profound gratitude for all that his art has revealed, this book, in which I have tried, quite imperfectly no doubt, to discover the secret of his immeasurable work.' In later years, Schloezer reversed his views on Stravinsky, writing to the composer on 18 January 1963: 'I have just heard *Danses concertantes*, and with what pleasure. . .'

7 'Since I am not a partisan of expressionism in music, I think that the role of music is not to express the meaning of a piece or the meaning of its libretto, and not to create an "atmosphere" for a spectacle. According to what principle do the play of the music and the action of the spectacle operate? My answer is: according to the principle of independence from each other. Every art is necessarily canonical, possessing laws of its own that rule and govern it. This applies to all theatrical spectacles, and I find no logical reason not to apply it likewise to all cinematographic spectacles.' (Unpublished note by Stravinsky, 1932, in the composer's archives.)

8 Suvchinsky had been to the USSR in 1937, according to his letter from Marseille on his return telling Stravinsky of the sense of relief at being back in France. Suvchinsky had sent Stravinsky the article in *Pravda* attacking Shostakovich, 'A Muddle Instead of Music' (18 January 1936), with the comment: 'Obviously written on direct orders from Stalin.' Stravinsky wrote in the margin: 'The muddle is in the head of the author of this article, who cannot distinguish the valuable and the worthless in contemporary music (*Lady Macbeth*). What an idiot.' Stravinsky underscored two statements in the article, one to the effect that Shostakovich 'has deliberately turned everything upside down so that nothing will remind us of classical operatic music,' the other the claim that the composer 'has the ability to express simple and strong emotions.'

9 In the Roland-Manuel Collection, Paris.

10 The Tuesday of the second week after Easter.

11 Daughter of the Russian-American pianist Leopold Godowsky. After Godowsky's death, on 21 November 1938, Alexis Kall wrote to Stravinsky: 'Not long ago, Godowsky dedicated a new edition of a piece of his to me; I went to the synagogue for his funeral, at which Edward G. Robinson read a beautiful speech.' In Stravinsky's correspondence with Kall

in Los Angeles, during the same period, the composer refers to Miss Godowsky as 'the dangerous person'.

12 In a letter of condolence, dated Belgrade, 15 July 1939, Stravinsky's Yelachich cousins refer to the deceased by the names 'Niuta' and 'Niutochka'.

13 It would be interesting to know exactly what Stravinsky had written to Suvchinsky, since the two words quoted from the letter are so utterly unlike anything the composer ever said on any other occasion. Stravinsky's late-in-life correspondence with Suvchinsky is disappointing, the composer refusing to be drawn out on any important subject.

14 In the manuscript, the appendix is in Suvchinsky's hand.

15 Stravinsky saw Valéry several times in the two weeks at Mlle Boulanger's before the departure for America.

16 Stravinsky had insisted that he lacked the time to prepare eight lectures, but Harvard did not agree to reduce the number to six until June 1939.

17 [In the margin:] Cycles: periods with precise beginnings and ends.

18 Roland-Manuel wrote '*Pulcinella*' here, but Stravinsky struck it out.

19 Roland-Manuel develops the dialectic of order and disorder but, unlike Stravinsky, does not go so far as to cite Scriabin as the embodiment of this disorder.

20 This refers to Weber on Beethoven, etc.: classics of critical gaffes that Stravinsky quotes in the lectures.

21 Jouvet, the stage and cinema actor, was a good friend of Stravinsky's niece Ira Belline.

22 Marcelle de Manziarly wrote to Stravinsky from Paris, 16 March 1947: 'It is astonishing, the influence that Schoenberg has on all of these young composers.'

23 Canudo had obtained an interview with Stravinsky on *The Rite of Spring* in May 1913. See 'Stravinsky at the Musée d'Art Moderne', page 311.

8

SUFFERINGS AND HUMILIATIONS
OF CATHERINE STRAVINSKY

Catherine Nossenko Stravinsky, first wife of the composer, is not mentioned by name in the three references to her in his *Chroniques de ma vie* (1935). Yet any full study of Stravinsky must include the stories of both his marriages, and while Vera Stravinsky's place in the composer's life has been partly established (in the book *Dearest Bubushkin*, London and New York, 1985), Catherine's remains almost unknown. If the deficiency is not rectified by the excerpts presented here from Catherine's letters to her husband, these passages should at least help to give some sense of her personality, as well as to contribute to an expanded and intimate view of his character. She was a thoughtful woman ('Life would be horrible if we knew exactly why it had been given to us,' she wrote to her husband on 10 November 1937), and a kindly, wholly unselfish person, utterly incapable of meanness.

Stravinsky almost never referred to his childhood and youth except as a period of unhappiness. Not only was he the least favoured of the four brothers – at any rate by their mother – but he hated school, where he was taunted because of his short stature. One exception to this unsympathetic treatment was the kindness, affection and encouragement shown to him by his first cousin Catherine Nossenko, eighteen months his senior, who was musically educated and may have perceived the genius not yet visible to others. Like Igor, she had a talent for painting and calligraphy and made copies of some of his earlier manuscripts including The Three Pieces for String Quartet, *Renard, Histoire du soldat*, and the Octet. Before showing his newly composed music to anyone else,

Stravinsky played it for Catherine,[1] as he did in later years for Vera.

Obviously Catherine was aware of Igor's explosive and tyrannical nature, and of the will that could crush any obstacle.[2] But she seems to have understood him, and during the summers of their late adolescence, these first cousins were as close as siblings, the more so, no doubt, because the 'brother' had only brothers, the 'sister' only another sister. Stravinsky's letters to his parents in July 1901 show that he both enjoyed Catherine's artistic companionship and was grateful for her goodness and generosity. In retrospect, it seems almost inevitable that she and Igor would marry, which they did in 1906.[3] She soon assumed a maternal role, addressing him in all her letters by the childhood nickname 'Gimochka', occasionally adding the endearment 'dunik'. This marriage within the family was practical and apparently successful until *Firebird* (1910) took him into a new, lionizing world and tuberculosis made her a chronic invalid, from 1914.

Fifteen years after wedding Catherine, Stravinsky met and became infatuated with Vera de Bosset Sudeikina. Telling Catherine that he could not live without this other woman, he expected his wife not only to accept the triangular relationship but also to join him in admiring and befriending the younger woman. Since Catherine had always subordinated her wishes to her husband's, he correctly anticipated that she would do the same in this new situation. It may be said that she had no alternative, for her illness precluded a full participation in his life, and divorce between two people so closely united was unthinkable. But these pragmatic explanations are less important than that of her absolute devotion to Stravinsky and to what she saw as his divine creative gift.

The new relationship does not seem to have altered Catherine's feeling for her husband. Her letters suggest instead that she, who always coddled him, regarded Mme Sudeikina as a partner for his help and protection.[4] Many of Catherine's letters begin with expressions of anxiety about the effect that the bad news of her illness may have on him: 'All I did was think of you and how my letter must have upset you. . .' (30 October 1937); 'I would so like to write something comforting, but I only distress you with all that I say.' (8 January 1938)

She shielded Stravinsky in other matters as well. One of the themes of her correspondence was that he should spare his energies for composing, and to that end she urged him to travel less and to ignore comments about himself in the press: 'So you plan to go to America again next winter. . . When will you ever have time to rest and to compose?'[5] (11 March 1935)

I understand why you are indignant, and how unpleasant all of this is for you, especially now with these silly newspaper articles. . . If I were in your place, I would withdraw the candidacy [for the Institut de France. What matters] is that this should not disturb your work. [18 January 1936]
  Mika[6] wrote that Schloezer[7] has published another unpleasant article about your [*Chroniques*]. But this is not worth getting excited about, since it is plain that he's always going to write unpleasant things. It's impossible to get away from this. There will always be such people. But, then, there are others. [3 February 1936]

Stravinsky had arranged for Vera and Catherine to meet, in Nice in March 1925, while he was in America. Vera wrote to Catherine from Paris at the end of December 1924, describing Stravinsky's departure for America:

Without any unnecessary words, I would like to express my gratitude to you, Ekaterina Gavrilovna, for giving me the opportunity of writing to you. It will be a great relief in this sad and troublesome time, and I am happy that this has happened. It is difficult to talk about all those moments that trouble or touch one and that give meaning to everything. But you will understand, since we have a common language. To whom should I write about what is dear to me except to you? And from whom but you can I receive news that is dear to me?
  I went to Le Havre on Saturday to see Igor off. Although it

was decided from the beginning that I was not going, he seemed so unhappy in the last few hours before his departure that I stayed with him until he left. Robert Lyon came along with us, and it was in his name that I sent you the wire saying that Igor had left in good spirits.

We were in Le Havre from eight to ten o'clock and were allowed to visit the ship and to have dinner on board. Igor's cabin is the best on the ship, in the exact centre, and with all conveniences. There was also a piano. Sabline was allowed to come from third class to help Igor install himself and to dress him. I am afraid Sabline will not be much help: he seems slow, sleepy, and not very intelligent.

Arriving in Le Havre, we learned that there was a great storm at sea; and everything around was shaking and tearing. Because of this, the life on board appeared strange. As soon as the passengers had gone aboard, music started playing, the restaurant and the bar were opened, and the boat looked like a large first-class hotel – all of this, of course, so that the passengers would not think of the stormy night and of the possible dangers awaiting them. That was my impression, but most of the American passengers did not seem to be bothered, and they certainly looked calm – almost too calm.

The ship was supposed to sail at ten but was delayed because of the storm. Visitors were asked to leave at ten, and we did. Igor stayed below in his cabin and did not come up on deck. He must have felt depressed. The experience of leaving like that can only be balanced by the joy of returning. Robert Lyon left with the night train. I spent the night in Le Havre and listened for the whistles to hear when Igor's boat was leaving, but I could not distinguish them from the whistles of other boats. [Original in Russian]

'If there has to be another woman, I am glad that it is you,' Catherine told Vera during the meeting in Nice, and, improbable as it may seem, the two apparently did become fond of each other. Most of Catherine's letters to Igor in the 1930s mention Vera or 'Verochka': 'How are things with Vera's new automobile? I kiss Vera affectionately.' (27 May 1933); 'God keep you both healthy.' (13 November 1933); 'I kiss Vera.' (17 November 1933); 'I was at Vera's recently. We sat and talked and then she drove me to the Beliankins'.'[8] On Christmas, her birthday, I congratulated her over the telephone, and sent some azaleas to her.' (8 January 1935, from Paris); 'I wrote to Vera before I left [for the sanatorium in Sancellemoz], and she answered with a very nice letter. . .' (21 March 1935); 'I am writing these lines while you are still sailing on the *Ile de France*. . . Vera will meet you in Le Havre on Saturday morning. . .' (April 1935); 'How did you like Bologna, after driving out of Venice?. . .I kiss Vera warmly and wish her a lot of pleasure from this trip. . .' (21 May 1935, sent from Sancellemoz); 'Yesterday all of the children and Yuri[9] were at Vera's, where they had tea. Perhaps Vera has already written. . .' (2 October 1935, from Paris); 'How is Vera? Has she given up her flowers, or is she still working on them?[10] How does she feel in this gloomy and foul weather?' (31 January 1936, from Sancellemoz); 'Advise Vera about this medicine [*extrait d'ail*]. . . After all, she likes to try all sorts of medicines, doesn't she, and this one is harmless and promising. . .' (29 July 1936); '. . .Right now Milene[11] is buying slippers for Vera. . . [Vera] said that she has so much to do that she has not written to you yet. . .' (12 December 1937, to Stravinsky in Tallinn).

But when Catherine expresses gratitude to her husband for his consideration toward Vera during his absence in South America for concerts, the reader can scarcely believe that the intention is not ironic:

How good that you have decided to make it possible for Vera to move to another apartment. Does she already have something in mind? . . . Apparently, otherwise you would not have decided so quickly. . . This is very good for Vera in many ways, first, for her health. . .and, second, for her spirits, since a change of apartments somehow always brightens one's mood. As she will be doing this while you're gone, the process of settling in will keep her busy and make the time of your absence seem shorter. . . [22 February 1936 from Sancellemoz]

Sufferings and Humiliations of Catherine Stravinsky

(This will remind some readers of Graham Greene's story 'Mortmain', in which a newly married man is bombarded by his former mistress with such messages as 'All I really wanted to say was: Be happy both of you.')

Three days after Stravinsky's departure for New York in December 1934, Catherine wrote: 'I gave Vera 6,300 fr. yesterday as you asked me to do. I asked her to come to the bank and we sat in the car for a while and talked. In a day or two we'll set a time for me to go and visit her.' (29 December 1934; and two days later: 'Your godson Alya Chekov says that the quantity of your gloves made a big impression on him.' (31 December 1934).

As might be expected, Stravinsky wrote more frequently to Vera than to Catherine: 'This morning. . .I talked with Vera on the phone and she already had a letter from you. She said that you had described the storm. . .'[12] (11 January 1935); 'Vera received a letter from you today but I still haven't got one. She received one before I did the other time, too. . .now I wait impatiently for my letter. . .' (18 January 1935); 'I wait for news from Lisbon or Madeira. Perhaps you wrote only to Vera from Lisbon, but I hope that when she receives the letter, she will call me. . .' (14 April 1936); 'Not having received a letter from you in 15 days, I asked Vera if she had got one. . . Vera wrote to me that you had written. . .' (25 May 1936); 'Neither Vera nor I [had] received anything since the letters of 7 March that you wrote on the train outside Los Angeles . . .[but] Svetik[13] has just come in and informed me that Vera has received a letter from you. . .' (30 March 1937);[14] 'I spoke to Vera on the telephone. She told me that she received a letter from you three days ago. . .' (20 April 1937).

Since Stravinsky's letters to Vera from North and South America reached her in Paris before his letters to his wife arrived in Sancellemoz, where she was confined for long periods during his 1935, 1936 and 1937 North and South American tours, Vera often telephoned his news to Catherine.

Stravinsky was in the United States in February 1937 when Milochka, Catherine's sister, suffered a brain haemorrhage, and her husband, Grisha, instead of informing Catherine first, telephoned Vera, asking her to find a doctor. Catherine wrote to Igor that 'dear Vera. . . helps the family in everything. Because of my lack of health I cannot be useful to them. . .' (3 February). On 9 February, the day before Milochka's death, Catherine wrote, 'Vera is there all the time,' and, on 19 February, 'Vera is still making arrangements for the family.'

On 10 April, Catherine wrote that she and Vera had received letters from Stravinsky on the same day, sent from Tacoma,[15] and went on to say that 'on Monday I arranged with Vera that I'll be with her.' (Vera's diary records that she received Catherine at home on 12 April.) By the summer of 1937, Catherine's health had deteriorated and her marriage had become almost purely vicarious: 'I really hope to receive something written from you. . . So far you've told me very little about how you are spending your time [in Italy with Vera].' (Letter of 23 September 1937) Six weeks later, on 6 November, she wrote: 'I imagine that Vera would want to come before you left, but perhaps she's going with you to Naples?'[16]

Some of Catherine's references to Vera contain revealing statements about Stravinsky's relationship with his mother, who did not know of his association with Vera: 'Mama already noticed Vera in church, and that means she still remembers her. She's already talked to me about her and she could begin to ask questions. . .' (18 January 1935); 'I'll write Vera tomorrow. [The letter was written on 6 August.] How long will she be there?[17] It occurred to me that if you will be receiving letters from her frequently, then Mama, who probably has morning tea earlier than you do, will notice that the handwriting on the letters is all the same. She always looks very closely at the mail lying on the table. . .' (3 August 1936); I called Vera twice and would love to see her. . .but it is always difficult for me because of Mama, since it would have to be after dinner. . . Vera and I have arranged to meet between 11 and 12 o'clock somewhere in a café. . .' (10 January 1937); 'I will telephone Vera early tomorrow morning from bed; it's unlikely that I'd reach her right now, and, what's more, Mama might come in . . .' (14 December 1937, from Paris to Stravinsky in Riga).

For more than sixteen years, the composer lived in dread of his mother's discovery of the liaison, and, though the secret was kept, her suspicions were aroused – once, apparently, when a photograph album with pictures of Vera on the same page with family groups had not been spirited away in time. Such friends as Samuel Dushkin and Baron Fred Osten-Saken, who knew Catherine, Vera, Igor, and his mother, have affirmed that he was intimidated by 'Moussechka', as she signed her letters to him, and that the two were constantly quarrelling. This is confirmed by Catherine's letter of 3 August 1935: 'I am afraid that an argument and conflict may arise between you and Mama. . . It's better to give in to Mama.' A week later, on 11 August, she wrote again: 'You usually spend Sundays with Vera, but I do not think that you should leave Mama alone today, her birthday.'

In other words, it is quite possible that Stravinsky would have left his mother alone if Vera had been in Paris, and the story that he refused to attend his mother's funeral (she died on 7 June 1939) until Vera persuaded him to go was well known to intimates.[18] That Mama was indeed dour is substantiated by Catherine: 'I begged the children to be a little more affectionate to Mama and indulgent of the hard side of her character, which always gets her into squabbles, and because of which she concludes that the children do not love her. They do not communicate in any way, since she cannot understand them in their youthfulness. That is where the conflict lies, and, in my absence,[19] it is very difficult for her.' (Undated)

Catherine understands both sides. But between her husband and her children, she is more protective of her husband. Nor do the difficulties inherent in being the children of Stravinsky seem to evoke any special sympathy from her, as if she had expected them to augment his glory and was disappointed after they failed to do so. When her pianist son,

Sviatoslav, wrote from Barcelona that he had made a mistake in a performance of the Capriccio under his father's direction, her concern was not for her inexperienced young son, and the possible traumatic consequences to him, but for her husband, to whom such incidents must have been routine: 'Svetik writes that he managed to get through this uncomfortable moment, but did his doing this frighten *you*?' (Letter of 20 November 1933)[20]

Nor does Catherine refrain from criticizing her son's playing to his father, though she takes into account some of the circumstantial difficulties that beset the younger Stravinsky, remarking, for example, that the real disadvantage of a forthcoming recital in the Salle Gaveau is that in the following week 'Rachmaninov will have a recital, and many people, especially Russian, will spend their money to hear him, rather than Svetik'. . . (letter of 5 March 1935). (Stravinsky himself had changed the date of a concert in Prague in 1930 because Rachmaninov was scheduled to play on the same evening.)[21] On 14 January 1935, Catherine wrote that 'poor Svetik was disappointed with Holland. There was a very small and cold audience and the reviews were bad.' Ten days later she observed that 'Svetik very much needs a few lessons from Philipp[22] before the recital,' and on February 11: 'At my insistence he took a few lessons from Philipp. . . On his return he'll study with Philipp again, but this time [he should concentrate on] technique, which, in my opinion, he has neglected.'

Two years later Catherine noted to her husband that their son, in a Salle Chopin recital, 'got a little lost in the Bach Suite and in an Etude by Liszt.' (Letter of 19 February 1937)

Catherine's mother had suffered from tuberculosis. In January 1914, following the birth of Milene, Catherine had to be treated for the disease, and her daughter Lyudmila died of it in November 1938.[23] Stravinsky himself had it in an active form in 1937, in 1939 – in which year he spent six months at Sancellemoz – and from July to December 1969. Catherine was continually ill with pulmonary disorders in the 1920s and early 1930s,[24] and tuberculosis was diagnosed in May 1925 when, in a disastrous attempt to accompany her husband to Rome, she became ill and had to return home, the last part of the way in an ambulance. In 1935 she was obliged to write to her husband in New York:

> Dr Lipschitz, Dr Sobesky, and Dr Parisco all emphatically denied that there was any trace of the disease, but Dr Rist immediately made an X-ray, which determined the tuberculosis and the lesion. He expressed great amazement that, until now, and with such a long history of illness and repeated pleurisy, a radiograph had never been done. He thinks that I never had influenza of any sort. . . He said that I should go to a sanatorium immediately. Even before they took the X-ray, Milochka realized that my lesion is the same as in 1914, since she well remembers the place on the picture that Dr Demiéville pointed out in her presence. [Letter of 17 March 1935]

Rist sent his patient to Sancellemoz, where she had first stayed two years before. 'It will be cheaper there than at Leysin,' she says in the same letter, 'and more convenient for you to visit me, since I will be there for several months.' Her sister stayed with her a short time, and wrote to Stravinsky on 23 March, reminding him that 'pulmonary tuberculosis is a serious thing. . . Katya will stay in the sanatorium for several months, and, after that, must remain in the mountain air, which reminds me of early spring in the North.' (This letter also mentions the tendency of Stravinsky's mother, an accomplished pianist, 'to give severe criticisms' of piano playing.)

All of Catherine's letters from February 1935 until her death on 2 March 1939, contain detailed medical reports, including almost hourly tabulations of her temperature, expectorations, and descriptions of treatments ('Lipschitz gave me some foul stuff extracted from the liver of an unborn horse'; 'the eucalyptus injections have had to be stopped'). Some of this correspondence is almost too painful to read:

I hope that, just as at Leysin [in 1914], I will soon stop coughing and spitting up blood. . . Dr Rist told me that I won't be able to have pneumothorax induced because of my pleurisy, but they have another method, operating on one of the nerves near the collarbone and thereby raising the diaphragm and compressing the lung. . . [21 March 1935]

Dr Tobé examined me. . . He remarked that the infiltration began to progress after my first cold, and even more after the second. Also, the cavity began to open again. He said that though I've got worse, I will recover. . . [15 January 1936].

But Catherine's loneliness must have been as hard to bear as her physical suffering. She begins a letter on her twenty-ninth wedding anniversary: 'At the very time I am writing this, you and I were going to the Finland Station. . . It feels like a very, very long time ago, much longer than all those years . . .' (24 January 1935).[25] On 8 March 1936 she wrote: 'I am so looking forward to the three days I'll have with you,' knowing that these days would be the only ones between January and late June.

Here are passages from other Sancellemoz letters:

What is most difficult for me is that you will return home and I won't be there. . . Perhaps you could come and see me, if even just for a bit. . . How wonderful it was when you were with me in Leysin and composed The Nightingale. . . [17 March 1935]

How I long for the Fourteenth of July to be over[26] and then you will come and, if possible, stay for at least two whole days. [8 July 1935]

After the 14th, I'll be waiting for you to tell me the date that you are coming to see me – only if this won't disturb your work. Please don't interrupt your work just to set your mind at rest about me. . . [12 July 1935]

I saw some gorgeous hyacinths, and I began wanting to have some in my room. But there's no pleasure in buying them for oneself. And then I said to myself that if you were to write to me and say that I should buy some flowers, then I'd feel that this would be your present, and I would buy them happily. . .[22 February 1936]

I hope that God gives me the consolation of seeing you. . .I'll spend three days with you, and I'll be home when you leave for Argentina, so I won't have to say goodbye from afar. . .but will actually hug you. . .[22 February 1936]

I must bear this cross of continued separation which God is sending me. . . At first there is always a prick of pain in the heart when I find out that another separation is at hand. . .[5 April 1937]

Occasionally the letters describe macabre events in the sanatorium, but so matter-of-factly that the effect verges on black humour: 'It turns out that while you were still at Sancellemoz, some poor young woman died, which I had already begun to suspect since we could not hear her anymore. . .' (6 October 1937)

Small wonder that in California, in the 1940s, free of the daily threat of morbid and depressing family letters,[27] and of ill and dependent in-laws, Stravinsky seemed radically different to friends who had known him in Europe during the previous decade.[28]

Whether or not in reaction to Catherine's letters, Stravinsky seems to have kept his terminally ill wife fully informed about his own most minor ailments: 'My poor dear, how terrible that you still have this pharyngitis,' she wrote to him on 21 March 1936. And, 'How is the abscess behind your ear?' on 26 July 1936. When he complained of a spell of high-altitude dizziness in Colorado Springs, she acknowledged his 'postcard from Texas', and added, 'What a shame that you had to be at such heights in Colorado. . .and it has already irritated your sympathetic nervous system' (17 March 1935); and on 10 July 1935: 'You write that you are feeling very nervous. . . But you are always more nervous when you compose. . .' One letter begins, 'What's this? Have you caught cold again?' (4 October 1935), and another, after receiving his first communication from South America, 'I am sorry that you had a sty' (27 April 1936). On one occasion, she notes that 'you are feeling poorly in general and had a headache for two days' (27 July 1936), but, though fatally ill herself, she goes on to say:

'With me it's all *des ennuis* and *de petites misères*, nothing serious, thank God. As for the unpleasant peculiarities from which you are constantly suffering, and which are distressing, better this than something serious. . .'

'Unpleasant peculiarities', indeed. Though fully aware of his hypochondria, she dares allude to it only through a reference to the same affliction in her daughter-in-law Denise: 'She looks for illness in herself, and this very thing *is* her illness, just as is the case with you. If it's not one thing that's bothering her, it's another, and she's always suffering from something – at age 23!' (Letter of 9 September 1937[29] from Sancellemoz)

The most puzzling feature of the correspondence is Stravinsky's lack of generosity to Catherine with money. In 1933, with the shutdown of Germany as Stravinsky's largest source of royalty and concert income, and the continuation of the worldwide depression, he was in financial straits. Already on 6 February he wrote to Misia Sert asking her to intercede with Chanel on his behalf: 'Chanel has not sent us anything since the 1st and so we are without a radish to live on this month. I ask you to be kind enough to mention it to her. . .' An exaggeration, of course, and before the end of the month he had received an advance on the commission for *Perséphone*, but until the 1935 American tour, his family, at any rate, felt a pinch. In June 1933, Mika was working for Chanel.

Catherine's letters are sad, and some are pathetic, even heartbreaking, as when, realizing that his sartorial tastes must have been changing,[30] she writes 'I would like to knit a scarf for you before your departure for South America, but if you don't like it. . .I won't be offended. . .' (8 February 1936). But if she had a desire to arouse feelings of guilt, this rarely comes into the open. It does, certainly, when she reports a conversation with a doctor, in dialogue form and in French, as if she feared to use Russian: 'I told him, "*Je suis une personne sacrifiée*"' (9 October 1937).

When Catherine wrote that 'Now, with my sickness, we have overloads on the budget' (21 March 1935), his earnings from concerts, broadcasts,[31] recordings, royalties, and commissions were substantial. In 1936, furthermore, he seems to have had a surplus. In a letter dated 6 March, she says that 'Svetik just wrote to me that you had extra money in Italy and that you bought silver.'

The frugality of her existence in a provincial sanatorium contrasts glaringly with the extravagance of her husband's life on his concert tours. Writing to her from Indianapolis in 1935, he complains that good wines are not available in the United States. During his next tour, in 1937, he arranged for Malayev – a friend of his younger son and originally credited as a collaborator on the *Jeu de cartes* scenario – to bring twenty-four bottles of Bordeaux from France. On 14 January 1937, Catherine wrote: 'Malayev was here . . . He said that he'll probably set out on the SS *Paris* on the 27th, and he will carry out your errand. He's confused about how he'll deliver the wine to you, but will in any case send a message by radio before he gets to New York. Either you must call yourself or send someone for it.' (In France, Stravinsky purchased his red wine – Marquiset 1929 – by the barrel, directly from Louis Eschenauer in Bordeaux.) On 26 January 1937, Soulima Stravinsky wrote that Malayev would not be making the trip, but that the violinist Jeanne Gautier[32] would be sailing on the *Paris* the next day, and that she had promised to bring the wine.

Many of Catherine's statements in her letters make the reader wonder about Stravinsky's control of the family purse strings: 'Fedik[33] [and his fiancée] are here. . . I'm sure that you've already forgiven me for the money spent on their food.' (11 June 1935); 'Tell Mama that I am without money and can't even buy stamps. . . When is Vera going to Italy?' (1 August 1935)[34]; 'I have already accumulated three bills. . . Please send money now before a fourth is added. . . God and the Holy Mother keep you. I kiss Vera.' (13 March 1936); 'In the light of your departure, what about the next bill? . . . Who will send money to me for the trip?' (21 March 1936); 'I will return the money to you that I don't spend, but it is better not to be caught short.' (10 September 1936); 'I'm afraid I won't be able to manage with just the 15 francs that remain.' (26 October 1937); 'Perhaps your trip to Riga was sent by God, since it was unexpected and came just at the time when poor Fedya has no money and it's imperative to help him.' (7 January 1938, to Stravinsky at the Hotel Excelsior, Rome).

Here are a few more excerpts concerning money: 'I'm sending you this very unfortunate bill from English imports; it looks very big, some 125 pounds. . . Those fleeting moments of your call yesterday. . . I gave you only brief answers. . .because you didn't want to go past three minutes.' (4 June 1933); 'If Fedya meets me – the train arrives in Paris at 7.20 – have him come to the Wagon-Lit 3rd Class.' (6 January 1934); 'I've been without money for the last few days. 3 fr. remain in my purse.' (12 February 1936); 'Dr Rist came and wanted to see me. I said that I had no means of paying for consultations.' (1 March 1936); 'Please send money. . .someday I'll free you from payment of all these large bills.' (13 March 1936).

Most astonishing of all are Catherine's pleas on behalf of Stravinsky's mother, then in her eighties: 'I understand [Mama's] fear of not being able to manage with the sum you gave her. I also understand *you* but I think you are burdening her. . . It seems to me that you've cut down a great deal on the money for expenses.' (26 June 1935); 'The poor thing barely manages, borrowing from [the housekeeper], giving it back to her, and borrowing again.' (6 July 1935); 'Mama is dreadfully worried about her hair, which is completely falling out. If she needs to get a wig, since she can't stay bald, perhaps you would pay for it and then she could pay back 100 or 200 francs a month from the household money. That's been worrying her a great deal.' (16 May 1935).

Catherine was intensely religious, increasingly so as her illness progressed:[35]

You say that you look forward to a normal life, but you won't find one, and we will bear this cross [TB] that God has sent us and we will not stop praising Him and thanking Him for everything. . . In your heart you know that what is important for you is how you stand before God. Temptations and trials are good for the soul. . . [letter of 17 March 1935]

In letter after letter she says that she is happier in church than anywhere else. When describing the consecration of a church in Paris in March 1937, she expresses some of the homesickness of exile: 'The walls are painted in light ochre with a pinkish tint, like some of the old buildings in St Petersburg. There is something very Russian and ancient in the form and the colour. There were about 500 people and [one's] heart rejoiced as the *Mnogiya lieta* was sung. . . Our names were mentioned among the donors.'

She quotes from the *Dobrotolyubiye*,[36] an essential book for anyone interested in Stravinsky's theological beliefs – in, for example, the Docetic Resurrection. Catherine drew a Greek cross at the head of each of her letters to Igor, and ended each one with blessings ('May the prayers of St Nikolai Chudotvorets keep you safe', or 'May God's holy servants [*ugodniki*] protect you'), sometimes adding, 'I will light the icon lamps[37] now and go to bed.'[37] She invokes a saint for every occasion and difficulty, beseeching St Expedite when her brother-in-law, who was in charge of Russian cuisine at the Café de la Paix, urgently needed money, and praying for '*la sainte indifférence*, about which St François de Sales talks so much'. (28 May 1935). She lives according to the observances of the Orthodox calendar – 'I am glad to be eating meat during these great days of the *sedmitsa* [Holy Week]' (25 April 1935) – and is constantly reminding her husband of forthcoming ones: 'Tomorrow there will be a service for the Archangel Mikhail's day'. (20 November 1935); 'Do not forget to kneel to the holy Plashchanitsa[38] and leave a candle' (13 April 1937); 'Do not forget that Mama's name day is the 22nd' (18 September 1937).

She tries to comfort him with the thought that prayers are constantly being said for him on his concert tours: 'On the holy Mount Athos, the humble elder, the Hieromach[39] Gabriel, prays for you as you travel. . .' (11 February 1935); 'Father Vassily will be here on Friday to lead a *molyeben* service to pray for you on your journey' (14 April 1936).

To his wife's deep disappointment, Stravinsky neglected the formal requirements of his religion.[40] Once she complained to him, 'You have for so long been leading a vain life, with your work, business, and people, completely without the church' (27 March 1935). But all who knew him closely were aware of his deep faith – Païchadze, for one, who wrote to him after the death of his sister-in-law: 'Your strong faith will help you through this time of grief' (20 February 1937).

Catherine's kindness is apparent throughout her letters. To give just one example, her sons, her young daughter, her niece Ira Beliankina, and her cousin Dr Vera Dimitrievna Nossenko all opposed Mika's marriage to Yuri Mandelstamm.[41] But when he first visited Catherine in Sancellemoz, she wrote to Stravinsky: 'Despite all that the children were telling me, I immediately felt in him not just the niceness, but also the complete goodness, of the man, to whom we can entrust our Mikusha not simply without fear, but rather with total trust. The impression that I got from my eyes is confirmed through meeting him. He is obviously intelligent and kind, and loves Mika with a genuine love' (21 May 1935).

Catherine's patience was tried almost beyond endurance but, in her letters at least, she seems never to have lost it, or her courage and hope, and, outwardly anyway, she continued to believe in an improvement in her condition, even in a cure.[42] So, far from despair, her letters radiate joy in the gift of life, even in a life of pain, and gratitude for any alleviation. Some of this feeling might be attributed to the euphoria said to characterize certain stages of tuberculosis, but surely the larger part of it is in the transcendence of adversity – and, in that, she can be described as saintly.

Catherine's death was hastened by that of her elder daughter. From Paris, on 1 February 1939, Stravinsky wrote to Willy Strecker:

Sufferings and Humiliations of Catherine Stravinsky

My wife is not at all well. Since our terrible unhappiness, her
lungs have become much weaker, and the lesion is larger. She
never leaves her bed and is further debilitated by a cough
that tires her in the extreme. In three weeks she has not been
able to recover from an exhausting grippe. We were to have
gone to Pau, where the air is supposed to calm the nerves and
soothe the irritation in the bronchial tubes, but in her state it
is impossible to move. What can I do? I wait, I hope, and I
am full of anguish. . . A huge discouragement strikes me
every hour, every day. I wait, I wait, I wait.

Notes

1 'I am so happy when I think about your present composition
[*Jeu de cartes*]. I liked what you played for me immensely.'
(Letter of 17 January 1936)

2 On his return from America in 1935, Igor received a letter
from Catherine in which she says that her sister, Lyudmila
Beliankina, and Irina Terapiano, sister of Stravinsky's sister-
in-law, 'have written to me that you are somehow completely
changed – even-tempered, calm, and kind.' Down-to-earth
Lyudmila attributed the transformation to an improved liver
condition; Irina, who was typing the composer's *Chroniques*,
spoke of 'a spiritual cause'. But the new character seems not
to have been long-lasting. Catherine begins a letter on 23
August: 'Forgive me for having been all wrong about [the]
telegram. . . I know how such things make you angry.'

3 Since parallel-cousin marriage was forbidden in Russia, the
Stravinsky–Nossenko ceremony was performed in secret. For
the Stravinsky family genealogical chart see my *Stravinsky in
Pictures and Documents*, New York 1978.

4 Both women made copies of the letters Stravinsky wrote when
he did not have a typewriter; and both performed sundry
errands. G. G. Païchadze, of Edition Russe de Musique, wrote
to Stravinsky in New York, 13 January 1937: 'In accordance
with Ekaterina Gavrilovna's instructions today, we sent the
Mavra and *Baiser de la fée* piano scores, and, as Vera
Arturovna telegraphed, we added the scores of your three
church choruses.' Two weeks later, Païchadze wrote again
saying that Vera Arturovna had relayed Stravinsky's
instructions concerning *Apollo* and *Fée*, the ballets that were

to complete the programme, with *Jeu de cartes*, at the
Metropolitan Opera in April. Païchadze added that the score
of the *Fée* had to be copied from the original manuscript.

5 That Stravinsky's concert tours did have an effect on his
composing, both in quantity and form, is indicated by his
letter to Ernest Alexandrovich Oeberg of Edition Russe de
Musique, 23 September 1925, saying that three parts of the
Serenade were finished and that 'in all probability there will be
six parts.' Two weeks later he had written the fourth
movement, destined to be the final one, arguably because of
interruptions for concerts.

6 Lyudmila ('Mika', 'Mikusha'), Stravinsky's elder daughter
(1908–38).

7 Boris de Schloezer (1881–1969), brother of Alexander
Scriabin's second wife, was the author of *Igor Stravinsky*
(Paris, 1929; English translation by Ezra Pound, *The Dial*,
1929). Schloezer's aestheticizing irritated Stravinsky, who
once wrote to Nicolas Nabokov: 'What rubbish the Russian
intelligentsia [Schloezer] represents.' (Letter of 15 December
1949.)

8 Lyudmila ('Milochka') Beliankina (1880–1937), Catherine's
sister; her husband, Grigory ('Grisha') Beliankin, a retired
naval officer; and their two children, Ira ('Irusha') and Ganya.
When Germany invaded the Ukraine early in World War I, the
Beliankins moved from Kiev to Odessa. After the armistice,
they fled through Germany to the Swiss border, where, after
Stravinsky posted a bond, and René Auberjonois (the Swiss
painter and lifelong friend of Stravinsky: he designed the set of
the original *Histoire du soldat* in 1918), and an official in
Bern, Louis Ador, intervened in the composer's favour, the
refugee family was admitted to Switzerland.

9 Yuri Mandelstamm (1908–43?) was employed in Paris as a
film critic by the Russian émigré paper *Vozrozhdenie*. Early in
February 1935 he met Stravinsky's daughter Lyudmila, who
introduced him to her mother on 14 February. By the end of
April, he and Mika planned to marry – after his conversion to
the Russian Orthodox Church. Before taking this step, he
wanted 'to discuss theological questions with Bulgakov' –
Sergei Nikolayevich Bulgakov (1871–1944), a friend of Biely
and Berdyaev, and the author of several books on theology –
'but Bulgakov told him to go directly to Father Vassily, who is

the one who will baptize him.' (Catherine's letter of 11 May) Catherine later reported that 'Yuri is somewhat disturbed by the dryness of the catechism', but the baptism took place on 12 September, the marriage on 23 October.

Mandelstamm ghosted Stravinsky's essay on Pushkin: 'Yuri has just written your article about Pushkin, and tomorrow is coming here to dictate it to Ira, who will type it on your machine as you asked.' (Catherine's letter of 3 January 1937)

Mandelstamm remarried a year after Mika's death (November 1938), but, as late as April 1939, Anna Stravinsky, the composer's mother, wrote to Igor that 'Yuri comes by on Saturdays when he is free from the editorial office.' An article on Mandelstamm by Yuri Terapiano appears in the book *Vstrechi*, New York, 1953.

10 Vera Sudeikina was self-supporting during the years between her Sudeikin and Stravinsky marriages. The reference here is to her boutique for artificial flowers, but her most substantial sources of income were from a fashion accessories shop, the 'Tula-Vera', and from the designing and making of costumes in an atelier that she supervised. Catherine wrote to Igor on 25 May 1936: 'Because of the political developments and the change in the Ministry, everyone is afraid about the future. . .and Vera writes that the number of her orders dropped immediately, but she has probably written to you about it herself.'

11 Milene, Stravinsky's younger daughter (b. 1914).

12 Stravinsky had written from New York after a rough transatlantic crossing on the SS *Rex*.

13 Sviatoslav-Soulima ('Nini') Stravinsky (b. 1910), the composer's younger son.

14 Stravinsky received this letter from Catherine at the Sulgrave Hotel in New York, 3 May, two days before his departure for Europe.

15 On March 29, Stravinsky and Samuel Dushkin were in Tacoma, where they gave a recital, one of thirty concerts and ballet programmes in which the composer participated on the tour, a large number for the era of train travel, especially since the orchestral and ballet performances required rehearsals.

16 Returning from Naples, Stravinsky went to Sancellemoz. A letter to Willy Strecker, Stravinsky's publisher at B. Schotts Söhne, sent from there on 17 November, reveals that the

composer had just added the last six measures of the first movement of the 'Dumbarton Oaks' Concerto.

17 After difficulties in obtaining a German visa, Vera spent the first three weeks of August 1936 at Kurhotel-Wolf, Wiesee, a health resort south of Munich. Stravinsky met her in Strasbourg afterward for a '*Nachkur*' reunion, as Catherine put it (letter of 6 September). He had remained in Paris, composing *Jeu de cartes* and taking English lessons from a Berlitz instructor. The previous summer Catherine had written, 'You are studying English in the evenings, but is it possible to do this on your own, especially the pronunciation? Don't overload your already so overloaded mind.' (14 August 1935) Stravinsky's English was evidently much improved by the time of his next American tour, in 1937. His friend Alexis Kall, a Greek scholar and philologist, wrote to him on 13 May 1939, advising him to read his lectures at Harvard in English: 'No more than 5 or 10 will understand you in French. You spoke English wonderfully when you were here [Los Angeles] last.'

18 On 17 June, back in Sancellemoz, Stravinsky wrote to René Auberjonois: 'My poor old mother has left me too. I have just come back from the funeral in Paris and am here in the sanatorium with Milene. My home, my family, are in ruins. I have left Paris. There is nothing for me to do there.' Stravinsky does not say that Vera was also with him, possibly because Auberjonois might not have approved of the relationship.

19 Catherine spent most of her time in the sanatorium at Sancellemoz, which her mother-in-law could not visit because of the altitude. Stravinsky's mother, wife, and children had lived together in Biarritz (from December 1921), Nice (from September 1924), Voreppe (from September 1932) and Paris, where Stravinsky lived at 21, rue Viète from 15 October 1933 to 20 June 1934, on which date he moved to 25, rue du Faubourg St-Honoré. He lived there with Walter Nouvel, working on the *Chroniques*, until 1 October 1934, when the family arrived from Voreppe.

20 Barcelona seems not to have been the younger Stravinsky's lucky city with the Capriccio. On 18 March 1936, Catherine wrote: 'Yesterday I received Vera's letter of the 14th from Barcelona, and today I received Svetik's of the 15th. . . I

already know from Mama how he, poor thing, lost count and got out of phase [in the Capriccio].'

21 Stravinsky ended a letter to Nicolas G. Struve, 6 April 1919, 'My regards to Rachmaninov', but by the 1930s the two composers were not on good terms. Surprisingly, however, until the 1940s Rachmaninov's royalties were not vastly greater than Stravinsky's. Païchadze wrote to Stravinsky on 8 April 1930: 'Columbia Records paid us $1,200 in American recording rights for *Petrushka* and this year they are paying us $2,000 for Rachmaninov's Second Concerto.' In Los Angeles, in 1942, Rachmaninov telephoned to his biographer, Sergei Bertensson: 'I know how much Igor Fyodorovich has always disliked my compositions. . . I am not sure whether I could invite him and his wife to my house – which I'd love to do – because I don't know how he would receive my invitation. Would you be so kind as to send out a feeler?'

Bertensson reported that he 'called Vera Arturovna and her immediate response was "Delighted!" Before dinner and during it. . .they talked about managers, concert bureaus, agents, ASCAP [the American Society of Composers, Authors and Publishers], royalties. Both composers were glad to have the old barrier broken down. The Stravinskys later returned the invitation. At the first dinner, Stravinsky mentioned that he was fond of honey, and within a few days, Sergei Vasilyevich found a great jar of fine honey and delivered it personally at the Stravinsky door. Rachmaninov played at Hollywood Bowl on 17 and 18 July [and dined] the following night with the Stravinskys and [Arthur] Rubinsteins. . .'

In Baden-Baden, in October 1951, Stravinsky dismissed a request to contribute 'a statement or article about Rachmaninov' with the remark, 'I knew Rachmaninov very little.'

22 Isidor Philipp (1863–1958), pianist and professor at the Paris Conservatory from 1903 to 1934.

23 On 18 August 1935, after consulting doctors on the medical consequences of Mika's forthcoming marriage, Catherine reported to Igor: 'She cannot have children for at least three years.' Mika gave birth to a daughter fifteen months after the marriage, and died the following year. In the same letter, Catherine says, 'I am certain that I also had a tubercular infiltration when I got married.' On 5 September 1935, she

told Igor that 'Dr Tobé attributes Mika's lung condition to a very long-range after-effect of a case or cases of pleurisy, but we know of only one instance of her having had pleurisy, when she was ten years old, whereas I have had such a condition all my life.'

24 In a letter to Païchadze, 25 July 1927, Stravinsky refers to the 'unexpected illness of my wife', a surprising choice of adjective, since, from her letters, it seems that in Catherine's case illness could never have been unexpected.

25 Catherine was born on 25 January, but, as she wrote to Igor on 11 January 1935: 'Since the day of our wedding, I always associate my birthday with the 24th.' She also celebrated the day of her engagement, 15 August (Old Style) – the Feast of the Assumption – 1905.

26 Catherine seems to have known that Igor regarded 14 July as the date of his 'marriage' with Vera.

27 During a short vacation with Vera, in Positano, in 1937, Stravinsky received no fewer than ten lengthy communications from Catherine, containing such information as: 'Yesterday I coughed up 19 times'; 'since it's cold at night I put on wool socks over my stockings'; 'Don't lie on the beach in the sun, as it could be very harmful to your lungs, liver, and nerves.'

28 On 17 February 1947, Stravinsky wrote to his sister-in-law Elena, widow of his brother Yuri, in Leningrad: 'I have enjoyed good health since I moved to California, and I compose and travel a great deal.'

29 On 1 September 1937, after a few weeks at Château de Monthoux, Catherine returned to Sancellemoz. Stravinsky accompanied her, then left with Vera for Venice on 7 September, Positano on 13 September, returning to Sancellemoz on 27 September.

30 Stravinsky was a dandy and sometimes a fop. On 20 July 1923, he ordered a 'black cashmere smoking suit' from his Paris tailor, James Pile, and on 27 September 'a green jacket and gray flannel pants'. Every few days, it seems, he bought neckties, scarves, hats. *Lidové Noviny*, the Prague newspaper, noted on 25 February 1930: 'He wore a pink shirt, silk tie, perfectly cut brown suit.' Many of his letters mention clothes, as, for example, when writing to his publisher on 6 October 1932, Stravinsky asks him, while in London, to fetch some linen shirts *tricotées* that had been ordered from Hilditch &

Sufferings and Humiliations of Catherine Stravinsky

Key. Scarcely an interview throughout Stravinsky's life fails to describe his apparel: 'A bowler worn to protect the neck, a yellow tie hidden by a dark blue pullover. . .and beneath that a light linen vest. . .' (*Le Soir*, Brussels, 15 January 1924); 'He was dressed in a brown and rose sweater, which replaced the colorful orange shirt and scarf and black ulster in which he landed from the liner *Paris* on Sunday' (*New York Times*, 6 January 1925); 'He wore a grey jacket, violet shirt, green tie, golden bracelet, and a monocle on a black tether' (*Die Stunde*, Vienna, 17 March 1926); '[He was] clad in a dark, double-breasted suit, with gray spats peeping beneath perfectly pressed trousers, and a white handkerchief dazzling in his pocket' (*Washington Post*, 24 March 1935); 'He was dressed in a white linen suit with a sport shirt open at the neck' (*Excelsior*, Paris, 11 September 1935). At Harvard, in 1939, on one occasion, 'Stravinsky's clothes [were] collegiate: a brown suit-coat, contrasting gray trousers, black shirt, grayish sweater.' Even in the American Midwest and South his garments attracted notice: 'He wore plain dark trousers, with a matching V-neck, slip-over sweater of soft wool, a checkered black and white coat, yellow socks and black oxfords' (*Urbana News-Gazette*, 3 March 1949); 'doffing a small black Homburg and a white muffler. . .smoking a Turkish cigarette' (*Atlanta Journal*, 27 January 1955).

In comparison, the wardrobe of his wife is pitiful: 'I am very ashamed to admit that I've ordered myself a skirt, as I've only one summer skirt . . .' (4 November 1937); 'My telegram gives you an account of money needs. . .because I have little left and want to buy a woollen shirt and sweater' (12 October 1937); 'I am going to ask you for a present when you come in November. Bring some boots of the same kind that you gave me before. . . We can dispense with considerations of elegance. I write about this now because perhaps it's better to buy such things in London than in Paris' (16 October 1937). Catherine Stravinsky once wrote to her husband: 'The prices at Pile's are frightful, but it's difficult to find another tailor after having dressed yourself there for so many years. Perhaps you could buy yourself a ready-made travelling coat, though, of course, they are never so good. . .' Pile's bill for May 1932 was 3,000 francs.

31 Fees for broadcasts started to become important to Stravinsky in 1930–31. A letter from Païchadze, 13 February 1932, reveals that the League of Composers (New York) paid $800 to perform *Oedipus Rex* and an additional $400 for the radio transmission of the work. On 11 February 1932, Païchadze sent 50,000 francs in performance fees, many from broadcasts, to Stravinsky's bank in Geneva.

32 In 1947 Jeanne Gautier collaborated with Stravinsky in establishing the violin part in his violin and piano transcription of the 'Ballad' from *Le Baiser de la fée*, and in 1954 she performed his Violin Concerto, under his direction, in Turin.

33 Theodore ('Fedik', 'Fedya'), Stravinsky's elder son (1907–89).

34 In this same letter, Catherine says that during the brief absence of Mlle Svitalski, the governess, 'all the servants will be home,' and that Marcel 'never leaves [Mama] alone and watches over things in the evenings, while you are gone.' In October, no doubt frightened by the danger of contracting tuberculosis, Marcel, Thérèse and Raymonde departed, leaving only the maid, Emma, and the new cook, Céline.

35 'Since I turned to God,' she writes on 11 March 1935, 'this is the first time that I've begun Lent without going to church.'

36 This is the Russian version of the *Philokalia*, the writings of the early Fathers, compiled on Mount Athos by Makarius of Corinth and Nicodemus of the Holy Mountain, and published in Venice in 1782. The book was translated into Slavonic in the eighteenth century; in the 1870s a five-volume Russian edition was published, and a three-volume edition appeared in Moscow in 1905. (In 1951, Faber & Faber published a selection in English, *Writings from the Philokalia*.) On 20 August 1936, Catherine wrote to Igor: 'I am reading the *Dobrotolyubiye* every day and comparing how these people with great souls and faith, who lived only in God and for God, talked, measured, and thought about life. How simple and clear everything was to them.' And on 9 October 1937: 'I'd like to have another volume of the *Dobrotolyubiye*, since I have already reread everything and am rereading everything again.' In one letter, she asks him to bring Viktor Ivanovich Nesmielov's little book (probably on Gregory of Nyssa). To judge from Stravinsky's extensive annotations in his copy of Nesmielov's *The Science of Man* (3rd edn, Moscow, 1905, 2

vols), this philosopher exerted a major influence on the composer's thought.

37 On 24 January 1935, Catherine wrote, 'I went to church. The holy wonder-working icon was there. Father Vassily and Deacon Pyotr will bring it home with us tomorrow and we will pray.' Nearly three years later, she wrote, 'Tomorrow Father Vassily is bringing a marvellous icon to me.' (14 December 1937)

38 Good Friday shroud. An effigy of St Plashchanitsa was carried from the church on Good Friday. 'Here in Paris they bring her out later than in Nice,' Catherine wrote to Igor on 26 April 1935.

39 A monk who is also a priest.

40 Religion was never far from Stravinsky's thoughts, nonetheless, as is shown in the following passage from a letter to Païchadze, after seven years of silence: 'Aged? Of course you have aged. We all have aged in these seven years. . . But, speaking for myself, it is difficult to say whether I have aged or not, since I do not think much about it: I do not have time. I live from year to year, as everyone does, in the emotional aftermath of events. But I am unlike everyone else because of the pressure I have been under from composing: a lot has been created and a lot performed in my concert tours during these years. I work independently of *reality* for, after all, music goes on independently of it as well. People say, of course: "He is against the expression of feelings in music and has made it so dry that it has no more spirit." When you encounter such judgements, it is impossible not to remember the distinction that the Apostle Paul drew between *emotional* and *spiritual*, a distinction that people continue to ignore after 2,000 years.' (11 April 1946)

41 Later, Catherine decided that Yuri had questionable taste: 'He even wanted to look [for an apartment] with his sister, who also, no doubt, has bad or mediocre taste.' (2 August 1935)

42 'Patience and more patience, that is what is essential. . . I think that this is all that God wants from us' (6 October 1937); 'The doctor told me: "You will always have bronchitis, but you have a good nature, and will bear it"' (28 October 1937). Once, however, Catherine did refer to another woman at Sancellemoz, 'who, poor thing, considers herself a lifetime patient, like me' (8 September 1937).

9

CHER PÈRE, CHÈRE VÉRA

As all historians know, our knowledge of the past
is based very largely on records of litigation;
and, as Mantegna was a tireless litigant, we know
an unusual amount about him at all periods.
Kenneth Clark, *The Art of Humanism*

My title is the salutation that begins most of the letters to Igor and Vera Stravinsky from his three surviving children and their spouses. Similarly, the contents of the correspondence seem to indicate that Stravinsky's children had genuine affection for his second wife. Whatever their true feelings, they must have recognized that their stepmother was responsible for the smoother periods in their relationship with their father, who would do anything for her, and for her alone. Everyone close to the scene knew that Vera Stravinsky regularly interceded on the children's behalf, exhorting their father to continue to provide them with money, or doing so herself when he refused.

On 7 July 1964, for instance, Mrs Soulima Stravinsky[1] wrote to the composer: 'At Ann Arbor [13 May 1964] I asked Vera if it would be possible for you to help us financially with the work at my home [in France], La Clidelle. Vera's response was so kind and so full of warmth that I now permit myself to broach the subject with you.'

Less kindly and warmly, Stravinsky wrote to his publisher in London: 'Ashamed to ask me directly, [Françoise] spoke about it to Vera, breaking down into tears. But give the money to the poor girl, since taxes will not allow me to take it to my grave.' (9 July 1964)

On 8 June 1951, Stravinsky wrote to Theodore, his elder son: 'Vera just received the letters from Denise and Kitty.[2] I understand your financial trouble resulting from the trip you are obliged to make to Vichy. As testimony to my sympathy, I enclose a payment order permitting you to withdraw 1,000 Swiss francs from my account in Basel before your departure.' The composer's heirs[3] understood implicitly that they would be wiser to address their requests not to *cher père* but to *chère Véra*.

On 10 October 1952, Stravinsky wrote to Theodore, then aged forty-five:

> You say that you do not have sufficient money to build the garage and the fence, and you ask me for another $8,000 or $9,000. Although I have already told you how difficult it would be for me to exceed the sum of $15,000, I shall once again explain the state of my finances. . . If I send the money you request, I would be reducing to a dangerous level the small amount that I have put aside for Vera and myself in the event of my incapacitation. Do not forget, I am seventy years old. I live modestly, and, if comparatively comfortably, this is only because I am still conducting. How long I shall be able to go on conducting without running myself into the ground, I cannot say; but I do know that without the conducting, it would be difficult to make ends meet. My earnings as a composer are not enough to live on, and I will not conceal from you that *I live in constant fear of having no security*. . . The greater part of the savings that I made have been for all of you. I gave each of you $15,000 to buy or build a house. My own house cost $13,000.[4]

Despite repeated declarations of this kind from the composer, he continued to send money, thanks chiefly – as I witnessed – to Vera Stravinsky, who prevailed upon him not only to help support his children, but also to give each of them the house that Stravinsky mentions, and an automobile.

A few excerpts from the myriad letters, covering more than forty of Stravinsky's later years, are sufficient to indicate that the flow of money to Theodore was regular and substantial:

Unfortunately, I cannot afford to continue increasing the sums that I send you monthly. . . My earnings have decreased, especially in the last year, owing to the crisis in (conducting) engagements, which were my principal source of income. In order to help you, I am using the francs in the Basel bank, which do not amount to much and which I had been saving for an emergency. It would be nice to replenish this sum with proceeds from the sale of the manuscript. (4 June 1950)

I see from your letter that I must immediately provide you with 4,000 francs for your naturalization. Since I do not want to send the money from here, and I do not have enough in Basel at the moment, I have asked [Erwin] Rosenthal, with whom I deal in selling my manuscripts, to send you this sum. (14 March 1962)

I received your letter and in immediate reply am sending 4,000 Swiss francs. (11 April 1962)

In this and other instances, Vera Stravinsky was Theodore's advocate. Notwithstanding, neither he nor his brother Soulima, nor sister Milene,[5] nor Igor Stravinsky's granddaughter, Catherine, acknowledged the composer's widow at his funeral. And shortly thereafter they retained lawyers to contest her right to inherit much of what he had willed her, an action that, in February 1974, developed into a lawsuit settled (in name only) six years later, to the advantage of no one except the several law firms involved.[6]

The documentation for this ugliest and most highly publicized chapter in Stravinsky's biography is found in correspondence and in the depositions taken during the litigation.[7] The latter, on file at the New York County Surrogate Court, are part of the public record.[8] The original language of most of Igor Stravinsky's letters is French, but some are written, partly or entirely, in Russian and English. The quotations from the depositions, and from notes and letters entered as evidence, follow the official, notarized texts and translations of texts.

Apart from Vera Stravinsky, I was the only person to whom Igor Stravinsky confided extensively *vis-à-vis* his children and who, at the same time, knew all of the litigants personally: Soulima Stravinsky since June 1948; Milene Marion since July

1948; Theodore Stravinsky and Catherine Mandelstamm Stravinsky since August 1951. Although the aim of this chronicle is to present an unbiased view of a segment of Stravinsky history, I concede that this is not possible; having lived with Igor and Vera Stravinsky almost every day for twenty-three years, I am naturally more aware of the perspectives of the elders than of the children. Yet I was fond of the children when I first knew them and felt at times that I was on their 'side', partly because we shared the same struggle to preserve our own identities. The children were deeply handicapped, being biologically pre-empted: nature had concentrated all of her power in the awesome father.

Only rarely do great artists make good parents, great art demanding of its creators no less than all they have to give. Stravinsky was no exception to this rule, and it seems to have made him a tyrannical father. During a visit in February 1916, Nijinsky observed that the composer 'is like an emperor and his wife and children are his servants and soldiers.'[9] Stravinsky's correspondence indicates that his imperiousness with his sons did not diminish when they grew up. Thus Arthur Lourié felt compelled to write to him, on 8 March 1930: 'I am a little worried about [Theodore's] personal affairs. . . Give him a few kind words of advice, dear friend.' And a week later: 'I am sorry for [your sons] because even the suggestion that they might be suspected of something bad causes them to despair.' In the same year, Theodore wrote to his father: 'You hang up the telephone on me, leaving me standing there. . . I was very hurt by that.' Once Stravinsky's wife actually had to remind him that 'you were off by an entire month in your birthday cable to Theodore. He was born on March 27 *not* April 24' (letter of 27 April 1937). A letter from Stravinsky to Theodore, 18 April 1961, reveals an asperity of a kind more likely to be found in a communication to an errant adolescent than to a man of fifty-four:

. . .I do not understand anything in your short note of April 14. . . What exactly is it that has been done 'according to my

instructions'?. . .I asked you to send the letter I
enclosed. . .which you failed to do for reasons unknown to
me. . . And what 'documents' are you keeping 'here for now'?
I did not send any documents but only that ill-fated letter,
whose reply I have awaited for three weeks. Can it really be
that you took my letter of instructions to be a document of
some kind? What thoughtlessness! Reply immediately and
explain this stupid misunderstanding.

That holy terror was one of the emotions Stravinsky inspired
in his offspring is best shown in an interview given by his
daughter in the 1982 London Weekend Television documentary on Stravinsky. There she recalls that when she was a child,
her father would sometimes ask her to join him at the piano
and play a few notes that he could not reach:

> He would play the lines for me two or three times so that I
> would have an idea [of the music]. . . It was just a few notes.
> Just the fear of not doing it right made me make mistakes. The
> first mistake, he was patient. He would say, 'Start over again.'
> Second time, mistake again, and I was trembling, and then he
> would show impatience. The third mistake he would just blow
> his temper.

Because of Catherine's chronic pulmonary condition, and
because the children were ill so much of the time,[10] Stravinsky
was obliged to repeat the pattern of his own childhood,
entrusting to governesses a major part of the responsibility for
the children's education and care. During their formative
years, his sudden celebrity as a composer, beginning in June
1910, required frequent separation from the family, at first
simply to attend performances of the Ballets Russes, but later
to appear as pianist and conductor in hundreds of concerts.
After the move from Switzerland to France (June 1920), the
family was deprived of his presence for long stretches. In
February 1921 he met Vera Sudeikina,[11] and from that year
until their marriage in 1940 he spent as much time with her as
with his family.[12] (Martin Garbus, in an affidavit, described
the couple as 'common-law man and wife' in the years 1921–

39.[13]). Following Stravinsky's emigration to America, he did not see his elder son and granddaughter for twelve years, his younger son and daughter for nine and eight years, respectively. In the thirty-two years from June 1939 to April 1971, meetings between Stravinsky and his children, with the exception of Milene Marion, who remained his Los Angeles neighbour from April 1947 to September 1969, were remarkably rare.

At Stravinsky's bidding, Catherine Stravinsky and Vera Sudeikina met, in his home in Nice, on 1 March 1925. Theodore must have surmised the nature of his father's relationship with Mme Sudeikina later that year when he accompanied them on an automobile trip, but in 1926, Tanya Stravinsky, one of the composer's Leningrad nieces, temporarily living in France, may also have intimated something of the liaison to her cousin, apparently having perceived it after a few meetings with her uncle and Mme Sudeikina in Paris. Soulima discovered the relationship himself by 1928. Mme Sudeikina's 1929 diary mentions lunches with him, and soon both sons were fulfilling errands for their father with regard to her. In a letter of 21 June 1931, Stravinsky instructs Soulima to 'call Ranelagh' – Mme Sudeikina's apartment was on this street – 'so that I do not have to repeat this dull account of my illness.' In a letter to his father from Sancellemoz, 9 February 1934, Soulima writes: 'Perhaps you and Vera could drive here in the automobile.' By the mid-1930s, Stravinsky, Mme Sudeikina, and Soulima frequently travelled together,[14] and in 1935, both sons accompanied the couple on an automobile excursion to Venice.[15]

The children's letters to their father, written when he was on concert tours in America and elsewhere, mention lunches, dinners, visits with Vera. The letters do not refer to requests to Vera for advice, evidently not available in the straitlaced Stravinsky home. Sometimes Vera's letters to Igor offer glimpses of her role as a surrogate mother, as when, in a letter to Igor of 18 January 1935, Vera reveals that Mika has sought her advice concerning how to deal with an unwanted suitor, a brother of Serge Lifar, as well as support in her determination to study drawing from live nudes, the thought of which had nearly provoked apoplexy in Stravinsky's mother. Mika wrote to her father in Scandinavia, 1 October 1935: 'Today Yura [Mandelstamm, her fiancé], Fedya, and I are going to Vera's for tea; I called her on the telephone yesterday and wished her a happy name day.' Theodore wrote to 'Popochka' in New York in February 1937: 'Vera is at auntie's all day long and helps out in every possible way.' Vera's letters to Stravinsky also mention his family, as in, for example, the one dated 11 January 1933: 'Give Katya my thanks for the chocolate, and then thank the children for remembering me and for their kind wishes on my birthday.'

Between November 1938 and June 1939, Stravinsky suffered the loss of his elder daughter (30 November 1938), his wife (2 March 1939), and his mother (7 June 1939) – three funerals in six months, three services in the Church of the Sign of the Holy Mother, 32, rue Boileau.[16] And in mid-March 1939 he himself was obliged to undergo treatment at the tuberculosis sanatorium in Sancellemoz. He was accompanied by Theodore and Denise, and later by Mme Sudeikina, who could hardly have gone there with him immediately after his wife's death; Mme Sudeikina was with him there after the funeral of his mother, in any case, and for the remainder of the summer.[17] Already at this time Theodore Stravinsky began to show resentment toward Vera, and so noticeably after the composer announced his intention of marrying her that he angrily asked his son to leave. (See Vera's letter to Igor of 28 October 1939, below.) Vera pacified Stravinsky and closed the breach,[18] as she was to do countless times in the future. But in fairness to Theodore and his wife, it must be said that they had recently been prejudiced against Mme Sudeikina by Arthur Lourié, who, it seems, had repeated gossip to them about her life in St Petersburg before the Revolution. (Though Lourié denied this when confronted by Mme Sudeikina, and though he continued to visit her in the fall of 1939, Stravinsky never forgave his former intimate friend and musical assistant, and during the next twenty-seven years, when they both lived in the United States, and most of that time not far apart, they never met.)

Another incident, which took place while Stravinsky was in America in the fall of 1939, can, in retrospect, be recognized as precursory to the rift that occurred twenty-eight years later. On 14 September, just before his departure for New York, the composer opened a joint bank account in Paris at the Crédit Commercial in the names of Vera Sudeikina and Theodore Stravinsky, with a cash balance of 139,329 francs. In October, Theodore transferred 112,000 francs of this sum to an account in his name in a bank in Le Mans, where he was living, and withdrew 19,000 francs for himself, his brother, the governess Mlle Svitalski ('Madubo'),[19] and to pay bills. Left with only 5,000 francs, Vera wrote to Stravinsky in Cambridge, Massachusetts, on 28 October:

I am obliged to tell you about a very unpleasant surprise. Fedya and Denise arrived yesterday from Le Mans. They had drawn all the money from the Paris bank and transferred it to Le Mans. Fedya passed by to tell me that my access to the account, as well as Madubo's, has been cancelled, and that from now on, if I need money I will have to address myself to [Theodore] – and, if he is conscripted, to Denise (!!!). The same is true for Svetik: I can imagine how outraged he will be, since they did not even consult him. Fedya manipulated all this because he had heard that our bank may fail, but I do not see why trustworthy banks should exist only in Le Mans. He could have left the whole arrangement as it was and, if he were really worried about our Paris bank, transferred the money to the Banque de France. Fedya said that, as the oldest, he has the right to arrange things, and that 'Papa would have approved my action.'

Not being a member of the family, I kept quiet. Also, I did not want to say that the whole thing was manipulated so that Denise could control the money. . .and everyone would be beholden to her. I hope that they will not do anything foolish and that the money will not be lost under their 'management'. Nothing can be done now, in any case, since the money has been deposited in their names in Le Mans. . .they returned to

Le Mans yesterday without waiting for Svetik's arrival on his twenty-four-hour leave. . .

Forgive me, dearest, for having written you this unpleasant letter. . . Fedya has nothing to do with all this, and if he had acted alone, I am sure that he would have done so more delicately. . . I wanted to say: 'First ask your father for his permission,' since, after all, the money is yours, and you are the only one who can dispose of it; but then I decided not to say anything. . .

On 4 November, Vera wrote to Stravinsky, in response to his cable: 'You ask me how much money remains in the Paris bank. I have absolutely no idea; you will have to ask the Theodores. Incidentally, Soulima finds that this story about the money is completely idiotic and that the Theodores behaved with very little consideration for any of us.' The remainder of the long letter makes no further mention of the affair.

On 5 November, Stravinsky cabled to Vera as follows: 'Demand immediate transfer for your needs three-quarters my money Paris Morgan your name and one-quarter remaining Le Mans Theodore's needs.' Vera answered on 13 November: 'Soulima and I decided to transfer the money not to the Morgan but to the Crédit Commercial, where it was before. I do not want to have the account in my name only. I sent Theodore a letter enclosing a copy of your cable. When everything is settled, I will probably send you a cable. In it, "*Tout fait*" will refer to the bank story.' On 16 November, Vera forwarded to Igor the excuse that she had received from Theodore the day before: 'Why did you not tell me right away that you did not agree?' (She had answered: 'This money was not mine but your father's; I simply informed him that the instructions he left had been ignored.')

Meanwhile, Stravinsky dispatched an angry letter to Theodore, in care of Vera, with instructions to her to forward it. She did not do so, but wrote to Stravinsky (22 November) defending Theodore and giving her reasons for not delivering the letter:

Dearest Igor,

I have replied to your two letters concerning the money affair and told you that I will forward your letter to Fedya. I have not done this, however, and for the following reasons. When people who are very close find themselves separated and living in nerve-racking circumstances (you because of your own cares and work, we because of the war and constant fears), they should not write such letters: your letter to Theodore was very harsh; I took pity on him. Also, endless explanations would begin, and now, with the termination of the Atlantic Clipper, these could have gone on for a year. Besides, he sent me two apologetic letters: he understood your feelings from your cable. Soulima, too, expressed his opinion to him. Now everything is settled: I have received the money, thanks to your cable, and everything is back to normal. I did not want to upset Theodore all over again with your letter. Consider only that he cannot go to you and explain in person, a terrible situation, and that you would be troubled by a whole month of correspondence. Should something happen to anybody, a life of very bitter feeling would remain.

Forgive me for writing such depressing things, but a war is going on here, and people are perishing every day. . . A nervous tension exists which we try to hide and to which we become accustomed; still, it is there. I see no point in writing about things that, thanks to your cable, have already been straightened out: so enough of it. If you would write to Fedya that you could not understand his behaviour, and that you disagreed with it, but that now everything is arranged – well, that would be sufficient. . . I think that even you could not explain things at this distance. I hope very much that you will agree with my decision and that you will write to me about it. . . Either I will forward your letter or burn it. I prefer the latter. If I were to receive even a hundredth part of your criticism of Fedya, I would lose my mind. . . Fedya is very sensitive and would suffer terribly. He is not stubborn and does not resist, as is shown by his efforts to explain to me and by his sending letters to me. Please, my darling, leave him in peace.

On 25 November, Vera wrote that she had deposited the money that Theodore had returned to her in the Crédit

Commercial in Paris, adding that 'his last letter shows that he realized his blunder.' On 11 December, Stravinsky wrote to her from San Francisco:

> Only yesterday I received the long-awaited letter from you. . . Since you never forwarded my letter to Fedya, and in view of your advice to me concerning it, I am inclined to approve, except that I feel the necessity of his answering the two questions I put to him: Why did he remove the money secretly and not tell you? And why did he take it to Le Mans? According to your advice, I agree and do not insist on sending any letter to him; you can destroy it. Still, I will remain unsatisfied until I receive an answer from him to those two torturing questions and an apology for his actions. Without that, it is impossible for me to write to him as if nothing has happened. I feel uncomfortable in my soul, and, not wanting to hurt him, I will write nothing. But I want him to know the reasons for my silence. I received a letter from Denise, but I read it with a heavy heart, for I no longer believe her.

A month later, Vera was in New York. She described her impressions in a letter to Soulima: 'So far, the hugeness, the lights, the crowds on Broadway depress me; I still have too many ties holding me to Europe. . . I loved so much to rush out into the street in Paris to buy a newspaper, to exchange a few words with a shopkeeper; but here, from the twentieth floor. . .' In March, Vera and Igor were married and lived in Boston until they moved to Los Angeles in May. Though both of them were in their fifties, they began life anew, entering into the spirit and excitement of the California of the time.[20] Thanks to a large refugee population, Los Angeles was a cosmopolitan city, the wartime home of many European musicians, writers, artists, and theatre people, some of them representing philosophies, views, and values to which Stravinsky had theretofore paid little heed. He began to change profoundly as a result of diverse influences in the new environment, which equally stimulated the intellectually liberated, socially popular, open-minded woman who was no longer simply a companion but now his wife. In 1945, after visiting the Stravinskys in Hollywood, Pierre Schaeffer, the promoter of *musique concrète*, published an article portraying the composer's 'euphoria' in his life there, adding that the *'sourire éblouissant de Véra. . .[a] aidé Igor Stravinsky,'* and even providing a photo of Mme Stravinsky, *'où figure ce sourire éclatant de joie de vivre, de forte tendresse.'*[21] Two decades later the Stravinskys' enchantment with Hollywood had vanished, but not their enchantment with each other, or their *joie de vivre.*

Although Igor and Vera Stravinsky could hardly be described in 1947 as assimilated Americans, they had nevertheless become accustomed to many American ways. The composer's aloofness had given way to an informality in his relations with people, as well as in his habits of daily life, style of dress, and entertaining. He now listened to ideas that he would have rejected outright in the 1930s – such as the Trotskyite polemics of his ex-Viennese physician – and was constantly inspired by the range of knowledge and interests of such friends as Aldous Huxley and Gerald Heard.[22]

Though I can judge the astonishing transformation in Stravinsky only from his correspondence and through those who knew him both before and after the first American decade, it is obvious that while he had once been dogmatic, closed to criticism, contemptuous of colleagues, socially comfortable only with the rich and titled, by 1950 those characteristics had all but disappeared.[23] Now he wore denim trousers, ate hot dogs in diners, and hobnobbed with Hollywood's rank-and-file orchestra players. Moreover, when Russia entered the war his political outlook was quickly reversed, and the rabid anticommunist rightist[24] of the decades before became a supporter of every organization helping the USSR. Most important, he listened to, played, and studied a great deal of new music of diverse tendencies. When, after an absence of twelve years, Stravinsky first visited Europe, he perceived the metamorphosis in himself, everywhere declaring that he felt more American than European.

The composer's three children, meanwhile, had not undergone such a change. At the beginning of World War II, Theodore was briefly interned in a camp near Vichy, moving to Switzerland in the spring of 1942. Since he remained in Europe following the war and had not seen his father after 1939,[25] the Americanization of his parent should have been more conspicuous to him than to his sister and brother, yet it was never acknowledged. Milene lived in Sancellemoz throughout the war and, while there, married Andre Marion, another pulmonary patient. Soulima lived in Paris during the Occupation, and, unfortunately, chose to perform there as pianist in Collaborationist circles, and even appealed to influential people inside the Third Reich to arrange concerts for him in Germany, to his father's great chagrin and embarrassment after the war. (In 1945, Darius Milhaud, in California, received a letter from Francis Poulenc describing the activities of French musicians during the Occupation. Milhaud read the letter to a group of friends that included Stravinsky, and when he read the part about Soulima, 'Stravinsky covered his head in his hands.')

From the beginning of the war to August 1941, Stravinsky sent money to Theodore through the mother of the composer Vittorio Rieti, and Vera sent it to Milene in care of Mrs E. Schreiber, Zürich. After that date, Mrs Olga ('Aunt Lyulya') Schwarz, 4, avenue d'Evian, Lausanne, acted as intermediary, and in August 1943, Stravinsky sent $600 for Theodore and Kitty in care of this relative.[26] In 1941, Stravinsky also began to send money to Theodore and Milene by way of Darius Milhaud's mother in Aix-en-Provence; Milhaud sent cables with the code words 'Stravinsky's health good', which meant that she was to forward 30,000 francs to Theodore from her own bank, for which Stravinsky would reimburse his colleague in California. Between June 1942 and November 1943, Milene received $1,800 by this means. Beginning in December 1941, Soulima received his father's French royalties, and after the war Stravinsky transmitted sums to him via returning refugees, among them Vladimir Golschmann.

At the end of the war, Vera Stravinsky invited the Marions to move to California,[27] looking to the future possibility of

Stravinsky's need for assistance if she were to become ill. She persuaded her husband to purchase a house for them nearby.[28] Partly for the same reason, and also to give Soulima a fresh start, Igor and Vera Stravinsky invited him, his wife, and their three-year-old son John to Hollywood, renting a home for them[29] and arranging an American debut as a pianist for Soulima.[30]

Vera and Soulima seem to have had a very friendly relationship in the 1930s, perhaps because she – not Igor – had attended the young man's first recital, in Valenciennes on 13 April 1930. In any case, he spent his first weekend leave from the army with her and Mlle Svitalski. Vera wrote to Igor on 13 November 1939:

> Svetik's visit was a great joy for us. We sat until midnight while he told us about his friends and his daily life. He really is touching in his boyishness, though at the same time you cannot imagine how he has changed, bearing all the difficulties and encouraging everyone else with his good spirits and positiveness. At 6 p.m., when he left for the railroad station, I felt very sad. He asked me to write to him every day and to send him preserves and chocolates. Since he is completely free on Sundays, I will be able to go there and take him to lunch in a restaurant. He is magnificent.

On 25 November, Vera wrote again: 'Just this minute I received a charming letter from Svetik. He lovingly thanks me for my letter, and he is so warm that he makes me happy.' Vera's first letter written on American soil, a lengthy account of her impressions of the United States, was sent to 'Dearest Svetik'. It concluded: 'I am writing this letter at a desk in Father's sitting room and with your photograph, from *Vogue*, in front of me. . . My dearest, I kiss you very, very hard.'

The Marions' transplantation proved to be a mixed blessing. Milene's relationship with her father now depended on her husband, who began to work as his father-in-law's secretary and thus became dependent on the Stravinskys. The interests and temperaments of the two men were incompatible, and the Marions took little part in the Stravinskys' social life, never going to concerts with them, let alone operas, museums, and the theatre. According to the composer, Marion accompanied him on the train from Los Angeles to Chicago, 22–24 October 1954, without uttering a single word. After one crisis, Marion asked his father-in-law for $10,000 with which to return to France, but this was a larger amount than Stravinsky was prepared to give, and Vera Stravinsky persuaded the Marions to stay. Finally, in 1954, Marion left his father-in-law's employ, except as bookkeeper, taking a job in a travel agency. Nevertheless, the Stravinskys remained the Marions' chief source of income.[31]

The relocation of the Soulima Stravinskys in California proved to be a great mistake, and they quickly realized that living close to Stravinsky *père* would involve the surrender of whatever professional and personal independence Stravinsky *fils* had attained. The family moved to New York, then to Urbana, where Soulima was engaged as a piano teacher at the University of Illinois.[32] Whereas in 1948–49, Stravinsky had procured concert engagements that included his son as piano soloist, the two appeared together after that on only three occasions: in Urbana and St Louis (March 1950), Hollywood (12 August 1952), and Chicago and Milwaukee (13–15 and 18 January 1954). Relations between father and son post-1949 can only be described as remote, and in the last ten years of the composer's life, Soulima saw him during only eleven brief encounters,[33] though meetings in the 1950s had been even rarer.[34]

Perhaps Soulima's potential for conflict with his father was greater than that of the other children simply because music was the younger son's profession. He suffered a crisis on this account when he was twenty-nine, as Pierre Suvchinsky described to Stravinsky in a letter of 23 May 1939.[35] The letter refers to an 'aggressiveness' on Soulima's part that may have consisted in his mention of his father's mortality in a letter earlier that month:

In the event of your death, not one of us would be able to touch a *centime* unless Kitty's guardianship is established. That is why the matter should be attended to, at your convenience, just to make provisions for the future, because Mr Mandelstamm could end up as the guardian.[36]

Of all the Stravinsky children, only Milene saw her father and stepmother with any frequency during the years 1947–68, or, rather, during the six months or so of each year that they spent in California. And since Milene appeared to be close to Vera, successfully appealing to her in every difficulty,[37] the younger woman's behaviour after 1968 is less comprehensible than that of the other heirs. Stravinsky's widow was very slow to believe that someone whom she had treated as a daughter, encouraging her talents and lavishing gifts on her, had been a secret enemy long before Stravinsky's death. Milene's deposition conjures a purely fictional Vera Stravinsky, one who asks her husband to 'make the record[ings] in London. It brings a lot of money.' Anyone who knew Vera Stravinsky in the mid-1960s, the time of this alleged statement, would remember that she bitterly opposed her husband's record making, no matter where, and would recognize that such a remark – unless intended ironically – would be wholly uncharacteristic of her. Precisely her *lack* of interest in money, and therefore in wills, was to cause Vera Stravinsky many difficulties in later life.

Stravinsky's daughter seemed to believe a fabrication to the effect that her father had whispered a message to his lawyer, William D. Montapert,[38] designating 'Mr W. Montapert to protect the interests of my children after my death. . . I want my manuscripts to go to my children, who are so dear to me. My wife will have plenty with the copyrights.' Milene did not claim to have seen Montapert's transcription of this message, but Denise, Theodore's wife, was supposedly shown 'one complete, crowded, typewritten page [actually a photocopy] . . .definitely signed by *Père*' and worded in the manner quoted above, as she recollected in a letter to Françoise Stravinsky [Exhibit K]. Marion further testified that this was 'a very good [signature]', which would not have been possible in the summer of 1969, when Stravinsky's handwriting was shaky. When solicited by the court, no such epistle materialized, of course. In this affair, both Milene and Denise displayed extraordinary ignorance of Stravinsky's state of mind, for by this time he deeply distrusted Montapert and would not have shared personal confidences with him. Anyone who knew Igor and Vera Stravinsky would recognize the story as utterly preposterous.

In the mythological tradition of favourite children, Lyudmila, Milene's older sister, was the Stravinsky child to die at a tragically early age. Though she has no direct part in the present chronicle, her influence pervades it. She appears to have had a pleasant nature,[39] good judgement, and talent as a painter, as well as courage, maturity and independence.[40]

Stravinsky seems not to have expected her death, even though his correspondence in the months before contains expressions of anxiety about her:[41]

> The condition of my married daughter, her health (lungs), distresses me. [Letter to Roland-Manuel, 24 November 1937]
>   You know that our poor Mika has been in the mountains for three weeks with her child. She has tuberculosis in both lungs and has been separated from her husband for a long while. [Letter to Strecker, 1 February 1938]
>   Tomorrow evening I go to [Sancellemoz] to bring Mika back home, because the mountains are not doing anything for her. She has a fever all the time, is losing weight, and has just had another bout with pleurisy. According to the doctors here, the brisk mountain air is not indicated for this painful malady, and they insist that as soon as possible she return to Paris, where we can give her more attention than she receives in that sanatorium full of sick people. Poor Mika – I am very sad. [Letter to Strecker, 20 March 1938]

Catherine's letters contain many blunt comparisons between Mika and Milene in which the former appears as a paragon, the latter as a problem-child: 'If it had been Mika, she would have spoken with [the young man's] father right then,

but of course not Milene. . . What a difficult child she is for us'
(30 March 1937). For manifold reasons, Milene's early years
do not appear to have been very happy ones, but they may help
to illuminate her later conduct. Catherine wrote to Igor on 10
March 1935:

> I feel that, *au fond*, Milene is melancholy. Apparently this is
> her nature, and when I go walking with her I cannot help
> remembering our walks together in Morges, when she was
> four, five, and six years old. She was then exactly the way I find
> her now. Then, just as now, I did not know what to say to the
> little one, or how to get her out of her solemn mood. . . But
> why should her nature be so burdened with guilt?[42]. . .I have
> seen this in her since childhood, even infancy.

Theodore, who was to become a professional artist, was also
unfavourably compared with Mika, whom her mother clearly
considered to be the more gifted child: 'Mika. . .was at the
home of Grandjean, who asked her to prepare two drawings
for him, which he selected from very modest notebook
sketches. . . Mme Normano finds that Mika is very talented
and has taste and imaginative ideas' (17 November 1933).
Theodore, in contrast, seemed to lack conviction. Catherine
wrote to Igor, 3 November 1937: 'How did you like Theodore's painting of the image of Saint Peter of Panteleimon?[43]
. . .Fedya's hesitation in his painting is, I think, a consequence
of his nature and character, and, probably because of this, he
finds it difficult to get on with his work. I think *he* feels this,
too.'

To return to the 1950s, Theodore saw his father during some
of his European concert tours, and, in aggregate, spent
considerably more time with him than did Soulima, who lived
5,000 miles closer to 'the parents'. But Theodore also remained
the more dependent son, and the composer was obliged to
support him all of his life, as well as to meet Kitty's medical and
other expenses.[44] When *père* and Vera were away, Milene

visited their housekeeper, Yevgenia Petrovna, and sorted the mail. While they were home, the two families occasionally dined together. Between 1952 and 1954, Marion accompanied Stravinsky on six short concert tours that Mrs Stravinsky thought would be too tiring for her. The relationship between 'the parents' and Milene was affectionate, but in actuality less close than that between the Stravinskys and such friends as Christopher Isherwood and Gerald Heard.

As for relations between Stravinsky and his sons, these were exacerbated in the mid-1960s by two events and only super-ficially mended thereafter. Both disturbances, which occurred almost simultaneously, revolved around grandchildren: John Stravinsky, born in France in November 1945, son of Fran-çoise Bon[45] and Soulima Stravinsky; and Catherine Mandel-stamm Stravinsky – Kitty – born in France in January 1937.

After the Soulima Stravinskys left California for Illinois, when John was four years old, the composer rarely saw his grandson. In the last seven years of Stravinsky's life, they had only four significant meetings: in July 1964 (Chicago); on 4 October 1964 (lunch at the Hotel Pierre, New York); on 26 July 1968 (Hollywood); and on 10 November 1969 (at the Essex House, New York).

The Chicago encounter, to borrow John's mother's word, was a 'disaster'. On 17 July 1964, the young man checked into the Ambassador East Hotel in order to see Stravinsky conduct in Ravinia the next night. John had also invited friends, and when he left the hotel after the concert, his and their expenses were transferred to his grandfather's bill. Stravinsky had been in Chicago since the 15th, and his mood could hardly have been worse, as was always the case when his wife was not with him. He was suffering from the heat, had been exhausted by the added strain of travelling back and forth from Chicago to Ravinia for rehearsals, and wanted desperately to rest before a recording session (*Orpheus*), scheduled for the Monday morning after the Saturday-night performance. He spent no time with John. The absence of Vera Stravinsky was truly unfortunate, for she would have entertained and looked after the young man, and the painful aftermath might have been avoided. Three months later, Stravinsky discussed his grandson with the boy's parents in a telephone conversation that left the atmosphere charged.

Stravinsky lacked any understanding of the problems that beset a nineteen-year-old at that time, to say nothing of the special problems inherent in being *his* grandson. During the telephone conversation, expressing concern about the boy's future, the composer criticized John's lack of persistence in his studies. Although his mother was disturbed by Stravinsky's indifference to the boy and hopelessly old-fashioned notions of discipline and education, she did not express this when they next met, on 12 May 1965, in the composer's suite at the Hôtel Plaza-Athénée, Paris. While Stravinsky was travelling to Switzerland, back to Paris, and then to Warsaw, she wrote him a long letter (7 June) from La Clidelle, elaborating her feelings, but also, and unhappily, using a tone that the composer never forgave.

This crucial document in Stravinsky's biography begins by referring to his 'cruel' telephone call of the previous autumn and goes on to explain that the past two years had been difficult ones for John and that he had been unable to concentrate on his work. Françoise then quotes from a letter that she and her husband had received from John in which he describes his visit to Chicago to see his grandfather as 'a depressing experience'. He had been unable even to reach his grandfather on the telephone, and he concludes: 'My grandfather can't be bothered to see his only grandson.'

Thus far the letter would not have provoked an irreparable upset, but then John's mother attacks Stravinsky personally, accusing him of telling people that his grandson only came to see him to obtain money, and saying that to learn of such comments has made her 'indignant'. (Stravinsky underlined this statement and wrote next to it, 'WHO?')[46] But the conclusion of the letter was even more injurious. Stravinsky's daughter-in-law declines his invitation to come to California and discuss the matter, ostensibly because she and Soulima lack the time, and she encloses a cheque to cover the expenses of John's 'disastrous visit to Ravinia'. The letter terminates with the request that Stravinsky speak as little as possible about John in New York and Paris, 'where you have already given him a terrible press.' The composer was stung to the quick by the insult of the cheque, and next to the words 'a terrible press' he wrote 'WITH WHOM?'.

Vera Stravinsky answered for her husband, gently reminding John's mother that 'Stravinsky is eighty-three, in poor health, and the letter gave him a dangerous emotional shock.' A note of apology arrived (24 June), but the incident effectively ended the relationship between Stravinsky and his daughter-in-law, whom he saw only twice more. Twelve years later, in 1977, Milene Marion was to recall that in the summer of 1969 her father said to her: 'Isn't Soulima's wife a very unsympathetic person?' Milene then testified that when she asked her father what made him say this, 'he answered me in Russian, "It is a kind of feeling."'[47]

The other bitter and long-lasting rupture in family relations resulted from a romance between Kitty and Pierre Théus, a married man with two sons. On 5 December 1963, the twenty-eight-year-old woman wrote to Stravinsky to thank him for a cheque, part of his money from the Sibelius Prize. Kitty also says in this letter that she has moved into 'a ravishing little apartment' – which is to say, moved out of the Theodore Stravinsky home – and that she feels a need to write to her grandfather directly about her 'terrible love affair, in the sense of its unbelievable intensity', which 'torments me' because its object, M. Théus, is married.

Stravinsky could hardly have been less sympathetic. He wrote a terse reply, but sent it (31 December) first to Theodore, along with a copy of Kitty's letter, asking him for more information. Theodore answered that Kitty lived only for Théus, a wholly inappropriate partner, and that, moreover, she was well aware that he had no intention of divorcing, although she pretended otherwise. Though she had 'violently' rejected the advice of Theodore and his wife, they thought that the young woman might listen to her grandfather, whose reply perfectly expressed their own views.

Stravinsky received his son's letter on 11 January 1964, in Philadelphia, where he was conducting concerts, and he sent the following message to Kitty the same day:

> Dear Kitty,
> Happy Birthday and thank you for the Christmas card. I did not reply to your letter of December 5 because I have been *totally* without time. But I must tell you what has been at the center of my heart since then: the urgent and absolute necessity for you to dominate your passions and not to allow yourself to be dominated by them. Your grandfather loves you very much.

The incomprehension, remoteness, and hurried, impersonal tone of this response from the grandfather she worshipped must have hurt the young woman deeply. Having lost both parents in infancy,[48] Kitty was reared first in a tuberculosis sanatorium in Leysin – partly under the care of Dr Vera Nossenko[49] – and second by her surrogate father and mother, a childless couple themselves. At age twenty, in London to study English and secretarial skills, she was boarded with an elderly couple, Dr and Mrs Ernst Roth (he was a director of Boosey & Hawkes; one of Richard Strauss's *Four Last Songs* is dedicated to him), who could hardly have provided very congenial companionship for a young girl. Worst of all, she was still plagued by ill-health; in 1964, after five years as a secretary at the Institut des Hautes Etudes in Geneva, she was obliged to give up her job for this reason.

In August 1964, Kitty wrote to Theodore and Denise accusing them of betraying her, of meddling, of breaking their pledge to remain silent, and of destroying her future with Théus. She sent copies of this declaration of independence to Igor and Vera Stravinsky, to the Soulima Stravinskys, and to the Marions, in each case with a note explaining that she was convinced that the essential motivation in her adoptive parents' behaviour was not moral strictness but embarrassment.

This time Stravinsky's response was utterly different. He came to Kitty's defence and ordered Theodore to leave her alone. The composer was so angered that he did not mention his next trip to Europe to Theodore.[50] After it, in California, Stravinsky increased his granddaughter's allowance and made her a beneficiary to his Swiss bank account on an equal basis with Theodore, though denying that the change had anything to do with the 'painful development in relations between Kitty and yourself. I have wanted to do this for Kitty for a long time, as I would have done for her mother, and Kitty is more than of age' (2 September 1964). Theodore was instructed to procure from Basel whatever papers were necessary to effect the change, and when Kitty signed these, Stravinsky sent them (25 October) to Soulima for his signature as well.

On 15 May 1965, Igor and Vera Stravinsky (with David Oppenheim of CBS and myself) drove from Paris to the Vevey Palace Hotel on Lake Geneva. Theodore and Denise were waiting for them in the hotel lobby, and the composer, tired after ten hours on the road, did not conceal his irritation at finding them there. The next day Kitty came for lunch – alone – and Vera Stravinsky invited her to visit them in California in the summer (which she did, 13–27 August). On 17 May, the Stravinskys left Vevey for Basel.[51]

The Stravinskys were in Paris again a year later, in June 1966,[52] when Kitty telephoned from Lausanne asking whether her friend Pierre Théus (alias Carl Flinker at that stage, since Théus was his married name), could come to see Vera Stravinsky on personal business. She agreed, and on 7 and 8 June talked at length to Théus, who confided to her that Kitty was pregnant and needed help. Although she privately concluded that marriage would not be a solution for the couple, Vera Stravinsky was sympathetic to Kitty's plight. Then, on 11 June, Kitty herself came to Paris, alone (as Stravinsky noted in his diary).

Four months later, on 10 October 1966, Henri Monnet[53] wrote to the composer saying that 'Soulima and Françoise' had brought his attention to 'the Kitty question' in the hope that, through business connections, he (Monnet) would be able to find Pierre Théus a decent job in Switzerland or France, or anywhere 'to get him out of Fribourg'. Taking advantage of a sojourn at Peter Ustinov's retreat in Diablerets to become acquainted with Théus, Monnet invited him there and later reported to Stravinsky: 'I do not see him as Romeo, but he is a serious and competent man.'

Monnet wrote again saying that Kitty had telephoned to tell him of the possibility of a quick and amicable divorce for Théus, and advising Stravinsky to send $6,000 to facilitate the divorce, 'not as a gift to Kitty but, rather, as a loan to Théus.' Stravinsky replied on 24 October 1966, declaring that he loved Kitty very much and promising to send the $6,000. (The cheque was sent on 8 November, and Monnet acknowledged its receipt in a note of the 11th.) On 13 December, Monnet informed Stravinsky that a job had been found for Théus in South Africa, 'which I will advise him to accept.'

Monnet's next letter, 8 January 1967, the key document in the relations between the Igor and the Theodore Stravinskys, discloses that 'Kitty, obliged – at least she believed so – to earn her living since the age of eighteen, preferred independent work in Geneva to performing more or less servile tasks for Theodore (or, rather, for his wife).'[54] The composer's indignation on reading this can hardly be imagined. In the same letter, Monnet explained that Théus's wife, learning now that Kitty had the financial backing of Igor Stravinsky, had decided to drive a hard bargain for the divorce; and that Théus, without a decent job, would not be able to support Kitty and also make monthly alimony payments. For this reason, Monnet's advice was to drop divorce proceedings for a time and, instead, use the $6,000 to supplement Kitty's monthly allowance of 500 Swiss francs. She had calculated that her living expenses would come to SF 1,250 a month, and Monnet suggested that an additional SF 750 a month be paid to her out of the $6,000; Stravinsky authorized this in his next communication. On 2 February, Kitty gave birth to a daughter[55] (this was announced to Igor and Vera Stravinsky in a cable signed

'Pierre'), and on the following day Monnet wrote to say that the godfather was Peter Ustinov. Two months later, Theodore wrote to his father that Théus's wife had finally heard about the baby and was 'making a scandal everywhere', and that, consequently, 'Kitty is going away for some months' (27 May 1967). On 18 June, Stravinsky received a cable for his eighty-fifth birthday from Neuilly-sur-Seine, signed 'Madeleine and Henri [Monnet], Kitty and Svetlana.'

Kitty, who soon became 'completely absorbed in the child', as Theodore wrote, spent the early part of the summer with the Soulima Stravinskys at La Clidelle. By this time her letters to California no longer refer to Svetlana's father, and only Stravinsky brought up the subject, tactlessly and icily, in what was to be his last message to his granddaughter: 'I am relieved because, like yourself, we do not see any future in a relation-ship with the father of your child'[56] (10 August 1967). The composer received Kitty and Svetlana in his rooms in the Ritz Hotel, Paris, on 9 and 10 November 1968, and again in Evian-les-Bains on 14 June 1970, but he never forgave his grand-daughter for bearing an illegitimate child. In the summer of 1978, Kitty married Michel Yelachich, a distant cousin, who had been in Igor and Vera Stravinsky's home in Hollywood on 17 August 1969, the most infamous date in this chronicle.

To return to the background of the litigation, on 27 September 1968 the Stravinskys and I flew from New York to Zürich to stay at the Dolder Grand Hotel. The composer's health had improved, and he no longer needed nurses. The weekly analyses of his blood were continued, of course, and a haematologist soon advised him that the treatment of polycy-themia, from which he was then thought to be suffering, was more advanced in the United States than in Europe, and that he should return to America in a month or two.

The first visitor to the Dolder was Theodore, who arrived on Vera Stravinsky's name day, 30 September, in time for her celebration dinner.[57] For the record, the Stravinskys' visitors at the hotel were: 1–3 October, Pierre Suvchinsky; 5–6 October,

Nicolas Nabokov and his future wife Dominique Cibiel; 6–11 October, Rufina Ampenoff; 11 October, Theodore and Denise; 17 October, Hayni Anda (wife of the pianist Geza Anda); 22 October, Henri Larese, director of the Museum of St Gall. (Larese appraised the works by Picasso that the Stravinskys had brought to Europe, as did Mme Christian Zervos, 30 October, in Paris.) Another visitor was the harpsichordist and founder of the English Bach Festival, Lina Lalandi. Telephone communications were kept up with many friends, including Paul Sacher in Basel, Lilli Palmer in La Loma, and Hermann Dubs in Zürich.

On 7 October, Stravinsky expressed the desire to visit his bank in Basel. Ampenoff telephoned for an appointment with Jean-Pierre Puenzieux, one of the directors of the Swiss Bank Corporation, and after lunch the Stravinskys, Ampenoff, and I drove to Basel. M. Puenzieux met the party at the door of the bank, but, to everyone's surprise, did not permit Mrs Stravinsky to accompany her husband into the inner sanctum. A minute or so later, the banker returned and escorted Mrs Stravinsky to her husband's side.

When the Stravinskys and Puenzieux emerged two hours later, Ampenoff and I learned what had happened: Stravinsky had been informed that his wife's name did not appear on his account and that, incredible as it sounds, his sole heir was Andre Marion.[58]

Hearing this, the composer burst into a rage, tore up the agreement, and instructed the banker to draw up a new one, replacing Marion's name with that of Vera Stravinsky.[59] Not yet suspicious of Montapert, however, and of the true nature of his relationship with Marion and Puenzieux, Stravinsky, following the banker's advice, did not cancel the lawyer's limited power of attorney, which the composer had granted on 12 February 1962. Thus Montapert, who should have been dismissed at this first detection of his blatant abuse of his professional duty, continued in Stravinsky's employment.

If Stravinsky had intended to leave his Swiss money in care of any *one* of his children, the choice would naturally have been his elder son, who had been his father's intermediary with the bank for many years; prior to December 1965, a majority of Stravinsky's letters to Theodore contain instructions *vis-à-vis* the Basel bank. Certainly Stravinsky would not knowingly have left the money to an in-law, especially one whom he only pretended to like for the sake of his daughter.[60]

Had Stravinsky forgotten that both he and his wife had given Marion full power of attorney? Clearly Stravinsky had not understood an agreement – concocted by Montapert and signed by Vera and Igor Stravinsky, 1 April 1962 – that would have given the Swiss money to Theodore, Soulima, Milene, and their spouses in equal amounts, but nothing to his wife. This paper had been written in such a way that Stravinsky refers to 'Vera and myself' at the beginning but fails to define Vera's position in the event that he should predecease her. Nor could Stravinsky have understood the new dispensation of 20 November 1964, which included Kitty as an equal party, for the text with respect to 'Vera and myself' is exactly the same as in the first document.

Marion evidently became the sole beneficiary in December 1965. At any rate, on 3 March 1966 Theodore wrote to the Swiss Bank Corporation asking why he had not received since 23 November 1965 any of the papers 'that you send regularly to my address by understanding with my father.' Stravinsky was not aware of this change to his son-in-law's advantage, nor did the bank inform the composer of it. But from this time, his Basel accountings were received by Marion through Montapert by way of an address in Mexico.

A second event that took place during the Stravinskys' stay at the Dolder was to become an issue in the litigation. On 9 October 1968, Ampenoff presented a letter to the composer for his signature authorizing Boosey & Hawkes to allot, from his royalties, an annuity of £3,000 to Pierre Suvchinsky, 'in consideration of [his] work in connection with my archives.'[61] Stravinsky thought this sum far too high, saw no reason why he should finance the project, and, in any case, had changed his mind about publishing his papers. He balked, until *chère Véra* convinced him that the agreement was simply a way of helping an old friend – one of many good deeds for which she would be severely punished. Ampenoff was discharged from Boosey & Hawkes in 1975.[62]

Exactly one year before this 'Dolder agreement', Stravinsky had been gravely ill with a circulatory ailment that Dr Edel, his physician, had misdiagnosed as gout. Thinking that her husband, bored because he was unable to work, might be diverted by Suvchinsky's companionship, Vera Stravinsky invited him to Hollywood and accordingly telephoned Boosey & Hawkes to ask them to advance money to him for the trip. Seeing this as an opportunity for Boosey & Hawkes to acquire the publication rights to Stravinsky's papers, Ampenoff promised Suvchinsky a contract naming him editor of the archives in exchange for securing Stravinsky's signature. Suvchinsky, who had a morbid fear of flying, had never been in an aeroplane, and had declined earlier invitations by the Stravinskys to visit them, promptly arrived in Hollywood on 27 October. He spent two days with the composer, whose condition suddenly worsened. On 2 November, Stravinsky entered Mt Sinai Hospital. Ampenoff's agreement for the archives arrived the next day, and, on a visit to the hospital, Suvchinsky persuaded Stravinsky to sign the paper, after which Suvchinsky promptly returned to Paris, on 9 November.

Here, for contrast, is Suvchinsky's version of the trip, in his report of a conversation with Vera Stravinsky at the Hôtel Ritz, Paris, on 19 March 1974 – except that to judge by the style and frequent lapses into the third person, the *de facto* author is Ampenoff. 'Suvchinsky' says that the purpose of the journey was 'to explain in detail his [*sic*, not 'my'] idea of the archives publication.' But at this date (1967) Stravinsky was not aware of *any* plan to publish the archives, and, since Suvchinsky had never seen them and had no concrete knowledge of their contents, he could not have entertained any 'detailed' ideas about editing them. The report does not mention that Stravinsky's acquiescence was obtained while he was ill and hospitalized. In fact, it was I who advised Ampenoff that Stravinsky's hospital signature would not hold up in court, since medical records would show that he was sedated throughout the period of Suvchinsky's California visit. As a result of my letter she prepared a new agreement, brought it to New York herself in October 1969 and obtained Stravinsky's signature.[63] Neither this nor the hospital contract mentions any payment to Stravinsky himself. But shortly after his death, during a press conference about the acquisition of the archives, a reporter from the *Manchester Guardian* addressed the following question to Ampenoff: 'Stravinsky was famous for driving hard bargains. Did Boosey & Hawkes have to pay a large sum for the publication rights to his papers?' 'Stravinsky was reasonable,' Ampenoff replied. The truth was that he had received nothing at all.[64]

One final incident at the Dolder must be mentioned because of the exaggerated significance attributed to it in the lawsuit. On 9 October 1968 Stravinsky telephoned from the hotel to Theodore, in Geneva, asking him to bring the manuscript of *The Rite of Spring* with him when he visited on the 11th. The score had been kept in a Geneva vault since 1962, when Boosey & Hawkes presented it to the composer on his eightieth birthday. During the litigation, lawyers on both sides endeavoured, unsuccessfully, to prove ownership. Theodore, in his deposition, replied hesitantly to questions concerning the manuscript:

> *Mr Garbus:* Did you ever tell your father that the *Sacre* was in your name, and not his?
> *Theodore:* There was trust between my father and me, and there was no need of precisions about that. . .
> *Mr Garbus:* Mr Stravinsky, you did not answer my question:. . .Did you ever write a letter to your father telling him that the manuscript was being held in a safe deposit that was under your name?
> *Theodore:* I do not remember having written such a letter.

The documents that would have established categorically that Stravinsky did not intend for Theodore to keep the score or the money from its sale were never produced. The first of these is a letter from Stravinsky to Theodore, 7 December 1962, giving him the

> address of Erwin Rosenthal's son, whose first name is Alby [*sic*]: 49A Belsize Park Gardens, London NW3. His father tells me that Alby is going to write to you, Theodore, and arrange a meeting with you, which might not be so easy, since you are in Leysin and the [*Rite*] manuscript (for which I want to obtain one hundred thousand dollars, to be deposited in your bank, and then in mine) is in Geneva.

The second document is a letter from father to son, dated June 1968, asking to have the *Rite* manuscript microfilmed and to send the *film* to Boosey & Hawkes for inclusion in the archives, which is tantamount to saying that Stravinsky did not consider the *original* to belong with his other manuscripts.

But to return to the incidents that took place at the Dolder Hotel in October 1968, Theodore duly brought the manuscript, and, on the afternoon of the 11th, in the presence of Theodore, Denise, Ampenoff, myself and his wife, the composer removed the brown wrapping paper from the red, imitation-Morocco volume. Leafing through the score, he was suddenly reminded of the premiere and insisted on rubbing the Parisian nose in the insults of 1913, and on expressing his bitterness in writing on the last page. Ampenoff tried to dissuade him from doing this, but he took the score and a pen to my room, which was across the corridor from his, and inscribed the final margin with an *envoi*. Theodore and Denise then drove Ampenoff to the airport, whence she took the late-afternoon flight to London. As soon as they had gone, Stravinsky made a gift of the manuscript to his wife.

Compare Theodore Stravinsky's testimony concerning these events. In the first place, he is uncertain whether he delivered the manuscript to his father on the 10th or the 11th,[65] though his father was not even *in* Zürich until late in the evening of the 10th, having spent the day in Lucerne and at Triebschen, where his signature can be seen in the visitors' book at the Wagner house. In the second place, Theodore recalled:

> When my father asked Miss Ampenoff and myself to help with writing these few words [at the end of the score], he had already worked at it himself. However, I cannot testify as to his doing it a few hours before or on the evening of October 11th. . . When we finished writing the text, he seemed. . .very much moved. . . If my memory does not betray me, what was written on the manuscript is exactly what I translated from the Russian text.

At this point, Theodore was interrupted by his own counsel:

> *Mr Higginson:* Was what was finally written in the manuscript by your father in Russian?
> *Theodore:* No. What my father wrote was in French.

What Stravinsky wrote *is* in Russian,[66] as Theodore should have known even though he was not present when his father wrote it: the manuscript was on display in Basel for three years before the date of this deposition. Asked who was present when the composer received his manuscript, Theodore answered: 'The suite was inhabited by my father, Vera, and Mr Craft. Miss Ampenoff came in and out, Mr Suvchinsky also. . .' (Suvchinsky was in Paris.)

Writing to Soulima's wife three years closer to the event, Theodore's wife describes the return of the *Sacre* score as follows:

> Vera asked us on *Père*'s request to give him back the *Sacre*. Theodore turned it over on 11 October 1968. . . *Père*, very embarrassed, said that maybe he would sell it to pay taxes (it was obvious that Vera had been working on him).

As for the later history of the manuscript, Mrs Marion's testimony is wrong in every particular:

> *Mr Garbus:* Do you know if the *Sacre* manuscript was in California at any time during 1969?

Mrs Marion: I learned that it was at Mr Craft's.
Mr Garbus: When did you learn that Mr Craft had the manuscript?
Mrs Marion: It was in the summer of 1969.
Mr Garbus: When did you learn that Theodore Stravinsky had given the *Sacre* manuscript to Igor Stravinsky in Switzerland in October 1968?
Mrs Marion: In the fall of 1969.

In other words, Mrs Marion knew that the manuscript was in Hollywood in the summer of 1969, yet did not find out until the fall of 1969 that it was no longer in Switzerland. But Mrs Marion's recollections of the summer of 1969 are remarkably selective. She recalls that once 'we were sitting at the dining room table, only Robert Craft and myself, and he was talking about travel.'

Mr Garbus: When was this conversation?
Mrs Marion: I don't recall. After 1969.

Mrs Marion never met me 'after 1969'.

Mr Garbus: Was it a practice that each day visitors came and had lunch with [Stravinsky] during that. . .period [12 July–15 September 1969]?
Mrs Marion: I don't know.
Mr Garbus: Did you ever have lunch with him during that time?
Mrs Marion: I don't remember.
Mr Garbus: Did you ever have dinner with him during. . .this period?
Mrs Marion: I don't remember.[67]

In fact, Mrs Marion did *not* dine with her father,[68] but if she remembered this, to have admitted it would have nullified her efforts to establish her closeness to her father at this period, the more so since he had frequent dinner guests.[69] Mrs Marion then suddenly came up with 'Dr Edel and the Liebersons' among the friends of her father who came during this period, though Edel's final visit to the house had been two years earlier, and only Mr, not Mrs, Lieberson called on Stravinsky (12 September). But Mrs Marion shows so little knowledge of her father's activities that she answered Garbus's question 'Do you know if he conducted any concerts in 1969?' with 'I don't recall,' and the follow-up question, 'Do you know when the last concert he conducted was?' with 'I don't know.' (He had retired as a conductor more than two years before.) Mrs Marion remembers 'one instance' when her father was hospitalized in the summer of 1969. 'Did you go to visit him?' Mr Garbus asked. 'No,' she answered, but the records show that Stravinsky was hospitalized twice, once at the UCLA Medical Center (12 July) and once at Cedars of Lebanon (16–19 July, for lung tomography), where she *did* visit him, an hour or so after he was admitted.

To conclude the story of the *Rite* manuscript, Mrs Stravinsky carried it back to California. It was not 'at Mr Craft's' but at the First Safe Deposit Company, 210 West 7th Street, Los Angeles, in a vault rented by, of all people, Mr Montapert. (Mrs Stravinsky's deposition confirms this and adds the explanation that Montapert had several large bank vaults in which he stored silver dollars.) On 30 April 1970, the score was removed by Mrs Stalvey, the Stravinsky's secretary, and Lawrence Morton, whose brother-in-law, Robert Cunningham,[70] then brought it to New York, where Lew Feldman, a well-known manuscript dealer, showed it to prospective buyers from the New York Public Library.

On 23 October 1968, the Stravinskys flew from Zürich to Paris. On 14 November they continued from there to New York, and on 18 November from New York to Los Angeles. At home, their first caller was a greatly agitated Mr Montapert, who warned them that the children were angry about the change in the Basel account. At this, the Stravinskys began to wonder why their lawyer displayed such concern for the children, who, so far as the Stravinskys knew, were not his clients. Moreover, the children could have found out about the change in Basel only from Montapert himself, who nevertheless seemed oblivious to this revelation of his complicity.

Marion, however, realized that the Stravinskys were beginning to understand the conspiracy, and from this point on his hostility was ill-concealed.

Simultaneously, Montapert began to court me, no doubt fearing that I might discover and begin to question his schemes, though I was never privy to the Stravinskys' financial affairs. He invited me to their next business meeting, at which convocation I discovered that the cohorts and their wives were receiving substantial salaries for questionable services in the Stravinskys' Arizona citrus groves and in such ghost corporations as 'Verigor International', an abandoned gold mine in the Mojave Desert on which the Stravinskys unwittingly spent $100,000 almost entirely in the form of salaries to the Marions and Montaperts. As the Los Angeles attorney David G. Licht stated in an affidavit:

> In October 1969, I was retained by Igor Stravinsky to prevent the theft or destruction of certain of his manuscripts which were then under the control of Andre Marion. . . Among other matters which Stravinsky asked me to investigate was the establishment and assets of a company called Verigor Incorporated [*sic*], which appeared to have substantial oil, gas, ore, and mineral leases. Igor Stravinsky knew nothing about the company or its assets, but believed that Montapert and Marion had used the company as a method of diverting Igor Stravinsky's funds for their own use.

Not until the end of the year 1969, when Mrs Stalvey sent some of Marion's cheque stubs to the Stravinskys in New York, did they discover the extent to which they had been fleeced.[71] The stubs record the $2,000 'management fees' that Marion paid himself every few weeks, the cheques made out to cash, and the cheques that he made out to himself for secretarial work that seems to have consisted of little more than writing cheques to himself, his wife, and the Montaperts. In 1968, for example, while the Stravinskys were in Zürich, Marion paid $15,000 and $5,000 of their money in one day (15 October) to himself, the first for the citrus groves and the second for Verigor, both soon to be acquired for himself and Montapert. It goes without saying that the Stravinskys had never seen the books and were never informed.[72]

In March 1969, Montapert urged the Stravinskys to give their Arizona citrus farms to the children, as compensation for the change in beneficiaries in Basel. Not recognizing any such obligation, Stravinsky objected. Since the fruit trees were worth at least $200,000,[73] and nearly as much again in tax deductions, and since Stravinsky's income from conducting and composing had come to an end, he saw no reason to divest himself of such an asset. Yet *chère Véra* finally persuaded him to do just that, and Montapert promptly prepared a deed of warranty – though not the one to which the Stravinskys had agreed. When they were at lunch on 3 April, Montapert appeared unexpectedly. He seemed to be in a great hurry, unable to spare even a moment for them to read what they were signing – which, he claimed, simply authorized the gift to which they had already consented. Covering the text with one hand and extending a pen with the other, he induced them to endorse a paper that did not, as they had intended, give their property in equal portions to Theodore, Soulima, and Milene, but instead transferred the entire property to the Marions only. Months later, when the other children inadvertently learned about this, they established new standards in gullibility by accepting Mrs Marion's story that 'V[era] being still hostile towards the children, M[ontapert] was able to obtain the gift of these plantations only for Andre Marion and Milene Marion (actually at the time this was done to neutralize [?] Andre)' (deposition, p. 111), and showed deep ignorance of the character of Igor Stravinsky, who would never knowingly have made such a gift to one child only.

On 20 April 1969, the Stravinskys flew to New York, intending to stay there a few days *en route* to Europe, where Stravinsky had promised to attend a festival of his music in Holland. Then, on 2 May, after tests made in New York Hospital, Stravinsky underwent an embolectomy on his left leg, a lengthy operation that, since a second embolism was discovered, had to be performed again twenty-four hours later. He was in intensive care for only two days, however, and the doctors were confident of his recovery. On 14 May, Mrs Stravinsky tried to reach Montapert, rumoured to be in Paris, to ask him to sell some of her and her husband's securities in order to pay the hospital, the doctors, the nurses, and the hotel and living expenses; but Montapert could not be traced. (On the 14th, too, John Stravinsky came to the hospital; unfortunately, Mrs Stravinsky was at the hotel at the time trying to telephone Montapert, and John's grandfather instructed the nurses not to admit him.) On the 17th, Soulima, on his way to France, visited his father briefly. On the 18th, when Mrs Stravinsky telephoned Mrs Marion to ask her to have her husband sell some securities, she was informed that Stravinsky's 'business manager'[74] of many years knew nothing about such matters.[75] On 20 May, Stravinsky had pneumonia. His wife wrote in her diary that night: 'Bob calls Milene and tells her to prepare for the worst.' But Stravinsky was back in his hotel in time for his birthday on 18 June. Meanwhile, Mrs Stravinsky had appealed to Boosey & Hawkes to advance part of a half-yearly bonus, which they did, but out of which, against the advice of a new lawyer and all of her friends, she kept only enough to pay the most urgent bills, sending the rest to Marion.

On 9 July, the Stravinskys and I flew to Los Angeles, where we were met at the airport not by the Marions but by a friend of the Stravinskys, Jack Quinn. In the weeks that followed, the composer's health improved, and he grew steadily stronger. What did deteriorate were relations with the Marions, Milene making a few token appearances and Andre appearing only once in the entire two-month period during which the Stravinskys remained in California.

When Montapert suddenly materialized, the Stravinskys were unable to obtain a financial statement from him. Instead, he came again and again to urge Mrs Stravinsky to remove the money from the Basel bank, arguing that if her husband were to die, the children would block the account. She did not take this bait – which Montapert could have construed as evidence that she intended to keep the money for herself – and day after day he would leave the Stravinsky house in a scarcely controlled temper, unable to fathom such exasperating indifference to money.[76] In truth, few people can have gone through life so utterly guiltless of greed as Vera Stravinsky.

On 18 July, Mrs Laure Lourié, whose husband was a long-time friend of the Stravinskys,[77] warned them that Montapert had tapped her telephone and was quite capable of doing the same to theirs. Soon thereafter, to prove that Montapert was wiretapping, Mrs Lourié arranged to telephone Vera Stravinsky while she was dining at Lawrence Morton's. On the following day, when Montapert repeated the contents of this call to Mrs Stravinsky, the composer and his wife finally decided to dismiss 'their' lawyer. They telephoned their New York lawyer, L. Arnold Weissberger, who met with Montapert in their home on 18 August and arranged the transfer of limited power of attorney.

By this time, the main event in this history had already occurred. On 16 August, by prearrangement, the Marions and the Soulima Stravinskys (accompanied by Françoise's children by her first marriage, who were touring the United States and Canada) had held a meeting in a motel in Cambria, a resort 250 miles north of Los Angeles, long frequented by the Marions. There the foursome made the shocking decision to sign a contract with Montapert whereby, employing his power-of-attorney, he would remove the money of Igor and Vera Stravinsky from Basel and divide it fifty per cent for himself and fifty per cent for the children. On the night of the 16th, after driving to the Marion home in Los Angeles, Milene, Andre, Soulima, and Françoise actually signed the paper. The next day, 17 August, Milene, Soulima and Françoise called on Stravinsky. He did not wish to see them and, to cut the visit short, went to bed, pretending to be ill. None of the three spoke to or even inquired about Mrs Stravinsky. (Whether or not by coincidence, Michel Yelachich – Kitty Stravinsky's future husband – a resident of Paris, paid a call in the afternoon and

was received by the fully-dressed composer in his downstairs
living room.) That 17 August 1969 marked the last occasion
that Soulima and his wife saw or had any communication with
Igor Stravinsky.

The above description of the hatching of the plot is taken
from the deposition of Milene Marion, who appears to have
had some qualms about her participation:

> *Mrs Marion:* I said I was against it. I was afraid to do this.
> *Mr Garbus:* Why were you afraid?
> *Mrs Marion:* I felt I shouldn't do it.
> *Mr Garbus:* But you did it?
> *Mrs Marion:* The Soulimas decided to do it, so I followed.
> *Mr Garbus:* You made a decision, after discussion with the
> Soulimas, to sign it?
> *Mrs Marion:* Yes.
> *Mr Garbus:* Were you told that any one of the people or
> signatories to that agreement can be charged with
> embezzlement?
> *Mrs Marion:* No.[78]

The continuation of the story comes from the testimony of
her husband:

> *Mr Garbus:* Was there no discussion at all concerning what
> would happen to the money after Mr Montapert removed it
> from the Swiss account?
> *Mr Marion:* I don't remember.
> *Mr Garbus:* Do you know if Mr Montapert ever removed the
> monies from. . .the Swiss account under the name of Mr and
> Mrs Stravinsky?
> *Mr Marion:* . . .Yes.
> *Mr Garbus:* Do you know what the term embezzlement
> means? . . . Did you ever discuss with your wife that either you
> or Mr Montapert were running the risk of being sued for
> embezzlement?
> *Mr Marion:* Yes, I did.
> *Mr Garbus:* Did you ever have any discussion with Mr
> Montapert whereby in exchange for any services that Mr
> Montapert would render he would get any fees out of the Swiss
> account?

Mr Marion: . . .Yes.

Mr Garbus: Do you recall signing a document with Mr Montapert relating to the Swiss account whereby he was to receive fifty per cent of the proceeds of that account?

Mr Marion: Yes.

Mr Garbus: When did you sign that document?

Mr Marion: In August 1969.[79]

Mr Garbus: Was Theodore ever told of that conversation?

Mr Marion: Yes, he was.

Mr Garbus: By whom?

Mr Marion: I do not remember.

Mr Garbus: Did you tell Theodore?

Mr Marion: I did not.

Mr Garbus: Did your wife tell Theodore, to your knowledge?

Mr Marion: To my knowledge, she did.

Mr Garbus: Did she do it in writing or orally?

Mr Marion: In writing.

Mr Garbus: When you had this conversation with Montapert, was he then Igor Stravinsky's lawyer?

Mr Marion: Yes. Yes, he was.

Mr Garbus: What happened after you had that conversation with Montapert? Did you agree on your behalf to give him the fifty per cent?

Mr Marion: Yes, we did.

Mr Garbus: And when you say 'we did', who is the 'we', you and Milene?

Mr Marion: That is right, yes.

Mr Garbus: And did Theodore and Soulima also agree?

Mr Marion: That is right.

Mr Garbus: And were any of these agreements written down?

Mr Marion: Yes, they were.

Mr Garbus: Was there a written agreement between Montapert and the children?

Mr Marion: That is correct, yes.

As Mrs Marion's testimony shows, Montapert actually did remove the money. And he did not return it until he was advised that, even though the Swiss account was illegal because of the purposes for which it was being used, he could be extradited and jailed.

Montapert did not go to Switzerland immediately, meeting

first with Weissberger, and, once more, on 20th August, with the Stravinskys and myself. On the 24th, Marion wrote to Theodore:

> Do you intend to remain in Geneva the next two or three weeks. . .because you will have an important visit from a personal representative of ours but not of Vera. . .[80]

Almost four years later, Theodore's wife, in a letter to Soulima's wife, recollected that

> We were in Basel with Montapert, and it was there that we met this man, Puenzieux. [We hesitated in] authorizing power of attorney to Montapert because his methods struck us as a bit odd, [but] we gave Montapert a general power of attorney for Basel. . . Then Montapert admitted to us that he gets along very well with Craft. 'I am playing both sides against the middle in order to help you.' Shady character, to say the very least. [22 March 1973]

Meanwhile, on Weissberger's advice, the composer and his wife decided to go to New York as soon as they could pack. Since one of their nurses from New York Hospital was holidaying in San Francisco, Mrs Stravinsky asked her to accompany them on the flight, but the presence of this woman does not account for the inaccuracies in Mrs Marion's testimony concerning the departure: 'The persons I recall seeing at the airport besides my father and myself were Vera, Robert Craft, and Rita, the nurse.' (Deposition, p. 204) 'Rita, the nurse' is a most peculiar apparition, since she was in Europe and had not even been in California in five months.[81] But then, Mrs Marion does not mention Jack Quinn and Edwin Allen, with whom she rode to the airport in the same car. When Mr Garbus asked Mrs Marion whether Mr Allen had been in the Stravinsky home at any time during the two-month period in the summer of 1969, she answered 'Yes':

> *Mr Garbus:* How many times was he there, if you recall?
> *Mrs Marion:* I don't recall.

Mr Allen *lived* in the Stravinsky home from 17 July to 14 September.

The Stravinskys were in New York only three days when Montapert telephoned to Weissberger requesting a meeting with him, Mrs Stravinsky, and myself. Weissberger consented, though thinking this irregular, since to his knowledge Montapert no longer had any connection with the Stravinskys' affairs. During the meeting (19 September), Montapert openly represented the children against the Stravinskys, negotiating in terms of 'what Andre will accept'. Marion demanded that no change be made in Stravinsky's will.[82]

After Weissberger left, Montapert requested another meeting, with the Stravinskys and myself alone. The purpose of this was to discuss the Swiss account, of whose existence Weissberger was unaware, Montapert having so terrorized the Stravinskys about the subject that they were conditioned never to mention it. ('I am interested in two payments made by the Hamburg Radio,' Stravinsky wrote to Theodore on 6 November 1965. 'Ask Basel if these have been received, and write your reply in Russian to Milene's address, taking care not to mention my last name.') At a third meeting, Montapert brought a letter, addressed to the Swiss Bank Corporation, transferring his power of attorney over the Stravinskys' Basel account to me. His rationale for this was that henceforth he would be too far away from the Stravinskys to work for them, whereas I lived with them and was also frequently in Europe. The Stravinskys signed the paper, which Montapert pocketed. He then left for Switzerland to obtain the signatures of the Theodore Stravinskys on the embezzlement agreement.

Here is Theodore's testimony, after he had confirmed that his conversation with Montapert 'was about the numbered account [formerly Secretarial II, 43656, now 47992][83] with the Swiss Bank Corporation. . . Mr Montapert had told me that everything was ready to empty this account':

> From the first time I met Montapert, I felt mistrust towards him. . . It was not difficult to notice. . .that he was not a

trustworthy character. . . He introduced himself as coming from Milene, Andre, and Soulima, saying that my brother and sister asked me to confide in him. He said 'I pretend to be good friends with Bob Craft, but I work with you, for your interests.' This already did not please us both [Theodore and his wife]. I let Vera understand that I mistrusted Montapert [two months later, in New York, in November 1969]. [Deposition][84]

On 28 September 1969, I flew to Berlin to conduct a concert (2 October). Montapert telephoned me there from Switzerland, insisting that I meet him in Basel to sign papers without which the New York letter giving me power of attorney would not be valid. Accordingly, at 5.30 a.m., Friday, 3 October, accompanied by the aforementioned 'Rita, the nurse', I flew to Basel, via Munich and Zürich, where I went to the Hotel Drei Könige and waited for Montapert's telephone call. This came in mid-afternoon, and, according to his instructions, I met him in the street outside the bank. Inside, we were ushered into a room where Puenzieux[85] had prepared papers for me to sign, transferring Montapert's power of attorney to me. Much later I discovered that one of them was 'a verification of account amounting to more than $400,000.' (Letter from Marion to Theodore, 27 November 1969)

As I was leaving the bank, Montapert told me that he had borrowed $10,000 of the Stravinskys' money, that this would show up in the accounting, and that he would return the sum before the end of the year.[86] Why, I wondered, was Marion drawing cheques on the Stravinskys' money without informing them, especially since he lived only a few blocks away?

The next day I flew to New York and advised the Stravinskys to repatriate their money immediately. We summoned Weissberger, revealed everything concerning the Swiss account to him, and I gave him my proxy. After consulting with his partner, Aaron Frosch, Weissberger retained a lawyer with dual, American-Swiss, citizenship,[87] and sent him to the Swiss Bank Corporation with instructions to purchase United States municipal bonds with all of the money in the account and to send these bearer bonds to New York. Stravinsky did not sign the final authorization for this until 26 November – Theodore was in New York and in the room at the time – and the bonds did not arrive until February 1970, at which time they were placed in two vaults in the 57th Street and Park Avenue branch of Bankers Trust Company.[88]

On 30 September 1969, Weissberger served Marion with legal notice that his power of attorney had been cancelled, while Stravinsky sent a letter to him demanding the return of his music manuscripts – which were in a vault in the Crocker Bank, Hollywood, in Marion's name – and of Marion's account books. Apparently waiting to consult Montapert, Marion disregarded these instructions until 12 October, when he met with Mr and Mrs Montapert, the three together drawing up a list of the manuscripts that were to be returned. On 28 October, Mrs Stravinsky wrote to Milene reporting on 'father's health' – though Milene had not inquired about it. Two days later, Mrs Stravinsky, open-hearted and trusting as always, wrote to Theodore and Denise: 'I would like so much to see you, to "unburden myself."' (Exhibit 4C)

On 3 November 1969, Stravinsky signed a new will, witnessed by Miriam Pollack (nurse), William T. Brown, and Samuel Dushkin. Shortly afterward, Marion refused to return the manuscripts,[89] which he intended to use as leverage in obtaining a general release from his father-in-law and a promise not to prosecute. At this, Stravinsky felt that he had no recourse but to institute legal proceedings. On 22 November (while Theodore was present), Stravinsky signed papers to sue Marion for the return of the manuscripts, an action reported in newspapers and on national television. Stravinsky also decided to make another will and to exclude Marion from it. This was signed on 9 December, the same day as Marion's release, which is a litany of the forms of his income from the Stravinskys:

AGREEMENT made this 9th day of December 1969 by and between Andre Marion of Los Angeles, California (hereinafter called 'Marion'), and Igor Stravinsky and Vera Stravinsky of New York City (hereinafter called 'Stravinskys').

For and in consideration of the delivery by Marion to Stravinskys of the attached list of manuscripts. . .Stravinskys do hereby release and forever discharge Marion individually and as agent and/or employee together with all persons connected with him in any transaction in which said Marion acted individually or as agent or employee for said Stravinskys for and from any and all claims, account damages, demands and causes of action of which the undersigned Stravinskys ever had, now have, or may hereafter acquire or become possessed of by reason of his employment by said Stravinskys as business and investment manager, holder of various powers of attorney, as bookkeeper, recipient and disburser of funds, as corporate officer and director of Verigor International, Inc., as manager of Stravinskys' farms [citrus groves] and in any and all other capacities or any connection therewith directly or indirectly including but not limited to any claim for salary or fees paid, expenses incurred, obligations undertaken or discharged in their behalf, or their successors in interest, amounts disbursed to himself or others, disbursements or transfers relating to investments, record keeping, acts done under powers of attorney, or otherwise or any claims to damages for anything whatever from 1947 to the present. . .

Stravinskys hereby expressly waive all benefits of Section 1542 of the Civil Code of the State of California which reads: '1542. A general release does not extend to claims which creditor does not know or expect to exist in his favor at the time of executing the release, which, if known by him, must have materially affected his settlement of the debtor.'[90]

Stravinskys hereby warrant. . .that this release is given, based on their knowledge of their business affairs, based on regular periodic review of all records including but not limited to canceled checks, records of disbursements and income, brokerage firm statements, deposit receipts, corporate minutes, bank and check books, and all other records regularly kept by Andre Marion. . . This is intended as a general release and not a mere covenant not to sue.

The manuscripts were returned three weeks later. When Martin Garbus asked Marion under oath whether he had consulted a lawyer on the issue of the manuscripts, he replied that he had consulted Montapert:

Mr Garbus: Did Montapert tell you in August or September of 1969 that he was not free to represent you because he represented Igor Stravinsky?
Mr Marion: I do not remember.
Mr Garbus: When did you learn for the first time that Montapert was no longer representing Igor Stravinsky?
Mr Marion: I don't remember.

On arrival at the Essex House on 18 November 1969, Theodore Stravinsky telephoned his wife in Geneva. She told him that his sister had tried to reach him by telephone before his departure in order to explain 'a matter of great importance'. Vera Stravinsky realized that the call her stepson had just missed was to tell him what he should have known six months before, namely that he had been given one-third of the Stravinskys' citrus groves. She informed him of the gift herself.

During this visit to New York (18–23 November), Theodore kept notes; he later denied this when questioned by Mr Garbus, but Denise had written on a packet of notes on Essex House stationery: 'Summary of the conversations between Vera and Craft during Theodore's stay in New York.' The jottings are of interest mainly because of the absence of any expression of concern for Igor Stravinsky. As Mr Garbus remarks in an affidavit: 'When Theodore Stravinsky visited [his father]. . .he reported back to his brother and sister – and made notes not of his father's health, but of the Respondents' shared financial concerns.' (No. 69) Mr Garbus also asked Theodore whether, during this visit, he had questioned his father 'about any of his business dealings with Andre Marion. . .' Theodore answered, 'No. My father was in too bad a state';[91] yet Higginson's affidavit of 27 November 1978 reads: 'It is apparent that Igor Stravinsky learned about Theodore's mistrust of Montapert from conversations held

when Theodore was at the Essex House in November 1969.'
(No. 46, p. 20) And at about the same time, Françoise wrote to
Milene that John had 'found *Père* better'. (Exhibit 36) Even
Denise was obliged to admit to Milene in a letter sent in the
summer of 1970: 'I believe. . .that it is true that *Père* is getting
better and better. He was definitely on the way lately here [in
Evian].' (Exhibit 30) Finally, the nurses' logbook for 19
November reads: 'I.S. fully aware and angry. Says he'd like to
"send some people [i.e., Marion and Montapert] to hell."
Talking now to son Theodore. Walked four times and played
the piano.' (Miriam Pollack, R.N.]

Theodore made a note on 21 or 22 November (he could not
remember which day): 'Vera declares that father alone has
access to the Basel account: "Even I, I cannot touch anything,"
[she said].' Though this demonstrates exactly how little Vera
Stravinsky understood both about the bank transaction and
about Theodore's motives, he evidently thought she was trying
to deceive him with the statement. But by this time all of the
children seem to have had an *idée fixe* about their stepmother's
character, as is portrayed in this letter from Theodore's wife to
Soulima's wife:

> M. Puenzieux, one of the bank officers. . .told us the story in a
> café in Basel. . . *Père* struggled with Vera for a half-hour.
> Clearly, he did not want to sign a paper to cut off his children
> from the account that was to be divided at the time of his
> death. But as M. Puenzieux told us, Vera spoke severely to
> father in Russian, and finally harassed him to the point of
> signing. Vera had got her way.[92]

This fantasy ignores the fact that the children were not named
as beneficiaries, but only Marion and Montapert. (Ampenoff's
presence is not mentioned.) In actuality, Vera Stravinsky was
wholly *un*interested in the Swiss money, except that she had
been disturbed for years about its illegality and wanted her
husband to repatriate it.

On 23 November, Theodore flew from New York to
Chicago for a meeting with his brother in Urbana, at which

time he also conferred with the Marions by telephone. A very different, less communicative Theodore returned to New York (25 November) and left the next day for Geneva. Stravinsky's health continued to improve: on 5 December he posed for photographs for *Time*, and on the 7th he met with Harold Spivacke of the Music Division of the Library of Congress for advice on the disposal of the manuscripts.

The year 1970 was less eventful than 1969. The composer was hospitalized (Lenox Hill) on 6 April with pneumonia, and discharged on the 29th. Dr Lax advised him to leave New York for the summer, recommending the Hôtel Royal in Evian-les-Bains. The Stravinskys flew to Geneva on 11 June, and drove from the airport to Evian. The composer enjoyed the summer there, when the weather was mild enough for him to eat out-of-doors and to take daily rides with his wife driving their automobile, which had been shipped over.

Theodore's Geneva doctor, Della Santa, visited the composer at Evian every few days, and the weekly blood tests were continued at a hospital in Thonon-les-Bains. (When Stravinsky returned to New York, his polycythemia, as it was then erroneously thought to be, disappeared, and no further treatment was prescribed during the remaining seven months of his life.) After Ampenoff had visited him in Evian, she wrote to me saying that she was happy to see him 'looking and acting so much better than in New York last October [1969].' Theodore and Denise came from Geneva, too, about every four days, but Stravinsky found their visits fatiguing, and a scouting system was organized with the aid of Marcel, a sympathetic room waiter, who warned the composer whenever the small car with the Swiss licence plates approached the parking lot. This was a signal for Stravinsky to take to his bed and feign sleep or illness.

Nevertheless, Vera Stravinsky felt that, in Evian, a relationship of trust had been established between her and Theodore and Denise, even if *père* had been less than eager to spend time with them. The citrus groves, bank accounts, and the suit against Marion to recover the manuscripts were never mentioned, and the only reference to a rift between the parents and the children was in Vera Stravinsky's repeated question: 'Why doesn't Soulima come to see his father, call, or send him a letter?' To this Theodore's answer was always the same: 'I don't know, and I myself no longer seem able to understand my brother.'

Shortly after the Stravinskys had reinstalled themselves at the Essex House on 26 August, Vera Stravinsky telephoned Geneva, reporting on her husband's improved health and asking for pharmaceutical products not obtainable in New York. A little later I wrote the Theodore Stravinskys a detailed letter, but this was never answered or acknowledged, nor was Mrs Stravinsky's letter of 13 October; and in the remaining months of his father's life, Theodore never communicated with him. The autumn was a busy time for Mrs Stravinsky. Because of noisy remodelling on their floor, the Essex House had become uninhabitable, and a decision was made to move. She personally inspected about twenty apartments until finding one she liked and, on 1 December, purchased.

On 3 December, a story appeared in *The New York Times* to the effect that Stravinsky's manuscripts and archives were being offered for sale for $3 million, and that the Soviet Union was among the bidders. Nothing in the report was true, though the sale of the manuscripts had indeed been entrusted by Weissberger to the aforementioned Lew Feldman, who had sold the T. S. Eliot collection to Houghton Library at Harvard, and the Evelyn Waugh collection to the University of Texas. In Feldman's opinion, this 'advertising' and the establishing of a price would stimulate interest in a sale, though in fact no tangible offer had been made from any quarter, and obviously not from the USSR.

Also on 3 December, I wrote to Theodore and Denise explaining the *New York Times* article, but apparently Ampenoff had already reached them by telephone and convinced them that a sale was a *fait accompli*. As a result, Theodore retained a lawyer, Jacques Borel, and sent an indignant letter to Mrs Stravinsky. She answered (15

December) with the help of Arnold Weissberger and myself.
The following is a draft of the letter that was sent:

I am. . .grieved by your breach of faith in consulting a solicitor
before speaking to me, and am therefore formulating my reply
with the help of my attorney, Mr Weissberger.

I recall your surprise last year when I mentioned that the
remainder of the manuscripts would have to be sold.[93] But
what did you suppose Marion intended to do with them, study
orchestration? . . . Certainly you know that your father
donated fifty-two of them to the Library of Congress, in return
for tax deductions on which our livelihood depended. . . and
you must find it perfectly logical for a man who has sold his
manuscripts at every opportunity all his life to continue to do
so in his old age, when his needs are greater than ever. . . But,
perhaps you are not aware of these things, having had so little
contact with your father for so many years that you could not
have any idea of his true thoughts and feelings. It is sad to have
to tell you that not once since his suit to recover his
manuscripts from Marion has your father mentioned the name
of any of his children. And sad to have to say that Marion's
behavior shocked but did not surprise him. . .

While your father's medical expenses are not likely to
diminish, his income from conducting and commissions has
ceased. All the same, I am determined to give him as much as I
can of the comfort he deserves – and would have if he had not
spent $100,000 on 'Verigor'. And, by the way, isn't it more
usual for fathers of eighty-eight years to be receiving aid from
children in their sixties, rather than the other way around?

. . .But I had better stop before I get into a pique. In fact, one
remark in your letter did annoy me: the compliment that you
approved of the way I took care of your father. What did you
expect me to do, treat him as his children have done? We now
hear that your brother excuses *his* neglect of his father with the
bogus claim that he felt restricted during his visits to him – of
which there have been ten in ten years. He was not restricted,
but even if he *had* been, surely this would not have stopped
him if he had any real desire to see his father .

Nor is the motive that you give for your own letter
consistent, convincing, or ingenuous. . . In short, I do not
believe in this sudden concern about your father's 'business

affairs' and in the sudden 'family feeling' about the fate of the manuscripts. This comes suspiciously late in the day.

Moreover, his affairs and well-being are inseparable from mine; and as I have received no help from his family in the past three years, I feel fully able to continue with my responsibilities alone. Forgive me if in fact I think that this anxiety about the sale of the manuscripts has less to do with your father's welfare than with your own financial future. After all, you did not even ask about his health.

Theodore answered the last criticism, saying he considered it inappropriate to mention health in a business letter – though he had not sent *any* letters in five months. On 10 February 1971, Mrs Stravinsky, again with Mr Weissberger's and my help, wrote to Theodore for the last time. Again, the following is a draft:

> First, a misunderstanding. I did not deny your request to see your father in New York Hospital in May 1969. The decision was that of his doctors, who wished to avoid any visit likely to upset him. So sensitive and suspicious a man as your father would have been quick to see a morbid significance in your presence, especially since your brother had just been at his bedside. I hardly need to add that if those visits had not been so rare, the danger of a sinister interpretation being placed on your sudden appearance would have been less likely.[94]
>
> Second, though no expert on the matter, I am inclined to agree that the state of health of a man of eighty-eight is probably 'irreversible'. But your father is an exception. His polycythemia has given up on him after a fifteen-year siege, and no sign of an occlusion has been detected in nine months. His only medical ordeals during the past six months were a bone-marrow aspiration, performed on 11 September, and, last week, the extraction of two teeth, which he bore extremely well.
>
> I am sure you will agree, on reflection, that the question of your father's awareness or nonawareness of the geography of Evian is trivial. After all, he did not know the town from the past and was transported there directly from a New York hotel room, seeing nothing familiar on the way. To me, it seems natural that the hospital ordeals of May 1969 and April 1970

would disorient him. Yet he has a clear sense of his actuality
here in New York. And I know that you will be pleased and
grateful to learn that, in order to spare your father any
disturbing new adjustment, we have reconstructed his
Hollywood studio in the new apartment.

But whether you agree or not, I shall continue to take care of
your father, just as I have done these last years (with no help
from his children). I have already cut our expenses, above all
the astronomical fees that analysis of our books shows we had
been paying our former lawyer, Mr Montapert, and our
former business manager, Mr Marion.

From this time forth, the only communications between
Stravinsky's children and their stepmother were a cable from
Theodore in August 1971 expressing shock at the death of his
cousin Ira Belline,[95] and an announcement of the marriage
(August 1978) of Kitty to Michel Yelachich.

To most people, Stravinsky's death (6 April 1971) was
probably not unexpected. He was nearly eighty-nine, and his
many illnesses since the major stroke that he suffered in Berlin
in 1956 had been publicized. Yet the death was a great shock to
Mrs Stravinsky for the very reason that her husband had been
ill so often and had always recovered, often against strong
odds. At the funeral service in New York she stood on one side
of the aisle, the children on the other, and no meeting took
place. During the service in Venice, Nicolas Nabokov stood
between her and the children, and, on the island of San
Michele, he escorted her, at the head of the procession, to the
grave – after an awkward fifteen-minute delay in the tiny dock
area, during which eyes were averted and no one spoke.

Soon after the will was probated, in New York in June 1971,
Mrs Stravinsky returned to Venice, to be near her husband's
grave. But the city oppressed her, and she went to Biarritz until
mid-August. While there, she learned from Weissberger that
the Marions and Soulima Stravinskys had retained a Chicago
lawyer, Milton Fisher, and Theodore a New York lawyer,

Francis Wendell, for the purpose of challenging Weissberger's accounting, her ownership of the *Rite* score, and the inventory of Stravinsky's possessions at the time of his death – three issues that were to constitute the basis of the lawsuit that the children brought against Vera Stravinsky three years later. They contended that everything Stravinsky had acquired before – and nearly everything after – his second marriage belonged not to his widow, but to them. A legal ruling on this was temporarily withheld.

In December 1973, Mrs Stravinsky sold the *Rite* manuscript for $220,000, a high price, considering that Ralph Hawkes, of Boosey & Hawkes, had failed to find a buyer for it at $12,500 in 1950, and that other *Rite* scores and sketches exist. Yet the children accused her of accepting a sum beneath the market value.[96] (On 19 February 1970, all of the hundred or so manuscripts together had been assessed by Sigmund Rothschild at $200,000.)

Virtually nothing happened in the case until 18 December 1974, when a deposition was taken from Weissberger. In March 1977, depositions were taken from Vera Stravinsky by Kunin, a man remarkably prone to forget his own questions, as well as wholly unable to communicate with Mrs Stravinsky. Had Mrs Stalvey been her secretary, he asked, and she answered 'Yes.' Had Mrs Stalvey been her personal secretary, Kunin went on, and she answered 'No,' by which she simply meant that her husband and others had also benefited from Mrs Stalvey's services; yet the record reads as if Mrs Stravinsky had contradicted herself.

My own depositions were equally unproductive, the first one being spent almost entirely in answering questions about works of art in the Stravinsky home. My attorney, Mr Garbus, is a trial lawyer, expert at keeping his clients from speaking at all.[97]

As the years went by, countless settlement proposals were drawn up, modified, and rejected. Lawyers' bills mounted, 'the children' entered their seventies, and by 1983 Arnold Weissberger, Vera Stravinsky, and Andre Marion had died. On 18

December 1975, Boosey & Hawkes informed Theodore that they would be obliged to suspend work on the publication of the archives, since 'rising production costs and slackening demand made a project of [this] dimension. . .impossible for anyone other than a richly endowed university.' Ampenoff had maintained that the Stravinsky–Ansermet correspondence was ready for publication, but Ansermet's Lausanne lawyer, J.-Claude Piguet, wrote that permission had never been given to publish his client's writings. Moreover, Mrs Stravinsky vetoed the project on the grounds that, as the first volume of a series, the letters present Ansermet as more important in Stravinsky's life than can be justly asserted, that Ansermet's letters greatly outnumber, and are much longer than, Stravinsky's, and that Stravinsky himself would not have wanted to be coupled with the conductor this way, especially in view of the hostility between them since 1937.

The litigation was brought to a deadlock on 14 November 1977, when Soulima filed a petition in a French court claiming all of his father's royalties from French-speaking countries. A law of 14 July 1819 (Article 2), was cited in support. This 'establishes a privilege and account of nationality and derogates from the application of foreign law.' In short, the provisions of a will filed in New York State in 1969 counted for little. An injunction, *pendente lite*, freezing the French earnings was entered, and French counsel advised that, however ridiculous the antiquated French law, American law was powerless against it.

Soulima's action provided Garbus with a new weapon, however. Soulima had violated Clause Ninth (K) of his father's will, specifying that anyone who attempted to block any assets that were to go to his wife on his death would be automatically disinherited. The *in terrorem* clause, Article Eleventh, disinheriting Soulima everywhere except in France, could now be invoked, and since the other children would obviously claim a share in Soulima's French royalties[98] – one million francs had accumulated at the time of the settlement, and the annual French income was approximately $200,000 – Garbus determined to prove that 'all of the Respondents would share the funds.' This was self-evident, but Garbus was dissuaded from following this course because (a) after six years of largely simulated litigation, the legal fees were already in the millions of dollars; (b) two or three of the Respondents would probably be dead before the case could be decided in the higher courts; and (c) Vera Stravinsky went to court herself in August 1979, prepared to testify, but returned home and instructed Garbus to settle, so horrified was she by the rudeness, vulgarity, and ignorance of lawyers scarcely able to identify the name Igor Stravinsky. She had learned the truth of Donne's 'If any man sue thee for thy coat, let him have thy cloak, too, for if thy adversary have it not, thine advocate will.'

In 1987, five years after Vera Stravinsky's death, a New York judge ruled that the French royalties, which amounted to about $2,000,000 by then, should be divided among all the heirs. Then, in 1990, in a final irony, the Stravinsky children claimed (and were given) copyright ownership of the five books published under my name and their father's, since he had copyrighted them in his name alone and the renewals would go to his children, even though he willed the rights to me.

Notes

1 Françoise, née Blondlat, wife of Soulima ('Svetik') Stravinsky. She had two children by her first husband, M. Bon, a daughter, Hélène Cinqualbre, and a son, Jacques Bon. Françoise Bon married Soulima (b. 1910) in 1946.

2 Denise, née (1914) Guerzoni, wife of Theodore ('Fedya', 'Fedik') Stravinsky (1907–89). Kitty, Catherine Mandelstamm Stravinsky Yelachich (b. 1937), is the orphaned child of the composer's elder daughter, Lyudmila ('Mika', 'Mikusha') and Yuri Mandelstamm; she lived with Theodore and Denise in Geneva and was adopted by them in 1952. The originals of Stravinsky's letters to Theodore are in the Paul Sacher Stiftung, Basel.

3 On 12 December 1979, *The New York Times* published a front-page story, repeated by television, radio and newspapers worldwide, under the headline 'Stravinsky Estate Fight Resolved'. The report must have perplexed all but a few readers, for it did not, could not, explain the complex background of the litigation, which is the aim of the following pages.

4 The actual purchase price was $13,607, but Stravinsky was obliged to take first and second mortgages amounting to nearly $11,000. From April 1941 to January 1948 he paid off the mortgages at $60 a month. On 16 December 1941, the Stravinskys were forced to move all of their money from a blocked Hollywood account because he had been a French national (although he had filed first papers for US citizenship in August 1940). In a letter to Vittorio Rieti, 10 March 1942, Stravinsky complains of having to 'fill in applications and reports for our blocked account, new applications now to unblock our account' (original in English).

5 B. 1914. She married Andre Marion in France in 1944.

6 In an affidavit of 27 November 1978, Martin Garbus, Vera Stravinsky's attorney since 1974, felt compelled to remind the court that 'litigation does not exist solely for the benefit of the lawyers.' Each of the lawyers at the depositions in this case received $100 an hour, in addition to $45 an hour for some utterly bogus 'preparatory study', and a fee for each note taken during the sessions – this in spite of a stenotypist ($600 a day, $2,500 to $3,000 for the transcript, and $500 for the Xeroxes). A two-day deposition – work that Judge Kaufman in a recent article in the *New York Law Journal* described as 'mundane', recommending that it be carried on by paralegal aides – cost $9,000. Vera Stravinsky was represented throughout by Mr Garbus, a member, when the case began, of the New York firm of Emil, Kobrin, Klein and Garbus, but who soon formed his own firm, Frankfurt, Garbus, Klein and Selz. Another attorney employed by Vera Stravinsky, Helene Kaplan, left Emil, Kobrin at the same time as Mr Garbus, but continued to work independently. In the first few years of the case, Stravinsky's children and their spouses were represented by Messrs Cramer, Kunin and Gleick of the New York firm of Kaye, Scholer, Fierman, Hays and Handler. Later the children replaced these lawyers by James J. Higginson and Francis Wendell of Appleton, Rice and Perrin (New York), by Milton Fisher and G.

Bobrinskoy (d. 1991) of Mayer, Brown and Platt (Chicago), and, in 1982, as appellants, by Proskauer, Rose, Goetz and Mendelssohn (New York). In addition, Theodore Stravinsky retained the Paris lawyer Jacques Borel and the Geneva lawyer Oliver Dunant.

7 In the present account, the excerpts from the letters of Stravinsky's children and their spouses, and Pierre Suvchinsky are paraphrased: the originals are in French, with a few passages in Russian. Theodore Stravinsky's deposition was taken in the Hôtel Mercure, Annemasse (France), 29 and 30 November 1976, by Martin Garbus, as counsel for Vera Stravinsky; James Higginson, assisted by Oliver Dunant, was counsel for the children. The depositions of Milene Marion and of the nonparty witness Andre Marion were taken at 1888 Century Park East, Los Angeles, 27 and 28 April 1977. The Marions were represented by Higginson, Bobrinskoy, and J. Swanson (a Los Angeles lawyer); Martin Garbus represented Vera Stravinsky. My deposition – like Marion's, that of a nonparty witness – was taken in New York, 31 March and 1 April 1977, by Higginson, Bobrinskoy and Fisher, and on 29 May 1978 by Bobrinskoy; Garbus represented me on all three occasions. Vera Stravinsky's deposition was taken in New York 6 and 7 March 1977, by Kunin; Garbus represented her. Some of the transcript of these two days could have been published in an anthology of unintentional humour, so complete was Kunin's and Mrs Stravinsky's inability to communicate. Here are some excerpts:

Kunin: I take it you had clothes in your suitcase. . .

Mrs Stravinsky: . . .usually no(t) closed. . .no lock.

Kunin: What kind of a suitcase was it?

Mrs Stravinsky: I have twenty suitcases. I don't remember what I had five years ago.

Kunin: Was it a suitcase?

Mrs Stravinsky: A suitcase is a suitcase. . .

Kunin: You (and your husband) were talking about your birthday, I gather?

Mrs Stravinsky: Name day.

Mr Garbus: Her name day.

Kunin: Which you say is a birthday.

Mr Garbus: No, it's better than a birthday, Mr Kunin. You only have a birthday, Mrs Stravinsky has a name day.

Kunin: 'Bapa' is you?

Mrs Stravinsky: Vera. . .in Russian. . .

Kunin: And the next (word) is?

Mrs Stravinsky: 'Hope', Nadiezhda. . .

Kunin: Who is that?

Mrs Stravinsky: The saint; we have saints in the Russian Church.

Kunin: That is all it means?

Mrs Stravinsky: You know. . .give me the blessings, Saint Vera, Saint Nadiezhda, and there is Charity.

Kunin: And that is all these things mean?

8 In addition, much tape-recorded testimony of witnesses, among them Lawrence Morton, Nicolas Nabokov, William T. Brown, and Marilyn Stalvey (the Stravinskys' secretary during their last three years in California), has been preserved in the office of Martin Garbus. This material will be made available to future biographers, but has not been used here.

9 *The Diary of Vaslav Nijinsky*, translated and edited by Romola Nijinsky (New York, 1936; Berkeley, California, 1968).

10 Their poor health persisted into later life. As Vera Sudeikina wrote from Paris to Stravinsky in Stockholm, in October 1935: 'It is difficult to reach anyone in your family on the telephone, since everyone is ill: Fedya is in the hospital practically all the time' – with Denise, who was there for several weeks – 'Katya is unable to come to the phone, Soulima has a furuncle, and Milene is in bed with a cold.' On 9 October 1937, Catherine wrote to Igor: 'My soul grieves for Theodore: he and Denise are always undergoing cures and with no end to it all.' In fact, three of the four children had had tuberculosis. Catherine's letter of 28 February 1937 states that Dr V. Nossenko (1882–1929, Catherine's cousin) 'did an X-ray of Theodore in Leysin, and it revealed that there were old scars on his lungs. . . Apparently his bronchitis came from an earlier tubercular condition.' Mika was severely ill (with pleurisy) for the first time in January–February 1919, and her TB was discovered in 1922. On 23 June 1935, Catherine wrote to Igor: '[The doctor] said yesterday that. . .the little problem [Milene] had was nevertheless the beginning of tuberculosis.' In the spring of 1939, a pneumothorax treatment was performed on her.

11 Born Vera de Bosset, 25 December 1888, in St Petersburg, daughter of Artur Efimovich de Bosset and Henriette

Malmgren. Vera lived at 3 Troizkaya Ulitsa, St Petersburg, until 1898, then moved with her parents to Kudinovo, near Moscow. For further details see *Igor and Vera Stravinsky: A Photograph Album, 1921–1971*, captions by Robert Craft (Thames & Hudson, London, 1981).

12 'I divide my time between Biarritz and Paris.' Interview in *ABC*, Madrid, 25 March 1925.

13 In this same affidavit, Mr Garbus says that 'the relationship between Vera, Igor, and Catherine, his first wife, exhibited a great deal of mutual understanding never shared by the respondents who now, nearly sixty years later, still hate their father for having left them. . . Their hatred has grown since the 1920s. And their father's success, their lack of involvement in his life, turned, in the last decades of [his] life, to a deeper hatred that "justified" the thefts, embezzlements, and blackmail.' (Page 34.)

14 Soulima wrote to Vittorio Rieti, 14 February 1936: 'My father asks you to send our railroad tickets, Paris–Rome. Mme Sudeikina will come with us, therefore three tickets with *wagon-lit* are required.' On 18 March 1936, Catherine wrote to Igor: 'Yesterday I received Vera's letter of the 14th from Barcelona, and today I received Soulima's of the 15th.'

15 Catherine's letters to her husband during this trip suggest that she was not aware that her sons were with him.

16 After the Church of Alexander Nevsky (rue Daru) recognized the primacy of the Metropolitan of Moscow, the Stravinsky family became members of the Cathedral of the Metropolitan Anastasy, on the rue Odessa. Both Lyudmila and Theodore were married there. In 1937 they became members of the diocese of the Church of the Sign of the Holy Mother.

17 Soulima wrote to his father from Paris, 17 June 1939: 'I kiss Vera. . .' This is when Stravinsky untruthfully told René Auberjonois, in a letter of 17 July, that he was living with his daughter Milene (see n. 18, p. 124).

18 Early in July, Stravinsky and Vera went to Aix-les-Bains to visit Koussevitzky, whom they saw again later in Bourges. At this time Stravinsky was trying to obtain a visa and *titre de voyage* for Mme Sudeikina to accompany him to America, but his efforts proved unsuccessful.

19 In his *A Family Album*, Theodore Stravinsky says that after the death in April 1917 of Bertha Essert, his and his father's nurse,

the Stravinsky home was a sad place, until 'Mina Svitalski [1892–1956] came to us as governess.' Actually, Mlle Svitalski had been employed by the Stravinskys since 29 March 1916. Catherine wrote to Igor on 18 March 1936: 'I would like to do something at the end of the month for the twentieth anniversary of [Mlle Svitalski's] service with our family – I believe the date is the 29th.' Theodore goes on to claim that Mlle Svitalski 'was to stay the rest of her life with one or the other of us.' In truth, she did not live with any member of the Stravinsky family for five of her seven years in America. Stravinsky wrote to Edouard Svitalski, 27 October 1953: 'When my daughter and her husband came to live in Los Angeles in 1947, I asked [your sister] if she would also like to transplant herself. . . her experience [here] proved to be negative. For one thing, her life, first in my daughter's house and then in my son's, was contraindicated by everyone involved. . . She continued to see as "the children" people who had grown up and were married. From 1949, therefore, she lived alone and earned her living as a dressmaker, quickly attracting a devoted clientele.' Stravinsky himself continued to support her, to the extent of paying for a room over a garage, rented for her from the film director Jean Renoir. Mrs Aldous Huxley employed her as a dressmaker.

20 Stravinsky had wanted to live in California since his first visit there, which began in San Francisco in the early morning of 13 February 1935. On his arrival from Chicago, he was met at the railroad station by a crowd of autograph seekers, and, according to San Francisco's Russian-language newspaper *New Dawn*, 'He signed 100 record jackets but refused to be taken to meet a crowd gathered at one of San Francisco's shopping centers.' (On the same day, Stravinsky and Samuel Dushkin gave a recital.)

21 *Opéra* (Paris), January 1946.

22 Stravinsky first met Huxley in London with Victoria and Angelica Ocampo in July 1934, Heard in Hollywood in 1950.

23 When I first met the Stravinskys, they were frequent guests of Elsie de Wolfe and Sir Charles Mendl, Atwater Kent, and other society figures, and the composer and his wife invited the likes of Baron de Meyer to their own parties.

24 A letter from his first wife, 20 January 1936, expresses the fear that Pierre Laval 'will be brought down by the radicals.'

25 Eugenio Montale interviewed Theodore in Venice, 9 September

1951: 'Theodore Stravinsky, a painter who lives in Geneva, has written a book, *Le Message d'Igor Stravinsky*. . .
Unfortunately, Theodore has not seen his father for the past twelve years and would rather talk to me about his painting. I ask him if he is an impressionist and gather from his start that I have committed a gaffe. Theodore has been profoundly touched by the *esprit de Genève*. . . When I try to lead him back to the subject, he puts great stress on Stravinsky's religiosity. . . I pocket the *Message* and take my leave. Aggressiveness has not been as productive as I had anticipated.' (*Prime alla Scala*, Milan, 1980).

26 Mrs Max Schwarz, née Nossenko (1872–1953), was a cousin of Stravinsky's first wife. The composer's payments were allowed only after the Bankers Trust Company, New York, applied to the US Treasury Department for a special licence on his behalf. On 6 August 1941, he answered an inquiry from the bank saying that Mrs Schwarz, a Swiss citizen and blood relative, 'is taking care of my granddaughter, a four-year-old child.' (On 29 October 1951, 'Lyulya' wrote to Stravinsky, who was in Switzerland on a concert tour, reminding him that they had not been together since Sancellemoz in the 1930s. She added that she wanted 'to see our dear friend from our youth, our "Gima", and not just the famous Stravinsky.')

27 The Marions were obliged to wait more than eight months for US visas. Since both of them had had pulmonary diseases, Stravinsky feared that on arrival in New York they might be detained at Ellis Island and returned to Europe. In January 1947, therefore, he asked for the help of his friend and patron Mrs Robert Woods Bliss, wife of the diplomat. On 31 January, she telegraphed her assurance that special arrangements would be made with the immigration officials to facilitate the Marions' entry into the United States. They were met at the dock on 7 April by the Dushkins, who entertained them and escorted them to the train for California.

28 'We bought a house in Hollywood, which Vera has charmingly decorated,' Stravinsky wrote to Mrs Bliss (January 1947). Before the arrival of the Marions, the Stravinskys used the address as a guest house, for, among others, Katherine Anne Porter and Alexei Haieff. In October 1980, the Marions sold this home, at 146 South La Peer Drive, and moved to 24312 Philiprimm Street, Woodland Hills, California.

29 Whereas the Marions had been French citizens, he by birth, she by naturalization (1934), Soulima did not acquire French citizenship until 30 December 1947. On 13 April 1948, Stravinsky sent the money for the Soulima Stravinskys' trip, Paris to New York, on 'French Airlines'.

30 At Red Rocks, Colorado, in July 1948.

31 Stravinsky not only bought their house, furniture, and automobiles for them but also paid the taxes and upkeep on their property and paid for their trips and their medical expenses.

32 In May 1978, the Soulima Stravinskys sold their Urbana property for $65,000 and moved to Sarasota, Florida.

33 16 August 1962 (Santa Fe); 8 December 1962 (Hollywood); 3 May 1964 (Ann Arbor); 12 May 1965 (Paris); 26 and 30 December 1965 (New York); 20–21 October 1966 (Hollywood); 29–30 December 1966 (Chicago); 25 January 1969 (Hollywood); 16 May 1969 (New York); 17 August 1969 (Hollywood).

34 8–10 December 1952 (Cleveland); 16 January 1954 (Urbana); 16 January 1955 (Chicago, between trains); August 1956 (Venice). According to Theodore's deposition, 'While [my father] was in Evian [in the summer of 1970], he continuously asked me where Soulima was, and why he was not there. I answered that for me it was easy to come and see him, as I lived in Geneva, while Soulima lived in Urbana.' But at that time Soulima was living in France, less than a day's drive away.

35 Suvchinsky had visited Stravinsky in Sancellemoz the month before (April 1939). Soulima visited his father there immediately after the composer's return from Italy in May, a meeting that left the composer disturbed.

36 Why Yuri Mandelstamm should *not* have been his daughter's guardian is unclear. A letter from Vera to Igor, 3 December 1939, refers to an invitation to Yuri's remarriage in that month.

37 That the Marions perfectly understood the method by which new cars, payments of taxes, and other gifts were obtained is evident from the following remark in a letter from Andre Marion to the New York director of Boosey & Hawkes: 'Explain the plan to Mrs Stravinsky first; you must leave it to her to convince Mr Stravinsky.' (18 December 1951)

38 Montapert, a graduate of the University of Southern California Law School, who also studied law in Switzerland, married

another attorney, the niece (d. 1970) of Harold English (d. 1953), a wealthy amateur painter and a friend of Igor Stravinsky for many years. In 1953 Andre Marion became friendly with Montapert, whom the Stravinskys retained as their attorney in February 1959 on Marion's recommendation.

39 On 19 May 1936, Catherine wrote to Igor: 'Mikusha writes to me that she keeps feeling happier and happier and is so satisfied with her life.'

40 Vera wrote to Igor, 18 January 1937: 'Mika, good sport, went on foot to the hospital to have her baby.' In May–June 1934, Stravinsky entrusted his twenty-six-year-old daughter – *not* one of her brothers – to go to Germany and bring back assets of his that the Nazis had blocked there. She stayed with the Willy Streckers in Mainz, and on 22 May had lung X-rays taken by a Wiesbaden doctor, L. Fursteran. Strecker wrote to Stravinsky on 11 June expressing pleasure in Mika's visit and regretting that she was not permitted to leave Germany with her father's money.

41 Stravinsky conducted a concert in Rome on 29 November, the day before Mika's death. (He was to have performed *Perséphone* there with, as narrator, Victoria Ocampo, who made the trip on the same train with him but who became ill at the last moment, forcing a change of programme.) Another concert, in Turin on 2 December, was cancelled. But letters from his wife and elder son between 25 and 29 November make one wonder why Stravinsky ever left Paris, both Mika and her mother being gravely ill. Catherine Stravinsky, whose own temperature was a constant 38.7 degrees Celsius, wrote to Igor in Rome on the 23rd: 'All I wanted to do this morning was cry. . .Mika's pulse is 120.' The next day's letter revealed that 'Mika is receiving morphine injections and her pulse is 126.' The letter of the 25th fills four pages with accounts of treatments and medications, and of the decision to ask Father Vassily to give the eucharist to her and Mika. Yet Catherine begins by commiserating with Stravinsky for a 'headache' about which he must have complained. On the 26th, she actually apologizes for writing so much: 'I am afraid you will scold me for wasting stamps.' (Some six months later, Vera wrote to Igor in America telling him that a past-due bill had arrived for him from Lanvin for 3,000 francs.) The next day Theodore wrote: 'Mika's pulse is 128 and there is no improvement in her heart

condition.' He wrote again on the 28th: 'There has been no improvement, the doctor is very worried about the heart, and this cannot go on indefinitely. It is disturbing,' he adds, '[to think that] you will be travelling even farther away [to Turin].' Catherine's last letter, of 29 November, is horrifying: 'One of Mika's lungs has collapsed, and she has coughed up part of her bronchiae; her pulse is 134. . . ; she is having a terrible, terrible time, and tomorrow, God willing, I want her to take the eucharist.' When she died, at 5 a.m. on the 30th, the family called Vera Sudeikina to fetch a priest. On reaching Turin, Stravinsky telephoned his wife from the railway station and heard the news.

42 Catherine does not explain her assumption that Milene was 'burdened with guilt', but it may have been that Milene's birth had reactivated her mother's tuberculosis.

43 Stravinsky did not answer the question.

44 Stravinsky was penalized for deducting these sums from his income tax, since the US Government did not allow deductions for relatives, even minors, living abroad. He wrote to Theodore, 21 July 1950: 'Until now I have deducted part of the costs of supporting Kitty on my annual tax return. . . But the law requires that the recipient live in the USA. Nothing has been said about this until the present, but now the tax inspectors have demanded an explanation. They do not accept my excuse that Kitty's state of health would not permit her to live in this country. . .and we must provide certification from a Swiss doctor testifying that Kitty has been his patient for ten years, that she is not completely cured, and that she could not risk the fatigue and changes of climate involved in moving here.' These certifications were obtained from Dr Vera Nossenko and Dr Maurice Gilbert, but still the deduction was not allowed.

45 Mme Bon's children by her first husband are a generation older than John.

46 Vera Stravinsky's diary, 2 June 1965, reads: 'Suvchinsky tells me about a long telephone conversation he had with the Soulimas concerning John.'

47 Deposition.

48 Her father, Yuri Mandelstamm, was deported from Occupied France and is presumed to have died in a Nazi concentration camp. A letter from Mandelstamm to Stravinsky, 10 August 1939, indicates that the composer had read his son-in-law's

poetry with appreciation. In the same letter, Mandelstamm thanks Stravinsky 'for your touching letter and for your offer to pay for my trip to visit Kitinka [Kitty]. . .which I gladly and gratefully accept.' Because of the international political situation, however, Mandelstamm did not take the trip, and he never saw his daughter again.

49 Dr Nossenko wrote to Stravinsky in October 1939, apparently unaware that he was in America, asking for money to have Kitty tutored in Russian.

50 More than once, Theodore wrote to his father in California while he was in Paris. Milene sent a letter to *père* and Vera in New York in June 1966: 'The fact that Theodore wrote to you here indicates that he does not know that you were in Europe.'

51 On the morning of 17 May, Theodore accompanied his father on a visit to 'Les Tilleuls', Clarens, where most of *The Rite of Spring* had been written.

52 Stravinsky's diary for 1 April 1966 reads: 'Sad news from Kitty, we sent Ampenoff a cable to send Kitty immediately $1,000.' The 'we' means that the decision was Vera Stravinsky's, as I witnessed. Miss Rufina Vsevolodovna Ampenoff was a member of the board of directors of Boosey & Hawkes in London.

53 B. 1896, lawyer. Monnet had known Stravinsky since 1928. In the letter Monnet mentions his home in Asolo and Stravinsky's visit there (22 September 1957) 'while the *savant* Mr Craft was at G. F. Malipiero's looking for a volume of Monteverdi.'

54 Vera wrote to Igor, 4 November 1939: 'Madubo is happy now in her independence. If she goes to live with Theodore, there will immediately be trouble with Denise, who likes to give orders and who will tell Madubo to 'do this' and 'do that'; in a week's time, she would be the cook, the housekeeper, the laundress.'

55 The child was baptized Svetlana Marie-Blanche. Blanche was the baptismal name of Théus's mother, Marie that of Denise, chosen as a gesture of conciliation.

56 'Unfortunately, Kitty is seeing Théus again,' Theodore's wife wrote to Soulima's wife, 22 March 1973.

57 Theodore, in his deposition, answered negatively to the question, 'Did you know when Mrs Stravinsky's name day was?'

58 Marion did not tell the Theodore and Soulima Stravinskys that he had supplanted them as sole beneficiary in 1965, a fact

revealed under questioning during the litigation. Garbus asked Theodore: 'Did you ever receive any letter from [Milene and Andre] concerning the disposition of the assets of your father after his death?' Theodore replied, 'No.' Marion himself testified that '. . .prior to their going to Switzerland in October 1968, Mr Stravinsky stated to Mr Montapert that Vera Stravinsky and Robert Craft always tried to interfere whenever he would have a chance of talking in private with me, and therefore he was asking Mr Montapert to see about taking the necessary steps to protect the money in the Swiss account for the children, because he knew that they [Vera S. and R.C.] were going to take him to Switzerland to try to change the status of the Swiss account in their favor.' But according to Marion's own agenda, in his handwriting, Montapert saw Stravinsky only twice in the month before the Stravinskys left California for New York on 8 September, both occasions being dinners at Chasen's with Mrs Stravinsky, Lillian Libman, and myself. Moreover, Stravinsky at this time had no intention of going to Switzerland at all; nor did he ever have business with Marion (or anyone else) that he would not have confided to his wife. It must be said that Marion's appointment books for the period agree with Mrs Stravinsky's and with mine, from Balanchine's visits in May to those of Alberto Moravia and Maya Plisetskaya, and, throughout the summer, Christopher Isherwood, Miranda Levy, Lawrence Morton and William T. Brown.

59 Ampenoff never testified in the case, but merely signed a written deposition of no value to either side (23 November 1977). If Garbus had subpoenaed her, he intended to ask: (1) Are you of the opinion that Mr Stravinsky was clear and mentally competent on the day of the bank visit?; (2) If he had not been, do you think he could have negotiated with Mr Puenzieux for two hours?; (3) Why is your presence at the bank never mentioned in any of the Stravinsky children's hearsay accounts of the visit?; and (4) Why did you take such pains to conceal the fact of your presence in your own correspondence with the children? Ampenoff's letters to the children were later to become exhibits in the suit.

60 When Milene had defended her husband in a letter to her father (6 September 1957) as 'simplement un grand nerveux',

Stravinsky had written in red pencil next to this phrase, '*un homme assez grossier*'.

61 François Lesure, in his book *Stravinsky: Etudes et Témoignages* (Paris, 1982), states that in a letter to Ampenoff, 9 October 1968, and in an earlier one to Suvchinsky, Stravinsky entrusted the editing of his archives to Suvchinsky. In truth, both letters were written by Ampenoff for Stravinsky's signature. Needless to say, Stravinsky did not typewrite letters to Ampenoff in English, nor did he use his California address in Zürich.

62 On the last day of her employment there, in December 1975, Ampenoff was observed destroying papers from her files. (Personal testimony of W. A. Fell, director of Boosey & Hawkes, Paris, December 1975.) Unfortunately, Ampenoff kept as personal property much of Stravinsky's correspondence to her while she was an employee of Boosey & Hawkes. For example, in June 1962 Jean-Pierre Laubeher of the *Gazette de Lausanne* wrote to Stravinsky in Hamburg proposing that Jean-Luc Godard make a film of *Histoire du soldat*. Stravinsky asked Ampenoff to reply for him and to negotiate a fee of 15,000 Swiss francs. When nothing came of the project, Stravinsky wrote (25 December 1962) asking her to investigate the matter. Her answer (2 January 1963) pretends that contractual difficulties had arisen with the publisher; but she also requests to be allowed to keep the original of Stravinsky's letter to her since it contains a striking use of a Russian word. On 8 January, Stravinsky asked for the return of his notes, since he had no copy, but he never received them. No doubt most or all of Stravinsky's Boosey & Hawkes correspondence directed to Ampenoff has been destroyed.

63 The reader must realize that at this time the Stravinskys did not know that Ampenoff had deep feelings of jealousy towards Vera Stravinsky and had sided totally with the children, as her letters to them were to reveal during the litigation.

64 In 1977, Vera Stravinsky bought back the publication rights from Boosey & Hawkes for $90,000.

65 This confusion is evident throughout Theodore's deposition. Thus, on page 21 he says that he saw the Stravinskys 'almost every day during the whole period of my father's stay in Evian [in the summer of 1970]. . . They came in July and left in the first days of September.' In fact they came on 12 June – how could Theodore forget his father's birthday party on the 18th?

— and returned to New York on 25 August. Moreover, as the nurses' records show, Theodore saw his father on only seventeen occasions during this seventy-three-day period. A little further on, Theodore says that 'the idea of making a book about [Stravinsky] did not come to me before his death.' But a letter, Ampenoff to Theodore, written before the death, unmistakably refers to the book.

66 See the reproduction of the final page of the *Sacre* manuscript in *Stravinsky in Pictures and Documents*, New York, 1978, p. 76.

67 The written testimony of the Stravinskys' secretary, Marilyn Stalvey, reads as follows: 'Milene did her duty, and often complained about that. Once Milene and I had a conversation in my office. She remarked on how time-consuming it was to come to the house. . .and that the visits made her late in getting dinner for Andre, which put him in a very bad humor.'

68 Mrs Marion seeks to give the impression (p. 195 in her testimony) that she was the only one who walked with her father in July–September 1969. The facts are that she was with him for a total of about twelve hours during the whole period, almost none of which time was spent in walking. He had nurses and a therapist at all times who helped him to walk.

69 The Stravinskys dined with, among others, William T. Brown on 11 July and 9 and 21 August; Lawrence Morton on 19 and 24 July, 22 and 25 August, 3 and 13 September; Christopher Isherwood and Don Bachardy on 19 and 26 August (Isherwood's birthday) and 10 September.

70 Stravinsky had known Cunningham and his wife for many years and, on 8 June 1958, composed a brief piece for them.

71 Here are some of Marion's stubs for a typical period in 1967:
10 January: $2,100 to Montapert for attorney's fees (unspecified)
10 January: $10,000 to Verigor
25 January: $2,000 to cash
30 January: $1,917.50 to Montapert
16 February: $1,200 to Montapert

72 Martin Garbus's final affidavit states: 'The total amount that the Marions took from Igor Stravinsky in the 1960s will never be known. . .Montapert had been hired by the Marions to do many things that Igor Stravinsky was not aware of, but was paying for. . . Montapert made unauthorized visits to the Swiss bank, and Igor Stravinsky never knew how much money

Marion and Montapert withdrew from the account.' Marion
testified that he had been in charge of the entire Stravinsky
bookkeeping from January 1955 until October 1969:

Mr Garbus: When you paid the monies to Montapert, either in
1966, 1967, or 1968, did you at that time ever tell Vera or Igor
Stravinsky that you were making those payments?

Mr Marion: No, I did not.

Mr Garbus: When you were making those payments [to
yourself] in 1966, 1967, or 1968, did you at that time ever tell
Vera or Igor Stravinsky that you were making those payments?

Mr Marion: No, I did not.

73 On 2 March 1978, Mrs Marion sold two parcels of this land,
one for $96,000 and the other for $40,000.

74 Theodore Stravinsky betrayed considerable surprise in his
deposition on learning that this was Andre Marion's official
title.

75 In October 1969, when the late Arnold Weissberger,
Stravinsky's New York attorney at the time, received Marion's
account books, he discovered that in a recent year in which the
income had been $300,000 – not including $80,000 deposited
in Switzerland – Marion and Montapert had sold $140,000 in
securities.

76 Marion actually testified that Mrs Stravinsky gave Montapert a
$10,000 check for his services in transferring the money from
the Basel account into another Swiss account under her own
name, and that her instructions to Montapert were written.
Needless to say, the evidence was never produced. Why
Montapert would have accepted $10,000 when, as will appear
later in the story, the Stravinsky children had offered him over
$200,000, Marion does not attempt to explain.

77 A letter from Stravinsky to his concert agent, Dr Enrique
Telemaco Susini, 18 February 1932, recommends the 'young
and very talented Russian painter Eugene Lourié, who most
recently achieved great success with his work in René Clair's
film *A Nous la liberté.*' Laure Lourié had been married to the
American painter John Ferren (1905–70). Lourié died in 1991.

78 The Marions' Chicago, New York, and Los Angeles lawyers
intervened at this point, but a letter from Milene to Theodore
had already been entered in evidence. She had written, in
October 1969, that 'M[ontapert] consulted lawyers in
Switzerland and New York [Samuel Byer, one of the Marions'

attorneys] and they all agreed that the position was indefensible and that he and Andre were running the risk of being sued for embezzlement.' At another place in her deposition (p. 118), Mrs Marion says: 'The money was replaced where it was originally, in the first bank. . .' Mrs Marion wrote to Theodore, 20 October 1969: 'M[ontapert] managed, through a great many acrobatics, to take out of the Basel account. . .the money that was there. . .by combining his own powers of attorney with those of Andre, since the powers of Andre had been taken away from him in October 1968, when [Vera] dragged *père* to Basel and made him put the account solely in the name of Vera and himself. . . Andre wanted me to tell you to be very careful when using the above information. . .the reason being that no one must be able to accuse Andre and M. to have plotted together (especially at the time when M. was the parents' attorney).'

79 In Petitioner's Exhibit 37, Mrs Marion states: 'At the time when M[ontapert] embarked upon this matter, Andre had agreed to remunerate him in kind if he were successful.'

80 *Mr Garbus:* Did you send Theodore a letter prior to the time that Montapert came over to visit him?
Mr Marion: I do not remember.
Mr Garbus: Do you know if your wife prepared such a letter?
Mr Marion: I do not know.
(Deposition, pp. 73–4)

81 Mrs Marion's deposition shows a slightly less hostile feeling toward me than toward her stepmother. For example, she testified that a part of one of her letters to Theodore 'refers to Bob loving and manipulating the first small sketches that my father wrote when he began to compose *Les Noces*. . . [Bob] found those little notes upon little pieces of paper made into little booklets were beautiful. . . It is the first idea that the composer writes down, and [Bob] found that absolutely beautiful, and he expressed it with love, I can say, and admiration.' (Deposition, p. 206)

82 In his own interest, Marion should have attempted to have the will changed, but he must have assumed that it was iron-clad, having been written by Montapert. According to the will, the only beneficiaries, after the death of Vera Stravinsky, are the children, grandchildren, and myself (in all the wills from April 1960). The new will, written by Weissberger, simply following Montapert's, is devoid of specifics (royalty income is not

mentioned!), and it encouraged the suit that the Stravinsky children eventually brought. In lieu of precise stipulations, this final will reduced Vera Stravinsky's lawyers to arguments about 'the intent of the testator'.

83 I do not know the date of the change in number; in a letter from Baden-Baden, 9 October 1957, Stravinsky questioned the identity of a new name, Roger Viollet, in his correspondence with the bank.

84 Milene wrote to Theodore, 9 October 1969: 'For the money in Switzerland, M[ontapert] incurred great risks and could be legally sued for misappropriation of funds. The others have taken away his proxy and given proxy to B[ob]. . . You should inform yourself there [in Geneva], if you could immediately block the funds in case of the death of Vera or of father. However, B[ob] is very well placed to take a plane the minute this happens and take the whole of the money. . .'

85 I still had no inkling of the alliance between the lawyer and the banker, even though I knew that Montapert regularly gave Puenzieux $10,000 'tips' from the Stravinsky account.

86 Montapert repaid the sum on 2 December 1969.

87 Elwood Rickless, the protégé of Samuel Pisar, of the Paris firm of Kaplan, Livingston, Goodwin, Berkowitz & Selvin. Rickless was also employed by the Stravinskys to obtain appraisals of their Picassos, which they placed in Geneva in August 1970. The paintings were later brought to New York by a daughter of the basso Andrew Foldi, whom the Stravinskys had known in Santa Fe.

88 The Basel money consisted largely of the annual bonuses from Boosey & Hawkes. Stravinsky's publishers paid him $25,000 in quarterly instalments, which he declared as income; if his music earned more than this, he received a bonus, which by the 1960s averaged $150,000 a year. Undoubtedly the sum that had accumulated in the Basel account was well in excess of $400,000, but Stravinsky did not keep any accounting of these monies. In 1969, after Weissberger succeeded Montapert as the Stravinskys' attorney, the Boosey & Hawkes bonuses were sent to New York and declared as income.

89 Marion testified that this refusal to return the manuscripts was prompted by Theodore and Soulima:
Mr Garbus: Did Theodore make the request to you in writing

or orally? Did Soulima and Theodore or Theodore and Soulima make that request to you?
Mr Marion: Yes, they did.
Mr Garbus: Both of them?
Mr Marion: Yes.

90 During Theodore's deposition, his counsel, Higginson, actually volunteered the information, now on the public record (p. 50): 'I felt the general release was at least partially related to the [Swiss] bank account question. . .'

91 At one point in the litigation, Stravinsky's children seemed to be on the verge of introducing the question of competence, but their lawyers must have advised them that this would only reveal how little they knew about their father and how infrequently they had seen him. Their lawyers surely realized, too, that Weissberger and Garbus would have obtained the testimony of qualified observers. In fact, Weissberger had a written statement from Dr John S. LaDue: 'I examined Mr Igor Stravinsky on 11 December 1969 and found him completely oriented with regard to time, place, recent events, past events and, in a word, in full possession of his mental faculties.' In 1973, Garbus obtained a tape-recording of Dr Henry Lax testifying that the composer's mind was fully alert in the last fifteen months of his life.

92 So much for the confidentiality of Swiss bankers! Puenzieux did not understand Russian, of course; 'Vera' was more likely arguing against any change.

93 Theodore had made a note of a conversation with his stepmother, 26 November 1969, according to which she answers his question 'Did you want to sell the manuscripts?' with 'If I could, I would frame them, but we need money. . . Poor, poor father, don't you feel sorry for him?'

94 Mr Garbus asked Mrs Marion to describe the substance of Petitioner's Exhibit 50, and she answered, 'The substance is Robert Craft being very worried because my father was very, very bad in the [Mt Sinai] hospital [November 1967]. . . Late in the evening Robert Craft and Vera came into our home after visiting *Père* in the hospital.'
Mr Garbus: When was this?
Mrs Marion: In October [*sic*] 1967.
Mr Garbus: When you say 'Bob was worried,' do you recall what he said?

Mrs Marion: He said 'It looks very bad. This is the end.' And then he said, pointing to Vera: 'She doesn't realize it.'
Mr Garbus: Do you know if Soulima came to visit [Stravinsky] when he was in the hospital at that time?
Mrs Marion: I don't know.
Mr Garbus: Do you know if Theodore came to visit him in the hospital at that time?
Mrs Marion: No.

95 Denise Stravinsky wrote to Françoise Stravinsky: 'We could be the ones to bring Ira's things to divide. . . As far as Ira's account in Geneva is concerned, it has not yet been released. . .' Ira had nothing but contempt for Stravinsky's children, except Lyudmila, and the only member of the Stravinsky family to whom she would have wanted any of her 'things' to go was Vera.

96 When Higginson asked Albi Rosenthal how he had determined a price for *The Rite,* the answer was: 'I took into consideration the sale I made to the Pierpont Morgan Library of the autograph manuscript of Schoenberg's. . .*Moses und Aron,* which was $100,000. I took into consideration the sale of Schubert's. . .*Winterreise,* which was at that time the highest price ever paid for a manuscript. . .[Also] there was a sale of a Brahms symphony [No. 2] for $75,000. . .' (10 July 1978)

97 Higginson's next affidavit asserts (para. 39) that Garbus had made a 'mockery' out of my deposition. Garbus responded that 'the deposition of Robert Craft was being conducted by a representative of a Chicago law firm not familiar with New York practice, and, it appeared, not familiar with trial practice.' (November 1978)

98 On 13 October 1978, Garbus had sworn and deposed for the New York Surrogate Court that 'in September 1978, Helene Kaplan, my co-counsel, and I met with James Higginson. . .I asked Mr Higginson. . .whether, irrespective of any settlement, the four respondents had agreed to share in the proceeds of the French proceeding. Mr Higginson said that all of the respondents would share equally. . .in the French proceedings.'

PART THREE

The Rite of Spring

GENESIS OF A MASTERPIECE

I

Certainly no one would claim that *The Rite of Spring* exerts any immediate influence on the new music of today, or at any rate on the new-fangled new music, except in the sense of an ancestor which, like a prize bull, has inseminated the whole modern movement. Composers, including Stravinsky himself, have tended to regard it as a dead end (bang rather than whimper) for at least the latter four decades of its existence, during which time the compilers of cinema sound tracks have diluted its originality and the 'titans of the podium' have added it as a trophy, or scalp, to the repertory. Its musical mysteries, since the publication of Allen Forte's landmark analysis of the harmonic language (see 'The Rite at Sixty-Five', below), are now profane knowledge and the desacralization is complete.

At the time of *The Rite*, Stravinsky's language was uncodified and his ambit unknown and unpredictable – all comparatively, since we might claim that in a reduced context the same holds true for his later years, for which reason the composer, who reflected as much of the century in which we live as an artist, continued to irritate musical historiographers by eluding the successive niches that they prepared for him. The composition process exposed in the *Rite* sketches is often akin to Debussy's in the development of harmonic and intervallic cells from small units to unity, but it is also and for the most part quite unlike anyone else's. In fact, the sketches could be called in evidence both for and against *facit e nihilo* explanations of the creation of the work, 'for' in those examples which seem to appear in bursts, fully formed, like asteroids, and 'against' in the pages that chronicle slower gestations. In many cases of the latter we are able to examine (and with little effort, thanks to a legibility compared to which Beethoven's manuscripts look like *tachiste* art) the nascent conception, and to trace it as it develops, transmutates, crossbreeds, or serves as springboard to other directions; and if we cannot actually invade the creating mind, we are able, as we watch its leaps of logic and the sharpening of images, to follow the mind's footsteps. To anyone interested in musical embryology, the facsimile pages of the *Rite* Sketchbook are a major document. The point of view of the following remarks is that of an observer in possession of an omnipotent advantage, the power of hindsight – historical superiority – which is also a handicap in that the investigations are deterministic: we are unable to imagine the completed *Rite of Spring* as other than inevitable.

II

Some of the musical resemblances between *The Rite* and *Firebird* are striking, especially the incidence, in both, of the Khorovod form; of the alternating metrical units of twos and threes; of the volcanic horn glissandos; of the use of the Wagner tubas at the entrance of the Kastchei in *Firebird* (No. 105) and of the Sage in *The Rite*; and of melodic content (cf. No. 182 in *The Rite*, and the beginning of the second tableau of *Firebird*). The young composer must have known Nicolas Roerich from at least the time that this painter, ethnographer and archaeologist designed Rimsky-Korsakov's tomb (1908). However that may be, Stravinsky remembered having confided his oneiric vision of the sacrificial dance to Roerich in March 1910, after finishing *Firebird*. This confidence was the most richly productive of Stravinsky's life, since Roerich's knowledge inspired the composer and helped to sustain his vision. Roerich was the catalyst of the subject, an incomparably more important function than that of set and costume designer by which he is remembered.

In midsummer 1911 Stravinsky and Roerich met at Talashkino, the home, near Smolensk, of the Princess Tenisheva, Diaghilev's patroness. Here they composed the scenario, Stravinsky, as he remembered it, contributing the idea of the division in two parts to represent day and night, Roerich suggesting the episodes based on primitive ceremonies; the anthropological titles, with the exception of a single word, are by Roerich. In early July Stravinsky had visited Diaghilev in Carlsbad, where the ballet was commissioned. The French title, *Le Sacre du printemps*, is found in the composer's hand in a receipt dated 19 November 1911 (whether Old Style or New Style is not indicated, though both are regularly given in the composer's Russian correspondence) for partial payment (4,791 francs).

Stravinsky spent the summer in Ustilug, his home in Volhynia, composing 'The Augurs of Spring', 'Spring Rounds', part of the 'Rival Tribes' and the Introduction. He kept Roerich informed of the progress of the composition, at least in its early stages:

Ustilug
13 (26)/IX, 1911

Dear friend,

. . .I have already begun to compose, and have sketched the Introduction for *dudki* [reed pipes] and the 'Divination With Twigs' in a state of passion and excitement. The music is coming out very fresh and new. The picture of the old woman in a squirrel fur sticks in my mind. She is constantly before my eyes as I compose the 'Divination With Twigs': I see her running in front of the group, stopping them sometimes, and interrupting the rhythmic flow. I am convinced that the action must be danced and not pantomimed, which is why I have connected – a smooth jointure with which I am very pleased – the 'Dance of the Maidens' and the 'Divination With Twigs'.

Stravinsky recalled that his first idea was the repeated chord of the 'Dance of the Maidens', that, as he remarked more than once, he could not explain or justify but his 'ear accepted with joy.' (T. S. Eliot: 'I am used to having my personal biography reconstructed from passages. . .which I invented out of nothing because they sounded well.') As a first idea, the chord's dominant-seventh superstructure and the major-seventh frame of the outer voices was indeed a discovery. The chord is reiterated for 280 beats in 'The Augurs of Spring' alone, interrupted in all that time by only a single bar of cadence, after which it forms a bridge to and becomes part of the substance of the next movement as well.

The remainder of Part One was composed in 'Les Tilleuls' ('The Lindens'), the *pension* in Clarens mentioned in the letter to Roerich, in the autumn of 1911 and January 1912. Part Two was begun at the same address on 1 March 1912, but, as the sketches show, at a later point in the score than the beginning as we know it. Part Two emerged in a more helter-skelter fashion than Part One: the 'Sacrificial Dance' was already in germination during the composition of the Introduction, and was completed before it. The final dances existed in outline by mid-April ('*Voilà* Le Sacre *bientôt fini*,' Stravinsky writes on 11 April to M. D. Calvocoressi, who was preparing the French translation of *The Nightingale*). But the full score was not completed until a year after that date.

By the end of January 1912 Diaghilev must have informed the composer that the ballet could not be produced that year, though in all probability Stravinsky would not have been able to finish the score in time even for an end-of-December performance. But the postponement did not slacken the composer's pace or result in a loss of momentum. Nor, in spite of 'everything that grows/holds in perfection but a little moment,' did it damage the time-scale. In fact, the interruption may have been necessary to the time-architecture of Part Two, in which *plateaux* of slower, less eventful music prepare for the high point of the final dance. Stravinsky always knew when he and his work required a change of scene, which partly explains his sudden, restless junketings about the globe. In 1912, owing to Diaghilev's ministrations, Stravinsky attended premieres and galas of *Firebird* and *Petrushka* all over Europe.

Between sojourns in Monte Carlo, Paris, and Venice, work went on apace,[1] more of it in Ustilug, where the composer returned for the summer, than anywhere else. By 17 November 1912, back in Clarens but now at the Hôtel du Châtelard, the end seemed to have been reached – the sketches contain three premature notifications of it. In Paris, earlier in the month, Stravinsky had unveiled the music in a piano reading to a group of friends, among them Florent Schmitt, Maurice Delage, and Ravel, the future dedicatees of the *Three Japanese Lyrics*. Schmitt, then music critic for *La France*, left his impressions of the occasion in the 12 November edition of his paper:

> . . .*je ne puis vous en parler que par oui* – [sic] *dire: à la même heure, en un lointain pavillon d'Auteuil, que désormais revêt à mes yeux la magnificence du plus somptueux des temples, M. Igor Strawinsky faisait entendre à ses amis* Les Sacres[2] du printemps *dont je vous dirai un jour la beauté inouïe et vraiment la révélation, quoique privée, de cette nouvelle preuve du génie du jeune compositeur russe avait à elle seule plus d'importance que toute la musique qui, pendant ce temps, pouvait se jouer dans l'univers entier, pour ce que l'œuvre contient de liberté, de nouveauté, de richesse et de vie.*[3]

We next hear of Stravinsky working at the orchestra score in a Lausanne-to-Berlin train; he attended the Berlin premiere of *Firebird* on November 21. While in Berlin he met Arnold Schoenberg, and the two composers heard each other's newest works, *Petrushka* at the Kroll Oper on 4 December, the *Lieder des Pierrot Lunaire* (as it was then called) at the Choralion-Saal on 8 December. By 18 December, back in Clarens, Stravinsky had composed the first two of the *Japanese Lyrics*, inspired, according to his own account, by *Pierrot Lunaire*,

though two of them were composed before he heard the
Schoenberg, and as we come upon these miniatures in the *Rite*
sketches they seem to devolve naturally from it. At the end of
December Stravinsky entrained for Budapest and the baptism
of *Firebird* there. He continued on 4 January to Vienna for a
stay of two weeks in the Bristol Hotel. A letter from Delage
reached him there with the news that Roerich's costumes were
ready and '*splendides*', but Stravinsky's own correspondence
at this time neglects to mention *The Rite* or, indeed, anything
other than the acrimonious treatment of *Petrushka* by the
orchestra of the Vienna Opera: '*J'arrive de Vienne où le
"fameux" orchestre de l'Opernhaus a saboté mon
Pétrouchka. On a déclaré qu'une aussi laide et sale musique
ne pouvait se jouer mieux. Vous ne vous figurez pas les ennuis
et les injures que l'orchestre m'a fait subir.*' (*La France*, 21
January 1913.)[4]

In an interview in the London *Daily Mail*, 13 February
1913, Stravinsky is quoted as saying: '*Petrushka* was performed in St Petersburg the same day as here and I see the
newspapers are now all comparing my work with the smashing of crockery. And what of Austria? The Viennese are
barbarians. Their orchestral musicians could not play my
Petrushka. They hardly know Debussy there, and they chased
Schoenberg away to Berlin. Now Schoenberg is one of the
greatest creative spirits of our era.'[5]

The triumph of *Petrushka* at Covent Garden was a pleasant
contrast to Vienna, as well as the most nearly unanimous
acclamation the composer had ever received. A number of
interviews with him appeared during this visit, some of them
surprisingly charitable about Wagner and *Tristan*, and including a variety of statements about *The Rite*: 'My new ballet,
The Crowning of Spring, has no plot,' he told the *Daily Mail*.
'It is a series of ceremonies in ancient Russia, the Russia of
pagan days.' The *London Budget* for 16 February quotes him
as saying that 'Monsieur Nijinsky has worked out the story,
and we are calling it *Le Sacre du printemps*, which might be
translated "*The Innocence of Spring*".'

III

All dances were originally sacred. . .any sacrifice
is the repetition of the act of Creation. . .all sacrifices
are performed at the same mythical instant of the
beginning; through the paradox of rite, profane
time and duration are suspended.

Mircea Eliade: *The Myth of the Eternal Return*

The title page of *The Rite* says nothing about a ballet, and the
word '*pictures*' in the subtitle is conspicuously non-choreo-
graphic. The sketches attest that Stravinsky's musical imagination was profoundly engaged by 'the story' and that he
composed with choreographic action as vividly and precisely
in mind as he did with the cinematographically synchronized
story-ballet *Petrushka*. Denotations for stage action are found
in them, and labels of assignment to one or another of the
thirteen descriptive headings are attached to most entries on
their first appearance. Later transplanting is rare. In the case
of the 'Ritual Action of the Ancestors', the sketches designate
the actual starting point of the action as the score does not, the
detailed stage picture having vanished from the composer's
mind, as he says, as soon as it had served its adjuvant purpose.

Stravinsky maintained that the French titles of the thirteen
subsections are largely inexact, and he preferred the Russian
title of Part One, 'Kiss of the Earth', to the unspecific French,
which means 'The Adoration of the Earth'. He also objected
to the first subtitle, '*Danses des adolescentes*', and to '*Jeu du
rapt*', even though the title in the sketches, as he translated it,
is 'Game of Chasing a Girl'. Stravinsky said that a ceremony
of young men locking arms in a circle around a young girl
survived in country weddings in Russia in his youth and that
he had once seen it, near Novgorod. At No. 37 the men
appear, each of them seizing one of the unbreached girls. The
next title, 'Spring Rounds', or '*Khorovody*', describes a form
of 'singing and dancing in a circle', '*khor*' meaning chorus,
and '*vod*', leading. Four small circles of dancers slowly gyrate
and at the end of the orchestral tutti coalesce into a single large

circle. During what Stravinsky called the Khorovod Chant (Nos. 48–9 and Nos. 56–7) the women stand apart from the men extending their arms in gestures of exorcism; at No. 57 they leave the stage and the men dance the orchestral coda (*Vivo*) alone. Choreographically speaking, the music of *The Rite* was conceived in terms of male–female dialogues.[6]

The English title for the next episode, 'The Ritual of the Two Rival Tribes', contains more information than the Russian original. The ritual is a tribal war-game, a contest of strength as determined in, for example, a tug of war.[7] Two sharply contrasted groups are identified, the first by heavy, comparatively slow figures in bass register (the first two bars at No. 57 and the brass chords before No. 59), the second by fast figures in treble register (the third bar of No. 57). The clash occurs (the fifth bar of No. 57) where the music of both is superimposed. The next event, the 'Procession of the Oldest and Wisest', is heralded by the entrance of the tubas at No. 64. A clearing is prepared at the centre of the stage, and the Sage's arrival there, with the women of the tribe in his train, coincides with the first beat of No. 70, the orchestral tutti signifying the gathering of all the people. Stravinsky translated the next Russian title (at No. 71) as 'The Kiss of the Earth (The Oldest and Wisest)'. The Sage, helped to his knees by two attendants, synchronizes his sacramental kiss with the chord of solo string harmonics. According to Stravinsky, the next title, '*vypljasyvanie*' ('dancing out'), was his unique contribution in this regard. He had imagined the dancers 'rolling like bundles of leaves in the wind' during the orchestral convulsions at the beginning of this piece, and 'stomping as if trying to put out a grass fire' during the latter part of it. The curtain cue is the second beat of the third bar before the end, as marked in the four-hand score, not, as in the sketches, at No. 78. Stravinsky had intended no more than a short pause between the two parts, but at the first performance Diaghilev called an intermission as a stratagem to defuse the audience.

As a title for Part Two, Stravinsky preferred 'The Exalted

Sacrifice' – rather than 'The Great', which suggests size. The curtain opens two bars before No. 91, at the word 'Night' in the four-hand score, during a Khorovod danced by six females. The French title, *Cercles mystérieux*, is ambiguous (problems of geometry?), while the English favoured in record notes, 'Mystic Circle of the Adolescents', is unhelpful. The dancers pace the perimeter of a circle, drawn on the ground and representing the cycle of nature, in which the *Elue*, the Chosen One, will die. The alto flute (at No. 93) and the clarinet duet thereafter accompany the movements of, respectively, one and two solo dancers. The Khorovod is interrupted at one bar before No. 101, then briefly resumed and abruptly concluded at one bar before No. 102 where, to quote the four-hand score, 'One of the maidens is chosen by lot to fulfil the sacrifice; from this point to the 'Sacrificial Dance' the Chosen One stands motionless.' During the ensuing orchestral crescendo the men appear at the sides of the stage, as though for an ambuscade, and during the eleven pounding beats the women retire.

Stravinsky conceived the next dance, 'The Naming and Honouring of the Chosen One', as a choreographic hocket, a ricochet of movement between stage left and stage right, the men on one side leaping during the rhythmic groups of threes, those on the other side leaping during the rhythmic groups of twos. 'The Evocation of the Ancestors', or 'Evocation of the Ancestral Spirits', is another male dance. At No. 125 the elders appear – five of them, like the ensemble of bassoons – and at No. 128 they squat before the sacred circle like a court of judges. Stravinsky recalled that he intended a type of ghost dance practised in archaic communities, performed by women while the men hovered at the sides marking time. At the beginning of the 'Sacrificial Dance', the Chosen One is alone with the elders. At No. 149, the men reappear and mark time to the ostinato figure; the quintuplet figure is associated with the Chosen One. Her dance resumes at No. 167 in the presence of the elders only. At No. 174 the men re-enter (with the bass and timpani figure). At No. 186 only the Chosen One moves. At No. 201, the elders stand like witnesses at an execution. They extend their hands towards the victim as she falls, in time with the flute scale.

IV

In great art chance and fancy are gone;
what is there is there of necessity.
Goethe

The sketches reveal that many of the composer's first notations were simple folk or folk-like melodies which he transformed by such devices as changing the note-order and grafting new rhythms and new characters of tempo. These transformations are sometimes so extensive that the original material seems to have been merely a point of departure, as is the case in the following source of the first subject of the 'Dance of the Earth':

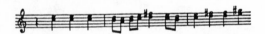

Here the paramount transforming tricks are the rhythmic overhauling and the changing of the tempo (if it *was* changed, but we tend to attribute a slow character to folk music sung by groups). The melodic substance of *The Rite* derives from actual Lithuanian, Russian and Ukrainian folk music and from inverted melodies following the same morphology: archaic, modal, simple in rhythm, restricted in range. In the case of this example, Stravinsky metamorphoses a simple melodic-harmonic choral passage into a fiercely fast dance of unprecedented rhythmic and harmonic modernity; translating the melody from the top to a middle voice; forming harmonic aggregates from it, superimposing the notes as if they were *appoggiature*; exploiting its whole-tone content (the harmonization in major thirds) in an ostinato-bass figure; and renovating the rhythm. That the rhythm was the most powerful transformer, Stravinsky realized when he wrote in the manuscript at this point: 'Music exists if there is rhythm, as life exists if there is a pulse.'

But while much has been written about Stravinsky's use of folk melody, his recapitulatory treatment of figuration is a neglected subject. In fact, no one seems to have mentioned the return of the following figure from the Introduction

just before the 'Sacrificial Dance'.

The pitch of an entry sometimes differs in early and final sketches, and the metronome marks are often at such variance with the score as to suggest a radically different conception of the musical character – a fact that must be emphasized because the composer may have a character in mind before he has a theme. Ideas do not always occur in the sequence of the completed composition, though this is not a phenomenon peculiar to Stravinsky. But the unfailing appearance, in the latter part of whatever movement he is composing, of a capsule sketch of the next movement, *is* extraordinary. Finally, while instrumental specifications are seldom drastically different between sketches and full score, some of the changes are substantial.

V

the mujic of the footure
on the barbarihams of the bashed?
Finnegans Wake

To sweep away the incrustations of the years and reconstruct the effect of *The Rite of Spring* in 1913 is impossible. (Cf.

Huizinga's classic discussion of the difficulties in trying to imagine the vividness of colour and sound in medieval life.) Moreover, the attempt to compare that remote musical age with our own would require a history of the art; and not only of the art, for if we can no longer imagine the original effect even of the sheer noise of *The Rite*, it is also because we have suffered so many louder and less musical concussions since then. We know that the music was in part intended, and certainly was received, as an act of iconoclasm. Stravinsky associated the creation of it with his hatred of the St Petersburg Conservatory and its academic tradition.

Let us try, nevertheless, to probe some of the reasons for the impact in 1913 of the dominant aspect of rhythmic novelty: no one was unmoved or uninfluenced by the rhythmic innovations. The first of these, the devices of ostinato employed in every dance, new not in kind but in extent, might not have provoked disruption in themselves. But consider the polyrhythms in the 'Procession of the Sage', and how they must have seemed to have had more in common with African and Asian than with other European music, though the vogue of the philobarbaro (Plutarch) was greater in all the arts in 1913, in the wake of Gauguin and Picasso's *Demoiselles d'Avignon*, than it is now. Imagine, too, how the mechanized, robotic beat, which at times holds the stage virtually by itself, must have seemed ultra-modern then; and contrast this with the recent past in which crude pulsation was melted away to the extent that the conductor had become a cue-giver, stopwatch watcher, coordinator, arbiter between chance effects and calculated and controlled ones. In these circumstances *The Rite* seemed remote.

With *The Rite*, music acquired a modern façade, a two-dimensional, icon-like objectivity (three clichés of the time) it had hitherto lacked. This made it seem newer than the music of Schoenberg, with its tumescent *Innigkeit* and paranoid self-consciousness – the period-piece adjectives – and *The Rite was* initially understood as a challenge to the emotion of Middle-European music. No wonder the new spirits in French music welcomed the young Russian as though he were a Second Front.

With *The Rite* Stravinsky became the patron saint of syncopation, irregular accent and metre; and the shifting of accents by varying the metres and dislocating the beat is the one ingredient of the early Stravinsky legacy that is still part of the canon of contemporary music, still in daily circulation. The most subtle aspect of this revolution in rhythm, however, lies in the virtual absence of dotted rhythms – they occur only during the 'Procession of the Sage' – the absence of the iambics of European classicism.

The Rite has become a classic itself, of course. It contains as much of the genius of its age, of the ethos of the twentieth century, as any one creation, and it has already demonstrated resilience to fashion: a '*Spring*' that survives its own investiture, let alone decade after decade of heavy season-to-season mortality, is already a *ver perpetuum*. Who, I wonder, would dare to predict anything about the world of music at the end of another comparable period of time – assuming there will *be* one, that the future will happen – and with results so perfectly on target as Florent Schmitt's crystal-gazing in *La France*, 30 December 1912:

> . . .*vers Noël 1960, leurs arrière-rejetons [du public] également en retard d'un demi-siècle, découvriront enfin. Debussy et Stravinsky devenus officiellement acclamables*. . .

Notes

1 Stravinsky to Andrey Rimsky-Korsakov, 27 March 1912: 'My God, what a joy it will be when finally I hear it. Come my dear, come. When you hear it you will understand everything. . . It seems to me that not two but twenty years have passed since I composed *Firebird*.'

2 Schmitt pluralizes the title in his every reference to the work even including his notice of the first performance (*La France*, 4 June 1913).

3 I can only tell you what I heard about it from others: at the

time, in a villa far away at Auteuil which, from now on, in my eyes takes on the magnificence of the most sumptuous of temples. Mr Igor Stravinsky was performing *The Rites of Spring* [*sic*] for his friends – a work whose incredible beauty I will one day tell you about; and, in truth, the revelation – although private – of this new proof of the young Russian composer's genius alone mattered more than all the music which could meanwhile have been played throughout the whole universe, because of the freedom, the originality, the richness and the life contained in this work.

4 I've just come from Vienna, where the brilliant Opernhaus orchestra has sabotaged my *Petrushka*. Such ugly, nasty music, it was declared, couldn't be played better. You cannot imagine the trouble and abuse the orchestra has made me suffer.

5 Several of the German reports of the premiere of *The Rite* bring in Schoenberg's name for homefront comparison; thus the *Allgemeine Musik-Zeitung*, 8 August 1913, states that '*Strawinski erfreut sich hier einer ähnlich exponierten Stellung wie in Deutschland Arnold Schönberg.*' The Stravinsky/Schönberg syndrome that imposed its nationalistic and deleteriously exclusive dialectical character on the musical thought of half a century seems to date from the aftermath of *The Rite*.

6 In Maurice Béjart's staging at the Paris Opera (May 1965), Part One was exclusively male. The sexes were united only in the 'Sacrificial Dance', but there so literally, with movements so unmistakably explicit, that they may have been serving notice of a tribal population explosion in *circa* three-quarters of a year. To match the *Elue* of Part Two, Béjart created an *Elu* in Part One, a reasonable notion given his male first half, though these twin *eloi* suppose an altogether different kind of drama (Adam and Eve). In general, the choreographer avoided 'choreography' in favour of various imitative actions which, except for a beautiful birdlike hopscotch by the *Elue* in the snake-charmer (next-to-last) dance, and a brilliant leap-frogging exit by the men at the end of Part One, were on the animated cartoon level.

7 Ritual combats between two opposing groups and the pursuit of girls are characteristic of New Year or 'renewal of the world' ceremonies in many primitive societies. (See Eliade, *op. cit.*)

THE PREMIERES

This 'anthology of music criticism'[1] purports to republish the most significant reviews of the first performance of *The Rite of Spring* in thirteen countries, although no critiques, but only dates, are given for Argentina, Hungary, Holland, and the United States (Philadelphia). The introduction, notes, and commentary are in French and English, though not all of the English is intelligible. Viz.: 'The articles are reprinted following the chronological order of performances, country by country, respecting the priority of publication of each one.'

What this means, the French text reveals, is that the reviews are grouped by country, and chronologically within each one. Thus the press coverage for Diaghilev's 1913 London ballet production is followed by that for Goossens's 1921 concert performance there, which is succeeded by two reviews of Koussevitzky's 1914 performance in Russia (albeit in the wrong order, Moscow in actuality having preceded St Petersburg).

Since the first-city-only format is suspended by the republication of reviews of a premiere in a second German city, Leipzig, and of a third American one, New York, the editor might have mentioned the amazing tally of performances in other German cities, beginning with Dresden (13 October 1924), Düsseldorf and Wiesbaden (1925), and, in the next five years, Duisburg, Munich, Karlsruhe, Bremen, Chemnitz, Frankfurt, Essen, and Cologne, the last three also having staged the ballet. The justification for including Leipzig is odd: the performance, conducted by Furtwängler, was 'all German', whereas the first performance in Germany, in

Berlin, was conducted by Ansermet. Yet Monteux conducted the Dutch premiere, and other non-nationals, most of those in other countries, including the Spanish, which took place in Barcelona[2] under Stravinsky, while the first 'all-Spanish' performance was in Madrid under Arbós.

The United States, Italy, and Switzerland present special cases. Reviews of Monteux's performance with the Boston Symphony in New York are included, but not those from the orchestra's home city, where the piece was first played. In Italy, two performances of Part One took place before the first complete one, in Florence in 1935 (three years after Oslo and nine after Prague, neither of which is mentioned). In a 1924 letter to Juan Mestres Calvet, Stravinsky had authorized performances of Part One only and had agreed to conduct it. Nevertheless, the first complete Swiss performance (Zürich, 1929, under Volkmar Andreae) is not listed, but only the incomplete one by Ansermet (Geneva, 1923), concerning which the press-book states that the conductor 'was compelled to make cuts in the second part.' No! Ansermet played Part One, as announced in the programme, and only the Introduction to Part Two, for which Stravinsky had composed a concert ending.

The reviews and interviews are published in facsimile, photographed from the newspaper and journals in which they appeared. This increases both the authenticity and difficulty for the reader, especially in the case of Karatygin's St Petersburg notice, some of which is faded and blurred beyond legibility. (Why were translations not provided? If the texts are not meant to be read, what is the purpose of the book?) A more serviceable publication would have been that of T. C. Bullard's dissertation (University of Rochester, 1971) containing the Paris reviews of the 1913 performances; this, at least, can be read by the Franglais public. Since Stravinsky was less interested in the local reviews of the event than in the Russian ones (not included in Bullard or the press-book), he preserved them, and their publication might eventually be expected. Among the worthwhile critiques of the Paris premiere not included in the present volume are those by G. Linor, Jean Chantevoine, Georges Pioch, and Reynaldo Hahn; but then, the most valuable of all the 1913 texts, Stravinsky's interview in *Gil Blas* the day after the premiere, is also absent.

The introduction claims that certain critics who had attended the Paris premiere wrote 'repentantly' after the revival there in December 1920, but the book offers no example of pre- and postwar reviews by the same person.

Notes

1 *Igor Stravinsky: Le Sacre du printemps, Press-book*, edited under the direction of François Lesure (Geneva, 1980).
2 22 March 1928. The press-book does not supply the full date. Stravinsky repeated the programme on the 28th.

12

THE RITE AT SIXTY-FIVE

The sixty-fifth birthday of *The Rite of Spring*, 29 May 1978, was marked by the publication of the most valuable study of this, or perhaps any other, representative twentieth-century masterpiece. Allen Forte has revealed the music's harmonic structure, identified its characteristic chordal formations, and mapped their relationships. His book[1] is of capital importance both because it provides the long-awaited analytical means with which Stravinsky's harmonic system can be understood, and because it throws new light on his mind, showing that what seemed to be most immediate was often most reflective. Everyone interested in contemporary music is indebted to the author.

Professor Forte's presentation is technical and directed to a small audience – which is even worse than addressing a large one, as Eliot wrote, adding that 'The only better thing is to address the one hypothetical Intelligent Man who does not exist and who is the audience of the Artist.' Yet the book's arguments and conclusions should be made available to a larger readership than that of Forte's fellow theorists. Commentators between the segregated worlds of the layman and the scholar-specialist, however, are more often barriers than bridges. My primary goal, therefore, is simply to attract readers to the book, and, secondarily, to raise questions about it.

The principal shortcoming of Professor Forte's study is a consequence of that notorious problem of scholarship, the over-narrowing of focus; but this does not affect his achievement, the codification of the harmony. Thus he postulates that the unity of *The Rite of Spring* is obtained 'not so much by. . .thematic relations of a traditional kind, as by the underlying harmonic units. . . A family of sets. . .serve [*sic*] to unify [the music] in the general harmonic sense.' But can the harmonic function be circumscribed to this extent, and can the harmonic relationships be proved stronger than the thematic ones, when neither melody nor harmony is always pre-eminent? As Stravinsky said a day or two before the first performance, '[at times] the dynamic power of the orchestra is more important than the melodic line itself.'

Forte also declares that he will not 'cover such features of the music as tonality, large-scale linear connections, register, or orchestration.' He might have added 'rhythm', which to most listeners is the most prominent feature of *The Rite of Spring*. Augmentation, it must be said, is a rhythmic as well as a harmonic event, and the two elements are inseparable. Professor Forte himself demonstrates the interlocking of rhythm and harmony in places where rhythmic variation introduces unfamiliar chords (cf. rehearsal number 99). Moreover, he shows that the essential sets, or chords, those defining the music's harmonic character, tend to coincide with the first, or accented, beat of the measure: '. . .metrically accented verticals are usually significant sets' (p. 48); '. . .metrically accented chords are now familiar sets. . .' (p. 56).

One must also question whether, without drastically limiting the perspectives, the subject of tonality can be avoided in a harmonic analysis of a piece that is 'characterized [by] the juxtaposition [of] diatonic and atonal components'; and whether the question of 'the function of. . .emphasized individual pitches' can be avoided, since, for example, 'the sustained E flat at 97 affects the harmonies'. Indeed. It changes them.

Professor Forte rightly warns the reader that Stravinsky's reminder, on one sketch, to 'transpose this to C sharp major' does not imply 'a traditional tonal orientation but [is] merely the only way [Stravinsky] would have to express the transpositional relation.' Yet the same cannot be said for other transpositions, such as that of the Khorovod tune in 'The Augurs of Spring'. The conventional, obsolete, terminology for the description of the beginning of the Introduction to Part Two, is 'a D sharp minor and a C sharp minor triad oscillating above a sustained D minor triad.' In Professor Forte's words and symbols, the music in this passage consists of 'two successive forms' of a set (6–Z48), a statement that contains more information ('Z' indicates a relationship), as well as a means, inaccessible to the older jargon, of associating the harmony with other constructions. Finally, Forte does not keep to his resolve not to 'cover' orchestration: his musical examples include the instrumentation, but superfluously, for the reader cannot follow the analysis without a full score; and sometimes erroneously (as when he assigns the uppermost line in Ex. 76b to a flute). And he does mention the influence of orchestration on harmonic structure in, for instance, a reference to 'the instrumentally determined component' of a set (6–248), though in what ways this component was determined is not explained – and cannot be, since the instrumentation is different in the earliest draft.

Professor Forte's approach to Stravinsky's creative processes is purely empirical, leaving no room for speculation about intuitive, precognitive, or preconscious processes. Forte focuses entirely on the logic of the harmonic construction. He views each 'compositional operation' as a reasoned step, and plainly does not believe in the single exception that he himself allows: 'The association of [two harmonies] may well be accidental, but nevertheless it is a demonstrable relation in the music.' (Page 56.) At one point he examines an *ad hoc* explanation', but quickly dismisses it as 'not convincing' (p. 110).

The book begins at the simplest level, with the chromatic scale and definitions of various ways in which its pitches are combined. The examples in music type, the diagrams, the charts and tables are admirably clear, far more so than the verbal explanations. In common with other academics, jeal-

Catherine and Igor Stravinsky,
Nice, October 1924.

Stravinsky and Vera Sudeikina,
Paris, June 1932.

Sergei Sudeikin (r.) and Zinovy Pechkov, 1917.

Stravinsky (seated, far right), with the author (standing, top right),
Andre Marion (standing, centre) and Eugene Lourié (seated, middle row).
Mrs Stravinsky is seated by her husband, with Milene Marion,
Stravinsky's daughter, centre. Mrs Lourié sits in front of
the author and Arminie Montapert far left in the second row.
Hollywood, July 1949.

The author, Vera Stravinsky
and Theodore Stravinsky,
Geneva, April 1952.

Munich, October 1951.
During a break in a rehearsal for *Oedipus Rex*.

Hollywood, 1952. Robert Craft
on the Stravinskys' front lawn.

Hollywood, July 1948.
With Stravinsky in front
of his rose trellis.

Hollywood, 1945.
Sunbathing at the foot of
the terrace behind the
Stravinsky home.

Hollywood, July 4, 1942. Stravinsky and gardener raising the flag in front of the composer's home.

Hollywood, 1948. The Stravinsky side porch.

Hollywood, 1952. With Stravinsky's daughter, Milene Marion, at her home.

New York, July 1948. Studying the score of the Symphony in C during a rehearsal break, with Alexis Haieff.

South Dakota, May 1950. Roadside stop between the Badlands National Park and Rapid City. Photo by Vera Stravinsky of her car and fellow passengers.

ous, perhaps, of an 'in-group' membership, accustomed to writing only for each other, and possibly inspired by such examples as Jacques Lacan, who has successfully promoted his work by boasting of its unreadability, Forte does not seem to recognize that the more difficult the material to be communicated, the more imperative the obligation to present it clearly. The reader must find correct forms of words for himself and even provide missing ones – 'a set type may be multiply represented. . .' ('a multiple'?); 'The accompaniment . . .is not the dyad B♭–D but the trichord A–B♭–D, which the melodic note D♭ creates the set. . .' ('which, with the melodic note D♭, creates. . .'?). Furthermore, subjects and verbs disagree ('all occur elsewhere. . .though none are. . .'), the misplacement of pronouns doubles the reading time, the diction is hideous ('the belongedness of a set'; 'the asterisk designates which of the larger sets is a superset of the main set in the set complex. . .'), and the word order is indirect, as well as, at times, hopelessly confusing: 'Several harmonies are found that do not relate to the basic structure of the work and that do not occur elsewhere in the music. The more familiar ones include. . .' One wonders how a harmony can be familiar if it is heard in only one place.

Finally, in an essay that depends on precision of language, the vocabulary is remarkably vague. Thus 'harmonies' is used interchangeably with 'sonorities', 'sonically' is suddenly introduced without explanation ('the hexachord. . .clearly refers sonically to the two variants'), and 'trilled' is intended to describe 'a figure of two slowly repeated eighth-notes [quavers] separately phrased on each beat.' And no sooner does the reader learn the new locutions than he is jolted by solecisms from the conventional ones: 'The interval between two notated pitches is measured by counting the number of half steps that separate them.' In the context, 'half steps' is an anachronism, none of the twelve equal divisions of the chromatic scale being the 'half' of any other.

The main part of the book, a 'Chronological Survey of the Work', starts unpromisingly:

[The opening melody]. . .is the source of the diatonic melodic
figures that characterize certain parts of the music. . .
(Clearly what Stravinsky wished to express with these
different diatonic formations is the folk mysticism of the
ballet. . .)

But do 'diatonic formations' express folk mysticism? And
how could anyone know what the composer wished to
express?

It seems plausible [Forte continues] that the Introduction to
Part I was written at a very early stage, perhaps even before
Stravinsky had the outlines of the entire work clearly in
mind. Two surface features render this convincing: nowhere
else in the piece is there an obvious use of familiar diatonic
formations together with primitive chromatic
progressions. . .

That Stravinsky did not have the outlines of the entire work in
mind until he began the last movement is obvious, but why is
it not plausible for the Introduction to have been written after
'The Augurs of Spring' and 'Spring Rounds', and in calculated
contrast to them, just as the diatonic second section 149 of
the 'Sacrificial Dance' was written after the chromatic first?
Stravinsky told one of his early biographers that this was the
order of composition, and the composer's correspondence of
the time does not contradict him. On 26 September 1911, he
wrote to Nicolas Roerich, co-author of the scenario: 'I have
sketched the beginning for *dudki* [reed pipes] and the "Augurs
of Spring".' The Soviet musicologist Vershinina accepts the
Russian word as referring to the first bassoon solo, but the
libretto that Stravinsky and Roerich had devised two months
before the date of the composer's letter states that *dudki* are
played in 'The Augurs of Spring' by 'the young men' (at 14).
Stravinsky rarely began a composition at the actual beginning,
because 'one has to know what one is introducing,' and 'to
find the entrance to a work is the most difficult task of all.' The
Second Tableau of *Petrushka* was written before the First, and

the Prelude to the next-to-last scene in *The Rake's Progress* before anything else in the opera. These and a hundred other examples do not rule out *The Rite* as an exception, but they do make Forte's conclusion somewhat less foregone.

What can be said with certainty concerning the extant notations for *The Rite of Spring* is that the first ones were not intended for the Introduction but for the 'Augurs', 'Spring Rounds', and possibly later movements. Yet even if the Introduction had been written first, this would not have been 'at a very early stage' but in the same three-week period as the 'Augurs', 2–26 September 1911; except for a few sketches possibly dating from 1910, the composition had not been started before Stravinsky's return to Russia on 2 September 1911 from a trip to Lugano and Berlin. A year earlier, three weeks before shelving *The Rite* to compose *Petrushka*, Stravinsky had written to Roerich: 'I have started work (sketches for *The Great Sacrifice*). Have you done anything for it?' (9 August 1910; the original of the letter is in the Tretyakov Museum, Moscow.) Roerich did make some drawings, at least two of which are known, but the composer's 1910 sketches, whatever they may have been, are apparently lost, and the one that follows seems to be the first to have survived:

The so-called 'Augurs of Spring' chord, which Stravinsky said he had discovered in July 1911, is a combination of the dominant sevenths in the treble part in the first two bars (pitch class[2] set 7–32 in Forte's nomenclature); the single dominant seventh chord (4–27) belongs to five principal harmonies in

The Rite. The complete first chord (*with* the bass) is an important harmony (both in this form – cf. 40 – and as the source of 6–Z43), especially in the 'Sacrificial Dance', while the chord at the beginning of the bottom line of the manuscript (a subset of 7–31) is no less crucial in the work as a whole. Also, the rhythmic and melodic designs of the sketch anticipate parts of the 'Ritual of Two Rival Tribes' and the 'Sacrificial Dance'. Thus this earliest known notation for *The Rite* contains the motto chord of the entire work, together with other basic harmonies.

Forte expresses a doubt whether 'one can assume that [the Sketchbook] contains a major portion of the sketches [and whether] the sketch pages (as is the case with many of the Beethoven sketchbooks) may not be correctly collated.' But one can be more definite on both questions simply by counting the passages in *The Rite* not covered in the Sketchbook, and by estimating the number of entries that must have been followed by others representing more developed stages. In addition, to judge by Stravinsky's drafts for instrumentation in other works, it seems safe to conclude that he made orchestral sketches for every section of *The Rite* before beginning the full score – of which he also finished a preliminary version for the whole of Part One. The Sketchbook contains only a few such drafts, none of them as complete as that for the 'Introduction to Part I'. As for chronology, the volume was neither compiled nor paginated by Stravinsky, and the presence of sketches for *Berceuses du chat* (1915) before those for the orchestration of passages from Part One is hardly reassuring. A letter to Stravinsky from the Paris representative of the publisher of the book, 3 February 1967, suggests that some of the pages might have been assembled in the wrong order after photographing.

In addition to the Sketchbook, Forte's texts are the four-hand reduction (1912–13), which, he wrongly says, was 'prepared for the ballet rehearsals' (a two-hand score was used, as a letter from Monteux to Stravinsky, 22 February 1913, confirms) and 'the 1921 orchestra score', even though, as he adds, 'one can assume that Stravinsky approved all changes [in subsequent editions].' Then why not consult these later editions, since this would have spared the reader much bewilderment? Instead, Forte treats seriously, as variant readings, the most obvious proofreaders' oversights, calling attention to 'an apparent [mistake] in clarinet 2', and devoting most of a paragraph to a note that is different in the piano and orchestra scores, despite the correction of both 'errors' in the 1947 edition. In one instance (Ex. B, p. 24), Forte actually discusses the harmony resulting from two typographical errors in the piano score that have been corrected in every edition of the orchestra score including the 1921, then acknowledges in a footnote that these 'differences' might be misprints.

With deliberate inconsistency, it seems, Forte refers to the 1943 version of the final movement on some matters but not on others. Affecting to be puzzled as to whether a note in the climactic chord is a misprint, and genuinely baffled in the previous bar as to 'what the main upper voice is intended to be,' he nevertheless refrains from peeking at the 1943 score, which answers both questions. Finally, when he concedes 'little doubt that' a certain trombone note should be changed – as it has been in all later editions – yet goes on to give the formula for the chord including the wrong note, the reader suspects that the Professor's interest in analysis exceeds his interest in music.

Pedantry is missing, however, where it is needed. Thus Forte writes that the final section of 'The Ritual of Abduction' 'presents no new music but repeats the introduction of the movement,' though in actuality the music from bar 3 of 'the final section' is transposed above the corresponding passage (at ⃞48⃞), in preparation for the following movement. And he writes that at two bars before ⃞22⃞, 'the violas should have an E natural and F sharp, not E flat and F sharp'; but the wrong note is in the second violins, not the violas. And, though he indicates near the beginning of the book (Ex. 13) that the second note of every trill is of equal importance with the first (and, in conventional language, a whole tone higher unless marked otherwise), he later defines the upper note of a trill as 'embellishing and hence secondary' (p. 60). In Example 30, he does not include the 'secondary notes' of any of the trilling parts, though some of these pitches are not in the sets.

The analysis of Part Two of *The Rite* is more intricate than that of Part One, in correspondence to the more 'sophistica- ted. . .compositional procedures', in which, for example, 'transposition and inversion' are more typical. The Introduc- tion to Part Two exhibits 'greater diversity' with respect to the chords used than any other movements except the 'Sacrificial Dance' and the 'Mystic Circle'. This Introduction is especially interesting 'with regard to the control of vertical succession. The verticals consist almost exclusively of sets that are significant throughout the work.' The section on the 'Sacrifi- cial Dance' is the most absorbing in the book, showing to what extent the mixture of new harmonies with familiar ones charges the music with its colossal energy. But, for a notion of the complexity of the structure here, the reader must turn to Forte's summary.

At one level, Professor Forte's achievement consists in having codified the harmonies of *The Rite* and traced the connections among them (by means of, for example, simi- larity relationships such as the linking of sets through subsets). At another level, his analysis exposes a few minor faults in the composition. For example, he shows that 'Two sets, 4–14 and 5–27, neither relate well at all to the other sets in the passage'; that, at one place, 'two thematic components do not fit well into the over-all harmonic sense'; and that an unimportant chord on the strongest beat (at $\boxed{92}$) raises a doubt about the metrical structure. Readers who turn to the music will no doubt find themselves in agreement, as well as pleased to have concrete explanations for felt but heretofore-not-understood weaknesses. This is the most valuable kind of music criticism.

More generally, Forte has provided the basis for a re- evaluation of the schematic side of Stravinsky's mind, which can now be seen to have resembled Schoenberg's more closely than has been supposed. Forte writes, in connection with a point that supports his thesis of Stravinsky's attraction, natural or logical, to certain basic vertical constructions: '[This] is significant insofar as it substantiates the extent to which Stravinsky worked out his sonorities within a specific scheme.'

The harmonic changes in the 1943 'Sacrificial Dance' strengthen this interpretation – as well as reveal the continuity of Stravinsky's musical thought at a time remote from *The Rite* in artistic philosophy. Forte reproduces a chord sequence from the Sketchbook, first conceived for the 'Sacrificial Dance' (at 161), and observes that 'Stravinsky's predilection for this progression' – he re-employed it in the Introduction to Part Two – 'very likely is based on the fact that it contains many, if not all, of the basic harmonies of the work.' The two early sketches show the evolution of the harmonic content, with only three of the seven chords of the ultimate version appearing in the first one. Stravinsky did indeed gravitate, instinctively as well as consciously, toward the music's fundamental combinations.

A synoptic study of *The Rite of Spring*, one that would consider all of its elements, remains to be undertaken. But Forte's book is the first that substantially helps to accomplish this goal. And, finally, his dissection does not reduce, but, on the contrary, greatly increases the mystery of the masterpiece.

Notes

1 *The Harmonic Organization of 'The Rite of Spring'*, by Allen Forte, Yale University Press, New Haven, 1978.
2 A 'pitch class' refers to, for instance, all Cs (in any register), whereas 'pitch' refers to, for instance, a specific C.

13

THE RITE AT SEVENTY-FIVE

The music. . .struck me as possessing a quality
of modernity which I missed from the ballet
that accompanied it. . . The spirit of the music
was modern, and the spirit of the ballet was
primitive ceremony. . . In everything in *Le Sacre
du printemps*, except the music, one missed
the sense of the present.

T. S. *Eliot* (1921)

The most written-about dance event of 1987, the Joffrey
Ballet's restoration of *The Rite of Spring*, requires still more
comment. Important historical aspects of the work have been
lost in the critical aftermath, which, moreover, has shown no
comprehension of what is wrong with the choreographic
syntax in the revival. If the great ballet of 1913 is to have a
future, its present form must undergo major repairs.

The New York Times, 25 October 1987, reported that
Millicent Hodson, the dance historian and choreographer
who guided the reconstruction, found two documents
especially valuable, one of them the score in which Marie
Rambert wrote down 'as much of Nijinsky's choreography as
possible', the other the score in which 'Stravinsky had written
descriptions of stage action above the music.' Having seen no
more of the Rambert score than the portion of a page
reproduced in her autobiography, I have nothing to say about
it except that her notes were not made 'during rehearsals', as
claimed in the Sotheby sale catalogue of 16 July 1968, but at a
distance of several months.

Concerning the score that Stravinsky prepared for Nijinsky, *The New York Times* quoted Hodson directly: '[The annotations] seldom mention specific steps, [but] they do indicate what happens by means of phrases such as "the men group together", "here they fall to the floor".' Let me add that the notes also describe movements, such as, for the women in Part Two: 'Walk in a bell-swinging rhythm.' But the real importance of the score is that it provides a map to the *musical* design of the choreography which shows that in rhythmic emphasis and phrasing, music and dance, as a rule, are in counterpoint to each other.

The score itself, as distinguished from verbal descriptions of its contents in a 1969 facsimile volume of the musical sketches, has yet to be mined for the full yield of its performance information. The reasons for this are that much of it is in coded or graphic form, and that the faded pencilling can be read only with the help of photographic boosting of contrasts. The score was shown to Jerome Robbins – for guidance, not reconstruction, which is for archaeologists, not artists – during the planning stages of the New York City Ballet's 1972 Stravinsky Festival, a *Rite of Spring* ballet having been momentarily considered with Robbins choreographing the groups, Balanchine the solo dance, the presumed division of labour in their *Firebird* collaboration. But Balanchine believed that *The Rite* should be heard and not seen.

The 25 October *New York Times* further reported that Kenneth Archer, art historian, described *The Rite* as

> Roerich's brainchild: Stravinsky often claimed that the idea for it came to him in a dream. Yet interviews in Russian newspapers of the time reveal that when Stravinsky finished composing *Firebird* in 1910 and sought ideas for a new ballet, Roerich suggested two scenarios. One concerned chess. The other was *Sacre*.

Hodson herself had written in the *Dance Research Journal* that an interview with Roerich in the St Petersburg press and other documentation show that he had already written a scenario when Stravinsky approached him with the notion of a ballet about archaic Russia. Roerich's scenario was entitled 'The Great Sacrifice' and it survives as the second act of what we know as *Le Sacre du printemps*.

Actually the interview with Roerich,[1] in the *St Petersburg Gazette*, in which he refers to the ballet-in-progress as 'The Sacred Night of the Ancient Slavs' – what we know as Part Two – appeared two months *after* Stravinsky had written to him on 2 July 1910, discussing their plans for the 'Great Sacrifice' – and, incidentally, revealing (to us) that work on the new ballet had begun even before *Firebird* was performed. Writing again on 9 August 1910, Stravinsky mentions the existence of musical sketches and not one but two versions of the libretto, in the second of which Fokine had participated. Fokine is never mentioned in connection with *The Rite*, even though as late as May 1912 he was to have been its choreographer. Whatever his contribution to the ballet, the 'mysterious circles' of Part Two are clearly descended from his Enchanted Princesses in *Firebird*, and so is the hand-to-cheek gesture (those shouts for '*dentistes*' from the first audience). Stravinsky might even have had Kastchei's court in mind when he wrote that aforementioned 'Fall to the floor' direction in the four-hand score. And some musico-dramatic axials between *The Rite* and the end of *Firebird* – ritual (celebration), dance form (rounds), rhythm (shifting metres) and even sonority (swooping horns) – are real and powerful.

Granted that Stravinsky's recollections were not always reliable, and that in the case of his mid-1930s condemnation of Nijinsky's *Rite* they amounted to a betrayal of his on-the-spot judgements of 1913. But his story of the vision of *The Rite* coming to him as he completed *Firebird*, and of seeking out Roerich, is documented in letters and interviews at the time: to André Rimsky-Korsakov, 7 March 1912: 'I am working on the piece that I conceived after *Firebird*'; to N. F.

Findeizen, 15 December 1912: 'My first thoughts about my new choreodrama *Vesna Sviaschennaya* came to me as I was finishing *Firebird*. . . I wanted to compose the libretto together with N. K. Roerich, because who else could help me. . . ?'

Whatever the contents of the 1910 libretto, the authors rewrote it a year later – at Talashkino, the Princess Tenisheva's estate near Smolensk, which is described in her memoirs as having burned down before that time and she herself as already living in Paris. What concerns us is that the July 1911 libretto is the one Stravinsky followed, and that it differs significantly from the two subsequent versions Roerich gave to Diaghilev, the first in the spring of 1912, the second undated but not earlier than March 1913. Whereas Stravinsky's copy of the 1911 scenario does not refer to Yarilo the sun god, Roerich's second version begins with him and excludes any mention of maidens with painted faces and even a ritual of abduction.

In November 1912, in Berlin, only days after completing the ballet in sketch-score form, Stravinsky received a letter from Roerich, in St Petersburg, announcing that he had 'changed the first act, and it is better now.' But of course the music could not be changed or revisions introduced, except to add programmatic significance. As surely as Roerich's knowledge of Russian prehistory had originally inspired Stravinsky, so was the composer deaf to his co-librettist's alterations. The statements on the title page of the four-hand score that *The Rite* is *by* 'Stravinsky and Roerich', the '*mise en scène* by Stravinsky and Nijinsky', confirm both that Roerich had no role in translating the libretto into action and that Stravinsky shared responsibility for the staging, a fact apparently unknown to ballet historians.

Bronislava Nijinska's memoirs attest to Roerich's influence on Nijinsky. We know from her and from Stravinsky–Nijinsky–Diaghilev correspondence that Nijinsky insisted on seeing Roerich's set and costume designs before beginning the choreography. No less certainly, Roerich's art and anthro-

pology inspired Nijinsky far more than Stravinsky's bewilder-
ingly new and terrifyingly difficult music.

In recent years, the music has been measured by new
analytical tools. One result is that its harmonic organization
has been quantified, revealing the fundamental combinations
and structures, and the interrelationships and frequency of
usage, of its vocabulary of chords. Another result is that the
folkloric origins of its archaic melodies have been traced. Still
another is that some light, but not enough, has been shed on
the rhythmic element, that unprecedented and unsucceeded
feature of the work. Publications of a more familiar kind have
accumulated, as well, offering fresh and not so fresh appraisals of the influence of *The Rite* on the other arts, along
with speculations about its significance as *the* representative
creation of the modern period, for no contender, not *Erwar-
tung*, or *Pierrot Lunaire*, not *Les Demoiselles*, Munch's
Scream, or Mondrian's trees, not even *Ulysses* has attained the
universality of Stravinsky's masterpiece, and maintained it for
seventy-five years.

Historical and other documenting has also proceeded
apace. Press dossiers of the first performance have appeared,
from which further information has been gleaned about the
staging, the dancing and the décors. Editions and revisions of
the music have been minutely compared, as have musical
interpretations, notably of Stravinsky's recordings and player-
piano rolls, and arrangements for different instrumental
combinations, from the disastrously misconceived orchestral
version by Robert Rudolph to the illuminating transcription
by Maarten Bon for four pianos, which shows that harmonic
perspectives change with the different weights and prom-
inences of the same notes in the orchestra and in the piano.

Exhibitions of the set and costume designs have also been
presented, as well as of the costumes themselves, the latter
most spectacularly in the Basel Kunstmuseum, where they
were suspended in a circle from the ceiling. And the Joffrey
Ballet has in places skilfully re-realized the pictorial
dimension, aided by Roerich's legacy, photographs of the

dancers taken at the time of the premiere, descriptions by participants and observers, Emmanuel Barcet's drawings and Valentine Hugo's drawings and pastels – though the promise in the pastels of stage depth, of diminutive figures in a spacious landscape, ill prepared the viewer at City Center, where the dance groups were cramped as well as too close to the audience. So, too, from the same visual and verbal sources, the Joffrey has reconstructed movements, the jumps and jerks, the shiverings and tremblings – with the entrance of the Sage – and dance postures, the legs and feet of the men, as Bronislava Nijinska recalled, 'turned inward, their fists clenched, their heads held hunched between their shoulders, and their walk on slightly bent knees.'

The Joffrey staging is exciting at the very end, where the paroxysms of the Chosen One are inevitably intensified by the music but also, and often, it is academic, that danger of revivals even of ballets whose choreographies are intact. At times, too, Russia forgotten, the viewer has the impression of watching Indians at a pow-wow in a kitsch Western, to some extent a fault of the costumes, albeit those of the young girls looked too neat and trim even for the movies, while 'the old men' wearing bear skins suggested a college fraternity caper with trophies borrowed from a hunting lodge. To these detriments must be added the scratch performance of the Rudolph version of the music – ragged ensembles, inaudible strings, a missing horn solo (a case of not giving a hoot?) – and the relentless synchronization between musical and stage event (except where necessary: the Sage planted his earth-kiss prematurely, during the creaky-knees music instead of with the celebrated string chord).

Marie Rambert does not date or locate the rehearsal she describes at which Stravinsky began playing the piano at double the speed the dancers had learned, but this could only have been at the beginning of February 1913 in London. Her account seems to imply that a two-hand arrangement was used, but Bronislava Nijinska remembered Stravinsky playing four-hands with one Steinman, actually Michael Osipovitch

Shteinman, whom Diaghilev had engaged as second conductor, in St Petersburg in October 1912. Nijinska recalled that Shteinman played alone only when trying to bang out the 'Sacrificial Dance' from the sketch for the full score, the only available version of the music before late March 1913, as a telegram from Nijinsky to Stravinsky asking for a piano score establishes. The sketch-score, which Serge Lifar finally surfaced and sold in 1982, ends with a note in Stravinsky's hand: 'That idiot Nijinsky has not returned the "Sacrificial Dance".'[2] The four-hand score, from which Stravinsky and Debussy played the not-quite-complete *Rite* months before dance rehearsals began, served for all other rehearsals.

On 4 January 1913, Emile Jaques-Dalcroze wrote to Stravinsky urging him to teach the music to his assistant Marie Rambert directly, sidestepping Nijinsky. But Stravinsky, preoccupied with the orchestration, did not answer. In a conversation with Romain Rolland after the premiere, recorded by him, the composer objected to the 'rhythmic gymnastics of Dalcroze' in the choreography, yet a trace and more of Dalcroze can be seen in Stravinsky's own instructions about counting beats. The autobiography of Nijinska, who opposed Diaghilev's decision to introduce Dalcrozian eurythmics to help the dancers learn the music, reveals that her brother did not have recourse to counting beats aloud until he came under the influence of the Dalcroze system. The annotated score shows how these beats were tallied. It also proves, if proof is still necessary, that Nijinsky was perfectly able to read the *musical* notation of beats and rhythms.

Decades after the premiere, Mme Rambert wrote:

> There was no melody to hold on to — so the only way to learn it was to count the bars all the time. The movements in themselves were simple and so was the floor pattern.
> But. . .the mastering of the rhythm was almost impossible.

This suggests that the radical rhythmic and harmonic newness had distracted the dancers to the extent that they could not hear melodies that were simple and far from new in kind. But surely, after three months of piano rehearsals, the greatest difficulty for the dancers was in the last-minute switch to the orchestra. The sonorities were entirely new, some of the figurations had either not been *in* the piano score or were unrecognizably transformed, and the dynamic and volumetric ranges were without precedent in music history. Shortly before the first performance, Stravinsky told an interviewer that '[At times] the dynamic power of the orchestra is more important than the melodic line itself.'

The Joffrey production follows the score in allowing the orchestral Introduction to be heard with the curtain closed, thereby obtaining the maximum contrast between the rhythmically free beginning – so supple in the first bars that even the notation is only approximate[3] – and the isochronous dance beat of 'The Augurs of Spring'. In this first section of the ballet, however and unfortunately, the dancers hop *with* each note and emphasize none of them. A glance at the following extract from the score shows that not only are the pencilled-in dance accents (∧) *against* the orchestral accents (>), but that the first accent is in the choreography. The music imitates the dancers' jump, and a *hoquetus* is set in motion between them, though not in the Joffrey performance, which leaves the orchestra to hiccup by itself.

The script at the top of the next extract, the beginning of 'The Ritual of Abduction', says '4 important accents' (found at the beginning of bars 1, 2, 3, and 7), and the Russian word in bars 2 and 3 identifies them as 'jumps'. As in 'Augurs of Spring', the dance accents are on, the musical accents off, the beat. The perspicacious London *Times* critic Henry Cope Colles noted in July 1913: 'What is really of chief interest in the dancing is the employment of rhythmical counterpoint in the mass for group movement.' The Joffrey reconstruction is totally devoid of rhythmical counterpoint. The words in the first bar say that 'a large group of men begin'.

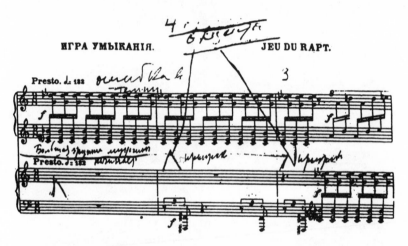

Here, for comparison, is part of the same page in Marie Rambert's copy of the score. The complete absence of accentuation is suspicious, since the three hammer blows in the orchestra (bars 2 and 3) can only be responses to choreographic emphasis. Rambert's handwritten recollections of Nijinsky's stage direction seem to support Stravinsky's later criticism that Nijinsky 'had complicated and encumbered his dances beyond all reason': the furiously fast music is too short for the stage business.

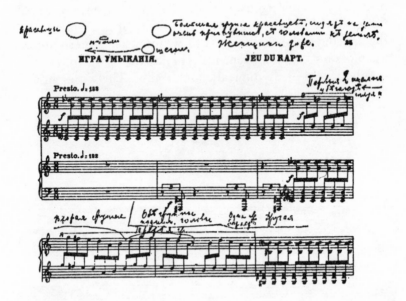

In the next extract, Stravinsky's pencilled-in notation above the first bar (which he had combined with the last bar on the preceding page) shows a different rhythmic grouping for the choreography: 'Cut these two bars in half', the Russian says. The minim tied to a semiquaver and the semiquaver tied to a minim form a retrograde rhythm (one that remains identical read backwards or forwards), a favourite Stravinsky construction, found in music as remote from *The Rite* as *Mavra* and *Apollo*. The direction in the next (and again in the fifth) bar is 'The answer of the women', and in the bar after that, 'Rhythm of men in two parts'. Remembering that Stravinsky later objected to the 'parallelism' in Nijinsky's choreography, we should note that parallels are specified here, and that these associations of music for male and female dancers, back and forth from groups of one sex to the other, are as traditional – masculine horn-call in the lower part, feminine skitterings in the higher – as in the ballets of Tchaikovsky.

The next two extracts, showing the polyphonic construction of the choreography in 'Spring Rounds', suggest that
Stravinsky had composed the choreography at the same time
as the music. The dancers are divided into three groups
entering at different time-intervals, like voices in a fugue; each
group, moreover, is identified with a different rhythm. The
written-in accents in the upper score define rhythm number
one, those on the right side of the lower score rhythm number
two. The word above bars 4, 7, and 8 says that all movement
stops during them, thereby dividing the otherwise monoto-
nous dance into interesting period-lengths. The Joffrey performance ignored this.

In the next extract, the single-line hand-drawn staves above the music chart the phrases of all three groups. The arrow in the first bar (bottom right corner) identifies rhythm number one as a retrograde and, at the same time, reveals how the 'fugal' distribution of the groups has shifted the dance rhythms into positions that contradict the metrical pattern of the music.

In the next extract, the Russian words assign the music to female dancers whose four-beat phrases are counterpointed against the musical metre. (The crotchet melody in the lower part, bracketed by twos, reappears seven years later in Stravinsky's *Symphonies of Wind Instruments*.)

'Music exists when there is rhythm, as life exists when there is a pulse,' Stravinsky wrote above one of his sketches for *The Rite*, and, in a letter, 'I sought to give the feeling of closeness between men and earth through a lapidary rhythm.' Sometimes, as in the following sketch for the most lapidary rhythm in the history of dance music, his first idea may have been purely rhythmic:

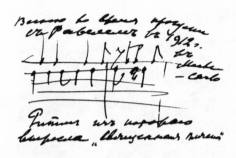

His Russian script says: 'In the spring of 1912 during a walk with Ravel in Monte Carlo. This is the rhythm from which the Sacred Dance grew.' The music that 'grew' is in the next excerpt.

The composition of the 'Sacred Dance', a dance piece from its inception, coincided with Fokine's departure and Nijinsky's arrival. All evidence indicates that the choreography was created in close collaboration between Stravinsky and Nijinsky during meetings in Bayreuth (!), Venice, Lugano, Monte Carlo, and Berlin: after returning to Switzerland from Berlin in mid-December, Stravinsky wrote: 'Nijinsky directs it with passionate zeal.' As in no other movement in the ballet, the orchestra in the second section has an accompanying role. The strong choreographic first beats in the following excerpt further show that Stravinsky adjusted his metrical system to the dance, since the corresponding place earlier in the movement is differently metred.[4]

Needless to say, the rhythmic pattern of the solo dance (7/8 ♩♩♪♩) is in counterpoint to the pattern of the orchestral rhythm. Regrettably, the Joffrey performance indicated no awareness of these ingenious designs.

The music was apparently heard for the first time in any form when Stravinsky and Claude Debussy played it four-hands, on 9 June 1912. Did the solo-instrument beginning, on this mind-boggling occasion, seem to the French master – as it still does to us – indebted to the example of *Afternoon of a Faun*? And what did Debussy, whose fluid music is forever overflowing its metres, think of the metrical tyrannies of the Russian master?

The reading took place in the home of Debussy's friend Louis Laloy, who wrote: 'We were dumbfounded, flattened as though by a hurricane from the roots of time.'

Notes

1 Roerich's veracity is nearly always in question. See the detailed investigation of this monumental con artist in R. C. Williams's *Russian Art and American Money*, Cambridge, Massachusetts, 1980, and Karl E. Meyer's 'The Two Roerichs are One' in the editorial column of *The New York Times*, 22 January 1988.
2 Pierre Monteux's reference to 'Nijinsky's two-hand score' (letter to Stravinsky, 22 February 1913) evidently refers to the sketch-score.
3 See the essay by Carl Dahlhaus, 'Problems of Rhythm in the New Music', in *Schoenberg and the New Music*, New York, 1987.
4 See Dahlhaus, *op. cit.*

PART FOUR

Perspectives

14

NICOLAI ANDREYEVICH
AND IGOR FYODOROVICH

'That blockhead,' Igor Stravinsky wrote to a friend who had called his attention to the publication in Russian (1959–60) of Vasily Vasilyevich Yastrebtsev's *Reminiscences of Rimsky-Korsakov*, nor was this verdict changed on acquaintance with the book. Twenty-five years later, this much abbreviated English version[1] will attract as many readers for the glimpses it contains of the young Stravinsky as for the portrait of his teacher, the composer of, and now almost exclusively known in the West by, *Sheherazade*. Yastrebtsev, a well-to-do amateur, had briefly been a Rimsky pupil.

The *Reminiscences* cover the last sixteen years of Rimsky-Korsakov's life. In Yastrebtsev's chronicle, Stravinsky enters five years before the end, on 26 January 1903 (whether Old or New Style is not specified), with some 'very charming and witty musical jokes of his own invention' performed for a gathering in the Rimsky-Korsakov home. Yastrebtsev's comment that the twenty-year-old composer was 'a man of undoubted talent' stirs a suspicion that it was not written at the time but added at a later date (Yastrebtsev died in 1934), both because remarks of the kind are out of character in the book, and since Stravinsky's juvenilia is remarkable precisely for the absence of indications of an unusual gift. Nothing in his music before 1907 points in the direction of the masterpieces that came immediately after and were to bury the works of Rimsky-Korsakov.

Yastrebtsev offers a glimpse of Stravinsky in the summer of 1904, living with the Rimsky-Korsakovs in their summer vacation home and scoring wind parts in the master's new opera. The pupil is also seen taking an active part in musical evenings in the Rimsky-Korsakov St Petersburg home, playing operas and symphonies at the piano, introducing a birthday cantata of his own composition for his teacher, even dancing the cakewalk. No close-up of Stravinsky's appearance is offered and no observation about his personality. But the book is short on description, and, as Gerald Abraham notes, Yastrebtsev's ears were 'pricked only for Rimsky-Korsakov', whose musical opinions it records, and not much else.

Yet how many of Stravinsky's opinions sound like echoes of those of his teacher! 'Beethoven was not a great melodist,' Rimsky declares, as the composer of *Firebird* did after him, no less inanely. When Rimsky berates a conductor for introducing 'an absurd ritard' and for beginning 'to sentimentalize' in the *Eroica*, even the voice reminds us of Stravinsky, who would also have said, with his teacher, albeit in sharper language and with a hand-on-bosom gesture, 'I'm no admirer of heart-rending sounds.' So, too, Rimsky's claim, while improvising a parody of Wagner, that 'given a certain facility for harmonization, there is nothing easier than to write recitatives in this style,' was Stravinsky's as well. Stravinsky's irony must also owe something to Rimsky's example, but Yastrebtsev, totally lacking the quality himself, is not alert to it in his idol.

Most of Rimsky-Korsakov's *obiter dicta* will appal the reader unfamiliar with the identity struggles of the Russian Nationalist School. In opera, Rimsky says, 'Wagner and Glinka achieved heights unattainable by Mozart [in *Don Giovanni*].' And though 'Beethoven and Glinka possessed inexhaustible technical resources,' in the domain of rhythm 'Berlioz is the only indisputable genius in all music.' A symphony by Rimsky-Korsakov should be played for the reason that it is 'no worse than those by Brahms.' Some of the 'technical' talk is equally naive – on relationships between tonalities and colours, for instance, where E minor is 'bluish', and A flat major, as the dominant of D flat minor, 'grayish violet'. No reader can help noticing that while Rimsky-

Korsakov is primarily a composer of operas, he says virtually nothing about dramatic concepts and constructions, but discusses at length musical effects that usually prove to be no more than orchestral ones. And what Rimsky means by good orchestration is, on the whole, simply the use of a novel instrument or combination of instruments.

Rimsky-Korsakov was commonsensical, and the *Reminiscences* should be read to savour this and his other earthbound qualities. A certain piece by Arensky 'is boring not because it's long but, on the contrary, long because it's boring.' To cut Schubert's 'heavenly-length' symphony is actually to prolong it because 'the elimination of the modulation or development section compels the listener to remain longer in the same key.'

When the musicologists of the younger generation publish their Russian-oriented books on Stravinsky, the debt of the composer of *Sacre* to Rimsky-Korsakov may be exposed as more profound than anyone has so far been aware, and, along with this readjustment, we may expect a new and higher appreciation of Rimsky-Korsakov himself.

Notes

1 *Reminiscences of Rimsky-Korsakov* by V. V. Yastrebtsev. Edited and translated by Florence Jonas, foreword by Gerald Abraham. New York, 1986.

15

STRAVINSKY AND ASAF'YEV

It has taken a centenary to bring out an English-language edition of *Kniga o Stravinskom* (*A Book about Stravinsky*) by Igor Glebov, *nom de plume* of Boris Vladimirovich Asaf'yev.[1] This brilliant interpretation of Stravinsky's music and its meaning for the twentieth century, appearing in Leningrad in 1929, was virtually banned on publication. In 1977 the volume was reissued in the USSR, with the music examples corrected, and now Richard French has translated it.[2]

After conducting concerts in Russia in the spring of 1928, Ernest Ansermet wrote to Stravinsky:

> There is no place where you are more loved and better understood than in Leningrad, at least among an élite, and notably by a man who is very close to your ideas and your tastes as well as to your music. Boris Asaf'yev is a marvellous human being, extremely sensitive and incredibly intelligent. Not only does he know you intellectually, but he also has an intuition of you. . .[3]

This last statement does credit to Ansermet's own perspicacity, despite Stravinsky's curt answer: 'You would think otherwise about Asaf'yev if you had been able to read him.'[4]

A Book about Stravinsky is a classic of criticism, the peer of that great work on Leonardo da Vinci by Asaf'yev's younger fellow-countryman, V. P. Zubov, which I mention because the strengths of both studies are in their insights rather than in their histories, and because both books continue to outlive more recent and exhaustive ones. The fifty-year delay in the publication of the volume in this country is partly the fault of the composer himself. Asked for a blurb to promote a proposed English edition, he refused, explaining that any interest in Asaf'yev was misplaced. This attitude is understandable in a man who hated the Communism and atheism of the new Russia that Asaf'yev represented and described as having been preceded by a 'millennium of credulous and naive faith'. Philosophically the two men could hardly have been further apart: a Christian who believed in the divine nature of artistic inspiration versus a dialectical materialist who sought to explain artistic phenomena in terms of a constructivist social theory. Indeed, the party-line polemics with which the book commences make one wonder why it was placed on the Soviet index, except that Stravinsky himself, a White Russian reactionary in the official eye – in Asaf'yev's, one of the greatest composers who ever lived – was considered an unsuitable topic. Clearly, the subject of *Kniga o Stravinskom* began to read it with strong political and religious prejudices.

Stravinsky's animus against his disciple had other causes as well, perhaps dating back to the time when both men were pupils of Rimsky-Korsakov. This possibility seems to be borne out both by the book's complete absence of biographical information and by two or three asides accusing Stravinsky of arrogance in a way that suggests a personal history. In May 1914 Asaf'yev came to Paris for the premiere of *The Nightingale*, armed with requests from Stravinsky's friends to admit the critic to rehearsals. But if a meeting took place then, no record of it has emerged, and, to Ansermet, Stravinsky denied ever having known Asaf'yev. Then, too, Arthur Lourié disapproved of this Soviet admirer: 'I read Asaf'yev's last article with revulsion, and to think that at one time we almost spoke the same language!' (Letter to Stravinsky, 14 April 1925) Finally, the chapter on *Apollo*, the next-to-last composition that Asaf'yev discusses, is lacking in perspective, expresses fears that Stravinsky could be in danger of losing his way, and compares some of the music to that in Pugni's ballets. This would have offended the composer, of course, but it seems doubtful that he read that far.

My explanation differs from these and is based on a trait of Stravinsky's character. He would tolerate no interpreter he could not control – hence his autobiography, and, in conducting, his preference for a mere craftsman. Whether or not Stravinsky was annoyed that an infidel Marxist, living so far from the centre and with only the rarest opportunities to hear the music, had penetrated it so profoundly, the composer freely admitted that Asaf'yev understood him as no one else did, least of all the authors of the French and Italian monographs published at about the same time and written quite literally under the subject's nose.[5] In a letter to Asaf'yev, 6 September 1934, Prokofiev wrote: 'We dropped in on Stravinsky, who is writing a concerto for two pianos. . .and a book about himself. When I asked him what was the best book about him up to now, he answered, the Glebov.' And on 26 October 1931, Asaf'yev had written to Miaskovsky: 'Have I told you that my book about Stravinsky was very much to his liking and that he was astonished how, without knowing him personally. . . , I figured out. . .his creative process?' Asaf'yev does not reveal his source for Stravinsky's reactions, which are true only in part. It may have been the composer's friend Jacques Handschin, who wrote to him from Zürich on 20 February 1931: 'I had the opportunity to translate Glebov's Mussorgsky article. . . I hope I will have the opportunity to do the same with his book on you. That would be very interesting.' But – to return to Ansermet's observations – to be completely understood by anyone is threatening, and who, least of all Igor Stravinsky, wants an alter ego?

In the spring of 1935, while Stravinsky was on a concert tour in the United States, his wife's sister, Lyudmila Beliankina, wrote to him from Sancellemoz that his young American friend, the pianist Beveridge Webster, had procured a copy of the book while on a recent visit to the USSR. In it, she says, Asaf'yev dwells at length

on *Noces*, *Soldat*, and *Mavra*. Up to this time I have not encountered such an interesting and intelligent critique of your music. I was especially struck by how subtly he evaluated *Mavra*. It was amazing that someone who has had no contact with you and no guidance from you understood your work so completely. He analyzed everything himself, and he warmly and intelligently defends you against the academic circles in Russia.

Let me say at once that the *Mavra* essay is a revelation, convincing me, for one, that the work fails in performance only because it demands too much sophistication from its audiences. Being unacquainted with the sources, we in the West fail to relate to the references, not only to such composers as Alyabyev, Varlamov, and Verstovsky,[6] but also to Dargomizhsky and Tchaikovsky.[7]

Stravinsky had actually read *Kniga o Stravinskom* years before, having purchased the book through his publishers in Berlin on 4 October 1930. His 1935 Ecole Normale lecture on the *Concerto per due pianoforti soli* seems to owe something to Asaf'yev's discussion of the etymology of the word 'concerto', and the composer's presentation of his aesthetics in *Chroniques de ma vie* might also have been influenced by the Soviet musicologist. In any case, Stravinsky was well aware that Asaf'yev had already disavowed *Kniga o Stravinskom* when underscoring lines, inserting question, exclamation, and check marks, and adding comments so consistently deprecatory that when the margins are blank, as in the chapter on *Renard*, the reader interprets the silence as signifying agreement, if not praise. Stravinsky entered a favourable word – 'important' – in only one place, yet this could be taken as a clue to his recognition of the true value of the book, since, if not Asaf'yev, only Stravinsky himself could have written the passage to which the word refers:

In instrumental music, pitches and rhythms are not used to compose sound complexes that have precise emotional connotations. Nevertheless, the choice of material must be made, and that choice inevitably produces an inner logic of its own and a precise sonorous image. . .a unique complex of intonational 'gestures' by which the character and pace of a piece are defined.

Except to correct mistakes in music examples, Stravinsky did not mark the book until the chapter on *The Nightingale*. He probably took exception to some conclusions concerning his three early ballets, but not, I think, to the charge that the unadventurous character of his music before *Fireworks* can be blamed on domination by Rimsky-Korsakov, who, says Asaf'yev, 'walked behind the times. . . Each new work of his represented. . .a *concession* to contemporary demands. . . The pupil was of necessity behind his times.' Asaf'yev's analysis of *Firebird* is conventional, but he was quick to see the technical superiority of the 1919 suite over the earlier one. In *The Rite of Spring*, he seems to have been the first to notice the construction of the melodic ascent toward the end of the piece, from bass A to treble A, A above the clef, then up through C, E, the pivotal F, and rapidly, in the last two bars, to F sharp, G, G sharp, A (the demisemiquaver appoggiatura), and the ultimate A, five octaves above the first one. Asaf'yev regards the music as 'tonal' and as resolving from dominant to tonic.[8]

What must be emphasized is that at a time when it was still necessary to defend *Sacre* against those who had 'not enlarged their ideas about what is permissible in music,' and to uphold 'the originality that proceeds from organic and natural premises,' Asaf'yev had grasped the logic, the substance, and the import of the work, proclaiming that Stravinsky's music is 'the child of the era that it has come to define.'

For the Westerner, Asaf'yev's most valuable chapters are the ones devoted to the Russian-language theatre pieces, *The Nightingale* not least among them. His analysis identifies not only the opera's specifically Russian features, such as the 'Russian rococo' in the Nightingale's aria in Act I, but also those of Stravinsky's music in general. Thus the bell-like sounds that become part of the substance of *Noces* are already present in the texture of *The Nightingale*, in harp and string harmonics, in the timbres of piano and celesta, not to mention the actual bells in the Emperor's court at the beginning of Act II and the funeral gong in Act III. Asaf'yev, who knew that Stravinsky would have heard the great bell of the Nikolsky Sobor in his cradle, could not have been surprised by the continuing evocation of bells in the later music[9] – in the second of the *Shakespeare Songs*, in the setting of Thomas Dekker's *Prayer*, in the *Introitus*, and in *Requiem Canticles*. The mention of the music performed for the composer's funeral in Venice, just before the ferrying to the grave, reminds me of his experiments with notations for the different speeds of the city's bells, since their rhythms absorbed him as much as their ring and the percussive articulation of mallet and clapper.[10]

Festive ritual, grotesquery, and the search for the primordial as well as for the new are integral elements of *The Nightingale* no less than of *Fireworks*, *Firebird*, *Petrushka*, and *The Rite*. What is new, according to Asaf'yev, is the composer's 'growing scepticism' and its 'deepening effect on his vital instincts' – remarks, together with some others hinging on the 'mature' attitude toward death in the new Russia, that provoke the first of Stravinsky's marginal graffiti:[11] 'Very little has changed in this sense since I left Russia twenty years ago.' Asaf'yev goes on to say that 'the subject of death has always stimulated Russian composers to write deeply felt music', and he includes the Stravinsky of *The Nightingale* in the statement. This seems like special pleading, since the idea of death has produced 'deeply felt music' from composers of all times and places. But Asaf'yev argues that 'life in Russia is so hard, many regard the gift of it as an unjust accident,' a fact he relates to the hysterical reactions (peculiarly Russian, he says) of a Gogol, a Dostoevsky, and a Tchaikovsky. Moreover, nightingales are messengers of Eros, and, in Russia, wedding rites and funeral laments are closely related.

In any event, the Act III death scene gives Stravinsky's opera the human dimension and the depth it would otherwise lack.

The struggle between the Nightingale and Death is the opera's dramatic and musical focus, and the Nightingale's aria about the garden in the cemetery is the best and most moving music. The first two acts are mere satire at the expense of the 'magisterial stupidity' of the Chinese Emperor and his courtiers, and of the Japanese and their Panasonic nightingale. Moreover, the music after the Emperor's recovery is an anticlimax; his last words, instead of an affirmation of life, are a 'puzzled interrogation', and the Fisherman's song is simply a colophon. When the Emperor's temperature returns to normal, Stravinsky's own 'nightingale fever' – to borrow Mandelstamm's phrase – also disappears, but the emotions aroused by the music of the death scene linger on.

Apart from his stand against the new 'mature' Russian attitude toward death, Stravinsky's criticisms of the chapter are minor. 'The voice of the Nightingale [is] first introduced instrumentally (an ornate improvisation),' Asaf'yev writes, and Stravinsky counters: 'It is a cadenza and not an improvisation' (as if, traditionally, cadenzas were not improvised). 'Kuzmin and Verlaine, Rimsky-Korsakov and Debussy' are among the influences on the opera, Asaf'yev states, and Stravinsky asks, 'What is Rimsky-Korsakov doing in this company?' (to which the answer is 'Very little,' yet Rimsky's influence on the music is undeniable). 'In the symphonic poem, *Song of the Nightingale*, the middle section of the [opera's] *entr'acte* is made over into a new episode,' Asaf'yev goes on, and Stravinsky rejoins: 'As if no one ever noticed that in the opera this is sung.'

In the next chapter, 'Toward the New', the smaller works composed between 1913 and 1919 are examined – and illuminated. But Asaf'yev's usually reliable sense of Stravinsky's chronological development is contradicted in the conclusion that 'the new style reaches maturity in *Noces*,' for we have since learned that much of the composition of that work antedates the *Berceuses du chat*[12] and *Trois Histoires pour enfants*. During World War I, Stravinsky was composing in different styles simultaneously, as is shown by the 1914–17 piano duets. On the other hand, Asaf'yev's remark that the piano accompaniment in *The Jackdaw* 'suggests orchestral sonorities' reads like a prediction, since Stravinsky scored the song after *Kniga o Stravinskom* had been published.

In 'Toward the New', Asaf'yev says that in Stravinsky's concluding chorus for Mussorgsky's *Khovanshchina*, 'the ornate development of the archaic theme is incongruous,' and that the composer 'desires to be impudent at all costs.' Since the piano reduction hardly justifies these reactions, the remarks compound our curiosity to hear the orchestra score, which remained in Diaghilev's possession after the few performances in June 1913. I should also mention that Asaf'yev writes unenthusiastically about Stravinsky's orchestral *Chant funèbre* for Rimsky-Korsakov, a still earlier lost opus that continues to excite speculation, since it represents the next step beyond *Fireworks*.

In this same chapter, Asaf'yev enumerates the features of the new style, the exploitation of the responsorial principle, the rejection of the large orchestra, of tonic–dominant formulas, and of metrical regularity (or alternatively, the introduction of unequal time-intervals, of figurations with different numerators from those of the metre, and other devices – comparable to the enjambment, dislocated syntax, and so forth of the Russian poets of the time). Most essential, however, is Stravinsky's 'new awareness of the functional relationship and interdependence of the various elements composing the texture of sounds.' What this means is simply that he has outgrown the rigmarole of academic composition and henceforth will follow only his own artistic logic.

Of Stravinsky's contemporaries, Asaf'yev alone seems to have recognized the importance of the eight *Easy Pieces* (1915–17), and that they reveal 'the shrewd and incisive intellect of a great artist. [This is music in which] no transplantation of the past can be found, but only contemporary life, with its cinematographic quality.' Asaf'yev points out popular elements in each of the pieces that most of us would otherwise miss, in the Balalaika, for example, the abrupt interruptions and turns, and the dynamics of the folk rhyme, and in the stretto movement of the Galop, 'the sixth figure of the quadrille'.

The essay on *Renard* is the only one that does the work justice, though this can be blamed on the nonawareness of non-Russians that *Renard* represents the revival of 'an authentic old Russian theatre', long suppressed because of its blasphemy, mockery, and anticlerical satire. *Renard*, a fourteen-minute romp that can be described as burlesque, masked buffoonery, mime, is enacted by clowns, actors, acrobats, dancers – anybody but singers. Based on gesture, it stands at the polar opposite of the narrative and descriptive tale of, for instance, Chaucer's Fox and Chanticleer. Stravinsky's singers impersonate the actors with shrieks and howls, measured speech, mock chant, and prayer: the unctuous tone in which the Fox, in nun's habit, confesses the Rooster ('You have wedded, you have bedded, too many wives') is one of music's most delectable lampoons of religious hypocrisy. 'Laughter is life's real mirror,' Asaf'yev says, 'its self-criticism.'

As for word accentuation, Asaf'yev describes Stravinsky's aim as simply 'to preserve the natural flow of the musical speech', which would be inconsistent, of course, with the association of every verbal accent with a point of musical emphasis. It follows, too, that the words must be independent of arbitrary metrical divisions. Near the end of *Renard*, with the arrival of the Cat and the Goat, the accents of the words adhere to the metre, but the dance conforms to a different beat, a counterpoint of accents. But of word setting, more in connection with *Mavra*. The analysis of *Renard* concludes with an out-of-date defence of the work as a 'deeply intellectual phenomenon' and the perennially pertinent observation that 'this frightens many people.'

Asaf'yev's 'fertility' interpretation of *Les Noces* ignited a virtual explosion in Stravinsky, but for all his objections to the obtrusion of the mistaken thesis, he offers no clue to the right one, simply answering Asaf'yev's statement that the subject of *Noces* is 'the confrontation of man and his instinct for procreation' with 'I do not agree.' Asaf'yev repeats his argument: 'One must not forget that *Noces* is the embodiment of the ancient cult of fertility and reproduction,' and Stravinsky rebukes him again: 'Better to forget, because this has no bearing on it.' When the critic reiterates that *Noces* is about 'human beings standing face to face with the act of procreation', Stravinsky objects, this time at greater length: 'I meant nothing of the kind: these statements, which I never expected from Asaf'yev, astound me. He has a great desire to find an orgiastic tendency that simply is not there.'

Next to a remark about the work's 'epic forcefulness and Euripidean rigour',[13] the exasperated composer asks: 'What is all this deep-thinking nonsense? And I, simpleton, was not aware of any of this.' When Asaf'yev praises Stravinsky's economy, the compression into four short scenes, the composer jests: '*What?* All of *that* into only four concise tableaux?'

The sexual interpretation puts the composer so out of sorts that he chides his champion for using the diminutive 'little berry' – '*Just plain berry*', according to Stravinsky – and at a reference to the techniques and thought processes of Raphael and Velazquez, the composer snaps, 'As if they were the same.' When a tendency toward symphonism is detected, Stravinsky exclaims: 'This is again your own improvisation, dear friend: symphonism is not my intention.' Seeing Bolshevism in a class-war reference to 'unfortunates and captives', the composer wonders 'Who?' and further vents his irritation in a rash of question marks. Asaf'yev's behaviouristic analysis of Stravinsky's irony earns the comment from its subject: 'A curtsy to communists.'

> It proceeds from pity and from envy. . .of people who, like children, can still find amusement in. . .toys because of the secret mechanisms that make them operate. The curious child breaks the toy open, but he does not uncover a secret thereby: the expert knows that there is no secret but simply a spring adapted to a form. He pities the child and wants to laugh.

Nevertheless, Asaf'yev's essay on *Noces* helps us to understand Russian wedding ritual as both tragic-ironic and grotes-
que, with threnody and buffoonery as its principal contrasting
stylistic elements. On the one side are psalmodic chanting
('*Chesu, pochesu*') and the lamentations associated with the
loss of virginity, as well as the bereavement of the two
mothers. On the other side are the paroxysms, the whooping
and shouting – during the ballad of the little swan, for
example – the rhythmically notated talk, the clapping, the
basso falsetto. The antiphons and responses, of course, derive
from peasant music as well as from the church.

That Asaf'yev does not elaborate on the traditions of
matchmaking and other rituals is understandable, since he
assumed his readers' familiarity with such matters. Nor did
Stravinsky ever discuss these elements of the piece, no doubt
having despaired of the work's ever being understood in the
West. Already in 1923 he had transcribed *Noces* for the
pianola – which is to say, eliminated the voices, as he was to
do with many of his Russian-text songs. By the time I knew
Stravinsky, he was bored with folk music and even more so
with the question of its connections to his work. No doubt he
interpreted, in a very different way from that which Asaf'yev
intended, the latter's sage remark that '*Sacre* and *Noces*, two
of Stravinsky's greatest achievements, are. . .tragedies of race,
not tragedies of destiny.'

Asaf'yev's observations on *Histoire du soldat* contain
flagrant instances of his habit of introducing subjective
interpretations, as when he writes of the opening March: 'The
soldier's head is full of random recollections – flashes of
barracks life. . .' This is the more surprising since he has just
said that 'Stravinsky's musical thought is extra-personal, just
as his music is extra-sensual (but not sensual-less. . .). . . . The
best of his works are not "reflections" of inner life; rather,
they incarnate the drive and appetites of life. . . It is not the
inner subjective experiences of people that fascinate him but
the styles in which the people display themselves.'

Asaf'yev considers the 'Little Concert', with its network of motifs from all of the preceding numbers, as both the musical and dramatic centrepiece and a 'synthetic, Lisztian-type' sonata-allegro, the first movement of a symphonic structure in which the Tango is the adagio, the Waltz the scherzo, and the Ragtime the finale. 'Dance is the primary agent of form and movement in Stravinsky's art,' Asaf'yev concludes, and, 'the primary law of all life is rhythm, since all of our senses are rhythmic.' In the 'Soldier's March', 'despite the moments of silence, the rhythm is not silenced.'

In the Tango, Stravinsky discovered the potentialities of an orchestra of percussion only, composing not just rhythm-lines for these instruments, but rhythm-harmonies as well, layers, or registers, of different timbres and intensities. The 'orchestra' of the Waltz suggests a band of street musicians, or a parody of one, through the ornamented, mock-virtuoso violin part. Here, and apropos of the Ragtime, Asaf'yev remarks astutely on Stravinsky's 'preference for sudden change, rather than long emotional intensifications and broad crescendi.'

In the Chorale, 'lines that have been moving toward the limit of individualized utterance' are brought together in tonic cadences that seem to be saying, 'Everything comes out well in the end.' But the last one is a suspension, a 6/4 chord, and Stravinsky's ultimate irony, for the Devil soon leads the doomed Soldier below, to the accompaniment of hot jazz drums. Comparing the death of the Soldier to the 'splendours of Isolde's last moments', Asaf'yev decides that the fate of Stravinsky's hero is 'the more tragic, by virtue of its simplicity.'

The *Pulcinella* chapter abounds in insights, both general ('The instruments are treated as characters in the comedy. . .the doubles of the figures on the stage') and specific ('The strings in the Toccata are used. . .to carry the movement from one *register* to another'). In the 1920s, however, when Asaf'yev wrote, it was not yet known that Stravinsky had not developed 'fragments' in *Pulcinella* but, instead, had arranged and orchestrated complete pieces, some by Pergolesi, seven (from the trio sonatas) by Domenico Gallo, and one by Count Van Wassenaer.

Turning to *Mavra*, Asaf'yev says that 'the whole composition is magnificent, and the melodic line is perfection,' which did not stop Stravinsky from scolding him for attributing the 'new level of intensity' in the Quartet to qualities of the deceased, for whom the singers repine. 'The observation of a fourth-grade schoolboy', the composer writes, though it is one of many helpful evaluations of the musical means with which he delineates character. Thus Parasha, whose prototype was Tchaikovsky's Larina, is portrayed by a gliding melody that avoids 'disjunct intervals and temperamental rhythms', and the Hussar by bold entrances and 'passionate cadences'. Stravinsky's second outburst comes at the end of the analysis, after the statement, 'The ingeniousness of reality finds a new and authentic musical utterance.' 'Only in this?' he demands. 'Is it worthwhile, then, to give birth to a musical mouse?'

Mavra's melodic sources and genres, and its 'musical speech', occupy a large and, for me, absorbing portion of the essay, but then, I know nothing of Apollon Grigor'ev and Polezhaev, and was only vaguely aware that, like Stravinsky, Tchaikovsky, in *Onegin*, was attacked for his 'misplaced accents, ungrammatical word-couplings, pauses in the wrong places, and metrical confusion.' Asaf'yev's rebuttal is that 'correctness' is not the issue:

The central problem is to define the music of speech – speech that differs in style according to epoch, rank, society, the personality of the individual. . . Speech. . .may be filled with interjections, exclamations, interrogations, declarations. The problem is to catch its whole excitement. . . The critics have applied standards of written style and the pathos of theatrical speech, whereas *Onegin* [and *Mavra*] derive wholly from the music of the speech of the Russian middle class. . . Words pour out in unbroken melodic lines, commas are ignored. . .and emotional tone and its nuances take precedence over sense. . .

After the *Mavra* essay, *Kniga o Stravinskom* is less reward-
ing, both because the subject matter ceases to be Russian and
because Stravinsky's 1920s, so-called international-style
music quickly attracted a host of younger devotees, including
a great many from the Western hemisphere, ready to pore
over every note. Yet the final pages contain keen perceptions,
both musical – 'the reduction in the use of the dominant
seventh in cadential formulas helps to unveil the tonic' – and
dramaturgical: '[Creon's] aria proclaims [the] inexorable
decree of the oracle in a brilliant and authoritative tone,
but. . .in such a way that, though [he] believes he is his own
master, to the listener he is made to appear as a plaything
. . .which has been set in motion and will go through its
mechanical operations.'

At the outset, Asaf'yev had distinguished two kinds of
composer:

> the imitative and the evolving. The imitative preserves – or,
> at best, varies – what has been invented by others. The
> evolving always struggles to master new methods, new
> expressions.

One feels that if Boris Asaf'yev had lived as long as his great
coeval, and not been the victim of Soviet mental misprision, he
would have celebrated Stravinsky's glorious evolution
through the music not only of the thirties and forties, the
Concerto per due pianoforti soli and the symphonies, but also
that of the fifties and sixties, *Agon*, Movements, the Variations. No doubt he would have made the same pronounce-
ment then that he did in his concluding remarks about *Les
Noces*: 'Our musical epoch is the epoch of Stravinsky.'

Notes

1 1884–1949. Asaf'yev is better known as one of the villains in
  the persecution of Shostakovich. See *Testimony: The Memoirs
  of Dmitri Shostakovich*, ed. Solomon Volkov, New York,
  1980.

2 Ann Arbor, 1982.

3 Letter of 10 April 1928, in which Ansermet also reports that *The Rite* and *Symphonies of Wind Instruments* were remarkably well played and received in Leningrad. He adds that Stravinsky's brother and sister-in-law there desperately want to emigrate, and that the composer's sister-in-law entrusted him with an icon for Stravinsky's mother, then living in France, but the picture was confiscated at the border. Ansermet was more successful in smuggling '*un ouvrage ancien*', presumably an early Stravinsky manuscript, between the pages of a score.

4 Stravinsky's library *c.* 1924 contained a volume of Asaf'yev's essays on Russian composers, including Stravinsky.

5 This is not true of Herbert Fleischer's 1931 German monograph, published (in an edition of a thousand copies) by the Russischer Musik Verlag in Berlin. As Stravinsky wrote to F. V. Weber, 29 September 1931: 'A month ago [Fleischer] wrote me a very kind letter in which he expresses ideas that do not concur in the least with that article of his in the *Berliner Tageblatt*. . . That excerpt from his book had such a negative effect on me because of its complete misinterpretation of my intentions in, let us say, *Petrushka* and *Sacre*; I was utterly bewildered and depressed. And what *is* one to believe, what he wrote in his letter, or what, to my horror, I read about myself in the *Berliner Tageblatt*, where, in his profound German-philosophical language, he characterizes my work as that of a thoroughgoing pessimist, a nihilist even, saying that I cannot believe – it is clear to him – in life beyond the grave, this and other arbitrary fantasies?'

6 A. A. Alyabyev, 1781–1851; A. E. Varlamov, 1801–48; A. N. Verstovsky, 1799–1862.

7 In March 1982, listening to *Perséphone* with George Balanchine, I was astonished to hear him exclaim 'Tchaikovsky' and 'Glinka' during melodies that to me seemed purely French.

8 In the 1943 score, the final bass note is not D but E. Asaf'yev seems to have used the 1913 four-hand score, but since the hemidemisemiquavers indicated for the flute are not found as shown in his book in any edition, I assume a misprint.

9 In a talk at the Cleveland Institute of Music in 1968, Victor Babin recalled a visit to Stravinsky in his Hollywood home

during which the composer 'showed me his *In Memoriam Dylan Thomas*. . .explaining to me how the four trombones sounded like funeral bells. . .' From *Victor Babin*, Cleveland, 1982.

10 One of the illustrations in Nathanial Spear's *A Treasury of Archaeological Bells* (New York, 1978) is a photograph of a bell discovered in the 1950s in a Sarmatian (first to second century) burial ground in the Dnepropetrovsky District of Stravinsky's ancestral Ukraine.

11 The originals of these are in Russian.

12 Stravinsky objects to the title '*Berceuses du chat*', as Asaf'yev writes it: 'Not lullabies *for* the cat but *by* him; it makes a difference.'

13 In the English text, 'Aeschylean rigor.'

16

CELESTIAL MOTIONS

Which composers since Beethoven can survive the exposure of seven one-man exhibitions seven days in a row? Schumann and Brahms would be among the contenders, of course, if *Lieder* and piano recitals were included along with the chamber and orchestra repertory; and Chopin and Tchaikovsky. But seven nights of unmitigated Brahms might be more of a test of our endurance than of his, while a Mahler cycle of that length, whether or not it would kill off the composer, could prove to be lethal (in the effects of so much *Weltschmerz*) to the audience. Richard Strauss, on the other hand, a more prolific composer than Stravinsky, would as surely not withstand so large a display without the help of his operas, while more than three programmes of any kind by Debussy, for whom less is more, would all but deplete him or, if not him, us. Yet Stravinsky survives and would have been in still better health if the exhibits had lasted a fortnight. Some of his most popular music, after all, including actual ballets such as *Petrushka*, *The Rite of Spring*, *Les Noces*, *Jeu de cartes*, was ignored.

Would even Stravinsky have come through unscathed, however, without the choreographic superstructure? The performances were not concerts but theatrical spectacles, and watching was at least as important as listening – in many cases more important, the music being subliminal, to judge by the musically deaf applause. (This is also a feature of opera, the prima donna's claques often being vociferously indifferent not

A view of the June 1972 New York City Ballet Stravinsky Festival.

only to the continuity of the score but also to the work as a whole.) But what *is* this superstructure, choreography being an independent art with its own techniques? And what is the relationship of choreography to music? My answers, limited to examples from the City Ballet's Stravinsky Festival, are that choreography ranges from distractions that impinge on the music (in which event one closes one's eyes), to aesthetic constructions that are justifiable in their own right. And at best, as in the best of Balanchine, choreography can provide equivalences to music, and illuminate and mirror music. Essentially, however, choreography is irrelevant, ballet being one thing, music quite another.

Stravinsky won the seven-day marathon partly because his music inspired delectable visual entertainment, that being due, in turn, to the music's diversity and wit, and to the composer's miraculous power to 'make it new'. It is almost incomprehensible that masterpieces so different as *Histoire du soldat*, *Pulcinella*, and the *Symphonies of Wind Instruments* could have been created within two years – not the quantity of the music, of course, but the abundance of the new. Stravinsky's art continued to mature with each opus, and to grow in spirit as well as in mastery, yet *Agon*, composed at seventy-five, is the music of a young man, a younger one, first-time listeners might reasonably suppose, than the sixty-five-year-old (official retirement age!) composer of *Orpheus*. Nor does the power of newness diminish in the *Requiem Canticles*, written at eighty-four, but in which age is betrayed only by the intensity of focus. Stravinsky came fresh to everything, in life as in art, and as a listener as well as a composer, being able to hear the Beethoven quartets again and again, for instance, but always for the first time. Whatever his other powers in comparison to those of the great composers, no one has equalled him in his capacity for rejuvenation.

One might adduce from this year's City Ballet Festival that not all of Stravinsky's music lends itself to choreography: the Octet, for example, the Concerto for Two Solo Pianos, and the Serenade in A, though one of the problems in this last was that the volume of the offstage piano was unable to compete with the thunder of the onstage hoofs. Yet it could be the choreographers who lacked the skill to borrow from Stravinsky, which is to say that the same scores might have stirred other imaginations to better effect. *Duo concertant*, one of Balanchine's new marvels, was no more promising as raw material than these other three concert pieces.

Clearly not all Stravinsky *should* be choreographed, including the early, and fitfully bombastic, Symphony in E Flat, which is not remarkably prophetic, and is too long for a mere lesson in origins. Few or none of the composer's characteristics (except one foiled sequence) are discernible in it, nor is it redeemed by his orchestral skill, in spite of Miaskovsky's remark after the first performance: 'More instrumentation than music.' Neither did *The Faun and the Shepherdess* add much. The performance was provided with scenery – a backdrop of Central Park in the still further polluted future (down to eleven trees), with the soprano pitched like a pup tent in the foreground. But if a concert piece, why not one containing more Stravinsky than Tchaikovsky? And when the verse is Pushkin's, why not sing it in Russian? One may as well not understand Russian as not understand English, and the first English word that I 'understood' was 'candidity'.

The festival being homage to a composer, the role of music in ballet was recognized before all else. But no musician, no conductor, followed Stravinsky *all* the way as did George Balanchine. When *Agon* and the Movements were new, and Variations was the piece that passeth all understanding, it was New York's resident dance company, not the Philharmonic or the visiting orchestras, which gave us the opportunity to hear them. Moreover, the ballet orchestra plays the music very capably even though it performs under great handicaps. The acoustics of the pit are an unbreakable sound barrier, isolating one section from another with deleterious effects on ensemble, balance, intonation. (The basses in the Exaudi of the *Canticles* could have played the A sharp in tune only by marking the string with chalk.) The orchestra is further hampered by an insufficiency of strings, especially violins, which can scarcely be heard in many tutti passages and which even when playing alone, in *Apollo* and *The Cage* (Concerto in D), sound as if they could be in a cistern. Contrast this with the percussion, every utility of which from knocked-over music stand to dropped trombone-mute resounds in the outer lobby.

It would be an impertinence to extol the dancers, whose *esprit de corps* (*de ballet*) explains why, in a sense, the week was no seven-day wonder. One observation that could be risked is that the balance of power between the sexes is shifting, that either the company's long tradition of female supremacy is being challenged or Balanchine is giving the male dancers greater participation. In any case, dancers, by themselves, are no more than intelligent acrobatic anatomies. Ballets are made by choreographers, and of these the City Ballet has all but cornered the market. Balanchine classicism is still the company's only style, despite strong offshoots by Robbins. All of the successes were products of one or the other, as well as triumphs of dancing over storytelling. But the failures (*Firebird*, in this version, and *The Song of the Nightingale*) and the mixed bags (*Pulcinella* and *Orpheus*) prove the same: plot pieces, pageants, the world of make-believe are not the City Ballet's forte. It follows, too, that costumes and décors are not only inessential but a liability. (In *Firebird* they were a disaster.)

The Nightingale should be given in the complete 1914 score, with the singers in the pit. Stravinsky was right in insisting that *The Song of the Nightingale* is not a ballet, but it could have been a better one on this occasion if the Nightingale herself had been more active and the Emperor rather less, for, though near death, he still fights several rounds of a wrestling match. Purely as music, however, the piece promises more than it delivers. As for *Pulcinella*, Eugene Berman's combinations of rags and riches, Piranesi and Callot, filled the stage and the eye, but play-acting is not for the City Ballet.

The difficulties with *Orpheus* may have begun with the casting of the title part. M. Bonnefous is a natural comic, darting here and there like Buster Keaton, then rapidly looking about to see if he is in the right place. Once he was not, having miscalculated his distance from Green Mountain, which he backed into instead of vaulting, but which a hand with 'the power to move mountains' quickly uprighted. The hard-labouring damned on the rock piles in Hades looked like weight lifters in a gym, while the stones themselves would have been more useful on Earth, replacing the attic staircase from which the god takes off for Parnassus in *Apollo*.

Not all of the successes and failures can be attributed to a position on one side or the other of the categorical fence between storytelling and classic dance. *The Cage*, for one exception, is a prime example of a mistaken tendency of choreographers to 'orchestrate' rather than to come in from an angle. And whatever the reasons for the failure of the Concerto for Piano and Winds, the ballet could have been improved only if the musicians had been on the stage and the dancers in the pit. The festival's biggest hit, for its length, was the *Circus Polka*, with Robbins as ringmaster and the Ballet School's little girls as powder puffs, that being what they looked like in their tutus. But its companion piece for grown-up little girls, *Scherzo à la russe*, failed to hatch. The accordion-style music seemed to require at least one male, the stage full of hens at least one rooster.

Next year's Stravinsky week should open with that perfect programme, untried even by Diaghilev: the complete *Firebird*, *Petrushka*, *The Rite of Spring*. Balanchine does not believe that *The Rite* can be danced, but he has not yet seen the recently recovered score of the Stravinsky–Nijinsky choreography. This outlines a strictly musical approach to the ballet, contrapuntal in movement and phrasing and with no attempt to imitate or match the images of the orchestra. The year 1973 is *The Rite*'s sixtieth anniversary. If only to render historical service, the City Ballet should produce this greatest of all ballets in the version in which it was conceived, Robbins choreographing the groups, Balanchine the Chosen One and the other solo parts. *Renard*, *Histoire du soldat*, and *Les*

Noces comprise a second natural, sequential programme, and *Les Noces* still awaits a performance based on Stravinsky's own stage directions.

A complete *Le Baiser de la fée* is also overdue. The four-movement symphonic-form *Divertimento* that Stravinsky excerpted from it is ruined by the peremptory ending. Balanchine's excerpts, though weak in musical shape, were one of the festival's peaks, nevertheless, which indicates that the whole would be a supersuccess. *Le Baiser* belongs on a programme with revivals of that first Stravinsky–Balanchine–Kirstein collaboration, *Jeu de cartes*, and the last, *Variations*. Room could be found on other evenings for *Perséphone*, not yet staged in New York (or anywhere, properly), and *The Flood*, which should appeal to Mr Robbins's genius as well as to his showmanship.

The Violin Concerto, *Duo concertant*, *Requiem Canticles*, 'Dumbarton Oaks', *Circus Polka* must be repeated, along with Capriccio, Movements, and the Trilogy, this last in the achronological order *Orpheus, Agon, Apollo*, as Stravinsky and Balanchine did it in Hamburg in 1962. (The birth of *Apollo* was more beautiful in the original choreography, incidentally, with the unswaddling of the god like the unwinding of a *geisha* from her *obi*.) Thus an even more dazzling celebration would be assured for next June. I can hardly wait for the mock-Bayreuth fanfare in the foyer, the entry into the arena, and the thumbs-up for the company that is America's greatest artistic pride.

17

THE RELEVANCE AND PROBLEMS
OF BIOGRAPHY

Reviewing a life of Wagner, W. H. Auden wrote that 'on principle, I object to biographies of artists, since I do not believe that knowledge of their private lives sheds any significant light on their works. . . However, the story of Wagner's life is absolutely fascinating, and it would be so if he had never written a note.'

But if Wagner had never written a note, would he have had that fascinating life? And, apart from the doubtful assumption that we read an artist's biography primarily for illumination of his work, is it always true that nothing 'significant' about the art is revealed from study of the life? Further, can it be taken for granted that public and private are always separable? They are not, at any rate, in the case of Igor Stravinsky.

A celebrated artist for more than sixty years, Stravinsky left an immense public biography. This can be found in newspaper files, in recorded talk, and on film[1] in the cities in which he performed, attended performances, and toured as a private yet always inescapably public person. Some of this public view of him blends into the private. It does not do so in a taped public interview such as he gave at the University of Cincinnati in 1965, for he was conscious of himself and the audience in his every remark. But the reels of the talk made during recording sessions in the 1960s contain glimpses of the private Stravinsky, since he was unaware that the machines had been

Read at Goldwin Smith Hall, Cornell University, 29 March 1973, and at Breasted Hall, University of Chicago, 10 April 1973.

---

left on when he was *not* conducting, and that in effect he had been Watergated.

The same can be said of at least some of the two hundred hours of film that CBS took of him in New York, Paris, Switzerland, Warsaw, Rome and Hollywood in 1965, as well as of footage, official and unofficial, from the USSR and other countries, by cameramen known and unknown, professional and amateur, including members of the orchestras he conducted.[2] No one can say to what extent Stravinsky may have been conscious of the lens, but it must be conceded that the line between public and private is difficult to draw. No less apparently, the forms of biography have changed. Ideally, Stravinsky's should be issued in cassettes with accompanying album notes.

But the intersection of public and private goes beyond these electronic encroachments. Stravinsky's art was directly altered by public events – unlike Wagner's, whose career was disrupted by the Dresden Revolution of 1848, but whose music does not seem to have been affected either in its course of development or in substance. The Russian Revolution, on the other hand, changed both the direction and content of Stravinsky's work, most importantly by depriving him of his mother tongue as the language of his vocal music, Russian being impractical for him in his life as an exile. What is more, this deprivation occurred just as he had begun to explore new possibilities of combining syllables and words with music, experiments that could not be pursued in the Latin, French, English and Hebrew texts of the post-Russia years, despite his contentions that his approach was the same in these other languages as it had been in Russian.

The Revolution of 1917 had indirect effects on Stravinsky's music. For one thing, the accidents of Russian birth and American residence, and the failure of the two governments to sign the Berne Copyright Convention, cheated him of the largest part of the income from his works. To try to remedy this, he rearranged most of his Russian period music for copyright purposes, often giving as much time to this task as he did to composing new music. On 17 August 1920, for instance, he informed a publisher: 'I have spent six months (October, November, December 1918, and January, February, March 1919) composing [the new *Firebird* Suite].' As a further result of the same copyright predicament, Stravinsky was forced to earn a living as a conductor. He enjoyed conducting his music and hoped to establish performing traditions by doing so, but to play Tchaikovsky's Second Symphony a dozen times, largely for money and because it could be rehearsed in less time than any of his own music of comparable length was another matter, and it kept him from composing. During the Second World War, when his European royalties were nonexistent and his ASCAP payments were in three figures, Stravinsky was better known in America as a conductor than as a composer.

During the forties, too, the kind of commission that Stravinsky sought and often accepted reflects these straitened financial circumstances. In pursuit of a popular, paying success, or an acceptable film, for which he would write a do-it-once-and-retire score, he was forever chasing wild geese, among them Paul Whiteman, Billy Rose, Woody Herman, and Sam Goldwyn. His most spectacular flops in this sense – the 1940 Tango, for one (Stravinsky's 'last tango', mercifully!) – were in fact openly aimed at the commercial market. As a result, the Stravinsky *Köchelverzeichnis* contains too many tiny, if genial, masterpieces-for-money – the *Preludium*, *Circus Polka*, *Norwegian Moods*, *Scherzo à la russe*, *Babel* – and too few larger works, or works born purely of inner necessity.

I do not wish to add to the history-of-what-might-have-been, yet circumstances unquestionably did send Stravinsky's genius along some strange detours. In contrast, one thinks of the no less impecunious composer of the early *Ring* operas piling up the creations of *his* inner world even without prospects of their performance – though neither the artistic dimensions nor the ethical systems of the two musicians are comparable, Stravinsky, unlike Wager, having been a firm believer in earning his own way and in paying his own bills.

Let me proceed to the 'problems' of my title as they confront the Stravinsky biographer. In 1965, moving to a new home, the composer marked the two largest packets of his personal correspondence: 'To Be Destroyed After My Death'. But since he was in his mid-eighties at the time, why did he not carry out this destruction himself, if that were what he really wanted? The answer, I believe, is that he *did* intend to read and destroy the letters, but lacking time he was determined to prevent anyone else from seeing them in the eventuality that his own opportunity never came. He wrote this testamentary instruction on a day when he had been destroying letters and papers by the bushel. Moreover, during the sixteen years before that, I often saw him read and burn old correspondence. Clearly he wished to preserve nothing personal in his so-called archives, and, if the occasion had arisen, he would have made an *auto-da-fé* of them.

So far from condoning any personal biography, if Stravinsky had allowed himself to think about it, he would have specified in his will that none be written. Further, I am bound to admit that he would have agreed with Auden on the *ir*relevance of biography. Several lives of the composer were published during his lifetime, after all, and in his opinion none of them was of the slightest use in relation to his art. It is hardly surprising that his autobiography is one of the least 'personal' books of its kind ever written, and I, for one, am convinced that his principal motive in writing this book was to bring in money, and that the formation of his artistic creed and the correction of facts about his life were less important to him. That the book signally failed to accomplish even the financial objective is patently due to this avoidance of the personal.

The microfilming of Stravinsky's archives was botched for the reason that the photographers, unsupervised in their work, copied not only priceless papers but also useless catalogues, programmes of concerts in no way related to

Stravinsky, and, in short, everything in the *omnium gatherum* of the storage area. At the other extreme, lacking a definition of the archives, the team neglected to reproduce photographs (some of which contain as much information as some of his letters), ignored the contents of his libraries and even failed to copy his piano and conducting scores. These last are rich in revisions and annotations that should be preserved in a variorum edition, but none was photographed, and during the dismantling of the composer's library in 1970, when he had moved from California to New York, many items disappeared. I hardly need to add that the microfilmers also overlooked his library of music by other composers, some of it with comments in his hand.

Stravinsky possessed few documents dealing with the years before 1911, and not many more for the period between that year and 1914, when he was already thirty-two. Obviously this first third of his life, whether or not it included his greatest compositions, was as important in the formative sense as it is in anyone else's. But the history of these years can be completed only by the cooperation of individuals and organizations in many countries, the Soviet Union above all. The composer's early and most interesting letters are there, along with his earliest manuscripts and all of the Stravinsky family papers. Clearly a full exchange with the USSR must take place before any biographical study can be considered.

Whether or not Stravinsky's 1962 visit to Russia was a turning point in the musical life of his homeland, it was widely regarded at the time as merely another in the composer's pattern of reversals. Hosts and guest alike had been pouring abuse on each other for forty years, and, by the date of the trip, neither side had recanted. Officially, Stravinsky was still the USSR's arch symbol of capitalist decadence, and as late as the late fifties his Harvard lecture on Soviet music was considered too 'reactionary' to be published in France. A *rapprochement* seemed improbable, to say the least. Yet the visit took place. And now, some of his concert music, at least, is played and recorded in the USSR, and his early compositions, his letters, and biographies and analyses of his work are published with ever greater momentum. The return of the native in 1962 provided the impetus, and a historical switch is occurring, not comparable to Constantine's conversion of the Empire, but certainly to the cessation of the persecution before it.

The following selection from the list of Soviet publications begins with two that Stravinsky himself knew, the volume of *Soviet Music* (Moscow, 1966) containing his letters to N. Roerich, and the monograph *Stravinsky's Early Ballets* (Moscow, 1967) by Irina Vershinina. The composer read the former in a fever of rediscovery, the latter with mixed emotions, for while its very existence was a proof of the growing popularity of his music in the USSR, the rudimentary errors annoyed him.[3] I should add that Russian recognition meant more to him than that of the rest of the world, a fact I myself failed to realize until 1962. Coming to the Stravinsky household in 1948, I did not perceive the degree of its Russianness and have only recently discovered that as late as 1947 (the year 1 BC), the language, friends, habits of life of the home were almost exclusively Russian. It follows that I was also unaware of the extent to which my American views, language, and attitudes were displacing their Russian ones. And, finally, I did not see that Stravinsky's constantly expressed antipathy to most things Russian was a question of protesting too much.

Among the Soviet publications to date, the following are especially important:

(1) *Creative Formative Years of I. F. Stravinsky* by V. Smirnov (Muzyka, Leningrad, 1970). This book contains a facsimile of a Piano Scherzo, composed in 1902.

(2) *F. I. Stravinsky: Essays, Letters, Memoirs*, compiled and annotated by L. Kutateladze, edited by A. Gozenpude (Muzyka, Leningrad, 1972). The book contains letters to F. I. Stravinsky (father of the composer) from Borodin, Stassov, Rimsky-Korsakov, Anatoly Tchaikovsky, Chaliapin, Cui – and the teenage Igor Stravinsky.

(3) *Dialogues*, an omnibus of volumes 1–4 of the Stravinsky – Craft conversation books, edited and annotated by I. Beletsky and I. Blazhkov (Muzyka, Leningrad, 1971).

First, a word about number 2, the book about Stravinsky's father. A booklet on the composer's parent appeared in 1951. Stravinsky read it without comment, probably because it consisted of little more than an outline of the eminent singer's career, a list of his sixty-six roles at the Maryinsky Theatre, and a garland of quotations from Tchaikovsky and others on the elder Stravinsky's remarkable artistic and intellectual qualities. Unlike the earlier publication, the new book looks at him as the father of the composer, though without slighting the achievements of the parent in his own right.

One of the outstanding opera singers and actors of his time, Fyodor Ignatievich Stravinsky was also renowned as a gifted graphic artist and a *littérateur* and bibliophile. I have often heard Stravinsky refer to his father's talents as a painter and watercolourist but had seen no example of his work until George Balanchine gave me a set of colour photographs of it that he had acquired in a Leningrad library. The most striking of these are self-portraits in the costumes of various operatic roles, of which the new biography reproduces thirty-two, but unfortunately not in colour. Of privately owned libraries, Fyodor Ignatievich's was one of the largest in all Russia, of such importance that in January 1919 the Ispolkom of the Union of Communes of the Northern Territory passed a resolution placing the Stravinsky St Petersburg apartment under protective guard. Three years later his widow bequeathed the music section to the Petrograd Conservatory. In 1941–42, during the siege of Leningrad, most of the remaining books[4] were destroyed.

The biography of Fyodor Ignatievich Stravinsky – bookish singer, actor in public, introvert in private – is indispensable to anyone interested in the son, for the composer inherited not only his father's musical gifts but some of his complex character as well. And Fyodor Ignatievich endowed Igor

Fyodorovich with other talents, too: histrionic (the composer's early letters describe his acting in amateur theatricals, and C. F. Ramuz's correspondence reveals that Stravinsky entertained the idea of playing the part of the Devil in the premiere of *Histoire du soldat*).

Before examining the Soviet edition of the Stravinsky–Craft *Dialogues*, I must explain that the junior partner in this collaboration always regarded the senior's recollections, with their exaggerations, distortions and other nuances of memory, as more important than the encylopedia facts. Junior thought that 'anyone' could dig out the dates and places, and though 'anyone' could not, Soviet musicologists could and did: I am grateful to them for their paralipomena.

Apart from the data on the composer's early years, the *Dialogues* offer several glimpses concerning the state of the arts in the Soviet Union in the all-too-recent past. Some of the cultural blind spots are familiar, and when the Soviet editors chide Stravinsky for his partiality to Kandinsky, Larionov, Malevich and other émigrés, while ignoring the Socialist Realist School, the reader feels that Zhdanovism is not altogether dead. When the editors identify Lourdes (which Stravinsky mentions in connection with Werfel's *Bernadette*) by referring to Emile Zola's writings on the subject, the effect is bizarre. Readers should be advised, too, that the Soviet text is not always reliable on Stravinsky's non-Russian music. Thus the Ugly Duchess, in Auden's first draft of *The Rake's Progress*, was not, as the Soviet editors suppose, based on Marguerite, Duchess of Tyrol (1318–69), the protagonist of Feuchtwanger's *The Ugly Duchess*. Stravinsky knew Feuchtwanger in California but had not read this novel. The conception and the name originated with Auden.

The book's scholarship on the Russian works is more sound. Stravinsky's songs of Yuletide divination for female chorus are traced to Afanasiev's *The Slav's Poetic Attitudes Toward Nature* (Vol. II, Moscow, 1868, p. 194), and the texts are analyzed both linguistically and in terms of their symbolism; by means of the former, one of them, *Chigisy Across*

Yauza, is identified as Central rather than, as Stravinsky mistakenly thought, Northern Russian. This is run-of-the-mill research, but a run no one else had taken. More legwork of this kind provides information concerning the concerts and operas the composer attended in his youth, his studies with Rimsky-Korsakov, and the discrepancies between Stravinsky's accounts of the stagings of his Russian theatre pieces and those of his collaborators.

These new corrections and amplifications do not alter our picture of Stravinsky in any fundamental, but they help to complete it, and they modify the colours of some of its details. When the composer led a search for the home of his birth, 5 October 1962, he was unable to find it because of a change in street names. The location has now been established as Khudyntzev Cottage, 137 Shveitzarsky Street (now Uprising Street), in Oranienbaum (now Lomonosov). Corrective dendrological surgery has also been performed on Stravinsky's version of his family tree, with the result that the two oldest branches have been regrafted. The great-grandfather who lived to a hundred and eleven was not Ignace Ignatievich Stravinsky, as the greatest of his great-grandsons wrote, but I. I. Skhorokhodov, the composer's maternal great-grand-father. Furthermore, this Methuselah reached the age of a hundred and twelve (1767–1879). Stravinsky's error probably occurred while identifying a medallion portrait of the centenarian on its reverse; he appears inadvertently to have switched the family names, both ancestors having the same initials. As for Ignace Ignatievich, he died in Tiflis, on 29 May 1893, an eighty-four-year-old stripling.

Stravinsky's memory of distances and dates has been extensively corrected but seldom in a subject of much consequence. And in at least one instance the Soviet editors base their rectification on a dubious premise. Stravinsky recalled that in his youth he had admired Tanaev's *Mobile Counterpoint of the Strict School*, but this treatise appears not to have been published until 1909, by which date, the editors reason, the composer would have been beyond consulting a textbook.

Yet Stravinsky was never above reading even the most elementary theoretical writings, and this was true throughout his life; at the age of seventy, for example, he was deeply influenced by Krenek's *Studies in Counterpoint*. Whatever Stravinsky's opinion of didactic music, he did not despise didactic books.

The addressees of Stravinsky's Russian letters include members of the Rimsky-Korsakov family, musicians, publishers, editors, artists of the Diaghilev circle, even government officials. To one of the latter, Commissar Arthur Lourié, Stravinsky wrote on 9 September 1920, asking for assistance in obtaining a visa for his mother to leave the USSR and move to France; in later years Lourié became the composer's musical secretary and *éminence grise*. Here is another note to an official, this one the Commissariat of Education, which I quote because it reveals the composer trying to keep the door open, and adds to the background of his return to Russia thirty-seven years later:

Paris, 18 August 1925

Owing to numerous prior engagements abroad, extending into the foreseeable future, I am unhappily obliged to decline your kind invitation to undertake a concert tour of Moscow, Leningrad, Kiev, and Odessa. I thank you very much for your kind words, in any event, and I hope that in the future it will be possible personally to acquaint my countrymen with my art.

Pray accept, Madame, assurances of my utmost respect.
Igor Stravinsky

P.S.: Forgive me, Madame, for not answering you in Russian, but I do not have a typewriter with Russian letters.[5]

Stravinsky's correspondence grew with his fame, of course, and by the twenties had reached unmanageable proportions. French superseded Russian as the language of the larger part of it, though important French letters were usually drafted in Russian. Moreover, most letters from the beginning of the

French years until the end of his life were written with secretarial assitance, from which point they decline in interest. This is partly because the letters of the Russian years were not concerned with posterity, and because, as he grew older, his disputes with publishers, conductors, and critics consumed time that formerly might have been spent sharing artistic conceptions with friends.

Stravinsky's letters to C. F. Ramuz, written directly in French, show contradictory sides of the composer's character as well as reveal the profound change in that character which took place when Russian influences began to give way to French. He writes with gusto about his ill health, as he continued to do up to his eighty-eighth year. Sometimes, but rarely, he states his grievances immediately. More often his true feelings can be found only between the lines. Rarely, too, is he generous with words, and most of the letters are more circumspect and stingy with them than the correspondence of any other composer. When Ramuz sent his *Souvenirs sur Igor Stravinsky*, the contents clearly surprised the composer, and not altogether agreeably. Perhaps I am reading too much into Stravinsky's answer because I know that he disliked the book and felt that it had exploited a private relationship. But the adroitness with which he avoids the larger questions, while meeting the request for criticism with only insignificant details, is typical of Stravinsky and rich in clues to his character.

The editorial difficulties presented by the American letters, because of the farrago of styles in both English and French and the ever-varying Americanisms, are almost insuperable. Stravinsky's principal scribe before 1947 was Mrs Adolph Bolm, from which date until 1969 the position was assumed by his son-in-law, an example of whose collaboration is apparent in a letter about Dylan Thomas published in the magazine *Adam* in 1954. Other letters of these years were written with my help, which is all too apparent in a note concerning Artur Schnabel written in 1961 and published in the London *Observer*. Both missives say neither more nor less than what Stravinsky wanted them to say, but they lack style, the true mark of personality which can be conveyed only by one's own writing and which *is* found in the letters to Ramuz.

The word 'problems' in my title refers in part to certain perplexing areas in Stravinsky's life and work. Too many even to be enumerated here, they range from such large questions as his religious beliefs to a host of relatively minor ones. Among the latter, for instance, I would classify the gaps in our understanding of Stravinsky's musical origins, for the leap from academic anonymity into *Firebird* is extraordinarily sudden.

Still another area to be explored is that of the genesis of Stravinsky's subject matter. André Rimsky-Korsakov broached this in the Russian magazine *Apollo*, no. 1, 1915, remarking that Stravinsky had begun with the fairy tale and 'progressed' to primitivism. But fairy tales were to remain a part of Stravinsky's imaginative world (in *Le Baiser de la fée*), as was primitivism, though under the larger concept of ritual, both secular (*Les Noces*) and sacred (the Mass). To these he was to add morality plays (*Histoire du soldat*, *The Rake's Progress*), myths (*Oedipus Rex*, *Perséphone*), and, finally, Biblical drama (*The Flood*, *The Stoning of St Stephen*, *Abraham and Isaac*).

Stravinsky's obsession with the player-piano is an enigma of a different kind, important only because the transcribing of virtually all of his music for this instrument, up to the late 1920s, occupied such a disproportionate amount of his time and energy. What continues to be enigmatic in these labours is his failure to exploit the machine's mechanical advantages, never venturing to devise complex rhythms for it (by subdividing the beat beyond the possibilities of human performers), or even to employ such an effect as a glissando for the entire keyboard in the fraction of a second. His *Etude* for Pianola (1917) and the pianola part in the penultimate version of *Les Noces* (1919) use the contraption only to economize on live pianists and to assure a rigid rendition.

Stravinsky's 'creative processes' are no less mysterious than those of any other great artist, but their patterns often contradict claims put forth by the composer himself. For example, he often declared that musical ideas always came to him in the timbres of particular instruments or voices, which he seldom changed in later stages. Yet his sketchbooks belie him. The String Concerto included winds in the original drafts, the *Symphonies of Wind Instruments* featured violin and viola, in what later became the duos for flute and clarinet, and the second section of the first movement of the four-hand Sonata was conceived and scored as an orchestra piece, in which form it has nothing pianistic about it but might be an offshoot of the Symphony in C.

A larger and more puzzling question than any of these is why, at the end of 1944, did Stravinsky, a communicant of the Russian Orthodox Church, compose a Kyrie and a Gloria for a Roman Catholic Mass? It was not in fulfilment of a commission and had not been proposed to him. His avowed reason, that he was inspired to write a more liturgical kind of music than he found in Mozart's Masses, is hardly a complete answer. So far as musical influences enter into the question, he was engrossed at the time in all the music he could find by Jacopo da Bologna and Machaut. Yet this Mass is no mere exercise in musical style but a work born of religious faith.

Having lived close to Stravinsky for nearly a quarter of a century, and much of that time in the same house with him, I knew him to be, as the expression goes, 'profoundly religious'. But what this means in his case I am unable to say. He believed in the Devil Incarnate, and in a literal, Dantesque Hell, Purgatory, Paradise. And he was deeply superstitious, forever crossing himself and those around him, wearing sacred medals,[6] and performing compulsive acts without which the auguries for the day were certain to be unfavourable. Furthermore, he believed in miracles, both large and of the Houdini sort, and never questioned the provenance of any sacred relic. Dogmatism was another part of his religion, as it was of Stravinsky himself. It is ironic that the opinions of this least syllogistic and, in method, least Socratic of men have appeared in the form of dialogues, though of course the form in this case is artificial, and, even so, was in Stravinsky's mind closer to Hebrew versicle and response than to Platonic question and answer.

That Stravinsky had reached a spiritual crisis in 1944 is evident in his reading, which consisted of parts of the *Summa*, Bossuet's *Lettres sur l'Evangile*, Bloy, Bernanos and T. S. Eliot.[7] In that year, too, Stravinsky visited Santa Clara, the Convent of Dominican Sisters in Sinsinawa, Wisconsin, and he was often with Jacques Maritain. At about the same time, Stravinsky read Ramuz's *Questions* and filled the margins with criticism of its Protestantism, while endorsing the Roman Catholic views of C.-A. Cingria in the margins of *his* books. Yet none of this accounts for the creation of that Mass for a church which Stravinsky never joined and which disappointed him by failing to adopt the work.

But a more powerful force than dogma in Stravinsky was his abiding intellectual curiosity, his openness to ideas and irresistible attraction to new ones, and his limitlessly receptive mind. The genius of his artistic instinct overrode all else.

Notes

1 Films of Stravinsky conducting survive from as early as the 1920s. His first television-broadcast concert took place on WGN, Chicago, 13 January 1954.

2 The Los Angeles Philharmonic violist, Philip Kahgan, recorded Stravinsky on film conducting in 1937, and the New York Philharmonic tuba player, Sam Butterfield, filmed Stravinsky rehearsing the *Symphony of Psalms* in 1966.

3 On page 137, Vershinina refers to a 'suite' from *The Rite of Spring*, and its wide performance during the years 1914–21, when the music was not performed at all. Stravinsky underscored this, and corrected it in the margin to 'the whole ballet'. On page 140 he changed Vershinina's comment on the reception of Nijinsky's choreography of *The Rite* from 'not just' to '*un*just'.

4 Among the few volumes in the composer's possession was a

copy of the original edition of the plays of Catherine the Great, stamped with the imperial seal of Tsarskoe Seloe.

5 Diaghilev found one in London in August 1928, and made a gift of it to Stravinsky, who typed all of his Russian letters on it thereafter, and who appears never to have made a typographical mistake.

6 An image of '*La Vierge de perpétuel secours*', with votary candle, stood in his home at 25, rue du Faubourg St-Honoré.

7 He underscored approvingly two passages in the essay 'Catholicism and International Order', in his copy of Eliot's *For Lancelot Andrewes*.

18

PLURALISTIC STRAVINSKY

The Apollonian Clockwork[1] is an exhilarating account of a search, external and internal, for Stravinsky, both as a composer and as a man. Following his own example in breaking from the traditional concept of the linear development of musical evolution, the authors suspend chronology and jump 'in open form' from one episode to another in the life and the music, making illuminating connections in new directions, in an ironic and witty way. The criticism, largely confined to music examples, is musical perception as profound as any in the academic studies implicitly mocked. One chapter is subtitled 'Gruelling Description of the Numbers 3 and 5 in the Oratorio *Threni*'. Another exhibits features of Stravinsky's 'style and manner' through the few altered and added notes in his droll arrangement for solo violin of 'La Marseillaise'. Still another finds characteristics of his musical personality in the intermittently wayward octave and unison doublings of melodic lines, as in the beginning scale of the Concertino (though one wonders why the example of not-quite-successive octaves at the beginning of *Symphony of Psalms* was omitted).

Messrs Schönberger and Andriessen must be thanked for two acts of iconoclasm performed, respectively, on the myth of Stravinsky's association with C. F. Ramuz and on the musical philosophy of Ernest Ansermet. The young Dutch authors have correctly surmised that the artistic limitations of the librettist of *Histoire du soldat* had begun to dismay the composer even before its premiere, and that Ramuz thereafter became a millstone. As for his book, *Souvenirs sur Igor*

Stravinsky (1929), its 'tone of pathetic simplicity, sentimental unaffectedness, and tormented humbleness, is unbearable' – a judgement that makes Pierre Suvchinsky's claim, quoted in François Lesure's *Stravinsky: Etudes et témoignages*,[2] that Ramuz was '*la plus grande amitié*' of the composer's life, raise doubts about how much this time-to-time Russian friend really understood about Stravinsky.

Turning to Ansermet's 1961 tome, *Les Fondements de la musique dans la conscience humaine*, Schönberger and Andriessen attack the 'incorrigible school teacher' and 'formalist' for setting out to demonstrate 'that dodecaphony was ipso facto nonsense':

> [Ansermet's] blind faith in. . .Husserl left no room for the notion that, precisely in art, wrong premises can lead to valid consequences. . . You remember such a book only for its rancour, its convulsiveness, its ideological fanaticism and its anti-Semitism[3] wrapped up in phenomenological terminology.

The Apollonian Clockwork should also be read for its comments on the *Requiem Canticles*, after which, the authors say, 'Anyone who writes a liturgical requiem for large choir and orchestra will look like a taxidermist.' Stravinsky's *Requiem* is not about the Last Judgement, for 'that could only come out positive; the Judgment didn't have to be feared. Death had already been celebrated too often':

> For the first time since [*Les Noces*], Stravinsky uses real clock-bells. . .playing together with two instruments, one of which (vibraphone) he had never used before. . . At the end of your life, doing things you have never done before – that's conjuring.
>
> In the closing bar, the strokes of the clock and the chord of Death come together for the first and last time, the twenty-third beat of Part B [occurs at the same time] as the thirty-third stroke of the clock. The Hour of Truth. Wasn't there

someone who died after 33 years? . . . The twelve strokes
that announce Shadow in *The Rake's Progress* are twelve
silent strokes in the *Requiem Canticles*: there are twelve beats
of silence in the Postlude.

The Apollonian Clockwork is the most ingenious, sharply
observed, and original book likely to be written about the
composer for a long time, though the authors believe that 'the
actual influence of Stravinsky has just begun'. Today's 'new
music', they write, places serialism as 'the farthest consequence of nineteenth-century music, in the mausoleum of the
past perfect tense.' The new generation, they say, is drawn
to Stravinsky, and away from, among others, Boulez and
Xenakis.

To turn from Schönberger and Andriessen to François
Lesure's thorny centenary garland is to move backward two
or three generations. The book features forty pages of reflections by Suvchinsky and a survey on the texts of *The Rite* by
Louis Cyr. The other contributors include Claude Helffer on
the 1924 Concerto, Célestin Deliège on Stravinsky *vis-à-vis*
Schoenberg in 1912, and Stefan Jarocinsky's 'Stravinsky as
an Apostle of Apollonian Art'. Not many of the views are
new, and only Cyr offers the results of research.

Suvchinsky's Stravinsky is still the Russian émigré of the
1920s and 1930s; or, at any rate, the phenomenal powers of
growth and renewal manifested in the later years are not
mentioned. Moreover, the composer remains the '*homme
simple*' of Ramuz rather than the multiform creative personality revealed by the Schönberger–Andriessen book. Not all
of Suvchinsky's conclusions are mistaken, as when he recog-
nizes that 'Stravinsky was as passionate in his abstract
speculations concerning philosophy and theology as he was
remote from social and political intellectuality' and that
'Stravinsky was no pessimist, but rather an "anti-optimist"
who, with wisdom, gaiety, humour. . .and profound sadness,

accepted the state of things that one cannot change. . .'
Suvchinsky believes that a crisis occurred in Stravinsky's life
when he discovered something so frightening that he determined not to think about it. Suvchinsky neither identifies nor
dates the experience, but surely it is related to 'the tragic
irony of [*Oedipus*], of the man who believes himself capable
of independent action, when in fact he is no more than the
divinely controlled agent of his own destruction.'⁴ In any
case, with the creation of *Oedipus Rex* Stravinsky renounced
all *sub specie saeculi* philosophies.

When Suvchinsky assures us that 'Stravinsky was indifferent to the pathetic plights of the people in Chekhov', I can
only declare a very different impression, one of a man who
read and reread the stories and letters, and who would go out
of his way to see the plays, even in bad English translations.
(He spent part of an evening in New York in September 1965
reading howlers in English versions of Chekhov to Elizabeth
Hardwick and Robert Lowell.)

Suvchinsky's factual misinformation is less consequential,
but he should not say that the original title of *The Rite* was
'The Great Sacrifice' (actually 'Holy Spring', *Vesna Sviaschennaya*), and that Scriabin and Stravinsky, 'these two great
musicians'—Stravinsky would hardly have appreciated that—
have at last 'been assimilated by the Russian conscience'. But
when did this happen? Actually, most of Stravinsky's music—
all of the Biblical kind and even that supreme expression of
Russian culture *Svadebka* [*Les Noces*]—is still unknown in
the USSR.

Louis Cyr should undertake, a full-length critical examination of the *Rite* texts, if only because his present essay is
outdated by the surfacing, in 1982, of the first orchestral
draft. Apart from that, Cyr shows good sense, for example in
supporting Ansermet's arguments in favour of the restoration
of the pizzicati in the 'Sacrificial Dance'. In revised versions,
Stravinsky required the strings to play arco only, for the
reason that the rapid switching between bows and fingers was
beyond the orchestral technique of 1913; but the alternating

modes of articulation are part of his original conception, as well as, so the Symphony in Three Movements confirms, an element in his style. The most important chapter in this much-needed book would be a detailed comparison of the 'Danse sacrale' in the earlier and 1943 scores, and a study of the drafts for the latter, including the Kestenbaum manuscript.

Though accurately describing Stravinsky's reactions to questions of performance as 'humbly acquiescent' one day and the opposite the next, Cyr mistakenly assumes that the composer was 'not interested in a critical edition of his works' or in 'establishing definitive versions' of them. (He met with his publishers in Paris in October and November 1968 with no other purpose in mind.) Cyr also suggests that the composer might not have made the two-hand reduction of the complete work, even though 'his' piano score is mentioned in letters as having been used during the first rehearsals, and though he had already acquired the habit, in Firebird and Petrushka, of preparing piano reductions as he composed; but the original manuscript, the scholar's corpus delicti, has not been found.[5]

The dust jacket of Stravinsky on Stage,[6] a reproduction of Goncharova's backcloth for the 'Kolybelnya' set in Firebird, is the book's most striking colour photograph, but the competition is close and includes a picture of the costumes worn by the Chosen One and the Sage in the 1913 Rite; Valentine Gross's pastel impressions of both tableaux in the same production; Bakst's design for Mavra; Dülberg's for the first scene of the 1928 Berlin Petrushka, which looks like an Atari game; Barsacq's Chirico-like scene for Perséphone; and several of Hockney's designs for the Glyndebourne Rake. Among the black-and-white illustrations, the greatest novelty is a selection of Matisse's drawings for The Song of the Nightingale. The last photograph in the book, of Balanchine and Stravinsky, has become deeply poignant.

The presentation of graphic art in Stravinsky on Stage is accompanied by valuable information about first performances and 'other major productions' of twenty pieces composed specifically for the theatre. Here, perhaps for the first time in book form, Vera Sudeikina, with Nicholas Galitzine, is given credit for the scenery and costumes of the first London staging of *Histoire du soldat*, on 10 July 1927. But it should also be noted that the original *Perséphone* (1934) did not run 'for only three performances': the production was revived for three more in the following year; that Rennert's 1963 *Oedipus* was given for the first time not at La Scala but at the Hamburg Opera; and that the unidentified 1948 New York revival of the same work, designed by Frederick Kiesler, took place at the Juilliard School.

In 'Stravinsky and Russian Pre-Literate Theater' (*19th Century Music*, Spring 1983), Simon Karlinsky observes that Stravinsky's stage works from *Petrushka* to the *Soldat* 'add up to a compendium of the native theatrical genres of old Russia.' 'Why,' Karlinsky asks, did 'this musical innovator choose to compose some of his most revolutionary works on subjects taken from archaic and, in his day, mostly defunct preliterary dramatized folklore. . . ?'; and his answer connects Stravinsky's approach to folklore with that of Symbolist poets and Modernist painters including Khlebnikov, Tsvetayeva, Remizov, and Chagall, as distinguished from the nineteenth-century 'hybridization with Western themes' of Pushkin, Glinka, and Rimsky-Korsakov.

The years 1909–17 were a period of new fascination with purely Russian art. Whereas Pushkin had borrowed 'The Golden Cockerel' from Washington Irving, and whereas even *Ruslan and Lyudmila* derives from Western elements as well as Russian folklore – like the music of Glinka's opera based on the poem – Stravinsky, in *Svadebka* and *Renard*, turned his back on the West. Karlinsky quotes the pianist Alexei Liubimov on these pieces: 'Archaism of melodies and dynamism of rhythms create an extraordinary impression of a natural grasp of the spirit and style of ancient peasant folklore.' By this time (1914–17) Stravinsky did not need the actual folk tradition but only the subject matter and the words (in 'phonetically transcribed dialect'). The result, Karlinsky writes, was 'dazzlingly original Russian music that was free of both ethnography and stylization.'

Turning to the *The Rite of Spring*, Karlinsky observes that 'with the introduction of the disciplines of anthropology in the nineteenth century, a wide array of seasonal folk customs and games were [*sic*] easily identified as direct descendants of ancient rituals. . .' With *Svadebka*, pagan survivals in Christian weddings, officially condemned for at least three centuries, are given permanent artistic form. Karlinsky remarks that when the basses sing the words '*Pod'na svad'bu*', which amount to a command to the Virgin Mary, we realize 'that the mother of the Savior is here replacing some ancient fertility goddess. In monotheistic religions, divinities do not get ordered about, but in *The Iliad* it was quite possible for a warrior to order the goddess off the battlefield.' The rituals and ceremonies of the Russian village wedding have been presented as staged theatre performances in the USSR as well as at Harvard University's Russian Research Center (May 1983), culminating in a performance of *Svadebka*.

Karlinsky devotes much space to correcting mistranslations of Stravinsky's Russian texts, a service for which we are grateful. But when he says that C.-F. Ramuz's French translations of Stravinsky's *skomorokh* (minstrel-buffoon) pieces 'deprive them of all connection' with their Russian meanings, we wonder if Ramuz can be blamed for what must have been Stravinsky's intention. After all, the translations are Stravinsky's in substance, and they date from the times of the compositions.[7] Clearly he was not then concerned to hide the anticlericalism of *Renard* – a 1930s letter, from Jacques Handschin, his St Petersburg friend of the *Firebird* period, reminds him that he used to be an ardent 'leftist' – or, forty years later, of *Svadebka*, when he wrote his own, most-unliteral English translation of the text, together with his phonetic version of the Russian into his orchestra score of the work.

But as Karlinsky points out, Stravinsky's own English titles of his *Podblyudnye* choruses belie their sense in Russian, including 'Podblyudnye' itself, which the composer translated as 'Saucers'. ('Dish-divination songs', Karlinsky proposes, though Webster's Dictionary gives 'dish' as both the first and second meanings of 'saucer'.) One of these choruses, 'Ovsen', is called 'Autumn' in the English edition – ironically, Karlinsky observes, since the Russian name is that of the first day of Spring in the pre-Christian calendar. Yet the piece was first published in German, at which time Stravinsky himself chose, or approved, the title 'Herbstlied' (1929 manuscript, now in Mainz); and the English was translated from the German, probably being thought suitable because of the connection with harvest. In any case, the question – why, when translating his Russian texts, did Stravinsky deliberately seem to ignore their original meanings? – is not fully answered.

Professor Karlinsky asserts that in the second decade of this century, when Stravinsky 'was creating these epochal scores, he was addressing a Russian audience. . .' Where? By Lake Geneva? True, for a moment in 1916 he had hoped for a performance of Renard in Russia, even though the piece was commissioned for presentation in a Paris salon. But by the time Svadebka was completed, and the Soldat – which Karlinsky likens to a folk play described by Dostoevsky as performed by convicts in a Siberian penal colony – Stravinsky knew that his audiences would be those of the Diaghilev ballet, which had never appeared in Russia, and after 1917 no longer aspired to go there.

The piano was the fulcrum of Stravinsky's musical thought, as Charles M. Joseph demonstrates,[8] and though his book naturally focuses on the keyboard works – solo, ensemble, and in transcriptions – it also helps to elucidate Stravinsky's music as a whole. Despite unreliable recent editing, the lack of a critical edition, and the inaccessibility of many of the original sources, Mr Joseph is a judicious guide from the sketches of the 'Tarantella' of 1896 to the last, unfinished, piano piece of 1967. His documentation is extensive, and some of it is new, such as the interview (New York, summer of 1981) with Juilliard professor Adele Marcus, who played the

Concerto per due pianoforti soli with the composer several times in the spring of 1940:

> Stravinsky sat very high at the piano. . . He was especially
> attentive to matters of rhythmic fidelity. . . He did not wish
> to rehearse very much and was nervous about performing. . .
> Before a performance, [he] would apply some concoctive
> paste to the pads of his fingers that would quickly dry and
> act as a weighting agent. . . It is known that Stravinsky
> seemed to be preoccupied with the element of key touch and
> weight peculiar to any one piano. . . It would appear that
> Stravinsky's mysterious adhesive substance was an attempt to
> counterbalance artificially the resistance of the piano's keys
> with which he found fault. . .

One of the most interesting sections in the book concerns the use of 'interval vectors' in analyzing the structure of the same concerto. Mr Joseph counts only six possible intervals – major and minor seconds and thirds, the perfect fourth, and the tritone – since he accepts the principle of complementary equivalency (e.g., a major sixth equals a minor third, and so on). But in the first bar, for example, some of us persist in hearing a minor tenth rather than a minor third, and, in the second bar, Piano I, a fifth, not its 'complement equivalent' fourth. Nevertheless, the approach enables the musical anatomist to show quickly how the notes in the first two bars, Piano II, comprising the vector 012120, are transposed to other parts of the piece.

Mr Joseph's coup is his discovery in the autograph piano score of *Firebird* – under our noses in the Morgan Library in New York – of major revisions no doubt undertaken in collaboration with Fokine during the creation of the ballet in the spring of 1910. Thus the six bars at $\boxed{46}$, leading to the 'Apparition of the Thirteen Princesses', were originally introduced just before the 'Apparition of the Firebird'; the 'Supplications of the Firebird' was only half as long in the first version; and the passage from $\boxed{103}$ to $\boxed{104}$ was a late interpolation from Kastchei's 'Dance', perhaps to anticipate that movement.

These *Firebird* repairs, probably made during the St Petersburg rehearsals of the ballet, vivify the description by Brussel, the French critic who heard Stravinsky play the score there for Diaghilev and others before the company came to Paris:

> We all met in the little ground-floor room on Zamiatin Perenlokm. . .the composer, young, slim. . .with vague meditative eyes, and lips set firm in an energetic-looking face, was at the piano. But the moment he began to play, the modest and dimly lighted room glowed with. . .radiance. . . The manuscript on the music-rest, scored over with fine pencillings, revealed a masterpiece.

The excerpts from twenty-two years of *Modern Music*[9] contain few judgments that have endured, but the book records one important musical insight, in Roger Sessions's 1928 essay 'On *Oedipus Rex*', and provides a gauge of the period as well as of the subsequent conquest of belletrist criticism by scientific musicology. Thus Robert Tangeman's 1945 article on the four-hand Sonata does not even refer to its Russian folksong sources, whereas anyone writing about the piece today would be obliged to speculate about the work that Stravinsky had originally thought of basing on them, 'Songs Lingering and Quiet' (a note in his hand, in Russian), for which he made a copy of No. 41, music in the character of the title.[10] (The composer found the Jurgenson volume *Russian Ballads and Folk Music*, title in English, in 1942, in a secondhand Los Angeles music store, priced $2.50.)

Stravinsky in 'Modern Music' reprints two minor classics, Lincoln Kirstein's 'Working with Stravinsky' (*Jeu de cartes*) and Frederick Jacobi's 'The New Apollo'. According to the latter, 'The composer indicated his desire that the first scene represents the birth of Apollo; that Apollo be born on the stage, springing full-grown from the womb of his mother. It was thought, however, not advisable to stage it in just this way

in Washington.' Sessions, following Arthur Lourié, wrote that
Oedipus is not

> tonal in the ordinary sense of the word. As in nearly all of
> Stravinsky's works, the shifting harmonies move around a
> clearly established harmonic axis. . . To give but one
> instance: the musical pages which embody the crucial
> moment of the drama are based on a persistently reiterated D
> minor harmony. The effect of such a style is one of great
> deliberation and stateliness of movement. Tonality. . .is in no
> sense a part of the structure of the whole.

This is central to the thesis, more than half a century later, of
the most important book so far to appear on the composer,
Pieter van den Toorn's *The Music of Igor Stravinsky*.[11] His
point of departure is that much of Stravinsky's harmony
cannot be described in 'conventional terms'. In a majority of
Stravinsky's works, van den Toorn writes, there is 'no
functional activity to legitimatize any C-scale tonally functional definition of. . .separate keys' which elaborates, in
different, more obscure language, Sessions's observation that
the magnetic attractions of harmonies to a triadic centre
should not be confounded with the larger, functional hier-
archical relationships of keys in the tonal system. This is not
true of all of Stravinsky's music, but the point is that he did
not think of his triadically pure cadences – 'terminating
conveniences', van den Toorn calls them – as keys. This is
proven by the composer's comments on Paul Collaer's notes
on the *Symphony of Psalms* in the original programme book
(December 1930), which attempt to explain that the first
movement 'modulates toward G major' and actually ends in
this key. Stravinsky vehemently recorded his disagreement in
underlinings and question marks.

So, too, twenty years ago, in 'Problems of Pitch Organization in Stravinsky', Arthur Berger understood that despite
Stravinsky's 'congenital orientation' toward 'traditional harmony', and the 'tonal bias' that obviously 'governed the

conception' of many pieces, the semblance of 'tonal functionality' in the bulk of Stravinsky's work is distinctly parenthetical.

Van den Toorn's analysis of Stravinsky's musical language is on a much higher level than any heretofore attempted, and his grasp of the composer's immense scope extends beyond that of any earlier writer. At the same time, van den Toorn's conspectus is not as comprehensive as it might have been, since he concentrates on twenty works which best demonstrate that 'octatonic' constructions are at the core of Stravinsky's technique of composition. Thus *Pulcinella*, *Mavra*, *Apollo*, *Le Baiser de la fée*, *Perséphone*, the piano music, *Jeu de cartes*, the Symphony in C and *The Rake's Progress* are scarcely mentioned, for the reason that they can be discussed in traditional terminology (which appears in this book only in quotation marks – 'dominant seventh', 'diminished chord', etc.).

Van den Toorn's quest for 'consistency, identity, or distinction in pitch organization' in Stravinsky's music led to the discovery that, more than any other composer, he made use of a referential 'octatonic pitch collection'. The author defines this as 'eight pitch classes',[12] which, exposed in scale form, alternate major and minor seconds in two symmetrical halves:

This symmetrical organization might seem to be confining, but when, in *Petrushka* (1910–11), Stravinsky began to combine triads related through the tritone (in the above example, from *Svadebka*, the interval between A and E flat; in *Petrushka*, the interval between C and F sharp), 'a new universe' was opened up, 'one that Stravinsky was to render peculiarly his own.'

Stravinsky inherited the octatonic collection from Rimsky-Korsakov, who had used it most conspicuously in *Mlada* and *Sadko*. This octatonic scale also corresponds to the second of

Messiaen's 'modes of limited transposition', and Messiaen was apparently the first (*c.* 1944) to perceive the extent of Stravinsky's exploitation of it. The term became general currency through Arthur Berger's 1963 essay, though Berger's description did not include the sequence of alternating major and minor seconds. Stravinsky himself never used the word 'octatonic', but his own expression '*leit-harmonie*', in his 1927 analysis of *Firebird*, amounts to the same thing, and the evidence for his awareness of 'the octatonic collection as a cohesive frame of reference', and of his 'life-long predilection for octatonic partitioning', is irrefutable.

Van den Toorn's observations range widely and are by no means restricted to the theoretical. It seems safe to predict that the book will change the world of musical analysis as profoundly as, say, Leonid Kachian's *The Polynomial Algorithm in Linear Programming* changed the world of computer analysis. Thus van den Toorn calls attention to Stravinsky's fondness for the octave and third (without the fifth) and points out a similarity of effect between a harmonic progression in the 1945 Symphony in Three Movements and the traditional Neapolitan sixth – this is a comparison of the conciseness of the *Symphony of Psalms* with the 'sprawling' impression given by the Symphony in Three Movements, in the sense of 'abundance and diversity of material, and in the referential implications'. In the serial music van den Toorn comments on the simpler rhythms and 'tighter delineations' (smaller intervals) in the vocal pieces versus the 'looser delineations' (larger intervals) and 'poly-rhythmic combinations of great complexity' in the instrumental music (Movements, Variations). In short, van den Toorn is more musician than theoretician, even declaring himself in sympathy with Stravinsky's 'suspicion that formal reckoning represented a kind of thinking about music rather than a thinking *in* music. . .that, unlike composition or peformance, such reckoning was not fundamentally auditive.' More than once a theorist colleague's error is attributed to his having 'trusted his eye rather than his ear.'

A full chapter and several digressions are devoted to Stravinsky's 'metric irregularity as opposed to regular metric periodicity', or, in other words, to 'beat' in relation to accent and phrase, and to 'off-the-beat/on-the-beat contradictions and reversals'. The question has not been studied as thoroughly before, though for some reason van den Toorn does not mention Allen Forte's landmark demonstration that greater harmonic density coincides with metrical stress. Perhaps not all readers will agree with van den Toorn that the horn swoops on the first beats of the seven/four bars in the *Firebird* finale remain anacrustic in feeling despite the shifting of the 'melodic downbeat' to the second crotchet.

Van den Toorn does not favour the music of any one of Stravinsky's periods or styles, and the book's conclusions about 'the startling variety from one context to the next' in the neo-classic music destigmatizes this label. Nor does van den Toorn believe that 'serialism. . .could in some ultimate sense threaten the legitimacy of all other processes of musical invention.' *Agon*, he writes, is 'well-nigh miraculous' because of the music's 'vast pluralistic reach in historical reference' and because the synthesis of serialism and 'the octatonic–diatonic interaction' works. The author never loses sight of the totality of Stravinsky's music, and if the octatonic perspective is overemphasized, it also provides a unifying view.

For me, the most absorbing part of the book is the last, dealing with the serial music. Van den Toorn traces the composer's development from 'untransposed melodic sets' (series)[13] to hexachordal units and transposition by means of a new technique of rotation. But whereas van den Toorn provides a solidly grounded guide for the serial construction of *The Flood*, the one for *Abraham and Isaac* is at sea, in at least two particulars.

Stravinsky began *Abraham and Isaac* (Santa Fe, 2 August 1964)[14] with notations for the original and inverted order of the series, then deployed the pitches partly from right to left, the Hebrew text possibly having suggested this to him. Van den Toorn asserts that 'the complete twelve-tone set' occurs in 'an ordered rendition only once, at the beginning of the piece'. But this first exposition is *not* strictly ordered (the music starts with the second note of the beta hexachord, continuing with the first note and the alpha hexachord in retrograde); the strict version, inverted order, first appears in the vocal part in the – supposedly nonexistent – second statement. Van den Toorn also remarks on the 'seemingly privileged F identification'; it does not 'seem', however, but *is*, for the reason that all rotations of the original and inverted forms of the series begin with F, and that four hexachordal sets conclude with it. Nor does the author explain that the F octaves are derived from the combined verticals of the first pitch classes of the original and inverted series.[15]

A result of the 'information explosion' is that increasing numbers of the most valuable publications, van den Toorn's among them, are becoming less accessible to general readers because they are not so much 'literature' as manuals of technology. But new and complex phenomena may well require new and complex means of expression, and the vocabulary of Donald Tovey cannot explain the pitch organizations of Stravinsky's music. Yet the musically sophisticated reader should not be daunted by the few additions to musical nomenclature required in order to follow van den Toorn's arguments, which deserve to be brought to the attention of the larger public before being sent off to solitary confinement in a journal of music theory.

Having said this, one must admit that the writing also presents unnecessary impediments to communication. Equating such crucial terms as 'dissonance' with 'friction' (to be 'harmonious' is to be 'frictionless') is not adequate definition. And many of van den Toorn's sentences are indigestibly long – often more than a jaw-breaking one hundred words. (Could this be a result of word processing? When Le Carré's 'little drummer girl' wonders why her interrogation is not being tape-recorded, Kurtz answers: 'The ear selects. . . Machines don't. Machines are uneconomical.') Furthermore, the language distracts: to describe 'diatonic penetration' as 'tonally incriminating behaviour' is to give moral overtones to what should be a purely musical matter. (The author is at his best when distinguishing the 'pulls and attractions' in octatonic progressions from tonally incriminating ones.) Worst of all, approximately half of the hundred or so music examples are marred by wrong pitches, clefs, rhythmic quantities, time signatures. Yet van den Toorn's understanding of Stravinsky's music as a whole rewards the effort of reading the book.

One of the gaps in Stravinsky literature is a study of his work in relation to contemporary musicology. For example, Manfred Bukofzer's 'Speculative Thinking in Medieval Music', which he sent to Stravinsky in 1942, had an effect on him comparable to those of Cingria (*Pétrarque*) and Handschin (*Gregorianisch-Polyphones*) a decade earlier. (Handschin may have given Stravinsky the *Dictionnaire de plainchant*, in which he entered a *clausula* of his own.) The whole subject of the influence of musicology on the composer, apart from some misunderstood analogies between late Stravinsky and isorhythmic motets and parody masses, is a neglected one. An exordium might be made with a history of his twenty-five-year association with Sol Babitz and his laboratory for 'old music' (largely sponsored by the composer), but then even the best of the musical collaborations with Babitz, the violin and piano arrangement of two of the *Pièces faciles*, are unknown.

The book I would most like to read would be a memoir of Stravinsky with his poet and painter friends and acquaintances in the Hollywood years, a circle that included Charles Olsen,[16] who actually bedded his towering frame on the tiny couch in the Stravinsky den; Theodore Roethke, whose dedication of his *Words for the Wind* – 'For Igor Stravinsky, master of finance, from Theodore Roethke, Baron von und zu Gar Nichts, February 1959' – suggests that he might not have been so mad as was once thought; and Kenneth Rexroth, who, after holding forth on Elgar at the Stravinsky dinner table one evening in November 1957, might have been writing for all of us when he inscribed a book: 'What can you possibly say? The thanks of a lifetime.'

Notes

1 *The Apollonian Clockwork*, by Elmer Schönberger and Louis Andriessen, translated by Jeff Hamburg, London, 1990.
2 *Stravinsky: Etudes et témoignages*, introduced and compiled by François Lesure, Paris, 1982.
3 On Ansermet's anti-Semitism, see *Les Fondements*, vol. 1, pp. 235, 423ff., 534.
4 From 'Stravinsky the Litanist', an unpublished thesis (1983) by Edmund Lee of London University. Stravinsky's religious life from 1926 until he left Europe in 1939 is an almost totally unknown subject, awaiting the publication of his letters to the Hieroskhimonakh Gerasim (Mount Athos), the Father Superior Sergei Zradlovsky (and his assistant, the Superior Igumen, Kozlovsky), Archbishop Seraphim (Paris), and, above all, the family cleric, Nikolai Podosenov (Nice).
5 In the most valuable recording of Stravinsky in rehearsal, the one released (1983) by the Educational Media Association of America, of the composer conducting *The Rite of Spring* in Stockholm in 1961, he tells the lower strings to play the glissando figure beginning at No. 33 (1943 score) *détaché* in order to increase the volume, a revision that should be observed, since the effect he wanted is demonstrated in the recorded performance.
6 *Stravinsky on Stage*, by Alexander Schouvaloff and Victor Borovsky (London, 1983).
7 Stravinsky wrote to Nicolas Nabokov, 10 May 1953: '*Renard* is impossible because of a French text that has no value as song and deprives the work of its literary value.' The composer's own French translations of his texts not only fit the music better than Ramuz's but are often superior as language. Here is Stravinsky's translation from one of the passages of his *Cat's Lullabies*, followed by Ramuz's revision:
   Aujourd'hui
   Le chat a mis
   Son bel habit gris
   Pour attraper les souris.
   (Stravinsky)
   . . .Pour faire la chass' aux souris.
   (Ramuz)
8 *Stravinsky and the Piano*, by Charles M. Joseph, Ann Arbor, 1983.

9 *Stravinsky in 'Modern Music' (1924–1926)*, compiled by
   Carol J. Oja, foreword by Aaron Copland. New York, 1983.
10 The first of Stravinsky's source books for *Mavra* (1922),
   especially concerning melodic style, was Danilo Kashin's
   collection of folk music, published by Simeon Selivanovsky in
   Moscow in 1833, and actually entitled 'Lingering Songs'.
   Stravinsky edited and rewrote lines of song texts in the Kashin
   book with a view to using them in *Svadebka*.
11 *The Music of Igor Stravinsky*, by Pieter C. van den Toorn.
   New Haven, 1983.
12 See footnote 2, page 232.
13 Stravinsky transposed the first series that he ever used, the
   'rows' in the Septet.
14 During the next stage of composition, in Venice five weeks
   later, Stravinsky introduced a unison chorus for the response
   '*Avraham*'.
15 All three examples in music type for *Abraham and Isaac*
   contain errors: the clef is wrong in part 1 of example 93; one
   of the rhythmic quantities in example 94 is a demisemiquaver
   short; and in example 95 the sharp is missing before the third
   semiquaver G.
16 See Olson's poem 'Igor Stravinsky' (6 April 1948).

19

STRAVINSKY AT THE MUSÉE D'ART MODERNE

'*Igor Stravinsky: La Carrière européenne*,' the title of the catalogue[1] of the Stravinsky centenary exhibition at Paris's Museum of Modern Art, is an impossible premise, since the composer's European and American careers cannot be separated by drawing a Maginot line through the year 1939. If his American concert tours prior to this date might be overlooked, the same is not true of the transatlantic commissions, *Apollo*, the *Symphony of Psalms*, *Jeu de cartes*, and the 'Dumbarton Oaks' Concerto. Nor can a sufficiently comprehensive presentation of Stravinsky conclude with the beginning of World War II. Moreover, the Paris homage was further confined to theatre pieces, little or no account being given of the concert music.

The catalogue's introductory statement by François Lesure, 'This exhibition. . .is limited to the European years of the composer's activity,' is baldfacedly untrue. For one thing, the catalogue ignores Stravinsky's work in Europe in the 1950s and 1960s, though parts of *Agon*, *Threni*, *Abraham and Isaac*, and other pieces were written in Venice. For another, a large portion of the materials dates from the post-1939 period, including half of the portraits in the section '*Visages d'une vie*', a gallery of twenty-six photographs, drawings, and paintings.[2] Likewise, half of the photographs in '*L'Héritage sonore d'I. Stravinsky*', a stunning mix-up of pictures and captions,[3] show him in New York between 1947 and 1965 (*not* 1966, the catalogue's choice of year for a snapshot with Benny Goodman).

Since the 1939 boundary is also violated by the art on

exhibit, notably in Tchelichev's décor for *Apollo* (Buenos Aires, 1942) and in two Giacometti drawings, one wonders why Marino Marini's red-ink drawing and bronze heads of the composer (New York, 1950 and 1951) were excluded, especially when the only interest in the portraits by Larionov, Bakst, J.-E. Blanche, and Gleizes (no resemblance to *anyone*) is in the subject. But the iconography is unaccountably poor. Where are the charcoal portrait by Ivan Thiele,[4] Tatiana de Jonquières's sculptured head, and the bust by Fiore de Henriquez? In the main, the stage and costume designs are holdovers from the Bibliothèque Nationale's 1979 Diaghilev exhibition. Of them all, Roerich's coloured drawing for the costume of 'the third maiden' in Part Two of *The Rite of Spring* would alone be worth the trip to the museum.

The catalogue's category '*Amis et interprètes*' is astonishing for the exclusion of Stravinsky's closest friends of the period and the inclusion of the 'interpreters' he most abominated. Thus Pierre Monteux, his name forever joined to *The Rite*, is not among the conductors, though space is devoted to, of all people, Furtwängler. ('I am not an admirer of this conductor,' Stravinsky wrote to his publisher, 20 March 1931.) Whatever the reason, the catalogue suggests that Stravinsky had no friends outside of music, though the opposite is nearer the truth. To judge by the correspondence, Mitussov, Argutinsky, and Cingria were at the top with the trusted and elect, yet on them the catalogue sheds no light at all.

Of musician friends, the warmest words are for Nadia Boulanger, though it must be said that her relationship was not so much that of the Egeria of the catalogue's description, as of a prodigious proofreader.[5] But why omit Lord Berners, surely a more genuine and enduring friend than Florent Schmitt? And if Vittorio Rieti, represented by a 1942 type-written letter from Stravinsky[6] – a strange choice in view of Stravinsky's calligraphy – then why not Arthur Lourié, who was closer to him during the 1920s than any other musician? Finally, the iconography of Balanchine, the most important of all of Stravinsky's '*Amis et interprètes*', consists exclusively of pictures from the American years, photographs of the 1949 *Firebird* and 1957 *Agon*, and designs from the 1941 *Balustrade*, which for some reason conclude the section '*Les Années françaises*'.

The authors of the catalogue deserve much praise for touching on the subject of '*Stravinsky et les poètes simulta-néistes*', even though limiting it to Sébastien Voirol's '*transposition synodique*' of *The Rite of Spring*.[7] Stravinsky had attended Ricciotto Canudo's *Simultanéist* functions two years before meeting Voirol, and Canudo's manifesto, '*Notre Esthétique: A propos du* Rossignol *de Stravinsky*', had the greater influence. The catalogue states that Stravinsky's connection with Dada was less significant than that with the *Simultanéists*, although it was the Dadaists who developed the *Simultanéist* idea, as is shown by the Dada programme for an event in Paris, 5 February 1920, that Stravinsky attended. Moreover, some of Dada's most prominent animators were Stravinsky's friends, among them Tzara, Picabia, Cendrars, and Alice Bailly.

Bailly[8] (the catalogue follows Stravinsky's misspelling, Bally) deserves a paragraph to herself, since the catalogue includes a facsimile of '*Les Cris de Pétrouchka*', accompanied by a misreading of some of its contents, but not by a single word of explanation concerning the circumstances of the manuscript – which is dated '*janvier 28*', not '*janvier 1918*', as the catalogue states. In Geneva, on 27 January 1917, the '*samedi dernier*' mentioned in Stravinsky's text, Ansermet conducted a performance of *Petrushka*. Calls for the composer were finally answered, but when he went onstage, saw a group of admirers approaching with a Petrushka doll, and heard the demonstration of approval increase, he fled in embarrassment. During the next day's atonement, he wrote and sent the manuscript to Alice Bailly, blaming 'the cruelty of the public' for preventing 'Petrushka' from thanking her '*comme il faut*'.

With only six graphic objects, the section of the catalogue called '*Stravinsky et les Futuristes*' is woefully inadequate.

The historical notes, by Giovanni Lista, state that after Stravinsky's meetings with the Futurists in Rome in February 1915, three soirées in honour of the composer and Diaghilev were held in Milan during 'le mois suivant (actually April 1915)'.[9] Lista repeats Marinetti's story that Stravinsky wanted to present the noisemakers in Paris, even though he was able to travel there himself only with the help of friends in diplomatic circles, but did not wish to use their instruments himself.[10]

As might have been anticipated, Lista focuses on Diaghilev's production of Stravinsky's Fireworks (Rome, 12 April 1917) with Giacomo Balla's composition of coloured lights moving at different speeds. But much more is now known about this than Lista imparts, thanks to the survival of Balla himself until 1958 – by which date interest in the Futurists had revived – and to the reconstruction of the spectacle in Rome in 1967 and 1968. The premiere of the four-minute opus having been aborted by 'a technical accident' – blown fuses? – Lista's appraisal of the event as 'a major one in the experimental, avant-garde theatre of the first half of the century' seems slightly exaggerated.

The remainder of Lista's text mentions some of Stravinsky's contributions to Futurist publications. But after the Fireworks fizzle, the reasons for the composer's involvement were personal and not owing to any lasting sympathy with the movement. Thus the page from Noces reproduced in La Brigata (Bologna, May 1917) appeared in an issue dedicated to Modern Russian art; Clemente Rebora, the Milanese poet who procured the illustration from the composer, did not even refer to Futurism. Similarly, the publishing of the page of Renard in Noi (Rome, January 1919) should be attributed to the effort of Bino Sanminiatelli, who went to Montreux and obtained the manuscript from Stravinsky himself.

Stravinsky's association with the 'little mags' of Orphism, Dadaism, and Futurism was in response to appeals from painter and writer friends such as Canudo (the exhibition should have included the crucial 29 May 1913 issue of

Montjoie!), Severini (*Noi*), Morandi, Chirico, Cocteau, and Ramuz, who wished to publish his and Stravinsky's translations of Russian folk poetry. Lista refers to the 'echoes' of *Fireworks* that appeared in the Paris review *SIC* (*Son, Idées, Couleurs*; the magazine was published from 1916 to 1920), but he does not say that its founder, Pierre Albert-Birot, and his assistant, Pierre Lerat, were acquaintances of the composer.[11] Claude Artout, editor of another Paris avant-garde *journal d'art*, wrote to Stravinsky on 10 June 1917 'on the recommendation of Cocteau', claiming Picasso, Bakst and Satie as contributors: 'It is known that you work with Ramuz; what we would like is a "*poème musical*" created in collaboration with him.' When two of these collaborations, '*Chant dissident*' and '*Le Moineau est assis*', were published in *La Revue Romande* (15 September 1919), the Swiss press ridiculed the second as a specimen of Dada.

Months before the opening of '*Igor Stravinsky: La Carrière européenne*', its organizers were obliged to announce that the USSR would not participate. The loss was crippling, especially of the costumes and sketches by Roerich for *Sacre* in the Bakhrushensky collection. To some extent this deprivation was offset by loans from Theodore Stravinsky, the exhibition's largest private source. These included one of his father's early landscape paintings and many photographs. Yet Theodore Stravinsky's greatest treasures were regrettably not on exhibit – his father's annotated volumes of Kireyevsky and Afanasiev, from which the texts of *Les Noces*, *Renard*, *Histoire du soldat*, and several songs were taken.

What most surprised visitors to the exhibition is the small number of non-French sources – still another sense in which '*La Carrière européenne*' is a misleading title. Italy could have provided much more than the few items displayed, Belgium more than the single programme, and Britain at least a wide representation of pianola rolls, one that would include the *Roi des étoiles*, cut by Esther Willis, Philip Heseltine's protégée.[12] The British Museum alone could have provided a broader selection of manuscripts.[13] (The one of the Capriccio is opened, in the catalogue, to a famous gaffe, the indication 'Doppio Movimento' – instead of 'Doppio Valore' – at $\boxed{33}$.) But the limitation of the contributions from Germany to some lithographs of Karsavina is baffling. B. Schotts Söhne, Stravinsky's chief publisher in the 1930s, could have stocked several showcases. And was no one among the organizers aware that *Histoire du soldat* and *Oedipus Rex* had triumphed in German theatres before these pieces had been staged at all in France? The celebrated 1923 Bauhaus production of the *Soldat* is not mentioned, while the date of the first and far from acclaimed performance, 1924, is termed 'the decisive year' for the opus.[14]

But neither the Meyer autograph full score of Part One of *The Rite*, nor the manuscript of the first draft score (complete except for the 'Sacrificial Dance', now in the collection of the Paul Sacher Foundation in Basel), is mentioned, although both of them are indispensable for the adequate study and comprehension of the work. (In the Sacher score, purchased by him on 11 November 1982, Part Two begins with the music for two trumpets – now after $\boxed{84}$ – and not with the Prelude as we know it; the E flat key signature does not obtain at two bars before $\boxed{22}$, and the string chord there is written in sharps, thereby confirming that the second violins should play E and not E flat; tempi in several places are faster or slower than in the final score; and the end of Part One is dated 24 February 1912.) Moreover, the manuscript of Stravinsky's orchestrations for *Les Sylphides* and of the Sinding pieces for *Les Orientales* were not exhibited.

The most puzzling section of the catalogue is François Lesure's preface, with its negative characteristics of Stravinsky's music and breathtaking errors of fact. When the composer 'fled' Europe '*en guerre*' in 1939, he was forty-three years old, Lesure writes. Stravinsky, fifty-seven, did not 'flee' but went to fulfil engagements in America with every intention of returning after them. Nor did he live in a '*luxueuse villa de Hollywood*', but, for twenty-four of his twenty-nine years in California, in a one-bedroom cottage, and in far from affluent circumstances. Lesure says, too, that Stravinsky's correspondence has not yet been published, which ignores the major selection that appeared in the USSR only one year after the composer's death.

But Lesure's unsympathetic attitude towards his subject is curious, to say the least. He quotes a 1937 Stravinsky letter to Ansermet as an example of the composer's harshness to his interpreters, remarking that Ansermet 'had thought he had acquired the right to formulate his observations on [Stravinsky's] new creations.' The point at issue, however, is not that of offering 'observations' about a new piece (*Jeu de cartes*), but of performing it, repeatedly and against the composer's express wishes, with cuts. Which composer would *not* have said, with Stravinsky: 'Play the piece uncut or not at all?'

In conclusion, Lesure writes that Stravinsky's music strikes us by '*son ironie, sa colère ou sa crudité*'. Irony, surely, anger sometimes, though tenderness – as in the lullabies 'by' a feline, for characters in fairy tales, a goddess of spring, an inmate of Bedlam – is a quality that comes as quickly to mind. Of crudity Stravinsky's music has not a particle: on the contrary, his tiptoe lightness, his elegance and grace are unique in twentieth-century music. Finally, what strikes us primarily in his music is its festiveness and joyfulness, the joy in making (*poiësis*), joy in belief and affirmation, joy in a circus as well as in a psalm, and simple *joie de vivre*.

Notes

1 By François Lesure and Jean-Michel Nectoux. Paris, 1980.
2 '1950(?)' is given for a view of Stravinsky in a 'Columbia studio', though he recorded exclusively for RCA at that time, and '1956(?)' is the date attached to a picture of him said to be conducting the Mass in Venice, a work he never led there.
3 The photograph reproduced in the catalogue as no. 356 matches the caption of no. 354 (except that the record company is Keynote, not Columbia), while photograph no. 354 fits no caption, though obviously intended for that of no.

353. This says that, '*très probablement*', the picture is of Stravinsky recording his Octet (which actually took place in May 1932). What the often-reproduced photograph *does* show is the composer recording the end of the first tableau of *Petrushka*. The same picture was reproduced in *L'Intransigeant*, 4 February 1929, with the caption 'Stravinsky conducting *Firebird*.'

The true story can be pieced together from the report in *L'Instrumental*, January 1929, of the Columbia Records Gala at the Théâtre des Champs-Elysées, 15 December 1928. On that occasion, a film was shown of Stravinsky 'in a sweater' conducting *Petrushka*, while his recording, 'perfectly synchronized', was played with the movie. After this, the audience watched an actual, live recording session of Stravinsky conducting *Firebird*. (He chose to record the original Suite, rather than the 1919 version, because the orchestra had been rehearsed for the Ballets Russes performances in Diaghilev's revival of the original work, 24 December 1928.)

4 Thiele wrote to Stravinsky (in Russian), 5 June 1913, saying that Koussevitzky wanted the portrait to be made. A letter from Thiele, 12 June 1934, reminds Stravinsky that the portrait was painted 'in Paris, twenty years ago, at the same time that I made the one of Debussy.'

5 Photograph no. 210, of Stravinsky and Nadia Boulanger, dated 'Cambridge 1937', was actually taken in the Cambridge home of Edward Forbes in January 1941. (The two musicians are pictured comparing scores of the 1940 Symphony.) The catalogue states that Boulanger was 'one of Stravinsky's closest friends from the time of his installation in France.' This would mean 1920, but the relationship was not close until a decade later. They first met at the time of the *Firebird* premiere.

6 The catalogue reproduces the last half of the letter, though the first half, which reveals that Stravinsky had agreed to write a ballet 'after' Donizetti (not, as stated in the caption, after Bellini), is the important one.

7 The catalogue does not explain the connection between Stravinsky and Voirol, which began on 24 June 1913, when the latter wrote to the composer in his nursing home in Neuilly: 'I and my friends, your fervent admirers, have learned

that at the very time we were ceaselessly acclaiming your name, you were gravely ill.' The letter also refers to a project, surely the '"*Sacre*" *synodique*', a poem of fifty-six pages, handwritten in violet, red, blue and green pencil and ink, and issued in Paris in an edition of fourteen copies; Voirol sent a copy to Stravinsky on 22 November 1913. The lines to be spoken simultaneously, by groups of individuals, are bracketed, but these are not numerous. Stravinsky and Voirol seem to have met for the first time in Paris in May 1914, possibly when Ravel, Casella, and Daniel Chennevière played *The Nightingale* six-hands (this event was reviewed in *L'Intransigeant*) at the home of Madame Valentine de Saint-Pont (the Futurist dancer, painter, and granddaughter of Victor Hugo, not to be confused with Hugo's daughter, the subject of François Truffaut's film). Stravinsky sent a manuscript to Voirol for publication by 'Les Editions M. Mouillot', as a letter from Mouillot to the composer, 14 July 1914, confirms. Voirol's last recorded meeting with Stravinsky was at the preview of *Mavra* at the Hôtel Continental, Paris, 29 May 1922.

8 Alice Bailly (1872–1938), painter and engraver. She and Cécile Cellier, the future Madame C. F. Ramuz, shared an apartment in Paris on the rue Boissonnade, where Ramuz lived from 1910. Stravinsky preserved Alice Bailly's letters to him from 1917, as well as two series of photographs with her, one with Ansermet, Werner Reinhart, Elie Gagnebin, and the publisher Mermod, taken in Winterthur on 17 March 1930, the second with Dushkin and Reinhart, taken in Zürich in March 1933. Reinhart wrote to Stravinsky, 5 January 1938: 'I went to the interment of Alice Bailly two days ago. . . She had been working for two years on the décor for the foyer of the Théâtre de Lausanne. A good friend has disappeared, one who participated in many of your successes in Switzerland and Paris, and at which I was also present.'

9 Lista describes Stravinsky's participation in the Milan gatherings from Pratella's memoirs, but the account by Francesco Cangiullo (1884–1977) is the more reliable. Cangiullo – spelled 'Canquillo' in the Bibliothèque Nationale's 1979 Diaghilev exhibition – visited Stravinsky in Milan in June 1963 and invited him to a show, '*Cangiullo futurista e passatista*'. The artist inscribed the catalogue of this event: '*Si*

ricorda, Maestro, a Roma, a Napoli, con Diaghilev', and drew a picture in which the smoke plumes from Vesuvius spell 'Napoli' and the initial 'C' forms the Bay of Naples shoreline. See *Yale Italian Studies*, Spring 1980, for a list of publications by Cangiullo and for the facsimile of his manuscript of *Viva Marinetti!*, in which the 'Stravinsky storm' is compared to the storm provoked by Matisse's *Red Dancers*.

10 A letter from Luigi Russolo's widow to Stravinsky in Milan, 21 April 1954, reminds him that he had heard and admired the 'Russolophone' (in April 1915).

11 Lerat wrote to Stravinsky from Rome, 4 May 1917, asking him to send a manuscript to *SIC*, and a letter from Albert-Birot to the composer reveals that he complied: 'Picasso is in Spain, and I have not received any word concerning the manuscript [which you sent to him, rue Victor-Hugo, on 4 May]. Just this minute I received the manuscript that you promised me in your last letter. I will publish it in the next issue. Would you give me the full name of the translator Ramous [*sic*]?' The May 1917 issue contained costume designs by Fortunato Depero for *The Song of the Nightingale*.

12 Constantin Braïloï's judgement that this piece *'annonce un bouleversement'* in Stravinsky's development might have been the result of listening to the pianola arrangement, probably made around 1915, in addition to studying the score. It should be mentioned that the version of Braïloï's essay that appeared in *La Tribune de Lausanne*, 24 September 1918, was much reduced in length, and that the complete text (unpublished) constitutes a remarkable piece of criticism for its time.

13 More interesting than any manuscript on view is the set of corrected proofs of *Petrushka* showing 'eight bars of the finale'. The catalogue identifies the passage as that in which 'the Moor pursues Petrushka to kill him: [Stravinsky] made an entirely new *rédaction'*. But the music is simply that of the concert ending.

14 From all accounts the most absorbing production of the *Soldat* was that by Pirandello in Rome in 1925, partly because of the superb translation by Alberto Savinio, Chirico's brother, whose qualities as a writer have only recently attracted English readers, in John Shepley's translation of Savinio's essay on Isadora Duncan.

20

THE STRAVINSKY *NACHLASS*
IN NEW YORK AND BASEL

'The Stravinsky *Nachlass*: A Provisional Checklist of Music Manuscripts', by John Shepard, in the June 1984 issue of the Music Library Association *NOTES*, purports to be a survey of Stravinsky's collection of his manuscripts and an account of its history. The account is inadequate in both respects. (Mr Shepard, a reference librarian in the Music Division of the New York Public Library, was employed in the removal of the manuscripts from the Stravinsky home at 920 Fifth Avenue, New York, to the library in late March 1983 pending their final disposition.) For openers, Mr Shepard states that the materials in the collection 'give clues' about 'the correct musical text of nearly every work [Stravinsky] composed from 1904 to 1966.' In actuality, the collection contains nothing of the original versions of *Firebird*, *Petrushka*, *The Rite of Spring*, *Zvezdoliki*, the Balmont songs, *Perséphone*, *Requiem Canticles*, and 'The Owl and the Pussycat'; only fragments of *Histoire du soldat*; no sketches for the 1924 Concerto and almost none for the 'Dumbarton Oaks' Concerto; nothing of the compositions with opus numbers; no juvenilia except the manuscripts for *How the Mushrooms Prepared for War* (described as 'unpublished' despite an excellent 1982 Soviet edition); no source materials for *Le Baiser de la fée*, and only very incomplete ones for *Pulcinella*.

Mr Shepard states that 'after the Library was given custody of the collection in late January, Thor Wood, Chief of the Library's Performing Arts Research Center, and the present writer worked in the Stravinsky apartment checking the music manuscripts against an existing inventory and producing a

———

preliminary inventory of the documentary archives.' What he neglects to mention is that I was present as well, as my signature next to each checked item attests, and that *two* inventories were used, the one he describes, compiled by Sigmund Rothschild, and another, compiled by Andre Marion, Stravinsky's son-in-law. (Rothschild, a certified appraiser, was employed by Arnold Weissberger, Stravinsky's attorney, in January 1970, and the task was completed in three weeks – most inefficiently, partly because Rothschild himself and the secretary who did most of his work for him could read neither music nor any foreign language.) The only comparatively complete and accurate inventory was a micro-film, made in 1967–68 in Stravinsky's Hollywood home and deposited in the Beverly Hills bank in which his manuscripts were kept. That Mr Shepard does not mention this is puzzling: it must have been obvious to him that the only useful survey of the *Nachlass* would have to be based on the microfilm, not on the two inventories; moreover, his Performing Arts Research Center had access to a copy of the microfilm from Stravinsky's children, who had had it for fifteen years and who were responsible for the court order transferring the manuscripts from the Stravinsky apartment to the New York Public Library.

Mr Shepard gives no account of the background of the collection, yet it is essential to an understanding of Stravinsky's American years to know that his manuscripts and his libraries of music, books, and personal and business papers were not in his possession from 1939 to 1949. Before leaving Europe for America in September 1939, he placed most of his full-score manuscripts in a Paris bank vault. Other manuscripts were stored in the cellar of his apartment at 7, rue Antoine-Chantin. During the war, many items from his collection were removed by his younger son, Soulima, accord-ing to Mina Svitalski, the Stravinsky children's governess since 1917, who, living at the address, reported this to a family friend, Olga Sallard, who informed Stravinsky in 1946 or 1947. After the war, Stravinsky's elder son, Theodore, shipped manuscripts, books, the collection of family photographs (formerly in the keeping of Stravinsky's mother), and furniture (including Stravinsky's Swiss work table and Swiss painted cabinet) from Paris to Geneva. (In the spring of 1950, Stravinsky asked Theodore for an inventory of manuscripts in his possession in Geneva, but no full accounting was ever received.)

In 1949 Stravinsky invited me to catalogue the manuscripts that had been sent to him from rue Antoine-Chantin and that he wished to sell. Until 1965 these were kept in closets in his home at 1260 North Wetherly Drive, Hollywood. Changing residences in that year, to 1218 North Wetherly Drive, he decided to place the manuscripts in a bank in Andre Marion's name. In October 1969, after moving to New York, Stravinsky asked Marion to send the manuscripts there, and when Marion did not comply, Stravinsky sued for their return. He received them at the end of December 1969.

The manuscripts in the *Nachlass* are not, despite Mr Shepard's assurance, those that Stravinsky 'chose to retain'. In the late 1940s, after selling a 1910 *Petrushka* sketchbook and the full score of the 1946 *Petrushka*, Stravinsky hoped to dispose of all of his manuscripts no less profitably. This was the raison d'être for the 1949 catalogue, bearing only my name but actually compiled by Stravinsky and myself together: Stravinsky wanted to provide prospective buyers with a descriptive brochure. This catalogue, updated to 1954, was published as an appendix to Eric Walter White's biography of the composer. Since the inventory is inaccurate, incomplete, and hopelessly out of date, one can only regret that Mr Shepard based his survey on it.

No more than a sampling of the numerous inaccuracies in Mr Shepard's discussions of individual works can be mentioned here. But among the howlers are his description of one manuscript as Stravinsky's 'realization of a canon by Schoenberg'. In fact the 'realization' was published in shorthand form by Schoenberg himself in 1928; I wrote it out in score form when I recorded it, while Stravinsky, who admired the piece, made a calligraphic copy of my manuscript. Mr Shepard describes a manuscript of the *Double Canon: Raoul Dufy in Memoriam* as the 'draft of an episode'. As in the case of the Schoenberg canon, the manuscript contains the complete four-part canon in shorthand form.

Mr Shepard perpetuates a serious misunderstanding by quoting Elliott Carter's recollections of Stravinsky showing him a book of sketches for *The Flood*. According to Carter, Stravinsky 'proceeded to explain how he chose fragments from his sketches, tore them out, shuffled them in different orders until he found one that satisfied him, and then pasted them down. I was genuinely surprised to learn of such an unexpected way of composing. . .' That Stravinsky never composed in this 'unexpected way' is obvious from a comparison of the sketches and the final score. From the time of *The Flood* (1961–62), Stravinsky sketched on any scrap of paper that came to hand – a sheet from a hotel telephone note pad, a paper napkin, his wife's stationery, the back of an envelope or a telegram – and pasted each lapidary notation in scrapbooks, one of which he showed to Carter. Whatever Carter thought Stravinsky had said about the contents of these pages, the sequence of the sketches was never in doubt in Stravinsky's mind.

Mr Shepard quotes a description from the 1954 catalogue of a large (12 by 15½ inches) Edition Russe de Musique full score of *The Rite of Spring*, remarking that this item has not been traced and was not listed in the Rothschild catalogue – which does not list *any* published music – and stating that 'plate 4 of a 1978 publication, *Stravinsky in Pictures and Documents*, shows page 48 of this score in full color. . .' In fact this plate was photographed, actual size, from a miniature score. The Stravinsky–Ansermet correspondence makes clear that the rubricated corrections in the timpani parts shown in plate 4 date from the summer of 1922 and are those contained in this miniature score. The very different timpani parts in all corrected *large* scores were inserted in 1926, when the work was in demand in several cities simultaneously. The large score mentioned in the 1954 catalogue is in Basel (Paul Sacher Foundation), but not all of the inserted manuscript is Stravinsky's. Pages 99–101, in sepia, are apparently in the hand of Serge Koussevitzky; they do not contain a single mark by Stravinsky. This is the 'big full score' mentioned by Stravinsky in a letter to Ralph Hawkes, 6 November 1948.

Mr Shepard erroneously writes: 'a draft of the second theme area of the first movement of the Sonata for Two Pianos (1943–44) begins with instrumental indications which show that that work was originally planned for orchestra. . .' The 'draft of the second theme area' does contain indications for instrumentation – it is written in short-score form – but this music was intended for a separate, autonomous piece, part of an aborted film score. Only later was the orchestral section incorporated into the Sonata.

A draft of the Etude for Pianola 'omits the final score's opening bars', Mr Shepard reveals. But what had not yet been composed could not be omitted: obviously the opening bars were *added*, though exactly when this took place has not yet been discovered. According to a letter from Stravinsky to Alfred Cortot, 18 December 1917, the holograph was sent to Madame Eugenia Errazuriz.

Mr Shepard's 'checklist' of the sketches and drafts often fails to note the real point of interest. It is not surprising that the volume of sketches for *Oedipus Rex* 'opens to reveal Latin text in IS's hand on the left page.' But what is to be made of the French translations that sometimes accompany the Latin? That Stravinsky was dependent on them? And how are we to account for the twelve-note series of Schoenberg's Quintet, Op. 26, on a sketch page of Stravinsky's Septet, but in a different hand?

Mr Shepard's most evident blunder is his identical description of forty pages of sketches for the 1931 '*Concerto en ré pour violon et orchestre*' (Violin Concerto) and the 1946 '*Concerto en ré pour orchestre à cordes*' (Basler Concerto).

The Russian text of *Les Noces* is interspersed with numbers that 'may' refer to sources in the Afanasiev and Kireyevsky folklore collections, Mr Shepard avers. But these sources exist in many libraries, and the originals are in the Theodore Stravinsky Collection. Further, Mr Shepard's description of the *Noces* materials is confusing. For instance, he distinguishes two draft scores of the '1st instrumentation for large orchestra'. In fact the archives contain three very different early score drafts, one with, and another without, two string '*quintuors*' (one playing arco, the other pizzicato), the third listing a harpsichord. Since the strings in all of these scores are soli, the ensembles cannot qualify as 'large' orchestras. Mr Shepard dates a chart showing Stravinsky's tuning of each string of a cimbalom from the time of the 1919 '2nd instrumentation' of *Les Noces*. But 1915 is a more likely year for the chart, since that is when Stravinsky learned to play the instrument and to restring it himself, before composing the cimbalom part in *Renard* in 1916.

Mr Shepard says that the *Petit Ramusianum harmonique* is unpublished, though Stravinsky's contribution is found on the first page of the volume for which it was solicited, *Hommage à Ramuz* (Lausanne, 1937, in an edition of eight hundred). Mr Shepard also lists as unpublished *Valse des fleurs* and *Lied ohne Name*, both of which are available in facsimile editions. Finally, he claims that '*Sagesse*' (Verlaine), from Two Songs, Op. 9, was never published in the original scoring, even though an excellent Soviet edition exists.

The chronological order of Mr Shepard's identifications of Stravinsky's sketchbooks is wrong: his A, B, C, D, E, F, should be D, A, B, C, F, E.

Referring to a 'smaller page' among the sketches for the *Three Songs from William Shakespeare*, Mr Shepard says that it contains a 'substitute four-bar passage'. What the smaller page actually contains is the missing music for a part of the text that Stravinsky had neglected to set.

'*Stravinsky: Sein Nachlass, sein Bild*', the Basel Kunstmuseum's exhibition (6 June – 30 September 1984), was lavish in both substance and presentation. Of the makers of the age, perhaps only Picasso could fill so much space with so much interest, as the forty-six works by him in this show attest. These include little-known gouaches for *Pulcinella* and sketches for the cover design of *Ragtime*, but his three portraits of the composer brought together on one wall provided a greater surprise. Though known to most of us only in similar-size reproductions, the drawing of Stravinsky seated is actually twice as large as the one in profile and three times larger than the frontal map of his face.

The dimensions of the three J.-E. Blanche portraits also differ greatly and, with his Redonesque *Karsavina as the Firebird*, add to his stature as an artist. Bakst, Benois, and Roerich were fairly represented, Auberjonois in huge disproportion, but justified in that the documentation of *Histoire du soldat* in his graphics and letters was the most thorough for any opus in the exhibition. The Giacometti room, in bleak contrast to those of the Russians, had drawings spread on all sides; this viewer, at least, would have preferred to see the tiny heads closer together. (All of these studies were assigned to 1957, though two of them date from May 1965; one other, not shown, and never reproduced or catalogued, was done from a photograph of the composer in his Hollywood studio taken nearly a year before the artist knew him.)

For an exhibition that emphasizes Swiss artists and collections, some omissions are puzzling. Thus Theo Meier and Steven-Paul Robert are here, but not Boris Solotareff, whose portrait was completed at the same time and place (1918, Lausanne) as the Robert sketches; and Hans Erni, who made an album of drawings of Stravinsky in Zürich in October 1961. Of set and costume designs, the most regrettable absences are Tchelichev's 1942 *Apollo* (or any reproduction of it) and Hockney's *Rake's Progress*, which would have been of greater interest than reproductions of the Hogarth engravings, which the scenario follows only loosely. And is there no maquette or photograph of *Histoire du soldat* as staged by Pirandello in Rome in 1925?

Separate rooms were devoted to *Renard*, *Noces*, and other theatre works, each of which were focused on sketches and drafts of the same passages in the music at different stages, supplemented by photographs, artwork, letters, and memorabilia. The displays for ballets and operas were naturally more abundant than those for concertos and cantatas, yet *Perséphone*, one of Stravinsky's few large-scale theatrical creations, was not represented at all. And the roles in Stravinsky's biography of those evidently not in favour with the exhibition's organizers were censored out, most glaringly that of the composer's second wife, whose image was limited to a single portrait from her pre-Stravinsky years. (Her designs for *Perséphone*, now in the Stravinsky–Diaghilev Collection in New York, were greatly admired in Berlin in 1961, when the Santa Fe Opera staged the work there.)

The *Sacre* room was the most stunning, with eleven colourful costumes from the original production suspended from the ceiling, and the draft and full scores beneath – on loan from the Paul Sacher Foundation, the exhibition's main source. Valentine Gross's pastels of the *poussettes*, or *khorovods*, were there too, further countering the strangely hard-to-kill notion that the 1913 *Sacre* was black and white, or brown and white, like Nijinska's *Noces*. The music, in the four-hand version, was piped in, but the volume was sub-restaurant level and the keyboard arrangement too unfamiliar to distract.

René Auberjonois emerged from the exhibition as a figure of larger dimension in Stravinsky's life than has hitherto been recognized. The composer often characterized him as 'sharp' and '*méchant*', but fondly, as a kindred spirit, and his letters help to explain the adjectives. ' "I squeeze the lemon to the last drop" ', the painter quotes Stravinsky on his music, and in a 1935 letter, Auberjonois asks his son Fernand, in New York, to try to discover something from Stravinsky, on tour there, about his adoption of 'an intensive, even bigoted, religion', and whether the contradiction between his religious beliefs and his 'extravagantly materialistic mode of life' has had an effect on his work. Not unexpectedly, Fernand did not succeed in broaching these matters, conversing with the composer about buffalo hunting instead.

Another Auberjonois letter describes a lunch at Ouchy with Stravinsky and Ramuz, on 3 August 1935: 'Stravinsky crossed the lake at Thonon and returned to the Haute-Savoie in the evening. Little, feisty Igor did not stop eating: fried foods on the boat; meats, salads, and cheeses at lunch; ice cream back on the wharf, where we participated in a travelling fair – at the booth of a colossal woman who asked us to feel her muscles.' Fernand has noted here: 'A drawing in the margin of the letter admirably contrasts the daring of the great Russian musician and the reticence of the Swiss painter when confronted by life in the raw.'

The Kunstmuseum's catalogue is indispensable to everyone concerned with music, ballet, and theatre décors of the period. Though published only nine months after the transferral of the *Nachlass* from the New York Public Library to Basel, and a still shorter time after the acquisition of such prime exhibits as the full score of *Agon* and the 1920 Errazuriz sketchbook (where is the one, mentioned in correspondence, from 1917?), no signs of haste are apparent in the production. True, languages are occasionally mixed ('Three Quatrains for Unaccompanied Voice auf Texte von. . .'); important dates are missing (such as when Stravinsky made his copies of Webern's orchestration of Bach and of Schoenberg's canon); performance information is garbled (the Serenade is listed as having been played by Stravinsky months before it was written); and misattributions occur (that the red crayon markings on the envelope shown on page 72 are not Stravinsky's but his son-in-law's is evident in their near obliteration of the composer's signature; also, the rehearsal number in the *Noces* score reproduced on page 89 is not Stravinsky's but Lawrence Morton's). Yet the mystifying identification of one composer as 'J. St. Smith' – a latter-day Anglican saint? – could have been an intentional kindness, to protect the perpetrator of the most-played national anthem at the 1984 Olympic Games.

During the last few weeks of the Basel Kunstmuseum's

exhibition '*Stravinsky: Sein Nachlass, sein Bild*', the composer's death mask, my gift to the Sacher Foundation, was displayed for the first time anywhere – a disturbing apparition, since the furrows from the tubes of an oxygen mask are still visible.

Stravinsky's Swiss decade, the natural focus of the show, was his most fertile and varied, encompassing the Second Tableau of *Petrushka*, most of *The Rite of Spring* and *The Nightingale*, all of *Renard*, *Histoire du soldat*, *Pulcinella*, *Les Noces* (except for the final instrumentation), and numerous songs and instrumental pieces.

Were the rich displays accompanying the music manuscripts of this period achieved at the expense of so important a later work as *Oedipus Rex*? Whatever the answer, the visitor could not have formed a notion of what *Oedipus* might have looked like at any point in its half-century in the theatre, and this though its designers have included Alfred Roller, Ewald Dülberg, Robert Edmond Jones, Cocteau, Manzù, and Hockney. Since Stravinsky considered Dülberg's set design for the Kroll Oper (February 1928) 'a perfect realization, the decorative sobriety and sensible positioning of the soloists and chorus resulting in a performance that was a logical extension of my score,' perhaps this might have been shown along with the other major loans from the Theatre Museum in the Victoria and Albert. Stravinsky did not see the Roller version at the Vienna Staatsoper, which scooped the Berlin stage premiere by three days, but a friend of the composer's described it to him as 'a *mélange* of Louis-Quinze and Hubert Robert'; the singing chorus was in the pit, in the tradition of Diaghilev's productions of *Nightingale* and *Noces*.

More has been written about the *Bild* aspect of the exhibition, the iconography and decorative art, than about the *Nachlass*, the manuscripts and archives, though Stravinsky's manuscripts must be regarded as calligraphic art in addition to the musical art that they notate. Yet the sumptuous catalogue devoted more full pages (sixty-eight) to illustrations of music sketches and scores than to portaits and theatre and costume designs (sixty-four). Inks, crayons, and pencils of more than one colour are used in most of the manuscripts, and these are faithfully reproduced. The reader of the catalogue can learn even from a single page. Thus, to compare the sketch and published score of the 1924 Sonata is to discover that piano fingerings were a part of the composing process, though Stravinsky might remove them later, as a builder does his scaffolding. (Stravinsky even revised Isidor Philipp's fingerings in his two volumes of exercises, which were part of the composer's daily piano practice.) The reader can also see how a chord has been revoiced, an orchestral balance adjusted, and a serial order or segment deployed. In one remarkable catalogue page, juxtaposing the sketches for the first and last versions of the ending of the second movement of the Violin Concerto, musicians can follow the act of imagination that expanded an unremarkable five bars into six marvellously vaulting ones.

Only a few errors are found in the catalogue text. The score of *Noces* shown on page 86 is not a holograph but a blue carbon of one, as the pencilled-over chord for woodwind and timpani shows. And, the florid script on the sketch for *Apollo* on page 114 is not Stravinsky's but Boris Kochno's (a greeting to the composer). Performance data are missing for the Tango – inexplicably, since some of it is to be found in Stravinsky's own hand on the verso of one of Picasso's *Ragtime* covers (no. 201 in the catalogue). And, on page 262, the 1965 orchestral Canon is confused with the *Introitus* of the same year.

Whereas some of the art has been borrowed from Britain, France, West Germany, and the United States, the provenance of the music manuscripts (with a single exception from the Picasso Museum in Paris) is unique and local: the Paul Sacher Foundation. No doubt the music will be exhibited in Basel again, in its own new home, and with the benefit of further acquisitions. Stravinsky's source books have not yet been collected, but in the future we may hope to be able to examine the Kireyevsky volumes containing the annotations for *Les Noces*, as well as such curiosa as *The Melodist* (New York,

1820), from which the composer chose model dance pieces to be used in the *Jane Eyre* film score, a project that absorbed him as *Wuthering Heights* did Balthus; Stravinsky copied out dialogue from the novel, kept on the wall of his studio Bramwell Brontë's drawing of himself and his sisters, and read Mrs Gaskell's life of Charlotte Brontë.

Perhaps at some future exhibition at the Sacher Foundation, Stravinsky's choice of excerpts from *Linda di Chamounix* for a projected 'Donizetti ballet' (1943), might be on view, and his arrangement for piano of the Overture to Weber's *Turandot*. Perhaps, too, the foundation will succeed in acquiring the manuscripts given to Ernest Ansermet (Three Pieces for String Quartet, *Pribaoutki*, *Berceuses du chat*), Giacomo Manzù (*Oedipus Rex*), Alexander Tansman (*Four Norwegian Moods*), Adriana Panni (*Canticum sacrum*), John Cage (*Fanfare*), Henry Moore (*Abraham and Isaac*), and Nijinsky (the orchestral draft of the 'Sacrificial Dance', missing from the Lifar *Rite of Spring* manuscript, now in the Sacher collection, and the most important Stravinsky manuscript still in private hands). No doubt a recording library is also being assembled, beginning with Chaliapin's 1910 disc of Stravinsky's instrumentation of Mussorgsky's *Song of the Flea*, and including the 1935 speech at MGM, in German, to a group of Hollywood refugee composers. The foundation has already acquired the vast Tony Palmer archive of Stravinsky on film.

To classify the photographic record may take several years. Since a representative selection could not be presented, the Kuntsmuseum confined this branch of the *Bild* to portraits by twelve acknowledged artists of the camera. The results are disappointing, Stravinsky having been overposed by Man Ray, Edward Weston, George Platt Lynes, and even Cartier-Bresson, all of whom also, disastrously, avert the composer's eyes. Auerbach, Langdon Coburn, Mili, and Beaton are not here, or Ruth Orkin, whose glimpse of Stravinsky motioning her to leave him alone at the Taverna Fenice reception after the premiere of the *Rake* recalls a whole vocabulary of his body language.

Picasso's Stravinsky is more real, even literally, than the thousands created by photographers. Otherwise, among the graphic images only a few Cocteau cartoons and Giacometti drawings are worthy of mention. Eugene Berman had more opportunity to observe the composer than any other artist, but was unable to draw faces, though he did leave a sketch of Stravinsky seen from an angle behind and below the podium that exactly captures the dome of the head, the large ears, and the hunched shoulders. Marino Marini's two skulls seem small in relation to the death mask, but they convey the qualities that the sculptor describes as having felt for this subject during those two (only!) modelling sessions in New York in April 1950: '*Stravinsky, personaggio cosi vivo, cosi nervosa, cosi apprensivo mi interessava per la sua forza cosi sensitiva, per cui procurava grandi difficoltà, e mi dava anche gioia.*'

PART FIVE

Music

21

SVADEBKA: AN INTRODUCTION

1. Avant-propos

Svadebka[1] (*Les Noces*) ranks high in the by no means crowded company of indisputable twentieth-century master-pieces. That it does not immediately come to mind as such may be attributable to cultural and linguistic barriers, and to the inadequacy, partly from the same causes, of performances. For *Svadebka* can be sung only in Russian, both because the sounds of the words are part of the music, and because their rhythms are inseparable from the musical design. A trans-lation that satisfied the quantitative and accentual formulas of the original could retain no approximation of its literal sense. Which is the reason that Stravinsky, who was not rigidly averse to changing sense for sound's sake, abandoned an English version on which he had laboured in the fall of 1959 and again in December 1965.

But performances are infrequent as well as inadequate. The four pianos and large number of percussion instruments that comprise the *Svadebka* ensemble are not included in the standard instrumentation of symphony orchestras and other performing units. Then, too, the piece by itself is long enough for only half a programme, while the few possible companion works, using many of the same instruments – Varèse's *Ionisation*, Bartók's Sonata for Two Pianos and Percussion, Antheil's *Ballet mécanique* (an arrant plagiarism hailed as an apostolic successor at the time) – derive from it as instrumen-tal example.

Lecture read at Emerson Hall, Harvard University, 8 August 1972.

As a result of the obstacles of language and culture, audiences do not share in the full meaning of the work, hearing it as a piece of 'pure' music; which, of course, and as Stravinsky would say, *is* its ultimate meaning. But Stravinsky notwithstanding, *Svadebka* is a dramatic work, composed for the stage, and informed with more meanings on the way to that ultimate one than any other opus by the composer. The drama is his own, moreover, and he is responsible for the choice of the subject, the form of the stage spectacle, the ordonnance of the text. *Svadebka* is in fact the only theatrical work by him, apart from the much slighter *Renard*, that combines music with a text in his mother tongue, the only work in which ritual, symbol, meaning on every level are part of his direct cultural heredity.

It is also, of all Stravinsky's works, the one that underwent the most extensive metamorphoses. The sketches are a study in the processes of growth and refinement that illuminate part of the path of Stravinsky's working mind. *Svadebka* occupied his imagination throughout a decade and, in aggregate, took more of his time than any other opus of the same length. (A later Russia would have awarded him a Stakhanovite medal for his industry alone, if that Russia had recognized *Svadebka*.) The reasons for the long gestation are, first, that Stravinsky several times suspended work to compose other music, which, each time, left him greatly changed. And, second, that he *was* creating something entirely new, both musically — its heterophonic vocal–instrumental style is unique in our music — and in theatrical combination and genre, an amalgam of ballet and dramatic cantata that he was himself unable to describe. 'Russian Choreographic Scenes', his subtitle on the final score, does not even mention that the subject is a village wedding and that the scenes or tableaux are four: at the Bride's (the ritual plaiting of her tresses); at the Groom's (the ritual curling of his locks); the departure of the Bride for the church; the wedding feast.

2. Calendar

On 9 September 1913, Stravinsky, his wife, three children, and nurse Sofia Dmitrievna[2] left Russia at Alexandrov, the border station, *en route* from their summer home in Ustilug to their temporary winter one in Clarens. In Warsaw, where he had obtained the necessary exit visas the day before, Stravinsky was joined by his friend and co-librettist of *The Nightingale*, Stepan Mitussov. Having resumed work on the opera after his return to Russia from Paris at the beginning of July, Stravinsky completed the mechanical Nightingale's music on 1 August, and, three weeks later, the true Nightingale's aria which precedes this *japonaiserie*. But another project had been taking shape in his imagination that must also have been discussed during the stopover in Warsaw. For it was Mitussov who, two months earlier, had supplied the manuscript for a song that occurs, virtually as he transcribed it, in the Fourth Tableau of *Svadebka*.

Stravinsky could not have turned his full mind to the new opus until *The Nightingale* was completed six months later. But he was thinking, and even talking, about it: a letter from Prokofiev to Miaskovsky[3] repeats a rumour that plans were afoot to mount it as early as the autumn of 1914. Work on the libretto probably began during May and June. Stravinsky wrote no music then, in any case, or since the completion of the first of the 'Three Pieces for String Quartet' on 25 April, and it is unlikely that he was idle as a composer during those two months, ceaselessly occupied as he was in the far less interesting world of music outside his own head. His notebooks of the time are filled with Russian popular verse, songs, and *chastushkas* (folk rhymes), most of them capped with his scansion marks.

The need for additional texts, in any event, was the principal reason for a hurried trip to Ustilug and Kiev between 2 July – on which date he completed the second of the string quartet pieces – and 14 July, when he was safely back in Leysin working on the final one.[4] Believing that war was

imminent – this was a few days after Sarajevo – he went first
to Ustilug to salvage some personal possessions, then to Kiev,
where he stayed at the home of his father-in-law, 28 Annens-
kaya Street, and where he acquired a volume of wedding
songs published (in 1911) as a supplement to *Pyesni sobranye
P.I. Kireevskim* – 'Songs collected by P.[eter] V.[asilievitch]
Kireevsky'. The songs in this volume served as the main source
of the *Svadebka* libretto.⁵ (Kireevsky, who died in 1856, was a
great Slavophile who compiled some twelve volumes of
Russian folk songs, drawing on the work of many other
collectors, including Pushkin.)

Once back in Switzerland, the song cycle *Pribaoutki* – on
texts from Afanasiev,⁶ the source, a few years later, of
Histoire du soldat – came first. During this time, however, and
during a sojourn in Florence with Diaghilev in September, a
version of the libretto was pieced together. And by November
Stravinsky had drafted some, possibly most of the music of the
First Tableau; or so I deduce from a sketch, dated that month
for the section at 21, though the date merely refers to a
succession of intervals on the same page that Stravinsky's then
seven-year-old elder son had sung (or whistled, or hummed),
and that his father, with the immemorial pride of the parent in
the prodigies of its offspring, had written down. On 15
November Stravinsky composed a Polka. Surprisingly remote
from *Svadebka*, it was the first of the *Three Easy Pieces* from
which, by hindsight, we can see the roots of his neoclassicism;
one part of his amazingly compartmented mind – in which
Renard and *Svadebka* were incubating at the same time with
no tangling of stylistic lines – was always several steps ahead.

At the beginning of January 1915, Stravinsky moved to the
Hôtel Victoria in Château-d'Oex, where, except for brief
trips, he remained until March. One night in a funicular near
Clarens, he found himself with two deeply inebriated Vaudois
for fellow passengers, one of whom sang a tipsy tune while the
other interjected an accompaniment of hiccups. Stravinsky
composed a hocket imitating this debauched duet, perhaps the
only *real* hocket ever written, though the name has been given

to a style of a long period of late medieval European music. He made capital use of it in the Fourth Tableau of *Svadebka*, increasing the suggestion of drunkenness appropriate to the wedding feast by shifting the music from thesis to arsis, and then, in a powerful unifying stroke, identifying the hocket rhythm with the motive of the Groom, Khvétis Pamfilievitch, which dominates the ending of the work. It hardly needs to be said that what was actually heard in the funicular must have been very different from the construction it inspired in *Svadebka*. But the incident is typical. Stravinsky was able to hear, and often noted down, the music in the rhythms and intervals of machinery, in street noises, in hurdy-gurdies and carrousels – and in troubadours, intoxicated or otherwise, such as these Vaudois.

On another excursion (28 January), this time to Geneva, Stravinsky dined with Ernest Ansermet in Maxim's Restaurant, where he happened to hear a cimbalom – which may not have provoked him to say 'Eureka', though that is what he thought. *Svadebka*'s original subtitle was 'Songs and Dances on Russian Folk Themes, for voices, woodwinds, brass, percussion, plucked and bowed instruments'. The plucked instruments were to have included balalaikas, guzlas, guitars, but these were replaced in the first scores by a harpsichord – a 'plucked' instrument – and a quintet of strings playing pizzicato. The cimbalom, which is not plucked but hammered with wood or padded sticks, nevertheless provided exactly the articulation Stravinsky required, as well as a harder and more resonant sound than the jangly balalaika of his native land. It is a large-size dulcimer[7] – the Biblical instrument, pictured on the Nineveh tablets, uncertainly invoked in *Ulysses* ('like no voice of strings or reeds or whatdoyoucallthem dulcimers'), and partly described in Pepys's diary, 23 May 1662: 'Here among the Fidlers I first saw a dulcimore played on, with sticks knocking on the strings, and is very pretty.'

That night in Geneva the player[8] favoured the composer – not knowing that it *was* the composer – with a demonstration of the instrument, and as a result Stravinsky purchased one for

himself and had it sent to Château-d'Oex, where he immediately added it to the orchestra of *Svadebka*. He taught himself
to play it, moreover, drawing a chart of its thirty-five strings
and notating the instrument's fifty-three pitches on them at
the places where they are produced on the actual strings. At
first the instrument is indicated in his manuscripts by its
Russian name, '*tympanon*', which is the name employed by its
master maker and master player – its Stradivarius as well as its
Paganini – Pantaléon Hebenstreit, whose patron had been
Louis XIV. (Pantaléon's only surviving tympanon, made in
1705, was among the effects of Pantaléon's descendant Sasha
Votichenko at the time of his death in 1971 in Scottsdale,
Arizona – one of the odder cultural properties to have turned
up in that state since the London Bridge.) In the next five years
the cimbalom was never far from Stravinsky's instrumental
palette, but he was obliged to abandon it after that because
too few players could read and play *his* music. Yet it remained
a favourite instrument, and that most genial of his works,
Renard, cannot be performed without it.

Two weeks later (15 February), Stravinsky was in Rome,
playing *The Rite of Spring* (four-hands with Alfredo Casella,
in a salon of the Grand Hotel), for a small audience invited by
Diaghilev and including Rodin.[9] At this time, *Svadebka* was
unveiled privately for Diaghilev (his letter of 8 March to
Stravinsky in Château-d'Oex) and Prokofiev,[10] who heard
further portions of it in the Hotel Continental, Milan, on 1
April, and – Diaghilev alone – in Montreux at the end of
April. But the only creative digression from *Svadebka* between
April and the end of the year was the composition of that
miniature masterpiece of musical catnip, the *Berceuses du
chat*, the first phrase of which so resembles the first phrase of
the soprano in *Svadebka* that the one could have suggested the
other – and perhaps did, sketches for both being found on the
same page. On 4 January 1916, however, in ever more
straitened circumstances because of the war, Stravinsky
accepted a commission to compose a chamber opera. This
supervention was *Renard*, some of which had been written a

year before; it could hardly have been a happier one, but *Svadebka* was shelved for seven more months.

Returning to it after that, Stravinsky was again and almost constantly interrupted, by the excerpting and reorchestrating of a symphonic poem from *The Nightingale* (completed 7 April 1917); by the composition of several short pieces including the Etude for Pianola[11] (completed 10 September 1917); by four changes of residence; by frequent travels (three trips to Spain in 1916 in addition to visits to Paris, Milan, Rome); by endless questions relating to the performance and publication of his ever more famous works, and by *pourparlers* concerning commissions for future ones. He had been asked, through Léon Bakst, to compose incidental music for Gide's *Cléopâtre*.[12] Replying to Bakst, in Paris, from Morges, 30 July 1917, Stravinsky telegraphed: '*Notions du réalisme et synthétisme pour la mise en scène ne m'explique [nt] rien. Attends Gide pour comprendre*' – and the demand for the concrete is so characteristically expressed that the message could have come from any year of Stravinsky's life, 1970 as well as 1917, *mutatis mutandis* in the matter of the authors.

In April 1917 Stravinsky played virtually the whole of *Svadebka* for Diaghilev, then living in Ouchy, after which, by all accounts including Stravinsky's, Diaghilev wept. A month later (30 May) the *New York Herald* quoted the composer as expecting 'to finish *Les Noces villageoises* this summer'. Yet the sketch-score was not completed until 11 October, a delay that is in some measure attributable to three shocks: the death of his beloved childhood nurse Bertha ('Bilibousch', 'Bertoshka') Essert[13] (28 April), the death of his younger brother Gury (3 August), and the death of 'his' Russia.

For though Stravinsky welcomed the Revolution during its first convulsions – telegraphing to his mother and brother at 6 Khroukov Canal, Petrograd, 20 March 1917: '*Toutes mes pensées avec vous dans ces inoubliables jours de bonheur qui traverse[nt] notre chère Russie libérée. . .*' – Stravinsky became a Ukrainian revanchist soon after that (even writing to Swiss newspapers on the subject), and then, and more lastingly, an anti-Bolshevik, denouncing 'Lénine' (in the same *Herald* interview) as a 'fanatic'. He quickly foresaw the consequences to himself of the sundering from Russia, in any case, and realized that his voluntary exile was over and that the involuntary one had begun. The lament in the epithalamium at the end of *Svadebka* is as much for the loss of Holy Mother Russia as for the virginity of Nastasia Timofeyevna, Stravinsky's stage bride.

The instrumentation was not yet finished on 11 October, however, nor was it to be for another five and a half years. Writing more than a year later (13 November 1918) to Otto Kling, of the English music publishers J. and W. Chester Ltd, Stravinsky refers to the score as if it were complete, but he was trying to secure a contract at the time.[14] In a letter of 6 April 1919, to Gustav Gustavovich Struve of the temporarily defunct Edition Russe de Musique, he refers to *Svadebka* as 'a cantata or oratorio, or I do not know what, for four soloists and an instrumental ensemble that I am in too great a hurry to describe.' But this ensemble, for which the music is fully scored to the end of the Second Tableau, is described in a letter of 23 July 1919 to Ernest Ansermet:

> I do not know what to do with the '*Noces*'. It is ridiculous to stage this '*divertissement*' – for it is not a ballet – without décors, although the décors would not represent anything – being there simply for decoration and *not* to represent anything – with pianola, harmonium, 2 cimbaloms, percussion, singers, and conductor on the stage, together with the dancers. . .

The addition of the percussion was inspired by *Histoire du soldat*, composed the year before: together with the pianola and cimbaloms, it shows Stravinsky well on the way to the *martellato* ensemble of the final score. He wrote to Kling again on 23 November:

> as for the '*Noces*', you must put in the contract that it is to be described on *affiches* and in programs not as a 'ballet' but

as a '*divertissement*'. Here is the complete title of the work: '*Les Noces* (Village scenes): *divertissement* in two parts with soloists and chorus and an ensemble of several instruments.'

The contract was signed on 7 December. But *Pulcinella*, the Concertino for String Quartet, the *Symphonies of Wind Instruments*, *Mavra*, and numerous smaller pieces were composed before Stravinsky could return to and complete the instrumentation. Still another letter to Kling (Paris, 26 May 1921) reveals the composer surrendering to the problem of synchronizing live instrumentalists with the machinery of the pianola:

> As for the '*Noces*', I am in effect completely reworking the instrumentation for a new ensemble of winds, percussion, and one or two parts for piano. I think that this new ensemble will suit us as well as the former version which includes mechanical instruments, something that could create all kinds of difficulties for you.

Winds or percussion, 'sounding brass or a tinkling cymbal'? But apart from the winds he is nearing the final stage and perhaps the most original orchestra in twentieth-century music. The volume of sound is still small, evidently, and in fact the third and fourth pianos were not added, nor the arsenal of percussion instruments expanded to include heavy armaments, until the final score. After beginning with an orchestra that virtually excluded percussion instruments, he ended with one of percussion only, and in the process arrived at the category of the actual orchestra of a Russian peasant wedding; for percussion instruments – pots and pans as well as drums, tambourines, cymbals – were bashed, hammered, clapped together, rattled, and rung throughout the ceremony and celebration, to drive away evil spirits.

Typesetting the Russian text created new and unforeseen difficulties. Writing to London from Biarritz, 29 August 1921, Stravinsky advised his publisher that

[although] the [proof] page that you sent to me is good. . .I
ask you to draw the attention of your proofreaders to the
Russian text. Literally not a single word is comprehensible. It
is an agglomeration of letters with no sense. You must have a
proofreader; so many Russians are without work at the
moment.

On 3 October, Stravinsky informed a London newspaper
that *The Village Wedding* was finished. But he meant the
vocal score, the final proofs of which did not come for another
seven months, during which he composed the one-act opera
Mavra. The full score was finally completed on 6 April 1923,
in Monaco, where the ballet – or *divertissement* – was already
in rehearsal. The first performance took place on 13 June, at
the Gaieté-Lyrique in Paris, a full decade after the work was
conceived.

Graphic analysis, in the case of *Svadebka*, is helpful as a guide
to chronology, for as a rule Stravinsky's Russian script, on the
more mature and final sketches, is printed, rather than cursive.
(I should add that he drew most of the staves with his own
stylus – a roulette, like a tiny, five-furrowed plough, invented
and patented by him, though the idea may have come from the
rastral, the five-nib pen used to rule music paper in the
eighteenth century. I should add, too, that he used transparent
coloured inks in some of the *Svadebka* sketches to facilitate
reading abbreviated scores; if trumpets and oboes alternate on
one line, for example, the music of the former might be
orange, of the latter, green.) What the sketches reveal, above
all, is that in the beginning was the word. In the very act of
copying a text, Stravinsky added musical notations, setting a
line of verse to a melody or motivic fragment, or giving it
unpitched rhythmic values, or designating intervals or chords
that had occurred to him in conjunction with it.

Stravinsky is at the opposite extreme in this from, say,
Janáček, who, so he said, discovered 'the musical motives and
tempos adopted to demonstrating [the emotions] by declaim-
ing a text aloud and then observing the inflections in my

voice.' Stravinsky's inspiration in his vocal works came directly from the sounds and rhythms of syllables and words, while structures of poems often suggested musical structures, wordless ones included, such as the imitation of a Russian Alexandrine by Pushkin in *Apollo*.[15] And it is also clear from the sketches that Stravinsky's musical rhythms and stresses are far more commonly suggested by the text than imposed upon it, and that his own claims to the contrary are greatly exaggerated.

In this manner the earliest of the musical notations sprouting directly from texts were used in the Fourth Tableau, which was the last one composed. (The first notation for the Fourth Tableau, the song contributed by Stepan Mitussov, occurs at about the halfway point.) But in more than one instance notations found on the same sketch page are widely separated in the final composition. Still, once having found his beginning, Stravinsky seems to have composed from beginning to end, though, of course, not bar for bar exactly as in the published score. The chronology can be determined by sketches evincing instrumental improvements from one draft to the next.

I should add that the sketches oblige all of us who have written about *Svadebka* to eat underdone crow, the largest helping of which is the reward of my own unwisdom; a statement published somewhere in my first year of working with Stravinsky actually claims that music and sound-image were simultaneous and inalterable occurrences in his imagination, which may be true with some of his music – how would anyone know? – but is monumentally *un*true in the case of *Svadebka*, in which the sonority is continually and, in the end, totally transformed.

3. A Note on Derivations

Stravinsky would never concede that the question of thematic origins was of the slightest importance, and though he was interested in ethnomusicology in his Russian period,[16] the subject bored him later in life and he would not discuss it. Yet it is no exaggeration to say that all of the melodic material in *Svadebka* is closely related to folk and church music. What has not yet been determined is how much was actually modelled and how much was 'innate', a combination of memory and stylistic intuition. I suspect that nearly all of it originated in Stravinsky's imagination. Musicologists have traced the phrase at two bars before 3:

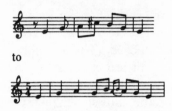

to

which is from Rimsky-Korsakov's *Polnoe sobranoe sochinenii* (1871). But Stravinsky's sketches reveal that he began with an E minor triad and even further from Rimsky's example than from his own final version.

Writing in 1931, Béla Bartók observed that

Stravinsky never indicated the source of his themes, no doubt because he wants to imply his indifference to the question. He has claimed the right to use any musical material in his works that he considers useful; and said that, once used, it becomes in some way truly his own. For lack of documents, I am unable to determine which are the themes he has invented himself, in his 'Russian' period, and which he has borrowed from popular songs. But one thing is certain: if among Stravinsky's themes there exist some which are his own invention, they are extremely clever and extremely faithful imitations of popular songs. Moreover, it is remarkable that in his 'Russian' period. . .the composer hardly ever uses melodies with closed structures, divided into two or three or more verses, but rather motives of two or three bars, repeating them in *ostinato*. These primitive, brief, and often repeated motives are very characteristic of a certain aspect of Russian music. . .[*La Revue Musicale*, 1955].

In one instance, however, it is possible to follow Stravinsky as he consciously transforms received material, for the music at [59]–[53] is derived entirely (and the music after [53] partly) from the Fifth Tone of the Quamennyi Chant,[17] which is sung at the beginning of the Sunday Dogmatik in the Russian Orthodox Service. Here is a fragment of the Chant:

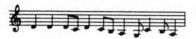

which, after several intermediate stages including experiments with triplet notation (a symbol for the Trinity at least as old as Philippe de Vitry), Stravinsky altered to

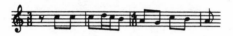

Another fragment of the Chant

is merely transposed and extended by Stravinsky to

while still another phrase of the Chant

he converts to:

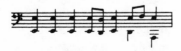

This last became the duet for the two priestlike basses (cf. 50),
which is as close as Stravinsky ever came to a representation of
the Orthodox service on the stage,[18] for the singers are
unaccompanied, following the Church rule, and they are the
only unaccompanied voices in *Svadebka*. Yet the entire
Second Tableau, with, at the end, a basso ostinato (A–C–A–
C #) imitating a great church bell, is 'ecclesiastical' music.

The critical bibliography is slender. The chapter on
'Wedding Ceremonials and Chants' in Sokolov's *Russian
Folklore* (Macmillan, 1950, for the American Council of
Learned Societies, pp. 203–23) is indispensable for the
background, nor does it go too *far* back. So is Birkan's 'On the
poetic text of *Les Noces*', in *Muzika*, Moscow, 1966, and
Russian Folk Poetic Creativity, Uchpedgiz, Moscow, 1956, p.
239. But the monograph 'Igor Stravinsky's *Les Noces*, an
outline by Victor Belaiev' (Oxford University Press, 1928) is
worthless as musical analysis ('The melos of *Les Noces*. . .
springs as it were, from a single melodic germ which is
presented in the opening bars') and misleading in most other
respects.

The only other essay worth the mention is in *Kniga o
Stravinskom* by Igor Glebov (see Chapter 16, 'Stravinsky and
Asaf'yev'). Glebov's analysis of the melodic content in terms of
'intonations', however, and of the rhythmic structure in terms
of numbers of bars, is irrelevant. Unfortunately, too, his better
insights are substantiated with false arguments; thus, he
understands the rhythmic mechanization as style but seems not
to have heard of the proportional system on which it is based.
He compares *Svadebka* to *The Rite of Spring*, almost inevitably at that time when even non-Russians *not* making a case
for the superiority of the composer's 'Russian' works were
raising the spectre of Antaeus. (By the mid-twenties even dug-
in Stravinskyans began to fear that without Russia the wells of
the composer's inspiration were in danger of drying up.)

But the two pieces can be more fruitfully compared for their
differences than for their similarities, their unities being of a
different order. *The Rite* is a succession of dance movements,

each, to a degree, complete in itself, and each manifesting a classical outline of a first section, middle section, recapitulation. *Svadebka*, in contrast, is nonstop; its materials are exposed in fragmentary as well as complete form, as a name is evoked by its initials (*pars pro toto*); and it depends on fusings, interweavings, trellises of cross-connection. And finally, no matter how much new ground is staked out in *The Rite*, its antecedents – in the Russian 'Five', in Debussy – are apparent. *Svadebka*, however, is all new.[19]

Yet Glebov's essay is valuable in its discussion of the 'anthropological background', the rituals and cultural traditions (of exogamous marriage, for one), or, in a word, for everything that Stravinsky took for granted but of which Western audiences are unaware. Glebov's emphasis is wrong, as when he exaggerates the role of the *skomorokh*[20] and misunderstands both the irony and the religion, greatly overdoing the pagan underground. Nor is he helpful with the text, even failing to mention Kireevsky. His terminology, too – 'psalmody', 'clausula' – is anachronistic and inapt. But he does understand the central role of lamentation, and his clues – that the *druzhka*'s (best man's) music resembles the music of Russian village street criers, that the Matchmaker may be compared to Nekrasov's character of that name – are illuminating for Western listeners.

Svadebka was new when Glebov wrote, yet he perceived its originality and its stature more clearly than any other critic of the time. This is doubly remarkable when one remembers that he was writing in a country that had begun to shut down against its greatest composer. The book was banned in the USSR, despite Glebov's telluric invocation to Stravinsky at the end of this chapter: 'Our musical age is the age of Stravinsky; *Svadebka* could have been composed only by a composer of a country in which the elemental power of communion with Nature [has] not yet been lost by the bourgeoisie.' The tone reminds us of Turgenev's deathbed letter to Tolstoy: 'Great writer of the Russian land. . .'

4. The Scenario

Stravinsky composed the libretto – selected, colligated, and edited it – from Kireevsky's collection of songs. But the first version was much longer than the final one, for Stravinsky had originally planned to dramatize the complete wedding ritual, and not to begin with the plaiting of the Bride's hair, where the score now starts. His first draft of the scenario is as follows:

SVADEBKA
Fantasy in 3 Acts and 5 Scenes
Act I
The Inspection
Act II
Scene 1
The Bargain
    a. At the Bride's
    b. At the Groom's (An Incantation Against Sorcery
       – see page 49 [in Kireevsky])
Scene 2
    a. Devichnik (The Bride's Party)[21]
    b. The Girls Take Her to the Bath
Scene 3
In the Bride's House Before the Departure for the Church
Act III
The Beautiful Table

Stravinsky soon scrapped this more comprehensive scheme and abandoned the preliminary matchmaking scenes, as well as the *devichnik* and the ritual dunking[22] of the Bride. The final version reduces this plan to four scenes: Act II, Scene 1a and b, Scene 3, and Act III; and it changes the content of Act II, Scene 1b, abandoning the Incantation in favour of more hairdressing. The reduction in size was accompanied by a drastic change in genre. Whether or not *Svadebka* was closer to opera in Stravinsky's mind than to the 'ballet cantata' it finally became, he appears to have begun with musical characterizations, in a conventional operatic way, fitting out the *druzhka*, for instance, with a hunting-horn fanfare – in his secondary role of master of ceremonies, the *druzhka* evidently blew a horn – which, transformed beyond recognition except for rhythm, became the music of the bass voice at 53.

In the final form, roles of this kind do not exist but have been replaced by voices, none of which is more than loosely identified with the stage characters. Thus the Bride and Groom may seem to be 'sung' by, respectively, soprano and tenor; yet no direct identification exists and the same two voices also 'speak' for the Bride and her mother (see 21). Even the Groom's final love song is 'impersonated' for him by the bass.

The change in genre led to greater abstraction in the stage movement. None of the four final scenes is actually depicted, enacted, or even narrated; by this time Stravinsky had substituted a collage of verse for narrative. In effect, *Svadebka* is a verse play for voices speaking out of turn. And as for stage action, the choreography was conceived as an extension of music: gesture and movement were to be stylized according to the rhythmic patterns of the music and not in imitation of popular or ethnographic dances.

As in *The Rite of Spring*, Stravinsky began with stage pictures in mind, even depending on them. But when the music had been completed he began to pare the stage directions away and to forget them, until no picture existed but only music. Many of his stage directions in *Svadebka* are quotations from Kireevsky. The following are from the sketches, all later than the scenario above, and intended for the four-tableaux final score, though only one of them appears there even in part. The first is an epigraph from Kireevsky that Stravinsky appended to an early draft of the full score:

> Two rivers flow together
> Two matchmakers come together,
> They think about the ashblond braid,
> How will we unplait this ashblond braid?
> How will we part the braid in two?[23]

First Tableau
The father and mother meet the Bride with an icon, when she
comes home from the bath. After the blessing, the
Bridesmaids seat the Bride on a bench at the table, and place
a dish before her, next to which they place a comb. Each
Bridesmaid approaches the Bride, takes a comb from the
table, combs her tresses, replaces the comb on the table and
leaves some money in the dish. [Kireevsky, p. 241.]

Second Tableau
The Groom's train enters. The cart is drawn by village
women from the opposite side of the stage from that on
which the Bride's cart entered. In the cart are the Groom and
his father and mother and best men. The mother is combing
his locks.

The mother combs Khvétis's locks, moistening the comb in
kvas.

At the end of the Tableau, Stravinsky marks the bar in which

The Groom's train prepares for departure. . .

and the bars during which

the Groom's train departs slowly, in their carts.

Third Tableau
Enter the Bride's cart (from the same side of the stage as in
the First Tableau), all glittering with icons and mirrors. The
characters (the same as in the First Tableau) are also dressed
in sparkling clothes.

Fourth Tableau
The backdrop is raised revealing a large room in a Russian
izba. It is almost entirely filled by a table, around which a
large number of people are seated. They eat and drink. A
door is open at the back showing a large bed covered by an
enormous eiderdown.

In the wedding parlour stands a table. On a table is a
karavay [very large loaf of bread] with various wondrous
decorations: the figure of a little man, a little bird, etc. This

karavay is surrounded by other, smaller *karavays*, and by honey cakes, cookies, sweetmeats. The table is made of wood. The mead is strong. The newlyweds eat the *karavay* first. The *karavay* signifies the marital union.

Svadebka ends with the following song, during which the *druzhka* and the *svaha* [female Matchmaker] lead the young couple to bed. When the *druzhka* and the *svaha* have put them to bed and left them, the parents of Khvétis and Nastasia close the door, place four chairs in front of it, and sit on them. The act is over. The curtain falls slowly. The music continues throughout. At the very end a solo voice [tenor] sings, in a saccharine, or oily, voice, drawing out the words:

> *Uzh i dushka, zhanushka Nastas'jushka,*
> *Pozhivem my x toboju xoroshenichka,*
> *Shtoby ljudi nam zavdyvali.*

Notes

1 'Little Wedding', a diminutive form of *svadba*, 'wedding'.
2 Sofia Dmitrievna Velisovskaya (d. 1917) was a relative of Stravinsky's first wife, as well as her nurse.
3 *Miaskovsky: Correspondence*, Moscow, 1969.
4 He was probably in Salvan (Switzerland) on 13 July. A cable addressed to him there on that date from Diaghilev, in London, expresses the hope that ' "*Svadebka*" suit son chemin'. On the 14th, Stravinsky wrote to Alexandre Benois proposing a collaboration based on *Koz'ma Prutkov*, a copy of which Stravinsky had brought back from Kiev; three musical sketches survive for the projected work. (It will be recalled that in *c.* 1901 Stravinsky had composed 'many comic songs' to the words of *Koz'ma Prutkov*, according to the composer's letter to Timofeyev, 13 March 1908.) Benois scotched this notion in a letter to Stravinsky, 23 July. See B. H. Monter's *Koz'ma Prutkov: The Art of Parody*, Mouton, the Hague, 1972.
5 The *only* source, apart from three lines in Tereshchenko's *Byt russkago naroda* (vol. II, p. 332, 1848 edn) used at 93, is Stravinsky himself, for he alone can have written the unidentified lines, the neologisms, and the many amendments

and modifications of the Kireevsky originals. I should also mention that one song used in *Svadebka*, '*Yagoda s yagodoi zakatilocya!*' ('A berry with a berry tumbled down!'), was set down by Pushkin and entrusted by him to Kireevsky; it comes from the vicinity of Mikhailovskoe. But Stravinsky was always entertained by the thought that an *original* line by Pushkin might be in the *Svadebka* libretto. The poet wrote to Kireevsky when giving his copies of folks songs to the collection: 'One day as a pastime try to discover which ones are sung by the people and which I wrote myself.' (*Works*, vol. III, Moscow, 1957, p.536.) Stravinsky might have said the same of some of the musical material.

At one time Stravinsky also planned to borrow a line (at least) from Sakharov's *Pyesni russkago naroda*, so marked by him in his father's bound volumes of the 1838 edition (Song 229, p. 331).

6 See A. Afanasiev, *Russian Fairy Tales*, translated by Norbert Guterman, commentary by Roman Jakobson, Pantheon Books, New York, 1945.

7 A trapezoidal zither with metal strings that are struck with a light hammer. According to Plutarch's treatise on music, the verses of Homer were sung at the public games to music composed by Terpander of Lesbos and accompanied by a zither.

8 Aladar Racz, whose account of the meeting ('I played a Serbian Kolo. . . Stravinsky wore a monocle, a red tie, a green waistcoat'), and, later, of Stravinsky purchasing a cimbalom (he 'prepared the flour-paste, and cleaned the rusty strings himself'), is published in the *Hungarian Book Review* for May–August 1972, together with some memoirs by Racz's widow. Both accounts contain chronological and other inaccuracies, however, as is shown by a letter to Stravinsky, dated 29 January 1915, from his friend Adrien Bovy.

9 Returning to Switzerland, Stravinsky described his Roman sojourn in a note to his mother sent from Milan, 18 February: 'I embrace you and Grusha and send uncounted kisses from Italy, where I have spent ten excellent days. I was at Diaghilev's in Rome. They put on my *Petrushka* at the Augusteum with smashing success. I took an innumerable amount of bows from the box. Our ambassador Krupyensky was present; I was introduced to him and spoke with him

during the entire intermission. After that many lengthy introductions continued in the corridors. All the Italian Futurists were at hand and greeted me noisily; Marinetti came especially from Milan for this.'

10 Stravinsky to Prokofiev, 12 May 1915: 'Someone told me that a note about my *Svadebka* appeared in the *Stock Exchange News*, and a rather well done one – was it from you? I would be grateful if you would send the note (it appeared, so they informed me, at the end of March or the beginning of April, our style).'

11 The instrument was used for rehearsals of the Diaghilev Ballets as early as 1912. In the fall of that year Diaghilev proposed that *The Rite of Spring* be 'recorded' on it for Nijinsky's rehearsals. An interesting letter from Ansermet to Stravinsky, 12 June 1919, deals with some of the mechanical problems of the Etude.

12 Stravinsky's diary for August 1917 includes a scheme for this. The project was not closed until December when Ida Rubinstein rejected Stravinsky's conditions.

13 Born 1845.

14 Stravinsky's contract with Diaghilev for the peformances was negotiated for him by Ansermet in London in June 1919.

15 Not that Stravinsky's musical imagination was dependent on words. In November 1947, after completing the scenario of *The Rake's Progress* with Auden, the composer immediately wrote the string-quartet Prelude to the Graveyard Scene, being inspired by its *subject* even before receiving the libretto.

16 From a letter to his mother, 23 February 1916: 'Musichka, Museecha, please send as quickly as possible (you'll find them at Jurgenson's) the folk songs of the Caucasian peoples recorded on the phonograph. Don't take anything but phonographed ones. Besides, if Jurgenson has any other songs phonographed, send them also. Don't forget that I have the first edition of *Great Russian Songs in Folk Harmonization* (phonographed by Linevaya). Are there no other editions?'

17 From the Oktoëchos or Book of Eight Tones. (Stravinsky no longer possessed his nineteenth-century copy of this Greek book in America, but in the early 1950s, the Byzantine monastery at Grottaferrata gave him an Italian translation of the *Ottoeco*. Russian ecclesiastical chant, which derives from the Byzantine, is based on a system of eight *echoi*. These are

the Byzantine modes, as distinguished from *tonoi*, the Greek modes, and each of them possesses different melodic formulas. Thus the Sticheron (Psalm tropes), Troparion (hymns sung between the verses of the Psalms), and Irmos (a Byzantine strophic chant) are sung to eight different 'Tones' (same sense as in Gregorian Chant), each of which includes three versions for the Sticheron, three for the Troparion, and three for the Irmos. Each, moreover, changes every week at Sunday matins. The Fifth Tone of Sticheron, the one Stravinsky chose, is sung after the matin Psalm, 'Lord, I cried unto Thee', and it occurs during the part of the service in which typological parallels are drawn between Old and New Testament prophecies.

18 He was appalled by Diaghilev's project to exploit the theatre of the Church – its gorgeous robes, and golden orarions – in a ballet.

19 Glebov likens it to Vecchi's *Amfiparnasso* (1594) – cf. Casella's monograph on Stravinsky (1926) – which is farfetched but may have been suggested by Stravinsky himself, who was fond of throwing out false trails of this kind.

20 An entertainer who performed at country fairs, singing, dancing, clowning, juggling.

21 *Dyevishnik* is Maiden's Day, the day before the wedding.

22 His sketches contain a note to the effect that 'among the songs collected by Pushkin, see pages 54–60 [Kireevsky]'; references are found to 'dancing in the bath'; and a reminder to 'See "Customs, Songs, Rituals, etc." in the Province of Pskov, pages 48–54 [Kireevsky]', which refers to the same thing. I should add also that the sketches contain several reminders to look up words in Vladimir Dal's *Explanatory Dictionary of the Living Great Russian Language*.

Professor William Harkins of Columbia University has remarked that at 52 'Stravinsky has retained the Pskov Dialect use of *ch* for standard Russian *ts* in *chérkov* for *tsérkov* ["church"] but corrected it elsewhere in the same quotation (*potselovat*, for Pskov *pochelovat*, "to kiss"). The apparent inconsistency is probably to be explained by the fact that the non-standard form *chérkov* is relatively more comprehensible, particularly in combination with *sobor*, "cathedral", than is *pochelovat*'.

23 Plaited hair is 'a fetish which Freud places at the origin of weaning (institutionally assigned to women). The braid

replaces the missing penis. . .so that "cutting off the braid",
whether on the level of play. . .or whether as social aggression
among the ancient Chinese, for whom the pigtail was the
phallic perquisite of the masters and the Manchu invaders, is
an act of castration.' Roland Barthes (*Erté*).

22

HISTOIRE DU SOLDAT:
MUSICAL ORIGINS, SECOND THOUGHTS

1. Musical Origins

Some of the thematic materials of *Histoire du soldat* come from sources in popular music. For one example, the melody at ⊞ in the music to Scene 1 is the well-known song

> I am pretty, I am pretty
> But I am poorly dressed
> And for that no one
> Will take a girl for his bride.

Stravinsky wrote these lines in Russian in the margin of his first sketch, and it is worth noting that throughout the sketches, more of the annotations are in Russian than in French. In one draft, beginning at the third bar of ⑤ in The Devil's Dance, he even refers to the Princess as the '*Tsarevna*'. (At this point, incidentally, at one bar before ⑥, a still earlier sketch contains the parenthetical indication 'Valse'.)

Stravinsky diverted to the *Soldat* music that had been intended for André Gide's version of *Antony and Cleopatra*. Still other music was taken from sketches written between 1915 and 1917. In late 1915, or early 1916, the composer was apparently planning a piece, 'Etudes and Cadenzas'. Among the sketches for this aborted work is the motive found in the *Soldat* three and two bars before ⑥, and in the second and third bars of ⑨, in the music to Scene 1.

Most of the motives that were later to form the music to Scene 2 were written in 1916. The following two bars occur in the sketchbooks no fewer than five times, in different registers and with minor differences in harmony and figuration:

The evolution of the music between [3] and [4] can be traced on two pages of a small sketchbook for *Renard* and on one detached sheet. In the first entry, the tonality is the same as that of the final score:

The final four bars of this last example were worked out in smaller notes:

Stravinsky added a question mark at the end of the upper line, then the word 'ossia' between the two upper staves, with the words 'Apparently so!' after it. He then crossed out both of these versions and wrote beneath the lower (third) staff: 'So' – and, after the music – 'Correct!' One wonders about the piece for which this music was originally intended.

The sketches for *Antony and Cleopatra* date from only shortly before Stravinsky began work on *Histore du soldat*. On 16 December 1917, he telegraphed Ida Rubinstein's agent, Charles Péquin: 'Please communicate to Madame Rubinstein that I will write the music for the Shakespeare drama only if she agrees to a payment of 15,000 Swiss francs, half payable upon delivery of the manuscript. Will work without percentage.' This message indicates Stravinsky's straitened finances after the October Revolution deprived him of all income from Russia. The question of the *Antony and Cleopatra* commission had been dragging on since 26 June 1917, when Péquin wrote to the composer proposing that he work on a percentage basis. Stravinsky rejected the offer, but continued to negotiate. On 15 November he received a letter from Péquin offering 7,500 presumably French francs, with a 5,000-franc advance. No money was forthcoming, however, nor any answer from Léon Bakst (who had involved Stravinsky in the affair) to a telegram from Stravinsky saying he was already composing and wished to know whether or not to continue. On 6 December Stravinsky telegraphed Péquin, requesting ten per cent of the box office and a minimum of 15,000 Swiss francs, 10,000 of which would be due upon delivery of the manuscript. Still no agreement came, and on 19 December Péquin conveyed Mme Rubinstein's regrets in not being able to alter her conditions.

The music in the following examples dates from November and December 1917, before the project was shelved. Proof of this is that some of it is found on the same page as a draft of the Berceuse, completed on 10 December, that Stravinsky wrote for his elder daughter; and that from the inception of the *Soldat*, in February 1918, Stravinsky understood that only a single instrument, a violin, would be used; he soon added a bass, a clarinet, a bassoon, a cornet, a trombone, and, on about 1 May, percussion instruments, but the *Antony and Cleopatra* ensemble would have been much larger.

Stravinsky's verbal notes for the *Antony and Cleopatra* music (red notebook, 1917–18, Paul Sacher Foundation) reveal that he intended to compose fanfares, marches, and dances. One of the first fanfares is a simple triadic bugle call scored for 'baryton'. Another, for small and large side-drums,

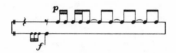

became the cornet tune in *Soldat*:

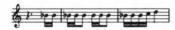

From a third fanfare

Stravinsky used the seven-note figure in reverse order in the harp part in the following sketch:

The harp motif is developed in a subsequent sketch that in some ways anticipates the *Symphonies of Wind Instruments*:

The relationship between this and the violin figure in the *Soldat* is evident:

The most interesting of the derivations of the *Soldat* from *Antony and Cleopatra* is that of the following melody:

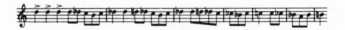

The rhythm comes from a piccolo, flute, and side-drum, while most of the intervals are derived from the fanfare for two trumpets shown above. The following Oriental dance for three trumpets and side-drum and bass drum in *Antony and Cleopatra* later became one of the principal motives in the *Soldat*:

The chronology of the composition and its instrumentation can be traced in a sixteen-page pocket-size *croquis* (sketch; Sacher Foundation), of which the Waltz fills about a third; the cornet enters in the final bars. Some sketches for the Ragtime follow, then notations for The Devil's Dance (between 4 and 5, and one bar before 8); for the Little Concert (from 9 to the second bar of 11, a version of the violin figure at 13, and the bass figure and chromatic violin figure at 7); for the Chorale (complete, but scored without the strings); and for the beginning of the cornet part at 1 in the Royal March, albeit with the first note of the second bar a step lower than in the final score. Some of the percussion part for the Tango appears on the penultimate page, and the coda is dated 16 March. The Little Concert (dated 10 August) is found on the detached sketch pages, as are the Triumphant March of the Devil (26 August), The Devil's Couplets (composed in September), and the Little Chorale (completed last of all).

When did it occur to Stravinsky to identify the repeated crotchet figure from the *Antony and Cleopatra* dance with the Devil in the *Soldat*? The sketches record considerable trial and error at the beginning of work on the Triumphant March. The first draft, below, marked 'for the ending', reveals the composer's sense of the need for an irregular rhythm:

Perhaps after writing this Stravinsky remembered the passage at ⟦15⟧ in the Royal March. In any case, the next draft shows his grasp of the theme, pitches, and some of the accompaniment pattern.

2. Stravinsky's Second Thoughts

The *Histoire du soldat* performed at the Théâtre Municipal in Lausanne on 28 September 1918 was very different from the work with which we are familiar today. Stravinsky began revising the score soon after this unique performance, as is shown by the manuscript of the version for piano, violin and clarinet of the Little Concert, completed on 1 December 1918, since it includes the music between 26 and 28 that he added to the full score after the premiere. Ansermet conducted the Lausanne stage premiere and the 20 July 1920 London concert performance from a copy of the manuscript made by the composer's wife, whose Russian script is found at the head of the second number. This score contains cues for Elie Gagnebin, the Narrator, and Closset, the violinist, participants in the premiere who never appeared in another performance together, as well as some revisions entered just before the London concert.

Stravinsky's revisions leave only the 'Scene by the Brook' and the Tango unchanged. The Royal March and the Triumphant March of the Devil underwent especially extensive overhauling, and the latter, which Stravinsky expanded from 71 to 114 bars, must have had a considerably less powerful effect at the premiere than it does today. Furthermore, the volume of the music was smaller in 1918, when the trumpet and trombone were muted, or *coperto*, almost throughout.

Most of the revisions were made in late June and early July 1920, in preparation for the London performance, but more followed in 1923–24. On 1 September 1923, Stravinsky wrote to Otto Kling, the publisher of the work: 'I have just returned from Weimar, where I introduced a very important change into the copy of the Triumphant March, which is now in Scherchen's hands. Since he is conducting the work throughout Germany, we will have to wait to get the score back from him before engraving it.' In another letter to Kling, 25 October, Stravinsky wrote: 'I have just completed the new instrumentation of the Triumphant March, which I will conduct when I perform *Histoire* on 7 November in Paris'. On 20 November, he wrote asking for 'the score used by Scherchen and myself. Since this score was used for a great number of rehearsals and performances, it has many more corrections than the one you sent me.' But the score Stravinsky wanted was in Leipzig for three performances there.

Some of the most substantial changes made in 1923 were in the music to Scene 2, where in the original score (unlike the published one) a pause is expressly forbidden before $\boxed{2}$; the curtain cue occurs at the beginning of the cornet solo; a complete break (silent bar with fermata) coincides with the entrance of the Devil at $\boxed{4}$; and the music does not resume until after the exit of the Devil.

The most important changes, completed by mid-July 1920, are as follows:

The Soldier's March (Part One): the violin and bassoon parts between $\boxed{11}$ and $\boxed{13}$ were entirely rewritten, conforming to the published score.

The Soldier's March (Part Two): in the first bar of the full score, in Stravinsky's hand, the trombone part at $\boxed{5}$ is marked 'cornet or trombone'. The bar includes a score for the Narrator, the upper staff marked '*libre*', the lower '*rhythmée*'. Kling, confused by Stravinsky's abbreviated directions at $\boxed{5}$, wrote to him on 28 October 1923: 'We believe that a passage is missing in the full score, in "Part Two, Introduction". The music stops after $\boxed{4}$ in the full score, but in the piano reduction you have added several measures [bars]. Should we delete these measures in the parts, or should they be added everywhere?' On 17 January, Kling sent the bars from the piano score and asked Stravinsky to orchestrate them. On 19 January, the composer wrote that 'these measures are exactly the same as in the first march of the Soldier.' Not until a month later did Stravinsky notice that 'in continuing to correct the proofs, I have discovered that the reprise of The Soldier's March is missing – the fragment concerning which we exchanged letters in January – although it is included in the manuscript full score. To my great surprise, this music was not engraved in the proofs that I now have. As I explained to you, it is exactly the same music found in the first march beginning at $\boxed{10}$. . . To guide you, I enclose the manuscript pages taken from the copy of the full score. Also, the pagination must be changed, since this fragment begins on page 16.' (19 February 1924)

Royal March: At $\boxed{5}$, the clarinet part in the original is given to the trombone, the violin part in the original to the clarinet. (Stravinsky, Ansermet, and the proofreaders overlooked the key signature in the trombone part, and as a result the Es and the B lack natural signs to this day – in the only score in print.) At one bar before $\boxed{7}$, Stravinsky changed the seven-note turn in the original bassoon part to a trill. The clarinet part in the second bar of $\boxed{8}$ was the trumpet part in the original score, and, at three bars before $\boxed{9}$, the trombone part was the trumpet part (an octave higher). The trumpet part at $\boxed{11}$–$\boxed{12}$ was originally played by the clarinet, and, in the original, the alternating and interlocking of the clarinet and violin parts in this passage were different.

Little Concert: In 1920, Stravinsky changed the barring before $\boxed{16}$; rewrote the bassoon part at $\boxed{21}$; reassigned the trumpet part to the trombone at one bar before $\boxed{21}$, and added the part for trombone from two bars before $\boxed{26}$ (though in one of the sketches this 'added' music is scored for bassoon). In Paris on 21 November 1923, Stravinsky inscribed a handwritten part containing these added bars: 'This conforms to the ensemble.'

Devil's Dance: On the same day he wrote on a similar manuscript of the percussion part between ④ and ⑧ in the Devil's Dance: 'The family of one of the players made this copy for him, writing it in a different manner from that of the score, but the result is in conformity with the ensemble.' Stravinsky wrote to Kling on 30 November:

> In the score of the *Soldat* that I sent to you via A. Bosc, you will find two manuscript pages, for the trombone and the percussion, on which I reply to your question about the noncorrespondence of the fragments with the score. . . Obviously the parts should follow the score, but the musicians of each ensemble in every country have left their own markings, which are not in the score. To establish the correspondence between parts and score is an immense task for which I do not have a free moment until June (and far beyond that).

Stravinsky added the cornet part at ② in 1920.

The Soldier and the Princess: The only change in the Tango is that the first part of the piece was originally titled 'Prelude'. The Waltz, in the original, began with a bass-drum downbeat, and in the original Ragtime the bassoon was alone in the last bar; the trombone was added in 1920 (but not yet the bass).

Triumphant March of the Devil: The lowest quavers in the bassoon part at the beginning were added in 1920; in the original this part had the same pattern as that of the trumpet and clarinet. In 1920, Stravinsky switched the bassoon and trombone parts in bars 2 and 3. (The trombone did *not* play the ascending quavers and the repeated D crotchets in the original.) The 'fade-out' music in the clarinet, bassoon, and cornet between ⑯ and ⑰ was added in Weimar, though a suggestion of it is found in an early sketch. In 1920, Stravinsky added the trombone to the bassoon at one bar before ⑬, hence the change to cornet must have been introduced at a later date. He also inserted off-beats to the bass music at ⎡13⎤. Most important of all is the addition of forty-one bars from ⎡3⎤ to ⎡9⎤. In the first sketch, the music at ⎡9⎤ is marked '*l'apel [sic] à l'enfer*', and, underneath the percussion part, Stravinsky introduces what may be a dance notation, with signs for the accented and unaccented notes.

The original score and earliest sketches require three side-drums without snare and a bass drum, and their parts are notated on four lines, large side-drum on the top, middle on the second, small on the third, bass drum on the bottom. Stravinsky added a verbal note in French at the head of the sketch:

> The notes with stems above are to be played with the right hand, the notes with stems below with the left hand. The bass drum should be placed to the left of the player, the large side-drum to his right, while the two other drums are in front of him, the smaller drum closer, the larger farther away, with their heads facing him. Timpani sticks made of hard felt are to be used.

Unfortunately, this arrangement is not followed consistently throughout *Histoire*. In the published score, moreover, Stravinsky changed one of the side-drums to a tambour and switched the positions of the large and middle side-drums on the staff. He later acknowledged that the percussion part should not have been written on a staff that might imply relative, high and low, pitches, and he wrote to Kling on 14 April 1925:

> I draw your attention to the engraved parts of the *Soldat*, which in many places do not conform to the engraved score.

Above all, this affects the percussion part, where there is a great confusion in the order of the different instruments. In addition to these faults, the last piece has the additional inconvenience of being unplayable: the musician must turn the page while executing the solo part with both hands occupied. Your engravers and proofreaders might easily have avoided that. Also, instead of printing the part of each percussion instrument on a staff of five lines (something perfectly absurd, since these instruments do not have definite pitches), your engraver could have saved space and avoided page-turns entirely. At my last performance, in Barcelona, and in the one last autumn in Berlin, I had to omit the final number.

The percussion part in the last movement contains many errors, and it lacks important markings found in the sketches – where, for example, the composer describes the sound of the drum solo at the fourth bar of $\boxed{13}$ in the Triumphant March as 'the heels of a dancer'.

23

'HYMNS OF PRAISE' FOR DEBUSSY: STRAVINSKY'S *SYMPHONIES OF WINDS*

The *Symphonies of Wind Instruments*, rated by many as one of Stravinsky's greatest works but heretofore confined to cult status, has lately been the subject of a Dutch film documentary, *The Final Chorale*[1], of a reconstruction of the unpublished original version[2], and of a milestone monograph[3] that includes facsimiles of both the draft and full manuscript scores, but, inexplicably, none of the sketches, which are of far greater interest. The facsimiles expose faint underlayers of pencil sketches invisible in microfilms, and in all other ways as well far surpass the standards of previous publications of the kind, including the Minkoff *Firebird*.

The authors of the book, André Baltensperger and Felix Meyer, provide illuminating commentaries on the form and compositional process without claiming to decrypt all of the mysteries of either the inner (germination) or the outer (publishing) history of the work. Following earlier critics, they touch on Stravinsky's use of the montage principle, the juxtaposition of self-contained segments, and the elements of repetition and reprise that replace the continuous development of first-movement sonata form and functional tonality. Beyond this, they chart a 'hypothetical "original state" of the score', delineating five sections subsumed under three larger units. '*Konetz 2omu slavleniu*' ('end of the 2nd praise', or 'end of the 2nd hymn of praise'), Stravinsky wrote on a sketch page for the end of the section before the final chorale. As the authors interpret this, the first hymn of praise *is* the chorale, since it was worked out first, but it could also mean that the first hymn consists of the music from the beginning up to the second hymn, the '2' requiring a '1' *before* it, at least in the final ordering of the score.

Moreover, the so-called bell motive, or 'invocation motive', as Baltensperger and Meyer identify the actual beginning, was composed before the chorale incipit, and may have been written soon after Debussy's death, 25 March 1918, which affected Stravinsky profoundly, despite a cooling in the friendship between the two composers by the end of 1916.

A note of 16 November 1916 from Louis Laloy to Stravinsky, during the latter's brief visit to Paris that month, invites him to dine with the French master and adds, 'Debussy feels you are avoiding him.' If in fact an estrangement was felt, the reasons might be that Cocteau had tattled to Stravinsky, 'Debussy says he is "tired of all these Russians",' and that Stravinsky's negative judgment on *Le Martyre de Saint-Sébastien*, no doubt confided to someone at the rehearsal he attended and later communicated to Diaghilev in Rome (letter of 21 November), had been repeated to its composer. But occasional strains in the relationship aside, Stravinsky's veneration of Debussy was lifelong, as is shown by correspondence, by Stravinsky's performances of *Nuages* and *Fêtes* in 1935, and by his participation in a Free France broadcast on the twenty-fifth anniversary (1943) of Debussy's death.

After completing the draft score of *Ragtime* for eleven instruments on 5 March 1918, and the full score on the 25th, Stravinsky filled six more pages of the same notebook (*Skizzenbuch* V in Baltensperger and Meyer) with sketches for the Piano-Rag Music. Suddenly he interrupted this work and entered the following startlingly different notations, the first perhaps suggesting clashing bells, the second, developing it, a keening chant:

The graphological evidence indicates that these motives were conceived shortly after Debussy's death, but in any case the next date in the notebook, 28 December 1918, found on the last of twelve sketch pages for *The Drake*, is in 1918, *not* in the spring of 1920, when Stravinsky was asked to contribute to a Debussy memorial album to be published by *La Revue Musicale*. From April to September 1918 Stravinsky was fully occupied with the composition of *Histoire du soldat*, and after that, and until March 1919, with the trio version of the *Soldat*, and *Four Russian Songs*, and the rewriting of the *Firebird* Suite.

He resumed the Piano-Rag Music in March 1919, finishing it on 27 June. The Rag sketches are followed by the first notation for the final chorale

and by a second notation for the bell motive, now connected to what Baltensperger and Meyer call the 'pendulum motive':

The chorale is remarkable in its diatonicism; its close, chant-like intervals and narrow melodic range; its austere harmonic structure; its restriction to three rhythmic units; and the dramatic pacing of rests toward the end. The resemblances to the bell motive in all except the last of these features are obvious, but Stravinsky developed and completed the chorale first, the request from *La Revue Musicale* being unrefusable. Much of the melodic, intervallic and harmonic materials of the opus derive from the chorale, which helps to account for the extraordinary inner coherence of what on first hearing can seem most disjunct.

The *Symphonies* is Stravinsky's most innovative and most compact formal structure. Composed backward from the chorale, so to speak, the draft score reveals Stravinsky's interpolation of anticipatory fragments of the chorale in preceding sections. Baltensperger and Meyer draw attention to this but, oddly, not to the relationship between the music that one of the anticipations replaces and the 'pendulum motive', namely the same rhythm and number of beats, the alternating B–F sharp and C sharp, and the F–G trill:

At this point, a digression on performance and publication history becomes necessary, for the reason that Baltensperger and Meyer present the case for the revised 1947 version of the piece over the 1920 original. For the premiere,[4] Queen's Hall, London, 10 June 1921, Stravinsky coached the conductor, Koussevitzky, during two rehearsals, but the performance provoked a scandal, the audience apparently agreeing with Sacheverell Sitwell's comparison of the beginning to the braying of a donkey. When Eugene Goossens conducted it in

London again, 12 December 1921, Ernest Ansermet wrote to the composer, 'There were simply no tempi at all. . .it was worse than Koussevitzky. "Twice as fast," I exclaimed at one point.' Ansermet conducted it himself in Geneva, 26 December 1921; in Paris, 26 December 1922; in Leningrad, March 1928; and in Brussels, 21 April 1928. Stokowski conducted it in Philadelphia, 23 and 24 November 1923, and in New York, 5 February 1924; and Germain Prévost conducted it in Brussels, 5 January 1924, with Stravinsky, in the audience, complaining that the performance was 'too gentle'. Three months later Stravinsky forbade performance by anyone except himself and Ansermet.

Stravinsky's response to a letter from Ansermet describing his Geneva premiere of the *Symphonies* reveals that 'minor accidents' had occurred. 'But what was the audience reception?' he asks. 'You do not say a single word about it.' Ansermet seems not to have answered, and his silence suggests that the music had created a ruckus, as it was to do in Philadelphia and New York. Stokowski wrote to Stravinsky, 24 November 1924, that the public was 'antagonistic . . .simply unable to understand the music at a first hearing', while the New York performance was greeted by 'a great deal of hissing'. On 3 May 1925 Stravinsky wrote to Stokowski asking him to bring the parts of the *Symphonies* to Europe with him: 'The work has not been published and there are many difficulties with it.'

Did Stravinsky have reservations about the wisdom of exposing the *Symphonies* to subscription-concert audiences? On 27 October 1924, Emile Giovanna, manager of the Orchestra de la Suisse Romande, wrote to him in connection with a concert scheduled for 29 November in the Salle de la Reformation, Geneva, in which he was to conduct his Octet and play his Concerto under Ansermet: 'For various reasons that [Ansermet] will explain later, he decided to replace the Symphony [*sic*] for wind instruments with the *Song of the Nightingale*.' But surely the Octet is part of the explanation: Stravinsky had evolved so far away from the *Symphonies*, and in contrast had enjoyed so much success with the Octet, that he had put the earlier work out of mind, and with it the painfully acrimonious newspaper exchanges with Koussevitzky it had caused.

To return to the chronology of the composition, the next twenty-seven pages of *Skizzenbuch VII* contain sketches for the *Symphonies of Winds*, albeit with specifications for harmonium and string quartet[5] attached to many of them. This would seem to indicate that they were composed as early as a year before the completion of the draft score, on 2 July 1920. The arguments for this, though hardly conclusive, are that Stravinsky is unlikely *not* to have worked on a new piece during the summer of 1919 (*Pulcinella* was not begun until September), and that the notations for harmonium registrations in the sketches coincide with the scoring for the instrument in the ensemble of the so-called 1919 version of *Noces*, which must have occupied him in July and August of that year, when he owned and played the instrument himself.

Whereas the failure of the piece with subscription audiences can be attributed to its radical newness, as well as to inept performances, its publication history is still an enigma. Why did Stravinsky, ordinarily impatient to publish, never finish correcting the proofs and fail to resolve conflicts between one set and another, while at the same time permitting the sale of a piano reduction that contained major errors? And why did the third proofs not become the basis for the score of the original version, instead of the disastrous second proofs? Whatever the answers, at some point the third proofs disappear from view. Were they in England for a performance just before or during the war? The 'corrections' of an English-speaking conductor, all of them mistaken, are found in Stravinsky's copy, sent to him from London in 1949. Who, moreover, is the editor of the pirated Kalmus edition of the second-proof score, which has hand-drawn corrections on every page but still teems with errors, some of them important?[6]

In June 1933, Ansermet was engaged in correcting the *Symphonies* proofs, the decision to publish the full score apparently having been made at that time. He addressed a number of questions to Stravinsky, some of which the composer failed to answer. In the following example, is the A natural in the second chord, and are the F sharp and E natural in the fourth chord, correct?

Stravinsky verified the F sharp and E natural but did not reply concerning the A, which the ordinarily perspicacious Ansermet then changed to A sharp, no doubt on the mistaken assumption that since the music is a sequence, an exact parallel to bar 8 of the chorale was intended. Reorchestrating the chorale, 11 December 1945, from a photocopy of the *Revue Musicale* album, Stravinsky changed the F sharp (bar 12 in the album) to F natural, and the natural obtains in his 1947 version of the *Symphonies*. The E is flatted in the album and in Arthur Lourié's 1926 piano reduction, but Stravinsky erased it (*c.*1920) in one of his copies of the album and cancelled it in his copy of Lourié's score;[7] the note is not flatted in the sketches and the manuscript scores. Emile Vuillermoz, who proofread the album for *La Revue Musicale*,[8] did not question the flat, and in 1945 Stravinsky himself, working from the erroneous album, erroneously incorporated it. Unfortunately, Stravinsky's 1947 rewrite of the complete opus, prepared from the first proofs sent to him from Paris after World War II, retains the error.

Writing on 30 June 1933, Ansermet wrote out three versions of the progression of trombone chords at [7] and asked if the last one is correct, 'since the interval of the fourth, C to G occurs everywhere else, or should it be G–B–G?' Stravinsky confirmed the C as correct, and, under the same question, wrote the simultaneous parts for the three trumpets, asking Ansermet to make certain that the third quaver of the second trumpet is G sharp (it is G natural in the piano reduction, which Stravinsky corrected, and where, too, the trombone chord is wrong). Another of Ansermet's questions concerns the chords in the treble at 14: should the lowest note in the second chord be C sharp instead of B, and the lowest note in the sixth chord, C sharp instead of D sharp? Stravinsky answered that both are C sharps.

In the same letter, Ansermet pointed out that the English horn and first trombone play B against the third horn's C in the penultimate chord of the whole work. Stravinsky did not respond, but he had added the B in pencil in the draft score and retained it in the full score and third proofs. In another letter, Ansermet copied a progression near the beginning that Stravinsky had notated in the lower margin of his first draft of the chorale as if he had intended to use it there, and asked the composer to verify the A flat (fourth chord, treble):

The A flat is correct, Stravinsky replied. In 1947, however, he cancelled both the D flat and the C flat in the second chord.

But to compare the original and the 1947 versions is a bewildering exercise and not within the scope of this review. The instrumentation is entirely different, and so is much of the metrical structure, the phrasing and articulation, the rhythmic figuration, and even the harmony. The most striking of the 1947 revisions in rhythm is the substitution of quavers for triplets in the first tutti – a figure that returns in another work of mourning at the end of Stravinsky's life, the *Requiem Canticles*. But the 1947 version weakens even the bell motive, with comparatively colourless instrumentation and the reduction of the number of 'peals' (*cf* 6 in the old version and 9 in the 1947).

Baltensperger and Meyer rightly characterize the 1920 and

1947 scores as 'two fundamentally different versions', the result of entirely different aesthetic approaches. They concede that the range of timbres is narrower in the late version than in the original,[9] but contend that the differentiation of tone colours at the beginning is clearer, that the switch from alto flute to bassoon in the 'pendulum motive' gives the principal line greater relief, and that the 1947 voicing of the first tutti chord is stronger and attains a higher level of dissonance. (In general, the simplified harmony of the 1947 score lowers the level of dissonance.) In any case, the original version has now been 'pushed aside', they say. More precisely, Stravinsky instructed his publisher to withdraw it from circulation, but the original is in the public domain in the USA, and several recordings of it have been issued there.

Baltensperger and Meyer mistakenly suppose that the score from which Stravinsky prepared the 1947 version was 'probably the third of the proofs'. It was unquestionably the first, the 'very dirty proof' mentioned in the composer's letter of 29 August 1947 to the present reviewer. It is covered throughout with editors' corrections, in spite of which, on 18 of its 39 unbound, blank verso pages Stravinsky introduced rebarring, as well as changes of pitches, instrumentation (3rd flute for piccolo between 24 and 25), and figuration (bassoon, bars 4−5 of 37, 63 in the 1947 score). The second proof score is simply an imperfectly corrected edition of the first, and, like the third, it contains no marking in Stravinsky's hand. The second and third proofs were apparently sent to Stravinsky in 1949 by Erwin Stein, the publisher's very acute editor, on the chance that the composer might check them against the 1947 version before it was published (1952), but Stravinsky, preoccupied with the composition of Act Two of *The Rake's Progress*, did not find time for this.

For this reviewer, the *Symphonies* in the third proofs is superior to the *Symphonies* in the 1947 version. The phrasing, articulation, and dynamic markings throughout are more sensitive and intelligent, as well as closer to the 1920 manuscript. Moreover, the third proofs follow Stravinsky's red-inked instruction on the manuscript to replace the horn parts by bassoons in bars 1–3 (and, by inference, 9–11 and 36–38). The third proofs and the 1947 version are identical in tempo relationships (72 for the crotchet, its sesquialtera, and its *doppio movimento*), yet the 1947 retains more fermatas, which seem out of place in music employing such strict, even mechanized, tempo controls. Not least, the third proofs embody the corrections discussed in the 1933 correspondence with Ansermet.

On 13 January 1948, Ansermet, in the Essex House, New York, wrote to Stravinsky in Hollywood announcing his intention of performing the *Symphonies* with Toscanini's NBC Symphony, 'which has a basset horn and an alto flute'. Ansermet says that he prefers to conduct 'the old version', partly because the new one 'seems to contain some mistakes'. He has already asked a publisher to send the parts of the latter from London – N.B., *not* the score, which he had with him, and which had to have been his copy of the third proofs. In a later letter he asks Stravinsky if he prefers to have the new version played, adding that 'Mr Krafft [*sic*] does not object to this since he has the first public performance.'[10]

Ansermet wrote again on 31 January 1948, acknowledging that the 1947 version is more powerful than the 'old' version in the 'savage' music, the dance section [51] to [56]. Perhaps. Otherwise he was right to prefer the old version, and right in remarking that the new one confuses principal lines of the original (*viz.* the missing melodic F two bars before [27] that a forgetful Stravinsky claimed had never existed – letter of 26 January 1948 – and the change in emphasis from E to D in the first horn part between [30] and [32]).

Above all, the original is richer and more varied in instrumental colours. Consider the flute and clarinet combinations, without oboes, in the 4 bars before [35], at [38], and at [41] – in contrast to the sharply accented and detached chords of the oboes and bassoons in the 1947 score – as well as the mellow trumpet of the last phrase before the final tutti, and the quiet open brass of the ending *vs.* the nasal muted brass of

1947. The softness of these sonorities, enhanced by legato phrasing, provides a change of feeling and a sense of progression absent in the 1947 score.

Notes

1 First publicly screened in Amsterdam in June 1991.
2 Recorded by the Orchestra of St Luke's, New York. Musicmasters, 1991.
3 *Igor Strawinsky Symphonies d'Instruments a Vent*, by André Baltensperger and Felix Meyer. Amadeus Verlag, Winterthur, 1991. Paul Sacher Stiftung, Basel. ISBN 3–905049–46–5.
4 The piano version of the chorale had been performed publicly in Paris, 24 January 1921.
5 The first sketches for the Concertino for String Quartet were composed either in the autumn of 1919, while Stravinsky was waiting for the *Pulcinella* contract from Diaghilev, or after the completion of *Pulcinella* in the spring of 1920. The Concertino was commissioned, in effect, by a letter of 17 August 1919, from Alfred Pochon, second violinist of the Flonzaley Quartet. Stravinsky wrote to Pochon, 25 February 1920: 'I am thinking about the music I will compose for you, not only thinking about it but. . .putting down on paper the things that come to me through my head, my fingers, and my ears.' Stravinsky eventually transferred one motive from the Concertino sketches to the *Symphonies*, that of the flute part at [9] in the original score.
6 The first bassoon's octave doubling of the second oboe (instead of the first) at [16]; the mistaken voicing of the flutes, oboes, and clarinets at [24] (the alto clarinet part at [24] in the third proofs does not follow the manuscript but doubles the English horn, presumably Stravinsky's revision); the wrong rhythm of the clarinets at [7]; the D natural (instead of D flat) in the third bar at [24]; the wrong flute figuration in the upbeat to [24]; the mistaken bass E flat in the third bar of [40]: all of these are corrected in the third proofs.
7 The rehearsal numbers that Stravinsky added in red pencil in his copy of the published piano score inserted in the proofs of the orchestra score.
8 According to a letter to Stravinsky from Henry Prunières, 17

November 1920. By this date, Stravinsky was completing the full score, which has E natural.

9 The text betrays some confusion about the instrumentation of both versions, in referring, as it does, to a nonexistent '4th trombone' and wrongly remarking that the 1947 score eliminates the third bassoon. Confusing, too, is the statement that Stravinsky drew staves with a 'special rastral' that 'produced a flexible image.' What seems to be meant is that Stravinsky drew staves of different sizes, but he did this with different sizes of stylus. Moreover, the statement, 'from the draft score to the full score, Stravinsky made a few minor changes,' is misleading, since he made major ones as well, as in the beginning of the 'pendulum motive', in the rhythm of the 'dance' after 32, and in the tempo at 20.

10 I had been introduced to Ansermet during the intermission of a Ballet Society performance at the Fifty-Fifth Street Mosque Theater. 'Krafft' is the name of a hotel in Kleinbasel that Ansermet may have known.

24

OEDIPUS REX, PERSÉPHONE, ZVEZDOLIKI

Oedipus Rex

Not critics but composers, among them Ravel, were the first to recognize *Oedipus Rex* for the masterpiece it is, Stravinsky's most powerful dramatic opus and one of his three or four greatest creations. After hearing Ernest Ansermet conduct it in London, 12 February 1936, the young Benjamin Britten noted in his diary:

> One of the peaks of Stravinsky's output, this work shows his wonderful sense of style and power of drawing inspiration from every age of music, and leaving the whole a perfect shape, satisfying every aesthetic demand . . . the established idea of originality dies so hard.

Leonard Bernstein was the first to identify in print the principal influence on the music:

> I remembered where those four opening notes of *Oedipus* come from. . . . And the whole metaphor of pity and power become clear; the pitiful Thebans supplicating before their powerful king, imploring deliverance from the plague . . . an Ethiopian slave girl at the feet of her mistress, Princess of Egypt. . . . Amneris has just wormed out of Aida her dread secret. . . . Verdi, who was so unfashionable at the time *Oedipus* was written, someone for musical intellectuals of the mid-twenties to sneer at; and *Aida,* of all things, that cheap, low, sentimental melodrama. [At the climax of *Oedipus'* 'Invidia' aria the] orchestra plays a diminished-seventh chord . . . that favorite ambiguous tool [*i.e.,* tool for the suggestion of ambiguity] of surprise and despair in every romantic opera . . . *Aida*! . . . Was Stravinsky having a secret romance with

Verdi's music in those super-sophisticated mid-twenties? It
seems he was. [*Norton Lectures*, 1973]

Bernstein is correct, of course, and he might also have mentioned the stylistic debt to Verdi in Jocasta's aria and duet
with Oedipus. A photograph of Verdi adorned the wall of
Stravinsky's Paris studio in the 1920s, and on his conducting
tours he would go out of his way to hear Verdi operas, even
to the extent of changing the dates of his own concerts, as he
did in Hanover in December 1931 for a performance of
Macbeth. Stravinsky's library of Verdi vocal and orchestral
scores is surely a unique collection for a modern composer.
In the early 1930s Stravinsky wrote to one of his biographers:
'If I had been in Nietzsche's place, I would have said Verdi
instead of Bizet and held up *The Masked Ball* against Wagner.' In Buenos Aires, in 1936, Stravinsky shocked a journal-
ist by saying: 'Never in my life would I be capable of
composing anything to equal the delicious waltz in *La Tra-
viata*.'

Other influences besides Verdi are apparent. The Messenger
and the Shepherd singing in duet remind us of the Cat and
Goat in Stravinsky's *Renard*, and the 'Gloria' chorus at the
end of Act One, the Messenger's music, and the choral music
in the Messenger scene are distinctly Russian. But the genius
of the piece is in the integration of its diverse materials.

The diminished-seventh chord, both harmonically and me-
lodically, pervades the entire score. It appears in most measures of the chorus part at the beginning. In contrast, Oedipus' first aria emphasizes the dominant-seventh, a means of
distinguishing his proud, confident manner from the frightened one of the chorus speaking for the plague-ridden people;
another means is his florid style in contrast to their unorna-
mented implorations. Creon's aria, characterizing his pom-
posity, contains several diminished-seventh constructions and
so does Oedipus' response, indicating that his suspicion has
been awakened. Oedipus' response to Tiresias, in the next
scene, and Jocasta's music in the scene after that, are charac-

terized throughout by diminished chords and diminished melodic progressions. Thereafter the *a cappella* chorus, before the announcement of Polybus' death, terminates with the word *'horribilis'* set to a diminished progression, while the chorus's *'falsus pater'* exploits the false intervals of the tritone, an incomplete diminished triad.

The rhythmic patterns are more simple than ever before in Stravinsky's music, but as an element in the dramatic tension rhythm is no less important than the diminished-seventh harmony. The vocal parts are always uppermost, the role of the orchestra secondary—the only purely orchestral passages are brief, pitch-establishing introductions and connecting links—yet much of the effect of the music is in the orchestration.

In at least two instances, a single note rings a powerful change. First, the move from the D major chord, over which the voices of Oedipus and Tiresias overlap, to the E flat a half-step higher, as Oedipus continues (in some of the most beautiful lyrico-dramatic music composed in the modernist period), and tells us that he is above Tiresias and still the king. Second, in the *'Sphynga solvi'* aria, Oedipus' D natural, after several measures of D flat, another upward half-step, is a resolution of great dramatic power. *'Sphynga solvi'*! Surely the canorous syllables determined the intervals, the character, and the tempo of the music.

But the most striking musico-dramatic moment in the opera—and *Oedipus Rex* is an opera, not an oratorio—comes just before the end, in the quiet C major chorus, *'Ellum regem.'* Here the first four melodic intervals are the same as those with which the work began, but in the minor mode, the B flat minor which is also the tonality of the Shepherd's revelations and of the Messenger's announcement of Jocasta's death. The major key brings catharsis worthy of Sophocles.

Hesiod tells us that the Sphinx, a winged monster, half maiden and half lioness, is the offspring of the goddess

Echidna, herself half woman and half reptile, and Orthos, her multi-headed son. Greek mythology tells us that Jocasta, wife of Laius, King of Thebes, frightened by an oracle saying that a son of hers would kill his father and marry his mother, condemns her infant son Oedipus to death by abandonment and exposure on Mount Kithairon with his ankles pierced and strung together. A shepherd, former slave of Laius, finds the infant and entrusts him to a younger shepherd (the Messenger in Sophocles' play), who gives the baby to his master, King Polybus of Corinth, who brings the boy up as his son. When a drunken companion of Oedipus betrays the secret and tells him that he is not his father's son, Oedipus goes to Delphi, hears the oracle himself, and in order to frustrate the prophecy resolves never to return to Corinth. Leaving Delphi, he encounters Laius, kills him in an argument, and proceeds to Thebes, which he frees from the Sphinx, whose 'jaws are bloody from human sacrifice,' by solving her riddle.

The *Iliad* mentions the funeral of the 'fallen' Oedipus but says nothing about how he fell. In the *Odyssey*, Odysseus, who has glimpsed Jocasta (Epikaste) in Hades, recounts the father-murdering, mother-marrying, and suicide part of her story, but says that Oedipus continued to reign as king of Thebes.

The source of the story of Tiresias, in whom truth is inborn, is Book III of Ovid's *Metamorphoses*. Walking in a forest one day and coming upon two monstrous copulating serpents, Tiresias thrust a stick between them and was immediately changed into a woman. He continued to live as one for seven years. In the eighth year, coming upon the same serpents engaged in the same activity, and again separating them, he was instantly changed back to his original gender. Called to settle a dispute between the gods over Jove's contention that women's pleasure in love-making is greater than men's, Tiresias agreed with Jove, whereupon Juno condemned him to eternal blindness. In compensation, Jove endowed Tiresias with the gift of prophecy.

425 BC is the generally accepted date of Sophocles' play; the plague that had wasted Athens in the second year of the Peloponnesian War flared up again in that year.

The first of Sophocles' many and multi-layered dramatic ironies is in the name 'Oedipus'. *Oida* means 'I have seen', or 'I know'. Nietzsche says (*The Genealogy of Morals*), 'We knowers are unknown to ourselves, and for a good reason: How can we ever hope to find what we have never looked for?' The full name of Oedipus means 'swollen foot' or 'witfoot': the king is still identified as maimed-footed.

Voltaire's *Lettre III* on Sophocles' play points out its inconsistencies, unrealistic details, and violations of common sense (while signally failing to perceive the overwhelming power of its ironies). But Seneca's adaptation of Sophocles (first half of the first century AD) had already addressed some of Voltaire's criticisms. For one, the Latinized Oedipus very reasonably asks Jocasta if Laius met his death alone; an aged king would hardly have been unattended. She replies that a few of his men were by his side, and that one of them fell 'as comrade of his fate'. (Sophocles' Oedipus kills all *but* one of Laius' company.) To locate the event in time, Seneca's Oedipus asks when the death occurred, and Jocasta answers that, since then, 'ten harvests have been reaped'.

Seneca further increases credibility by briefly expanding the Shepherd's narrative to include a description of the onset of what the Greeks called *tetanos*:

> A slender rod of iron his ankles pierced,
> And bound his limbs. This wound produced a sore
> Which by contagion spread through all his frame.

In one instance, however, Seneca's commonsensicalness undermines the belief system of the play. In her final exchange (*stichomythia*) with Oedipus, begging him not to leave, Jocasta says, logically in view of his technical innocence,

> What thou deplorest is the fault of fate.
> A fated crime can leave no stain of sin.

Seeking the truth, Seneca's Oedipus sends Creon to Hades to confront Laius' ghost, whose speech reminds us of the ghost in *Hamlet* (Eliot: Shakespeare's 'voice in poetry is, in the most serious matters of life and death, most often the voice of Seneca'.):

> But 'tis thy bloody King.
> Who as the prize of savage murder done
> Hath seized his father's sceptre and his bed.

When Creon repeats this to Oedipus, after much hesitation, Oedipus arrests him.

What most puzzles modern audiences in Sophocles' play is the role of the gods. Whereas Homer's deities occasionally look down on mortals with compassion (in Pope's rendering of the *Iliad* the gods 'lean forward from the sky', a phrase that reminds us of Juliet's 'Is there no pity sitting in the clouds'), Sophocles' gods are remote. Apollo, for reasons comprehensible only to the god himself, is Oedipus' demon, his enemy. Near the end of the play, Oedipus says:

> It was Apollo, always Apollo
> Who brought each of my agonies to birth.

But when the chorus asks him 'what demon lifted your hands [to your eyes?]', Oedipus claims human responsibility for this one act: 'But I/Nobody else/I raised these two hands of mine/ . . . I stabbed out these two eyes'. Creon's refusal to grant Oedipus' wish and drive him from Thebes, for the reasons that 'there are no precedents for what has happened', can only mean that he believes this, believes the self-blinding to have been Oedipus' own, god-free act.

In Seneca, the gods are quite simply equated with fate. Sophocles' theology is far more profound, if fathomable at all. Paradoxically, ironically, Sophocles' Apollo is also *in* his Oedipus, in the hero's *hubris,* in his individualism, in his having been chosen for a fate so extraordinary.

*   *   *

Stravinsky described the language of his *Oedipus Rex* as Medieval Latin, but the sentence structure, the placement of modifiers, and the use of the historical infinitive are features of Golden Age Latin, Ciceronian in the invocation of the gods who—an oddity of Jean Cocteau's libretto—are Roman (Minerva, Diana, Jove), despite the Greek place-names. The conspicuous exception is the theological word 'omniscius', probably introduced after the death of Boethius (sixth-century); the anachronism might be a slip on the part of the translator, Jean Danielou, who was a member of the College of Cardinals in Rome.

The Speaker's part both in Cocteau's original and in e. e. cummings's English is often confusing: 'After the Sphinx, a plague breaks out. The chorus implores Oedipus to save his city. Oedipus has vanquished the Sphinx.' But 'after' and 'vanquished' are imprecise. Oedipus saved Thebes by solving the Sphinx's riddle. The Speaker then tells us that 'Tiresias decides to speak. And this is the oracle.' But the words are Tiresias's, not the oracle's. In Cocteau's text, King Polybus of Corinth is first mentioned in the Messenger's announcement of his death, and, in the same sentence, Oedipus is revealed as Polybus's adopted, not his real, son. Obviously, the Polybus-Oedipus relationship must be explained in the previous speech. Further, this same 'death-of-Polybus' speech begins with the mis-statement: 'The witness of the murder steps from the shadows. A Messenger . . .' But the murder was not witnessed by anyone in the play. The Messenger and the Shepherd, who step forth, are witnesses of the survival of the infant Oedipus, and the Shepherd is additionally a witness to the truth of the child's parentage.

According to another speech, Jocasta is said to prove that oracles lie, but in fact she merely asserts this. The turning point in Cocteau's libretto, as in Sophocles's play, is Jocasta's revelation that the scene of the crime is 'where three crossroads meet.' But Cocteau omits the irony of Jocasta's prayer to Apollo to help rid Thebes of the plague, answered by the arrival of the Messenger, the consequences of which are her death, Oedipus's blindness and exile, *and* the end of the plague.

Perséphone

Melodrama in Three Parts for récitante, tenor, mixed chorus, children's chorus, orchestra

The stage drama that André Gide developed in 1933 from his early poem, *Perséphone,* is based on the fourth of the so-called Homeric Hymns celebrating the Eleusinian mysteries of the cult of Demeter. Its three parts correspond to Dante's *Inferno, Purgatorio,* and *Paradiso,* and, like them, provide the frame of a quest and a journey, round-trip in the case of Gide-Stravinsky. Perséphone's descent to the Underworld, during the orchestral interlude between Parts One and Two, evokes the stark, frozen world of winter in harshly accented wind-and-piano chords. Her victorious return is reflected in the stately march for full orchestra between Parts Two and Three. The pace of Perséphone's journeys is slow, like the pace of her longer melologues, but these are offset by animated choral dances and Eumolpus' allegro aria characterizing Mercury.

Whereas Perséphone and the chorus enact the drama, Eumolpus, son of Poseidon and Priest of Eleusis, the narrator-commentator, stands apart from it. *Perséphone*'s greatest 'numbers' are his arias, *'Pauvres Ombres,"* above all, and the trumpet-obbligato 'Tu viens pour dominer'. Eumolpus introduces each of the three parts with the same music, some of it exactly the same (*cf.* 6 , 72 , 199), in the sense of tempo, tonality—which is also the tonality of the end of the work—and the punctuation by percussive piano appoggiaturas.

Perséphone, Stravinsky's most consistently lyrical score, contains the longest-line melodies he ever wrote, and the most mellifluent sonorities: the string quartet accompaniment to the goddess's speech, *'Où donc avez-vous fui',* for one example, and the blend of four horns in unison with the chorus in '*Si tu contemplais*', accompanied by alternating harp and pizzicato string chords that suggest an ancient lyre.

At the beginning, the vocal line exactly follows the alexandrine of the text, with the caesura at the end of the sixth syllable, but it soon departs from the verbal rhythms. The tempos of the melologues are indicated by the music, but the rhythms are not notated.

At another level, most of the melodic substance of *Perséphone* is related by subtle means. One example is the figure of falling fourths heard near the beginning and, later, in shorter note values, as an accompaniment to the first and last melologues:

Less obvious are the derivations from the intervals of Eumolpus' first three notes, a minor second down and a minor second up. These recur some 160 times throughout the work, in numerous transpositions, in major and minor contexts, in different rhythmic guises, and, in most instances, at the beginnings of pieces or sections. Here is its first statement, and the repeats near the beginning of Part II and the end of Part III:

| *Part I* | *Part II* | *Part III* |

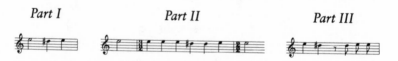

The first chorus of the Nymphs derives from the same intervals in the major mode,

and so does the dolorous music at the beginning of Part Two,

where, in correspondence to the change from summer to winter, Stravinsky inverts the figure:

The rhythm and accentuation of the motive are altered again in the second chorus of the Nymphs, now in minor mode:

The same tonality (the example sounds a fifth lower) occurs in two later transformations of the motive, the first of them in the orchestral introduction to Eumolpus' 'Mercury' aria,

the second in the ostinato accompaniment to the final melologue:

Eumolpus' music near the end of Part One exposes the motive in three different forms:

In Part Two, the motive's first two notes stand out from the diatonic contour of the melody and are repeated 18 times:

Still another form appears in the orchestral music following this lullaby:

The orchestra repeats a D minor form of the motive 15 times in the ballet Sarabande,

and this form returns in Part Three at the beginning of the chorus, *'chaque geste'*:

The motive appears in several more configurations, including the beginning of the Part Three chorus, *'Encore mal reveillée'*:

The orchestral tutti introducing Part Three, the dynamic climax of the work, identifies the motive as its nuclear theme; it is reiterated here fifteen times in the same tonality:

One other form, introduced in Part One, returns at the end of Part Three,

and so does the choral melody,

whose return near the end of Part Three, rounds out the form of the work and completes its cycle-of-the-seasons symbology:

Zvezdoliki

Konstantine Balmont's Symbolist poem, *Zvezdoliki (The Star-Faced One)*, the text of Stravinsky's 1911 cantata for male chorus and orchestra, dedicated to Claude Debussy, may be translated as follows:

His eyes were like stars, like flames which furrow space. His visage was like the sun when it shines at its zenith. The luminous colors of the heavens, purple, azure, and gold, dappled the gorgeous robe he wore to be reborn among us. Around him the thunder rolled in the ravaged, storm-rent sky. Seven halos of brilliant stars shone around his head. Lightning struck the hills and brought forth Spring flowers. 'Do you keep the Word?' he asked. And we all replied, 'Yes, always!' 'Alone and invisible I reign', he said. The thunder rumbled louder. 'It is the hour', he said in his glory: 'The harvest waits.

Amen'. Piously and fervently we followed him. Lightning cleft
the clouds. Seven halos of brilliant stars showed the way
through the desert.

Zvezdoliki alludes to Debussy in its orchestral shimmering
(string tremolos, harp glissandos) and repeated-note (F sharp)
rhythmic figure in the horns, and its quotes him literally in
the final section. Harmonically, in the successions of 7-note
chords, it abuts *The Rite of Spring*, and the passage invoking
the 'purple, azure, and gold' of the heavens, with its 9- and
10-note chords is the densest music, corresponding, harmonically and rhythmically, to those rich colors that Stravinsky
wrote before his 1964 *Variations*.

Like *The Rite,* Stravinsky's next work, begun in July 1911,
Zvezdoliki conveys an inner ecstasy, partly through the radi-
ance of its orchestral timbres, especially in the wind-instru-
ment chords at the center of the piece. It begins with the
unaccompanied male chorus singing a 'motto' in six harmonic parts. The motto's three melodic intervals are repeated
nine times in the body of the short cantata, and its first
harmony returns in a seven-octave wind chord at the climax
(and half-way point), heralding the Voice of the 'lodestar':
'Do you keep the Word?'

Unique in Stravinsky's music are the uncontrasted slow
tempo, the quiet dynamic level, the sostenuto style (no stac-
cato, no accents), the absence of a motoric rhythm (the
'purple, azure, and gold' passage exposes five different rhythmic figures simultaneously), and the sonorities: choral hum-
ming, fluttertonguing in clarinets (as well as flutes), muted
oboes, the 'bridge' effects in the strings (muted throughout),
and the wide spacing of the eight horn parts in the chords at
the center of the work. Also to be remarked in this first
surviving Stravinsky choral work is the use of four-part vocal
harmony for the third-person lines, and of octaves and uni-
sons for the first-person, the Voice of the 'lodestar'. Konstantine Balmont's mystic, quasi-religious poem (the word 'Amen'

may be the only one that the listener with no Russian understands) inspired one of Stravinsky's greatest works, perhaps the most perfectly unified of them all in that the harmony is inseparable from the instrumental color, the melody from the harmony. The melodic pitches identified with the word 'lightning' in the first part of the piece return with the same word at the end (oboe solo).

INDEX